The Play of
Musement

Advances in Semiotics   Thomas A. Sebeok, General Editor

The Play of Musement

THOMAS A. SEBEOK

INDIANA UNIVERSITY PRESS

BLOOMINGTON

For E

—who equals the mass of her matter
multiplied by the speed of light squared

This book was brought to publication with the
assistance of a grant from the Andrew W. Mellon Foundation.

Manufactured in the United States of America

Library of Congress Cataloging in Publication Data
Sebeok, Thomas Albert, 1920-
    The play of musement.
    (Advances in semiotics)
    Includes bibliographical references and index.
    1. Semiotics—Addresses, essays, lectures.
I.Title. II.Series.
P99.S33 001.51 80-8846
ISBN 0-253-39994-7 AACR2
1 2 3 4 5 85 84 83 82 81

Contents

Acknowledgments

My work on this book—among a host of other projects—was completed in the course of a year's residence, during 1980-81, at the National Humanities Center. At the same time, I enjoyed an extended sabbatical leave of absence from Indiana University, as well as a second fellowship from the National Endowment for the Humanities. The combined generosity of these three institutions is herewith acknowledged with utmost appreciation.

Particular thanks are due to Dr. Jean Umiker-Sebeok, for her collaboration on chapters 2 and 8; to Miss Harriet Margolis, for her collaboration on chapter 3; and to Professor Emeritus Max H. Fisch, for his setting chapter 2 in context and much else.

The text will reveal how much I have profited from recent critical opinion of my books on semiotic subjects by Eugen Baer, Paul Bouissac, John N. Deely, and Martin Krampen.

For additional details, see the note placed on the opening page of each chapter and appendix.

My overall indebtedness to Jean Umiker-Sebeok—by far my acutest critic—has been and continues to be of inestimable value.

THOMAS A. SEBEOK

NATIONAL HUMANITIES CENTER
April 1, 1981

The Play of Musement

Chapter 1

Introduction: *Ludens in orbe terrarum*

THE KEY TO the title of this book is to be found in Peirce's profound study, in 1855-56, of Friedrich Schiller's concept of *Spieltrieb*. In his *Briefe über die ästhetische Erziehung des Menschen* (1794-95), Schiller presented an analysis of human nature as comprising three "impulses": *Stofftrieb*, the drive for diversity, forever striving for change, contrasted with *Formtrieb*, the demand for "form" in the abstract, alien to time, hence oppugnant to change (this pair corresponding to Kant's well-known dualism), plus a third component he himself dubbed *Spieltrieb*, or play (*ein ernstes Spiel*)—the aesthetic tendency, mediating and harmoniously reconciling the twofold way of sense and reason on the level of the individual's faculties (microcosmos, the particular) as well as those of society (macrocosmos, the lofty). Schiller (1967:331) defined *Triebe* as "bodily needs inasmuch as they represent an incentive to mental activity," but then went on to use his compound in a substantially wider sense, continuously adapting it to his own purposes. In consequence, *Spieltrieb* has been much misunderstood (ibid.:clxxxvif.), although emphatically not so by Peirce, intent, as he was, "on uncovering the method and the message" of Schiller by a critical examination of his language (ibid.:clxxxviii). He undertook to expound the work to his classmate Horatio Paine, spending "every afternoon for long months upon it, picking the matter to pieces," eventually—no less than 47 years later—concluding that though "esthetics and logic seem, at first blush, to belong to different universes . . . that seeming is illusory, and that, on the contrary, logic needs the help of esthetics" (Peirce 2.197). Or again: "When our logic shall have paid its *devoirs* to Esthetics and the Ethics, it will be time for it to settle down to its regular business" (2.200). The two editors of Schiller's *Letters* point out the implied sequitur: "that logic rested on ethics, and ethics on aesthetics . . . " (1967:clxxxix). Further, Wilkinson and Willoughby underline the historically interesting fact that Peirce's "hierarchical structure" was very much akin to Schiller's own. At the same time, the most crucial and fundamental equation—of logic being only another name for *semiotic* (Peirce 2.227)—eludes them entirely. This is most unfortunate, and for two quite different reasons: First, because it blinds his astute editors to the possibility of an intellectually exciting semiotic revaluation of Schiller's philosophy—an opportunity that they missed, although they do hover at the very edge of discovery when they note that some recent investigations of both human and animal play have revealed it to be

1

"one of the primary message-systems, a means of communication" (Schiller 1967:clxxxvf., cf. Sebeok 1981). Second, they do not apprehend that Peirce imparted to Schiller's basic idea a voltage and dynamism precisely by virtue of its incorporation into what he called the third Universe of Experience, which is constituted of "everything which is essentially a Sign—not the mere body of the Sign . . . but . . . the Sign's Soul" (6.455).

Peirce replied to Lady Welby, on December 23, 1908: "As to the word 'play,' the first book of philosophy I ever read . . . was Schiller's *Aesthetische Briefe*, where he has so much to say about the Spiel-Trieb; and it made so much impression upon me as to have thoroughly soaked my notion of 'play' to this day" (Hardwick 1977:77). He toys with the captivating conceit of the "Play of Musement" in connection with an argument for the Reality of God (6.486; cf. MS 843), and variously associates this resplendent genitival phrase (repeated from 6.460) with Pure Play (which "bloweth where it listeth. It has no purpose, unless recreation . . ."; 6.458), Meditation (6.458, 483, 487), and Reverie (6.458) ("Reverie-meditation being a species of *solitaire*" [MS 843]), then explains further: Musement "is a certain agreeable occupation of mind. . . . The particular occupation I mean . . . may take either the form of aesthetic contemplation, or that of distant castle-building (whether in Spain or within one's own moral training), or that of considering some wonder in one of the Universes, or some connection between two of the three, with speculation concerning its cause" (6.458). By "Universe" Peirce meant "a receptacle or class of Subjects" (4.545), and proceeded to identify three Universes as being familiar to us: "The first comprises all mere Ideas, those airy nothings to which the mind of the poet, pure mathematician, or another *might* give local habitation and a name within that mind" (6.455). The second Universe is "that of the Brute Actuality of things and facts" (ibid.). The third Universe is, as already noted, the semiotic one, which "comprises everything whose being consists in active power to establish connections between different objects, especially between objects in different Universes" (ibid.). The Sign's Soul, Peirce remarks, has in its power the capability of mediating between its Object and a Mind: "Such, too," he amplifies, drawing impartially upon artifacts of Nature and Culture, "is a living consciousness, and such the life, the power of growth, of a plant. Such is a living constitution—a daily newspaper, a great fortune, a social 'movement'" (ibid.). Peirce directs the Muser how to find universe-wide phenomena as they will strike his attention: "Let him, then, for example, after well considering, in all its breadth and all its depth, the unspeakable variety of each of the universes—even that of minds—turn his keen mental gaze to those phenomena that are of the nature of homogeneities of connectedness in each Universe in turn, and what a spectacle will unroll itself!" (MS 843; cf. 6.464). Speculations on the homogeneities of each Universe will naturally draw the Muser to the consideration of connections between two different Universes, or among all three. At last, "in the Pure Play of Musement the idea of God's Reality will be sure sooner or later to be found an attractive fancy, which the Muser will develop in various ways. The more he ponders it, the more it will find response in every part of his mind, for its beauty, for its supplying an ideal of life, and for its thoroughly satisfactory explanation of his whole threefold environment" (6.465).

The only ordinance that applies to Pure Play is the law of liberty. Illustrations of this principle abound as much in physical science as in detectival ratiocination. Peirce notes (adducing here "The Murders in the Rue Morgue") that "problems that at first blush appear utterly insoluble"—anomalies, antinomies, perplexities, such as the quantum-mechanical paradox known as "observer-participancy," which imparts tangible reality to the cosmos (and which is the ultimate subject of Sebeok 1979: chap. 5 and chap. 8 of this book)—"receive, in that very circumstance . . . their smooth-fitting keys. This particularly adapts them to the Play of Musement" (6.640). In brief, the faculty of Musement—which Bronowski later, but more pallidly, chose to call *imagination*—"is the common root from which science and literature both spring and grow and flourish together" (1967:39). Bronowski used "image" as his coarse and unneedful synonym for Peirce's "sign," without regard for either its sensory quality or the wealth of distinctions Peirce drew among different species of signs (ibid.:34).

Peirce's Argument, in connection with which he brings the Play of Musement forward for consideration, can be loosely characterized as a "process of thought reasonably tending to produce a definite belief" (6.456). Accordingly, some of my readers may choose to skim through the following chapters with no higher expectation than may be required by Play—that is, by exercising their powers in as lively a fashion as they can work up while browsing. In stricter semiotic parlance, an Argument, for its Interpretant, is defined as "a Symbol, or Sign whose Object is a general Law or Type" (2.253). These essays can, therefore, also be registered more earnestly, in persual of the progression roughed out for anyone "determined to make trial of Musement as a favorite recreation. . . . It begins passively enough with drinking in the impression of some nook in one of the three Universes. But impression soon passes into attentive observation, observation into musing, musing into lively give and take of communion between self and self. If one's observations and reflections are allowed to specialize themselves too much, the Play will be converted into scientific study; and that cannot be pursued in odd half hours" (6.459).

It is the Play of Musement, then, that both animates and articulates the thirteen essays in this book. Their overall selfsameness was to be swathed by a seamless, if not always readily transparent, semiotic fabric whose strands are interwoven from filaments plucked from what I earlier identified as the major (i.e., biologically scrupulous) tradition of semiotic inquiry (Sebeok 1979:4ff.). But since Foreplay is the natural and legitimate prelude to semiotic (no less than somatic) arousal, I feel obliged to mention that I regard these amalgamated texts—all of them written or rewritten in 1980—as the climactic topping off of a trilogy consisting, in addition to the aforementioned essays, of the eleven pieces included in my *Contributions to the Doctrine of Signs* (1976) and the nineteen featured in *The Sign & Its Masters* (1979). The pivotal motive pervading the Argument of this entire trilogy and interfused throughout all of these papers is my "absolute conviction that semiotics begins and ends with biology and that the sign science and the life science ineluctably imply each other" (Sebeok 1979:xiii; cf. Baer 1979 and Bouissac 1979, for inspired comments). John Greenleaf Whittier put the matter, in his characteristically homespun fashion, in the simplest of terms: "For nature speaks in symbols and in signs,/ And through her pictures human fate divines . . . " ("To Charles Sumner," 1854). This millennial metaphor of "the book of nature" goes back to the invention of writing and the influence that had on Mesopotamian divination. Of this convergence, Ginzburg (1980:13) justly remarks: "It gave the gods . . . the power of communication with their subjects through written messages—on stars, human bodies, everywhere—which the diviners had the task of deciphering" (cf. Sebeok 1976:28).

The virtuoso methodological device, or, if you will, semiotic ploy, into which Schiller's *Spieltrieb* ripened in Peirce's authoritative hands is far from being the only modern expression of the theme of the Play of Musement. Its most complex artistic realization is to be found in Hermann Hesse's multiply ambiguous utopian fantasy, *Das Glasperlenspiel* (1943), rendered but roughly as the "Glass-Bead-Game," but usually referred to in English contexts by the Latin title of the hero, Joseph Knecht, as *Magister Ludi* (Hesse 1949). Hesse scholars commonly claim that Huizinga's famous (but, I fear, enormously overrated) *Homo Ludens* (1938; 1949) contributed to the novelist's concept of "play" as the highest manifestation of culture (Field 1970:153, 185-186n16). Yet it strains credulity to doubt Hesse's intimate familiarity with Schiller's *Letters*, and, as a corollary, to exaggerate his reliance on Huizinga, who demonstrably distorted Schiller's theory "in a way that is only explicable on the assumption that he can have read little more of the treatise than the single Letter [XIV] to which he actually refers" (Schiller 1967:clxxxvi). A perceptive passage in one of Thomas Mann's letters (cited by Field 1970:154), expressing his delight in the "sober playfulness" (*ernste Verspieltheit*) of Hesse's novel, itself contains an informed echo of a phrase made famous by Schiller. The Ludi Magister explicates the serenity of the so-called Castalian Order, in which is incorporated the faculty of the Bead Game: "With us it is the cult of truth closely bound up with the cult of the beautiful and, in addition to this, with the contemplative care of the spirit, and thus can never entirely lose its serenity; but our Bead Game unites within itself all three of these principles—science, reverence of the beautiful and meditation" (Hesse 1949:287). The point of Mann's remark was that, beyond this unifying principle that relates all knowledge

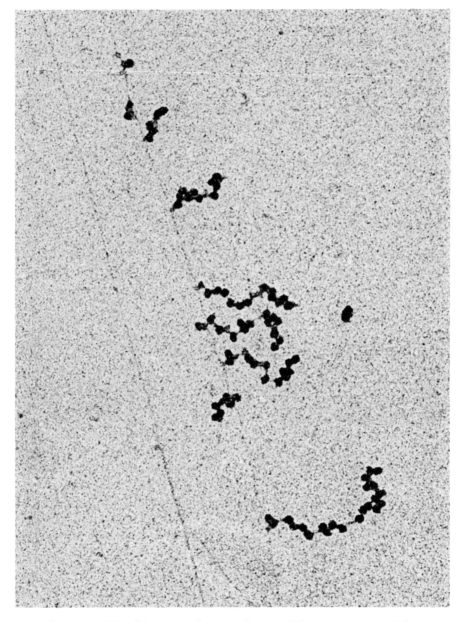

FIG. 1.1. The ultimate bead game: clusters of ribosomes, as revealed
by the electron microscope. The ribosomes are connected in a
series by a long nucleic acid molecule, which passes through each
ribosome. The cluster resembles a gigantic assembly of beads on a
string. Thus nucleic acid molecules serve both as part of the
structure of the ribosome (the bead) and as the string that connects
the beads. Illustration from O. L. Miller, et al., "Visualization of
Bacterial Genes in Action," *Science* 169 (24 July 1970):392-395,
copyright 1970 by the American Association for the Advancement
of Science. (See also Feinberg and Shapiro 1980:61f.)

to a central theme, Hesse's novel itself was a Bead Game, a "playing with all the contents and values of our culture" (Field 1970:154).

When the Game began, it had been a mere structure, an "arrangement, a grouping and opposing of concentrated performances from many fields of thought and from the beautiful. . . ." Gradually, however, "the concept of contemplation had entered the game . . . the greatest care was devoted to the art of . . . meditation. In this manner the hieroglyphics of the Game were prevented from degeneration into simple letters" (Hesse 1949:38). Later still, "This Game of games, under the hegemony of now this, now that, science or art, has developed into a kind of universal speech, through the medium of which the players are enabled to express values in ludic symbols and place them in relation to each other" (ibid.: 39). The figures and formulas of the Bead Game are constructed in a metasemiotic—the "universal speech" of signs and symbols, of the riddling oracle game (*alla sēmainei*), indeed, of the nature of reality itself (e.g., ibid.:119)—"composed from all the arts and sciences and striving toward perfection, being pure and reality" (ibid.:40). The players called this accomplishment "realisation," being the path from the possible to the real.

For Peirce, man is a string of signs, a text (cf. Sebeok 1979:61f.); for Hesse, man is a traveler, an essay (1949:75). Hesse's Game is a cosmic ecumenical semiotic suffused by the incandescence of subjective intensity, a glow that some—Northrop Frye comes immediately to mind—would call the essence of romance. It is hardly surprising that the Master cautions young Joseph: ". . . everyone is not in favour of the Bead Game. They say" (and who among us has not heard this semioclastic censure before: "que la science sémiologique n' avait pas trop bien tourné: elle n'était, souvent qu'un murmure de travaux indifférent, dont chacun indifférenciait l'objet, le texte, le corps" [Barthes 1975:163]) "that it is a substitute for the arts, and that the players are belletrists who cannot be regarded as being actually inspired but only as artists of free fantasy and dilletantism" (ibid.:75). The Master then warns Joseph to prepare for conflict. His next words should be committed to memory by every apprentice semiotician:

> One thing is certain: the Game is not without its dangers. . . . But you
> must never forget that what I have so often told you: our object is to
> discern opposites correctly, in considering them primarily as opposites but
> eventually as poles of a single unit. This applies also to the Bead Game. . . .
> You will get to know these antitheses, and will in time discern that they
> are not objective but subjective, and that, for example, an artistic dreamer
> does not avoid pure mathematics or logic because he has recognized and
> found it contradictory, but because his leanings are instinctively else-
> where. . . . Mark well: one can be a strict logician or grammarian and
> yet be full of fantasy and music. One can be a musician or a bead-player,
> and yet be devoted to law and order. The man whom we take to be our
> ideal and try to emulate should be able at all times to exchange his art or

science for any other, should allow the most crystal clear logic to radiate from his Bead Game and display the most creative fantasy in grammar. That is how we should be, and we should be prepared at any moment to be transferred to another post without opposition or allowing ourselves to become confused. [Ibid.:75-76]

The action in Hesse's utopian novel takes place in another century— around 2400 A.D.—as the sophistication of the Game approaches an ideal state of perfection under the superintendence of the Magister Ludi. We, the contemporary players, who are not yet prepared, hark back to diverse —even competing—traditions, varying in breadth of scope, flexibility in employment, and maturity as to conviction. For some, semiotic studies are nothing but child's play—no more than the discernment of "opposites correctly" (cf. Claus 1976). Such is the chilling conclusion I came to on a frigid Saturday afternoon in Toronto soon after I returned home from having acted as companion and guide to a young lady, who had just barely pushed past the age of four, at a tense viewing of *The Empire Strikes Back*. The precocious lass is a fervent admirer of Darth Vader's martial skills and stunning weaponry, although his wheezing metonymic malevolence and one breathtaking glimpse of his phallic *pars pro toto* head, caught in the act of sheathing, will cunningly continue to feed on her (and my) fancy as the rest of the epic unfolds and maybe beyond. (*The Empire Strikes Back* is not, as I had, in my innocence, assumed, Episode II of *Star Wars*, but Episode V, following hot upon what had retrospectively become Episode IV!)

The mythic overtones that encumber the second installment (i.e., Episode V) of the saga make it a prime candidate for the kind of global interpretation whose operative antithetical constituents—whether in the armature (Greimas 1970:187f.) or the code (ibid.:189-197) or the message (ibid.: 188f.) of its narrative structure, or overdetermined by a plurality of the aforementioned—are of such stupefying generality as to inspire deft parodic inventions, topped by Woody Allen's *Love and Death*.

In the course of a series of evening seminars conducted by my youthful escort, we chanced to hit upon the passport to the plot of *The Empire Strikes Back*. The film is, at bottom, we came to believe, a metacommunication about *communication* in its multiform galactic gradations ("le mythe lui-même . . . j'appelerai méta-langage, parce-qu'il est une seconde langue, dans laquelle on parle de la première" [Barthes 1957:222]). Since our dialogues and their tentative resolution may have some bearing on several themes recurring in this book and its two related predecessors, I thought I would pass on the substance of our deliberations in the hope of shedding some more light on the issues treated therein and for their inherent methodological import.

This story, as unfolded in this particular installment, is populated by five principal groups (Tesnière's *actants*) of creatures (*acteurs*), distinguished one from another in terms of the semiotic competence and functions of each class. Toward the center is an assembly of more or less "normal" men and women, constituting Group II, who all speak fluent, if, by and large, tediously slangy, English. Linguists might call the speech level of Group II a "restricted code" (Bernstein 1974:1551ff.) or the low variety of diglossia (Ferguson 1971:3). As Bernstein emphasizes, this does not mean that speakers will at no time use other variants—the choice of dialect depends on the context. Here belong Han Solo, the Princess Leia Organa (the only vocal female in this film), Lando Calrissian, the Nazi officer types running Darth Vader's Star Ships, miscellaneous extras of the Rebel forces, the human but bizarrely amoral bounty hunters, and, at this stage of his personal development, Luke Skywalker: as the Dark Lord of the Sith, the antagonist, is a former Jedi Knight, the protagonist, young Luke, reciprocally, is a Jedi Knight in the making. Some Group II characters are Good (+), some Bad (−), or, like the master of the City of Clouds, some Dubious (±).

Above this ordinary medial group there looms a handful of Jedi Masters, members of Group I, each in his way a Magister Ludi, each presumably a male, but appearing to be a sexless neuter (one being a mere manikin, one but a shade, and one often heard but hardly ever seen, as it were, "in the buff"). The Masters are not merely alive; Yoda claims, "Luminous beings we are, not this crude matter." Two of them are Good; one is Evil (on the light side and the dark side of the unifying principle—known as the Force—respectively). You recognize Jedi Masters mainly by virtue of the fact that they often speak in an elaborated code (Bernstein 1974:1551ff.), or the high variety in diglossia (Ferguson 1971:3); in other words, they cultivate the mannerisms of some characters out of *The Lord of the Rings*. The homunculus Yoda, the most venerable of the Masters (Yoda trained Ben, who trained Vader; both Ben and Yoda are training Luke, and Vader would like to), is only two feet tall, but over 800 years old, mutedly Oriental, and, as befits a gnome, given to gnomic utterances. (Luke: "I don't believe it." Yoda: "*That* is why you fail.") Yoda also tends to talk, in *Time*style, "backwards": "No good is this . . . what know you of ready? . . . Tried have you? Always with you it can't be done. Hear you nothing that I say? . . . Try not. *Do, do*. Or do not. There is no try.") Yoda also has a soulful and expressive gaze, notably long, mobile ears, movements of which, baton-like, punctuate his verbal apothegms. The spectral Ben (Obi-Wan) Kenobi, as enacted by Guinness, cannot help sounding like Sir Alec. The utterances of the Lord Vader are, of course, doubly marked: + heavy-breathing, to denote controlled malevolence; and + grandiloquence, to signify his social status, which is, well, imperious. Luke, advised by Ben to "unlearn" what he has learned, is edging toward the Upper Class, and this upward mobility is occasionally reflected by his verbal, though more often by his heroic non-verbal, behavior; at any rate, it shifts in that direction as the plot develops. The nefarious Darth Vader may even be the exemplary Luke's real father, but we cannot be sure as yet how the present myth will finally articulate either with Oedipus (although its Sophoclean associations are obvious) or with Percival (although its Wagnerian resonances cannot be overlooked either). (Cf. Sebeok 1979:177.)

Sharply demarcated from the two Upper Classes, both endowed with innate verbal propensity, one high, the other low, is Group III, the members of which are called Wookiees, most prominently embodied (personified?) by Chewbacca. The Wookiees are speechless creatures, but these brutes do grumble, gurgle, grunt, bark, and howl a lot, can communicate with ease by averbal means, and seem to possess a moderate degree of intelligence as well as an impressive budget of irrational loyalty. Wookiees can be taught splendid technical skills, such as co-piloting at least some primitive sorts of spacecraft. They remind one, in short, of the Smart Simians discussed in chapter 8 of this book (I was especially struck by the resemblance at the moment when the Princess Leia rejects her human suitor, Han, with the immortal refusal, "I'd just as soon kiss a Wookiee"—more than a hint, surely, of the miscegenetic Beauty and the Beast motif).

Wookiees are alive but necessarily speechless. The robots, or droids, of Group IV, on the other hand, are biologically inert computers that, nonetheless, can be programmed to communicate with the world of the living, as well as with each other, in several alternative ways. The surgeon-droid, 2-1B, for example, speaks, in an authoritative manner, a high-prestige technical idiolect, interlaced with medical cant: "Commander Skywalker has been in dormo-shock but is responding well to the bacta." The anthropomorphic C-3PO also converses by means of a natural language (English), supplementing his vocal commerce by a stiff mimicry of human gestures. Both droids have synthesized voices. But C-3PO has been overeducated: this droid is so excessively loquacious that it has to be disengaged at critical moments (Han Solo: "Either shut up or shut down"). Too, its speech sounds elaborately genteel—to American ears, insufferably like comical-British.

By contrast, R2-D2 interfaces with humans by means of a kind of Yerkish, consisting, in the acoustic channel, of beeps and especially whistles, which, accompanied by expressive visual displays, act as a speech surrogate (Sebeok 1976: chap. 11). The transmutation of the squat droid's messages is accomplished with the aid of miniature computers; Luke's X-wing fighter, for instance, carries an attachment capable of transcoding them onto a control panel view screen in English sentences.

C-3PO tries to rise, unsuccessfully, up the semiotic ladder and is punished for this transgression—is, in fact, temporarily junked altogether on the planet Bespin. R2-D2 is content to stay a mechanical but superior conversant droid and is continuously rewarded, like a pet dog, with affection.

Group V consists of an olio of men, monsters, and machines whose common property is that all of them approach semiosis degree zero. They are, because of this handicap, ineffably sinister and malefic. Here belong

Vader's Hitlerian storm troopers, who can receive verbal orders but carry them out in disciplined silence. Like a superorganism of army ants, they lack individual traits: these soldiers seem like an aggregation of cellular units whose component parts seldom even try to exchange messages averbally. In these respects, these animate soldiers are no different from the inanimate, insectiform Probe Droids, which are endowed with, among other such appendages, a set of auditory sensors.

The Wookiees are not to be confused with the speechless domesticated chimera—the Tauntaun, or growling snow-lizards, being ridden over the frozen landscapes of Hoth in the opening scene—or with the sporadic monsters (the dreadful Wampa Ice Creatures, the squishing Mynocks, the swinish Ugnaughts, or the titanic Space Slug) befouling the galaxy. These feral outer-space predators are mostly vermin that would rather consume than reason with you.

To summarize: The members of Groups I-III are all animate. The linguistic competence of Group I is elaborated, of Group II restricted, and of Group III nonexistent. The members of Group IV are all inanimate. They may be general- or special-purpose computers, programmed, accordingly, to produce a suitable level of synthetic speech. Others may be programmed to produce a speech surrogate, which has to be encoded and decoded by appropriate peripheral devices. The members of Group V, whether organic or inorganic, perform semiotic displays minimally, if at all.

This analysis does not begin, nor was it meant, to exhaust the deep structure of *The Empire Strikes Back*. For one thing, it hardly touches on the film's multifaceted, pregnant intertextuality. Sophocles, Wagner, Tolkien, and the Muppets (Frank Oz was the creator and the voice of Yoda) have already been alluded to; many other films could be mentioned, notably *The Wizard of Oz*, any number of World War II movies, with maybe a touch of Charlie Chan flicks. More important, we are, by definition, dealing with an *open* product, in Eco's sense, not merely "on account of its susceptibility to countless different interpretations" (Eco 1979:49), but quite literally, because of the text's interdependence with *Star Wars* as well as with perhaps as many as seven other installments yet to be produced, some to take place before, others after, the action allotted to this specific segment; truly, this is a situation in flux, a "work in progress" (ibid.:65). So we are left, provisionally, with an open narrative sequence, the elementary structure of which is quite transparent. Its binary semic organization can, as well, be displayed in sets of homologous four-term oppositions and contradictions, the outcome of each of which is a logical rectangle, or a scheme Greimas calls a semiotic square (*carré sémiotique* or, sometimes, *modèle constitutionnel*) (e.g., 1970:135-155, 157-183), and Segre condemns as "a redundant tool" (1979:51), but the underlying representation of which goes back to at least Roman rhetorical practice. This paradigmatic structure of signification is always laid out in terms of two polarized semes, in which each character set is assigned a thematic label, and the other set is assigned the opposite of that label. The plot of the narration involves the superimposition of time over the paradigmatic conflict, and this syntagmatic narrative transformation ("stretching out") comes to its eventual climax with an inversion of the initial configuration of the groupings of the *dramatis personae*.

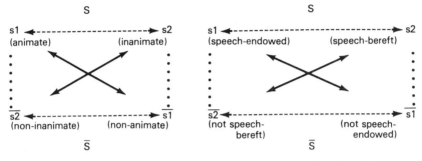

FIG. 1.2. S = Zoetic   FIG. 1.3. S = Semiotic.

The attentive reader should now be able to generate a complete universe of meaning, starting from any point in either Fig. 1.2 or Fig. 1.3 (or several other squares that could readily be constructed). With a little bit of ingenuity, and by unleashing the Pure Play of Musement, the spawning of endless movie scripts for further sequels and prolegomena to *Star Wars* should also be a romp.

Once before in this Introduction, the twin locutions "microcosmos" and "macrocosmos" have cropped up, but, as Heraclitus already well knew, there is a structural isomorphism between the inner personal world of the psyche and the vaster natural order of the universe. This central insight was summed up in his aphorism xxviii: "I went in search of myself." A paradox of this sort belongs with Kant's antinomies about space, time, and causality. What Heraclitus meant was that once he encountered the law of the microcosmos within himself, he discovered it anew in the external world (cf. Diels 1901:vii). Heraclitus supplies—if in fragmentary fashion—the essential link between the biosphere and the semiosphere, which is perfectly condensed by Thom's translation of the Heraclitean logos as "form"; and recall that it was the late Barthes who affirmed that "La sémiologie est une science des formes . . . " (Barthes 1957:218). We know that Heraclitus juggled with logos in at least four of its senses all at once: he intended by the term (1) his own discourse, (2) the nature of semiotic systems in general, (3) the composition of mind, and (4) the universal principle in accordance with which all things come to pass. Thom is absolutely correct, therefore, in interpreting *logos* as "the formal structure that assures for any object its unity and its stability" (Thom 1975:329n5; cf. Sebeok 1979:289n6). And Heraclitus thus marks the beginning of Hesse's unification of opposites in the Game: "It is wise, listening not to me but to the report [*logos*], to agree [*homologein*] that all things are one" (aphorism xxxvi). The reconciled antithesis between the themes of isolation and the community of *logos* is then triply applied to the Universes that Peirce alluded to, which, in Heraclitus, appear as (a) the semiotic production, (b) the private personality (mind), and (c) the communal domain. By its rational structure and its public function of the art and thought of Heraclitus, "language becomes a symbol for the unifying structure of the world which wisdom apprehends" (Kahn 1979:131). The superformula $E = mc^2$, which expresses the unifying structure of the world—the relationship of mass to energy—is intimated in the dedication of this book.

In chapter 2 we show that Peirce's uses of the Play of Musement bear a more than casual resemblance to Sherlock Holmes's advocacy of imagination (the specifically human faculty "to make images and to move them about inside one's head in new arrangements" [Bronowski 1967:39]), intuition and speculation (cf. Peirce 5.213n1), or extreme languor. Ginzburg (1980:12) independently reaches the same conclusion that we did, recognizing the emergence, toward the end of the nineteenth century, of a semiotic paradigm based on the interpretation of symptoms, features, clues, in a word, *indices,* and shows how this model, rooted in medical semiotics, became influential throughout the human sciences at large. Its transfiguration can be traced from primitive hunting cultures and, quite specifically, Mesopotamian divinatory doctrine, to the modern sciences, and, moreover, this progression from the mantic to the rational can be understood best in terms of semiotic principles, systematically applied (Bottéro 1974).

In chapter 4 I deal with the artist, romancer, and necromancer Morris, who himself could well have qualified for membership in the Castalian order: with this serene encyclopedist, who endeavored to dovetail all the scientific disciplines, "the cult of truth [was] closely bound up with the cult of the beautiful and, in addition to this, with the contemplative care of the spirit...." And in chapter 5, I turn to Bühler, under Meinong's sway, who wrote so eloquently about the role of play (*Spielräume*) in the vernacular, in the language of the poet (often in heightened fashion), as well as in the language of scientific works (Bühler 1965:171f.).

I return to a consideration of *Spieltrieb,* in somewhat more detail, in chapter 9, citing Spencer as having propagated, in 1897, the union of the play-impulse with aesthetic feelings and sentiments—a point of view widely advanced among contemporary biologists to account for and define art. I neglected to add that, churlishly, Spencer refuses to acknowledge by name the source of his argument, which was, unmistakably, Schiller.

In short, the contents of this book were shaped to exemplify the Play of Musement as a species of reverie on the threshold of scientific study. Its end is to meditate upon connections among the Universe of Signs and other Universes, to provoke, and to speculate—tempered by critical discussion—concerning the causes for such associations. The essays focus on the wellsprings and vital foundations of several major types of semiosis:

1. In the averbal domain, on architecture, dance, music, painting, and behavior generally (chap. 9, Appendix I).

2. In the verbal domain, on an (to me, autobiographically consequential) aspect of the verbal art (chap. 3), and—rather extensively—the alleged bent of several species of animals toward language (chaps. 6, 7, 8, Appendix II). We also discuss certain crucial problems in logic, notably abduction (chap. 2), both in fact and in fiction.

3. Self-referentially, I take up the dialectic of semiotic inquiry itself, particularly as exemplified by Peirce (chap. 2), Morris (chap. 4), and Bühler (chap. 5).

4. Finally, in one essay (chap. 10; cf. Appendix III) I attempt to trace out links between two seemingly very different Universes: the intimately coupled worlds of the mind and of the brute neurochemical blob enclosed in and radiating from the human cranium. Among other enigmatic oppositions I try to conjecture about in this work, none remains more profoundly puzzling and unresolved. Schrödinger, Wigner, and Popper and Eccles have all expressed the view that "there is need for some revision of physics in order to allow for the interaction of mind and matter in some special regions of the brain" (Eccles 1979:4). Monod, on the other hand, pejoratively labeled those who hold a belief in "dualist interactionism" as animists. My personal biases strongly incite me to adopt—to be sure, provisionally—a variant of the dualist-interactionist hypothesis, one which is closest to a theory maintained by J. Z. Young. This theory involves the principle of double coding and control. Quite briefly, according to this model (substituting my terminology), the mind is a system of signs—hence an immaterial order that upholds order. The mind is "the manifestation of the information coded within our physical brains" (Young 1979:45). Signs, although they are never material, can only be actualized and carried by material systems, whether static or dynamic. Signs pervade all of life (Sebeok 1977c) "as the encoded information that directs those ordered activities so that life continues" (Young 1979:45).

At present we know virtually nothing about the manner in which information is coded and controlled in brain operation, but Young's way of looking at the problem pinpoints at least the right questions to ask, which are, essentially, semiotic in character. His view implies that although mind and body are in a sense distinct, they can never be separated. I totally concur with his conclusion that, instead of postulating a distinct body and mind, "we can usefully consider that life is an activity that continues because it is directed by the symbolic non-material information about order, as embodied first in DNA and then in brains" (ibid.: 54). It will not have escaped the reader's attention that Young's model is itself derived from comparison with the coding operation semioticians employ when dealing with human communication.

In conclusion, I should like to return to the Magister Ludi's haunting admonition to Joseph: "the Game is not without its dangers. . . . " An especially perilous area of application is that of confidence games, which are very ancient but are, today, enhanced—and, by the same token, veiled—by the tools of modern technology. It is fascinating to learn from Maurer's classic book that competent con-men find a good deal of diversion in "playing the con" (Maurer 1974:89), presumably for the sake of Pure Play, as it were, besides the more tangible rewards of their kind of work. At the end of a con game, after the sting, it is of the essence to cool the mark out—that is, to pacify the victim after the fleecing, to stop him from complaining ("beefing") to the authorities.

When a con game is exposed, the informer is in double jeopardy: on the one hand, from the con mob itself (ibid.: chap. 5 and p.273); but even more so from Mr. John Bates, as the mark is commonly named in the big-con lingo. When he finally is convinced that he has been swindled, he is often "incapable of speech. He is sickened by what he has been through" (ibid.:69). Yet the hatred the addict nurses is seldom directed at the insideman (ibid.:279f.). As Northumberland tells Morton, ". . . the first bringer of unwelcome news/ Hath but a losing office; and his tongue/ Sounds ever after as a sullen bell,/ Remember'd knolling a departing friend."

Certain facets of the story of the Clever Hans Phenomenon—the effect and the fallacy (which are by no means synonymous)—are examined in several chapters of this book. Hans, the eponymous stallion, died early in the century. Or did he? He seems, rather, to have become a shape-shifting revenant, a ghost animal returning to complete his unfinished business of épater le bourgeois. A notable attribute of revenants is that, like poltergeists, they make noise: "they groan, cry, scream, yell, moan, wail, howl, holler, and sigh; they curse, laugh, whoop, whisper, cough" (Jones 1950:934)—or they simply paw the ground, or, aping the deaf, they "sign." Hans, indulging in such distasteful semiotic comportment, sometimes reappears as another horse, as a pig or a dog, more recently as a porpoise or a primate, or, in more modest guise, a tortoise or a woodpecker. Many educated people are quick to believe in the "accomplishments" of the avatars of Hans, especially when their faith is reinforced by the media—particularly popular television—acting as accomplices, or shills, for the act (Sebeok 1979:282n4). (For example, the opening segment of Those Amazing Animals, on WRTV-ABC Indianapolis, aired on August 24, 1980, featured a miniature mare, Kristina, that solves math problems, just as Morocco did in the seventeenth century. Kristina, like Lady and Weeping Roger [Sebeok 1979:90, 28n3] before her, was billed as "a mind-reading horse with ESP," although she was reacting to the most blatant gestural signs imaginable. I should perhaps add that this show is a spin-off from an earlier one, aptly titled That's Incredible.)

Our really very humble analysis of the Clever Hans Phenomenon and its all too easily recognized exploitation in current investigations of the alleged linguistic capacity of chimpanzees and gorillas has taught me how hazardous an undertaking it is to attempt to play the Game in straightforward fashion: we aimed our studies at scholars who dared face the facts as they are, rather than as they would wish them to be; at responsible, not avid, journalists; and at laymen who prefer the path of sanity to that of credulity. The greasy alarums and excursions—although their noisomeness was, fortunately, enlivened by farcical overtones—that ensued upon the heels of our early publications on this subject cannot be summarized here. I am saving this chronicle for another book, now in the making, to be devoted entirely to the saga of Clever Hans, his antecedents and his followers in its full implications for human affairs, including the murky corners of academic fraud and the far more commonplace intricacies of scientific self-deception.

Let me merely call attention here to one beacon shining through the miasma of contention about this phenomenon that, for me, unexpectedly clarified a host of previously mystifying attitudes in respect to the facts of the matter and the lines of argumentation used by our adversaries. In a recent notice of our book, *Speaking of Apes* (1980a), the sociologist Truzzi independently confirmed this flash of insight: "The arguments found in this [area of research] sharply parallel those between critics and advocates in psi research." *Psi research* is a cover term for telepathy ("mind reading"), clairvoyance ("second sight"), precognition ("divination"), and psychokinesis (e.g., "levitation"). All four have long been part and parcel of folklore and superstition; none of them, in a century of unremitting research, has ever enjoyed empirical verification (Hansel 1980; Marks and Kammann 1980). However, the advocates of psi research have developed a set of standard rules obtaining to their dialectical wonderland. This means that if you want to engage with them in argumentation, you must abide by the assumptions of the logic they constructed for their world's benefit. What is utterly amazing is that the ape "language" investigators and those engaged in comparable explorations with other animals have adopted psi logic. This astounding tendency—which has, since May 1980, been widely perceived—has certain highly interesting consequences that I also intend to examine in my next book. For the time being, and with deep apologies to Eliot, I am forced to close this issue:

> I have seen the primates signing, each to each.
> I do not think that they will sign to me.

For a writer of my temperament and my predilections, one of the greatest gratifications in assembling the materials for different portions of a book of this kind derives from the now this, now that coterie of people—experts and charlatans, scholars and conjurers, academics and circus folk, observers and fanatics—with whom one has the privilege of intermingling over weeks or months at a time. Many friendships are forged, many enmities begotten, both to be savored for a lifetime. What other profession would simultaneously impel one to plunge into the interlocked brotherhood of the Baker Street Irregulars of New York, the Napoleons of Crime of Detroit, the Red Circle of Washington, and the Sherlock Holmes Society of London, with one compartment of one's mind, and, with another, to become ensnarled in the festering twilight zone inhabited by enslaved Wookiee-like chimeras out of *The Island of Dr. Moreau* and those exercising supercilious mentorship over their fate? Always with benevolence, though often backed up by electric cattle prods, endowed with ample public and private funding, these men, women, and couples, in deadly competition with one another for their share of attention and resources, constitute a formidable phalanx of specimens of a sort I have previously encountered only at such fringes of the Universe of learning as celebrations of ESP and orgies of UFOlogy, or among students of the Bermuda Triangle, Big Foot, and the Loch Ness Monster. These are all great stories, and I relish their exoticism as long as these childish amusements are not mistaken for the extremely unlikely. The Play of Musement has, so far, led me to excitingly novel encounters at the borderline of biology and semiotics, in frequently surprising, sometimes relishingly controversial, but most often unfamiliar meeting places in the Universe of contemporary experience.

Chapter 2

"You Know My Method":
A Juxtaposition of Charles S. Peirce
and Sherlock Holmes

> "I never guess."
> —Sherlock Holmes
> in *The Sign of Four*

> But we must conquer the truth by
> guessing, or not at all.
> —Charles S. Peirce, Ms. 692

INTRODUCTORY NOTE

WHO IS THE most original and the most versatile intellect that the Americas
have so far produced? The answer "Charles S. Peirce" is uncontested, because any second would be so far behind as not to be worth nominating.
Mathematician, astronomer, chemist, geodesist, surveyor, cartographer,
metrologist, spectroscopist, engineer, inventor; psychologist, philologist,
lexicographer, historian of science, mathematical economist, lifelong student of medicine; book reviewer, dramatist, actor, short story writer;
phenomenologist, semiotician, logician, rhetorician, metaphysician—and,
the Sebeoks now add, detective! He was, for a few examples, the first
modern experimental psychologist in the Americas, the first metrologist
to use a wave-length of light as a unit of measure, the inventor of the quincuncial projection of the sphere, the first known conceiver of the design
and theory of an electric switching-circuit computer, and the founder
of "the economy of research." He is the only system-building philosopher
in the Americas who has been both competent and productive in logic,
in mathematics, and in a wide range of the sciences. If he has had any
equals in that respect in the entire history of philosophy, they do not
number more than two.

The materials constituting this chapter, written in collaboration with Jean Umiker-
Sebeok, originally appeared in *Semiotica* 26:203-50 (1979). They were subsequently
incorporated into a monograph, rearranged, enhanced by additional illustrations, and
graced with the illuminating introductory note by Max H. Fisch. This hardback
edition was undertaken at the invitation of Jack Tracy, and appeared in his series,
Gaslight Publications (Bloomington, Indiana, 1980). Arrangements have, so far, been
completed for the publication of a Japanese version, and are currently in progress
for German, Italian, and Portuguese versions as well.

17

Peirce (pronounced *Purse*) was born in Cambridge, Massachusetts, in 1839. His father was professor of mathematics and astronomy at Harvard College. Charles thus grew up in the Cambridge scientific circle. He took his bachelor's degree at Harvard in 1859, and a graduate degree in chemistry *summa cum laude* at the Lawrence Scientific School in 1863. His longest employments were (1) as a research scientist in the Coast and Geodetic Survey, 1859-60, 1861-91, and, in conjunction therewith, as observer in the Harvard College Observatory, 1867-75; (2) as reviewer, primarily of philosophic, scientific, and mathematical books, for *The Nation*, 1869-1908 (along with the New York *Evening Post*, 1890-1908); and (3) as Lecturer in Logic at The Johns Hopkins University, 1879-84. He gave courses of lectures at Harvard University in 1865, 1869-70, 1903, and 1907, and at the Lowell Institute in Boston in 1866, 1892-93, and 1903; a course of "Cambridge Conferences" in 1898; and occasional lectures in other places. He was a principal contributor to *The Century Dictionary*, in six volumes, 1889-91, and to Baldwin's *Dictionary of Philosophy and Psychology*, in two volumes, 1901-2. He was elected a Fellow of the American Academy of Arts and Sciences in 1867, a member of the National Academy of Sciences in 1877, and a member of the London Mathematical Society in 1880. His service in the Coast and Geodetic Survey involved five periods of transatlantic duty adding up to nearly three out of the thirteen years 1870-83. He represented the United States at meetings of the International Geodetic Association and thereby became the first American delegate to any international scientific association. Well over a hundred Ph.D. theses, thirty books, and a thousand articles and chapters have been written concerning various aspects of his work.

The most extensive editions of his writings are (1) the eight volumes of *Collected Papers* (Harvard University Press), Vols. 1-6 edited by Charles Hartshorne and Paul Weiss, 1931-35, and Vols. 7-8 by Arthur W. Burks, 1958 (commonly cited by volume and paragraph number); (2) the four-volumes-in-five of *The New Elements of Mathematics* (Mouton) edited by Carolyn Eisele, 1976; and (3) the three volumes of *Contributions to "The Nation"* (Texas Tech Press, Lubbock) edited by Kenneth L. Ketner and James E. Cook, 1975-79. The largest deposit of Peirce's manuscripts and correspondence is in The Houghton Library of Harvard University; see Richard S. Robin's *Annotated Catalogue of the Papers of Charles S. Peirce* (University of Massachusetts Press, 1967) and "The Peirce Papers: A Supplementary Catalogue" (*Transactions of The Charles S. Peirce Society* 7:37-57, 1971). A Microfilm Edition of the greater part of these papers is available from the Harvard University Library Photoduplication Department. There is also a nearly complete Microfiche Edition of the writings that Peirce himself published, accompanied by a printed *Bibliography*, both primary and secondary (Institute for Studies in Pragmaticism, Texas Tech University, Lubbock), edited by Ketner and others, 1977. A new printed selection from Peirce's writings, published and unpublished, in a single chronological order, in fifteen volumes, will begin appearing in 1981 from Indiana University Press. Volume I will cover the years 1857-66, and most of its contents will be appearing in print for the first time.

The episode in Peirce's life which moved the authors of "You Know My Method" to compare him with Sherlock Holmes took place a century ago, in 1879, in the service of the Coast and Geodetic Survey. That was one of his most productive years. Two brief examples: (1) His "Note on the Theory of the Economy of Research," which opened a new branch of economics, appeared in the Survey's annual report for 1876, which came out in 1879. (2) "A Quincuncial Projection of the Sphere" appeared in the *American Journal of Mathematics*. (During the Second World War, the Survey published a new and much enlarged edition of the map, under the title "Peirce's World-Quincuncial Projection," as being the best on which to chart international air routes. And in 1963 the Survey launched a research vessel named for him, which is now in the service of the National Oceanic and Atmospheric Administration.)

Peirce had been initiated in methods of detection twelve years earlier, in the spring of 1867, by his father, Benjamin Peirce, the leading mathematician of the day, who had recently become Superintendent of the Coast Survey. The occasion was the Sylvia Ann Howland will case. This was one of the most famous cases that ever came to trial, and the most famous of the many famous things about it was the testimony of the Peirces. The questions at issue were (1) whether Miss Howland's signatures to the two copies of the "second page" codicil of an earlier will were genuine, or were forged by tracing her signature to the will itself, and (2) whether, supposing them genuine, the codicil invalidated a later will much less favorable to her niece, Hetty H. Robinson. The Peirces addressed themselves to the first of these questions. Under his father's direction, Charles examined photographic enlargements of forty-two genuine signatures for coincidences of position in their thirty down-strokes. In 25,830 different comparisons of downstrokes, he found 5,325 coincidences, so that the relative frequency of coincidence was less than a fifth. Applying the theory of probabilities, his father calculated that a coincidence of genuine signatures as complete as that between the signatures to the codicil, or between either of them and that to the will in question, would occur only once in five-to-the-thirtieth-power times. The judge was not prepared to base his decision on the theory of probabilities, but he decided against Miss Robinson on the second issue. (Nevertheless, she married Edward H. Green later in 1867 and, as Hetty Green, was on her way to becoming "the witch of Wall Street.") In a long article on "The Howland Will Case" in the *American Law Review* (July 1870), it was said that: "Hereafter, the curious stories of Poe will be thought the paltriest imitations."

Among the surviving Peirce manuscripts, the earliest account of the 1879 episode that he intended for publication was in a 1904 draft of a paper "On the Simplest Possible Branch of Mathematics." Other parts of that paper appeared for the first time in 1976, in *The New Elements of Mathematics*, Vol. I, pp.158-69.

Much the fullest account, and the only one so far published, was in an essay entitled "Guessing," which he wrote in the spring of 1907, twenty-eight years after the episode. It was first published in the short-lived magazine *Hound and Horn* in 1929, fifteen years after Peirce's death and fifty after the event. (Other parts of that essay were reprinted in *Collected Papers* 7.36-48 in 1958, but that central part was omitted except for brief mention in an editorial footnote.)

Very few Peirce scholars have gone back to the *Hound and Horn*. So it has remained for the authors of *You Know My Method*, a century after the episode, to take us back to "Guessing," and thereby to introduce Holmes buffs to a great philosopher, and at the same time to equip Peirce buffs to read his other writings with fresh eyes.

The extreme diversification of Peirce's work had a focus and a purpose. The focus was in logic, conceived at first as a branch of a branch of semiotics, but eventually as nearly coextensive with it, though with a distribution of emphasis different from those of semioticians who are not logicians. The purpose was to distinguish the possible kinds of semioses or sign-functions, and, among them, to make the most thorough study he could of arguments in particular, and above all of their functions in mathematics and in the sciences. His major single discovery was that what he at first called *hypothesis* and later *abduction* or *retroduction* is a distinct kind of argument, different both from deduction and from induction, and indispensable both in mathematics and in the sciences. This discovery came at least as early as 1866, and one of the chief interests of Volume I of the new edition will be in the steps that led him to it.

Whatever the technical name and definition of this third kind of argument should be, and the exact working out of its relations with the other two, an essential element of it is something for which the colloquial name is *guessing*. Comparing the historical Peirce and the fictional Sherlock Holmes as detectives and as elaborators of the theory of detection is therefore not just an entertaining diversion for Holmes buffs, but the best possible entry into Peirce's philosophy for readers not yet acquainted with it.

For the most part, even those who *are* acquainted with Peirce's work know only detached fragments of it. A philosopher, for example, is most likely to know of him as the founder of pragmatism, and a semiotician as the founder (or one of the two or three founders) of present-day semiotics. But neither the philosophers nor the semioticians seem aware that his pragmatism was a theorem of semiotics, and that much of his labor on semiotics was for the sake of perfecting his proof of that theorem. Perhaps the most lucid exposition of the argument was the one he composed in the spring of 1907, in the form of a long untitled Letter to the Editor of *The Nation*. "Guessing" was an offshoot of that letter which could not be reduced to its scale. About the time the letter was finished, Peirce heard that Bliss Perry, the editor of the *Atlantic Monthly*, was interested, and he sent him both the letter and "Guessing." Neither was accepted. By the time Peirce got them back and sent the letter to *The*

Nation, Paul Elmer More had succeeded Wendell Phillips Garrison as editor. The letter never appeared, and, so far as we know, it was never returned to its author. But three hundred and fifty pages of drafts survive in Manuscript 318, and the editors of the *Collected Papers* spliced two drafts just before the last sentence of *CP* 5.481 to form what they called "A Survey of Pragmaticism" (*CP* 5.464-96). The best parts of Manuscript 318 remain unpublished, and though perhaps most readers get some sense of the relation between the semiotics and the pragmatism, they get none of the relation between either of them and the role of "Guessing" in detection. So the fragmentation continues.

Where, then, should a beginner begin? With "You Know My Method," I suggest, followed by *CP* 7.36-48 for most of the rest of "Guessing"; for, as the Sebeoks' Peircean epigraph puts it: "We must conquer the truth by guessing, or not at all."—MAX H. FISCH

C. S. PEIRCE—CONSULTING DETECTIVE

On Friday, June 20, 1879, Charles S. Peirce boarded the Fall River Line steamship *Bristol* in Boston, bound for New York, where he was to attend a conference the next day. Upon his arrival in New York, the following morning, he experienced what he describes as a "strange fuzzy sensation" in his head, which he attributed to the stale air of his stateroom. He hurriedly dressed and left the ship. In his haste to get some fresh air, he inadvertently left behind his overcoat and an expensive Tiffany lever watch which had been purchased for him by the U.S. government for his work with the Coast Survey. Soon realizing his oversight, Peirce rushed back to the boat only to find his things gone, at which point, faced with what he felt would be a "life-long professional disgrace" were he not able to restore the watch in as perfect condition as he had received it, he tells us that, having "then made all the colored waiters, no matter on what deck they belonged, come and stand up in a row. . . ."

> I went from one end of the row to the other, and talked a little to each one, in as *dégagé* a manner as I could, about whatever he could talk about with interest, but would least expect me to bring forward, hoping that I might seem such a fool that I should be able to detect some symptom of his being the thief. When I had gone through the row I turned and walked from them, though not away, and said to myself, "Not the least scintilla of light have I got to go upon." But thereupon my other self (for our communings are always in dialogues), said to me, "But you simply *must* put your finger on the man. No matter if you have no reason, you must say whom you will think to be the thief." I made a little loop in my walk, which had not taken a minute, and as I turned toward them, all shadow of doubt had vanished. There was no self-criticism. All that was out of place. [Peirce 1929:271]

Taking the suspect aside, Peirce was unable to persuade him, either through reason, threat, or promise of fifty dollars, to return his belongings to him. He then "ran down to the dock and was driven as fast as the cabby could, to Pinkerton's." He was taken to see a Mr. Bangs, the head of the New York branch of that famous detective agency, and reports the following interview:

> "Mr. Bangs, a negro on the Fall River boat, whose name is so-and-so (I gave it) has stolen my watch, chain, and light overcoat. The watch is a Charles Frodsham and here is its number. He will come off the boat at one o'clock, and will immediately go to pawn the watch, for which he will get fifty dollars. I wish you to have him shadowed, and as soon as he has the pawn ticket, let him be arrested." Said Mr. Bangs, "What makes you think he has stolen your watch?" "Why," said I, "I have no reason whatever for thinking so; but I am entirely confident that it is so. Now if he should not go to a pawn shop to get rid of the watch, as I am sure he will, that would end the matter, and you need take no step. But I know he will. I have given you the number of the watch, and here is my card. You will be quite safe to arrest him." [1929:273]

A Pinkerton man was assigned to his case, but instructed to "act upon his own inferences" rather than follow Peirce's surmises about who the culprit was. The detective, looking into the personal background of each Fall River waiter, began shadowing a man other than Peirce's suspect, and this proved to be a false lead.

When the detective thus came to a dead end in his investigation, Peirce returned to Mr. Bangs, and was advised by him to send postcards to all the pawnbrokers of Fall River, New York, and Boston, offering a reward for the recovery of his watch. The postcards were mailed out on June 23. The next day, Peirce and his Pinkerton agent recovered the watch from a New York lawyer, who directed them to the pawnbroker who had responded to his offer of a reward. The pawnbroker himself "described the person who pawned the watch so graphically that no doubt was possible that it had been 'my [i.e., Peirce's] man'" (1929:275).

Peirce and the detective then made their way to the suspect's lodgings, with the intention of also recovering the missing chain and overcoat. The detective was reluctant to enter the premises without a warrant, so Peirce, disgusted by the agent's ineptitude, went in alone, confidently telling the agent that he would return in exactly twelve minutes with his property. He then described the following sequence of events:

> I mounted the three flights and knocked at the door of the flat. A yellow woman came; but another of about the same complexion was just behind her, without a hat. I walked in and said, "Your husband is now on his road to Sing Sing for stealing my watch. I learned that my chain and overcoat which he also stole are here and I am going to take them." Thereupon the two women raised a tremendous hullabaloo and threatened to send instantly for the police. I do not remember exactly what I said, I only know that I was entirely cool and told them they were quite mistaken in thinking that they would send for the police, since it would only make

matters worse for the man. For since I knew just where my watch and overcoat were, I should have them before the police arrived. . . . I saw no place in that room where the chain was likely to be, and walked through into another room. Little furniture was there beyond a double bed and a wooden trunk on the further side of the bed. I said, "Now my chain is at the bottom of that trunk under the clothes; and I am going to take it. . . ." I knelt down and fortunately found the trunk unlocked. Having thrown out all the clothes . . . I came upon . . . my chain. I at once attached it to my watch, and in doing so noticed that the second woman (who had worn no hat) had disappeared, notwithstanding the intense interest she had taken in my first proceedings. "Now," said I, "it only remains to find my light overcoat." . . . The woman spread her arms right and left and said, "You are welcome to look over the whole place." I said, "I am very much obliged to you, Madam; for this very extraordinary alteration of the tone you took when I began on the trunk assures me that the coat is not here. . . ." So I left the flat and then remarked that there was another flat on the same landing.

Although I do not positively remember, I think it likely that I was convinced that the disappearance of the other woman was connected with the marked willingness that I should search for my overcoat through the flat from which I had emerged. I certainly got the idea that the other woman did not live far off. So to begin with I knocked at the door of that opposite flat. Two yellow or yellowish girls came. I looked over their shoulders and saw a quite respectable looking parlor with a nice piano. But upon the piano was a neat bundle of just the right size and shape to contain my overcoat. I said, "I have called because there is a bundle here belonging to me; oh, yes, I see it, and will just take it." So I gently pushed beyond them, took the bundle, opened it, and found my overcoat, which I put on. I descended to the street, and reached my detective about fifteen seconds before my twelve minutes had elapsed. [1929:275-277]

Peirce's remarkable aplomb is given charming expression in a letter he sent to Superintendent C. P. Patterson, of the Coast Survey, later in the day:

I have to report that I arrived here last Saturday and my watch, the property of the Survey, was stolen from me . . . at the instant of my arrival. I at once set to work to find it and was so happy as to succeed this afternoon. I strongly hope to capture the thief tomorrow morning before seven o'clock. . . .

The next day, June 25, Peirce wrote to Superintendent Patterson that "The two negroes who stole the watch were today committed for trial. Everything had been recovered. The thief is the very man I suspected throughout contrary to the judgment of the detective."

As noted in a much later letter to his friend and disciple, the Harvard philosopher and psychologist William James (1842-1910), this story of detection was meant as an illustration of Peirce's "theory of why it is that people so often guess right." "This singular guessing instinct" (1929:

281), or the inclination to entertain a hypothesis, more commonly referred to by Peirce as *Abduction*[1] or *Retroduction*, is described as a "singular salad . . . whose chief elements are its groundlessness, its ubiquity,
and its trustworthiness" (Ms. 692). As to its ubiquity, Peirce writes:

> Looking out my window this lovely spring morning I see an azalea in full
> bloom. No, no! I do not see that; though that is the only way I can de-
> scribe what I see. *That* is a proposition, a sentence, a fact; but what I
> perceive is not proposition, sentence, fact, but only an image, which I
> make intelligible in part by means of a statement of fact. This statement
> is abstract; but what I see is concrete. I perform an abduction when I so
> much as express in a sentence anything I see. The truth is that the whole
> fabric of our knowledge is one matted felt of pure hypothesis confirmed
> and refined by induction. Not the smallest advance can be made in knowl-
> edge beyond the stage of vacant staring, without making an abduction at
> every step. [Ms. 692]

If all new knowledge depends on the formation of a hypothesis, there
nevertheless "seems at first to be no room at all for the question of what
supports it, since from an actual fact it only infers a *may-be* (*may-be*
and *may-be* not). But there is a decided leaning to the affirmative side
and the frequency with which that turns out to be an actual fact is
. . . quite the most surprising of all the wonders of the universe" (8.238).
Comparing our capacity for abduction with "a bird's musical and aero-
nautic powers; that is, it is to us, as those are to them, the loftiest of our
merely instinctive powers" (1929:282), Peirce notes that "retroduction
goes upon the hope that there is sufficient affinity between the reasoner's
mind and nature to render guessing not altogether hopeless, provided
each guess is checked by comparison with observation" (1.121).

Peirce maintained elsewhere that the ability of a newly hatched
chick to pick up food, "choosing as it picks, and picking what it aims to
pick," while "not reasoning, because it is not done deliberately," is nevertheless "in every respect but that . . . just like abductive inference," and
he further traces the physical and social sciences back to the animal instincts for, respectively, getting food and reproduction (Ms. 692). Retroduction is a type of instinctive behavior two classic examples of which
are the migration of robins and the hive building of bees. Peirce called
the seemingly intelligent behavior of the lower animals *il lume naturale*,
which he considered indispensable to retroduction.[2] Peirce spoke of
rational, animal, and vegetable instinct; as Maryann Ayim notes (1974:
36), all levels of instinctive activity "have this feature in common—the
activity caters to the survival and well-being of the species as a whole
by enabling species members to react appropriately to environmental
conditions"; this holds, as well, for man-as-a-scientist.

In today's popular view of the Victorian world, man-as-a-scientist
means, above all others, Sherlock Holmes, the first practitioner of scientific crime detection, and inventor of the celebrated "Science of Deduction

and Analysis." In allusion to Holmes, Norwood Russell Hanson had made the interesting observation that: "Often the thrust of Holmes' comment, 'Simple deduction my dear Watson' [*sic*][3] is to the effect that the reasoning in question has proceeded from the previously accepted to what should be expected. But just as often the mathematician and the scientist will argue from the bottom of the page 'up' " (Bernstein 1965:59). This is one of the things Peirce identifies as "retroducing." It proceeds from an unexpected anomaly to a premiss cluster, most parts of which are already accepted.

> A given object presents an extraordinary combination of characters of which we should like to have an explanation. That there is any explanation of them is a pure assumption; and if there be, it is some one hidden fact which explains them; while there are, perhaps, a million other possible ways of explaining them, if they were not all, unfortunately, false. A man is found in the streets of New York stabbed in the back. The chief of police might open a directory and put his finger on any name and guess that that is the name of the murderer. How much would such a guess be worth? But the number of names in the directory does not approach the multitude of possible laws of attraction which could have accounted for Keppler's [*sic*] law of planetary motion and, in advance of verification by predications of perturbations etc., would have accounted for them to perfection. Newton, you will say, assumed that the law would be a simple one. But what was that but piling guess on guess? Surely, vastly more phenomena in nature are complex than simple. . . . [T]here is no warrant for doing more than putting [an abduction] as an interrogation. [Ms. 692]

Abduction, that is, retroduction—"a poor name," Peirce himself confessed—is, according to one of Peirce's later formulations, which would appear to owe much to the British philosopher George Berkeley (1685-1753), a means of communication between man and his Creator, a "Divine privilege" which must be cultivated (Eisele 1976, vol. III:206). For Peirce, "according to the doctrine of chances it would be practically impossible for any being, by pure chance to guess the cause of any phenomenon," and he therefore surmises that there can "be no reasonable doubt that man's mind, having been developed under the influence of the laws of nature, for that reason naturally thinks somewhat after nature's pattern" (Peirce 1929:269). "It is evident," he writes, "that unless man had had some inward light tending to make his guesses . . . much more often true than they would be by mere chance, the human race would long ago have been extirpated for its utter incapacity in the struggles for existence . . ." (Ms. 692).

In addition to the principle that the human mind is, as a result of natural evolutionary processes, predisposed to guessing correctly about the world, Peirce proposes a second conjectural principle to partially explain the phenomenon of guessing, namely, that "we often derive from observation strong intimations of truth, without being able to specify what were the circumstances we had observed which conveyed those intimations" (1929:282). Peirce, to return to the story of the missing watch, was unable to determine on a conscious level which of the waiters of the Fall River boat was guilty. Holding himself "in as passive and receptive a state" (1929:281) as he could during his brief interview with each waiter, it was only when he forced himself to make what appeared to be a blind guess that he realized that in fact the crook had given off some unwitting index and that he himself had perceived this telltale sign in, as he put it, an "unself-conscious" manner, having made "a discrimination below the surface of consciousness, and not recognized as a real judgment, yet in very truth a genuine discrimination" (1929:280). The processes by which we form hunches about the world are, in Peirce's conception, dependent on perceptual judgments, which contain general elements such that universal propositions may be deduced from them. On the basis of his experimental work on the psychology of perception, conducted at The Johns Hopkins University with the well-known psychologist Joseph Jastrow (1863-1944), then his student (1929; 7.21-48), Peirce maintained that these perceptual judgments are "the result of a process, although of a process not sufficiently conscious to be controlled, or, to state it more truly, not controllable and therefore not fully conscious" (5.181). The different elements of a hypothesis are in our minds before we are conscious of entertaining it, "but it is the idea of putting together what we had never before dreamed of putting together which flashes the new suggestion before our contemplation" (5.181). Peirce describes the formation of a hypothesis as "an act of *insight*," the "abductive suggestion" coming to us "like a flash" (5.181). The only difference between a perceptual judgment and an abductive inference is that the former, unlike the latter, is not subject to logical analysis.

> [A]bductive inference shades into perceptual judgment without any sharp line of demarcation between them; or, in other words, our first premisses, the perceptual judgments, are to be regarded as an extreme case of abductive inferences, from which they differ in being absolutely beyond criticism. [5.181; cf. 6.522, Ms. 316]

Concerning scientific method, abduction is, according to Peirce, "merely preparatory," or "the first step of scientific reasoning" (7.218). The other "fundamentally different kinds of reasoning" in science are deduction and induction (see 1.65-68; 2.96-97; 5.145; 7.97; 7.202-207). Briefly, the step of adopting a hypothesis or a proposition which would lead to the prediction of what appear to be surprising facts is called *abduction*. The step by which the necessary and probable experiential consequences of our hypothesis are traced out is called *deduction*. *Induction* is the name Peirce gives to the experimental testing of the hypothesis.

Peirce also calls abduction "Originary Argument" since it is, of the three forms of reasoning, the "only kind of argument which starts a new idea" (2.97), and, in fact: "Its only justification is that if we are ever to understand things at all, it must be in that way" (5.145). Similarly, "neither deduction nor induction can ever add the smallest item to the data of perception; and . . . mere percepts do not constitute any knowledge applicable to any practical or theoretical use. All that makes knowledge applicable comes to us *via* abduction" (Ms. 692).

Abduction is an instinct which relies on unconscious perception of connections between aspects of the world, or, to use another set of terms, subliminal communication of messages. It is also associated with, or rather produces, according to Peirce, a certain type of emotion, which sets it apart from either induction or deduction.

> Hypothesis substitutes, for a complicated tangle of predicates attached to one subject, a single conception. Now, there is a peculiar sensation belonging to the act of thinking that each of these predicates inheres in the subject. In hypothetic inference this complicated feeling so produced is replaced by a single feeling of greater intensity, that belonging to the act of thinking the hypothetic conclusion. Now, when our nervous system is excited in a complicated way, there being a relation between the elements of the excitation, the result is a single harmonious disturbance which I call an emotion. Thus, the various sounds made by the instruments of an orchestra strike upon the ear, and the result is a peculiar musical emotion, quite distinct from the sounds themselves. This emotion is essentially the same thing as in hypothetic inference, and every hypothetic inference involves the formation of such an emotion. We may say, therefore, that hypothesis produces the *sensuous* element of thought, and induction the *habitual* element. [2.643]

Hence the pronouncement of a certain confidence and conviction of correctness which Peirce makes in relation to his detective work.

SHERLOCK HOLMES—CONSULTING SEMIOTICIAN

Peirce's account of the method by which he recovered his stolen watch bears a striking resemblance to Dr. Watson's descriptions of Sherlock Holmes in action, although there is, to our knowledge, no direct evidence that Peirce had read any of the Holmes stories or that he had met Sir Arthur Conan Doyle. It is likely, however, that Peirce heard something of at least the early Holmes stories. *A Study in Scarlet* was published in New York by Ward, Lock in 1888, and in 1890 *The Sign of Four* appeared in *Lippincott's Magazine*, the major contemporaneous rival to the *Atlantic Monthly*, which we know Peirce did read. In addition, there was already a vogue for Doyle in the United States by 1894, when the celebrated writer spent two months there giving a series of lectures and meeting his American compeers. Peirce had grown up in the company of writers of fiction and artists as well as scientists. In a letter of January 31, 1908, he wrote:

> But my father was a broad man and we were intimate with literary
> people too. William Story the sculptor, Longfellow, James Lowell, Charles
> Norton, Wendell Holmes, and occasionally Emerson, are among the figures
> of my earliest memories. [Hardwick 1977:113]

As an adult, Peirce appears to have kept abreast of contemporaneous
developments in the verbal arts, for he frequently mentions both European
and American authors of his time in his reviews in *The Nation* (Ketner
and Cook 1975). Edgar Allan Poe (1809-1849), moreover, seems to have
been one of his favorite writers (1.251, 6.460; Ms. 689, Ms. 1539).

Judging from his references to Poe's "The Murders in the Rue
Morgue," Peirce certainly had a taste for detective stories. Of course, it
is generally recognized that the character Sherlock Holmes is partly
modeled after Poe's Chevalier Dupin (see Messac 1929:596-602; Nordon
1966:212ff.; and Trevor Hall 1978:76), but J. L. Hitchings, in his article
on Holmes as a logician, makes the good point "that in contrast to Dupin,
who is the brainchild of a mathematician and a poet, Sherlock Holmes,
even at his most theoretical, is the offspring of a doctor's brain, and
always has his feet firmly planted on the ground" (1946:117). In addition
to his specialized medical training, Arthur Conan Doyle was caught up
in the general enthusiasm for science in the England of his day. By
the middle of the nineteenth century, science had become a solid part of
English thinking at all levels, and there was generally a "dominant tone
of positivist rationality" (Messac 1929:612; cf. Nordon 1966:244). Conan
Doyle himself reports: "It is to be remembered that these were the years
when Huxley, Tyndall, Darwin, Herbert Spencer and John Stuart Mill
were our chief philosophers, and that even the man in the street felt the
strong sweeping current of their thought . . ." (1924:26). Hitchings
explicitly compares the logic of Holmes with that of Mill: Holmes's
"habitual method of solving these difficult problems is by his own extended version of Mill's Method of Residues" (1946:115). Hitchings is,
however, on the wrong track when he claims that "Most of Holmes's
reasoning is causal," citing the detective's own remark that "reasoning
from effect to cause is less frequent and thus more difficult than reasoning
from cause to effect" (1946:115-116).

There are frequent allusions in the Sherlock Holmes saga to Holmes
as a fox-hound—particularly in *A Study in Scarlet, The Dancing Men,
The Bruce-Partington Plans,* and *The Devil's Foot.* For example, in *The
Boscombe Valley Mystery,* Watson writes:

> Sherlock Holmes was transformed when he was hot upon such a scent
> as this. Men who had only known the quiet thinker and logician of Baker
> Street would have failed to recognize him. His face flushed and darkened.
> His brows were drawn into two hard black lines, while his eyes shone
> out from beneath them with a steely glitter. His face was bent downward,
> his shoulders bowed, his lips compressed, and the veins stood out like
> whipcord in his long, sinewy neck. His nostrils seemed to dilate with a

purely animal lust for the chase, and his mind was so absolutely concentrated upon the matter before him that a question or remark fell unheeded upon his ears, or, at the most, only provoked a quick, impatient snarl in reply.

Referring to this passage, Pierre Nordon comments: "Here we see a man transformed with all speed into a fox-hound before our very eyes, until he seems almost to have lost the power of speech and be reduced to expressing himself by sounds" (1966:217), heeding instead his instinctive, nonverbal powers of perception and abduction.

It is from such intuitive clue-gathering that Holmes is able to formulate his hypotheses, although he tends to subsume both the perceptual and the hypothetical processes under the rubric of "Observation," as in the following passage from the chapter entitled "The Science of Deduction" in *The Sign of Four,* where Holmes and Watson are discussing a French detective named François le Villard:

> [Holmes]: "He possesses two out of three qualities necessary for the ideal detective. He has the power of observation and that of deduction. He is only wanting in knowledge. . . ."
> [Watson]: ". . . But you spoke just now of observation and deduction. Surely the one to some extent implies the other."
> [Holmes]: "Why, hardly . . . For example, observation shows me that you have been to the Wigmore Street Post-Office this morning, but deduction lets me know that when there you dispatched a telegram."
> [Watson]: "Right! . . . But I confess that I don't see how you arrived at it." . . .
> [Holmes]: "It is simplicity itself . . . so absurdly simple, that an explanation is superfluous; and yet it may serve to define the limits of observation and of deduction. Observation tells me that you have a little reddish mould adhering to your instep. Just opposite the Wigmore Street Office they have taken up the pavement and thrown up some earth, which lies in such a way that it is difficult to avoid treading in it in entering. The earth is of this peculiar reddish tint which is found, as far as I know, nowhere else in the neighbourhood. So much is observation. The rest is deduction."
> [Watson]: "How, then, did you deduce the telegram?"
> [Holmes]: "Why, of course I knew that you had not written a letter, since I sat opposite to you all morning. I see also in your open desk there that you have a sheet of stamps and a thick bundle of postcards. What could you go into the post-office for, then, but to send a wire? Eliminate all other factors, and the one which remains must be the truth."

Watson then presents Holmes with an even more difficult task, and, when the detective again excels, asks him to explain his process of reasoning. "Ah," Holmes replies, "that is good luck. I could only say what was the balance of probability. I did not expect to be so accurate." When Watson then asks if "it was not mere guesswork" he says, "No, no: I never guess. It is a shocking habit—destructive to the logical faculty," and attributes his companion's surprise to the fact that "You do not follow my train of thought or observe the small facts upon which large inferences may depend."

Despite such disclaimers, Holmes's powers of observation, his "extraordinary genius for minutiae," as Watson puts it, and of deduction are in most cases built on a complicated series of what Peirce would have called guesses. In the preceding example, for instance, Holmes can only guess that Watson actually entered the post office, rather than having merely walked in front of it. Furthermore, Watson might have entered the post office to meet a friend rather than to conduct some business, and so forth.

That Holmes was convinced of the importance of studying details for successful detection is brought out in the following passage from *A Case of Identity:*

> "You appeared to read a good deal upon her which was quite invisible to me," I remarked.
>
> "Not invisible but unnoticed, Watson. You did not know where to look, and so you missed all that was important. I can never bring you to realize the importance of sleeves, the suggestiveness of thumb-nails, or the great issues that may hang from a boot-lace. Now, what did you gather from that woman's appearance? Describe it."
>
> "Well, she had a slate-coloured, broad-brimmed straw hat, with a feather of a brickish red. Her jacket was black, with black beads sewn upon it, and a fringe of little black jet ornaments. Her dress was brown, rather darker than coffee colour, with a little purplish plush at the neck and sleeves. Her gloves were greyish, and were worn through at the right forefinger. Her boots I didn't observe. She had small, round, hanging gold ear-rings, and a general air of being fairly well to do, in a vulgar, comfortable, easy-going way."
>
> Sherlock Holmes clapped his hands softly together and chuckled.
>
> " 'Pon my word, Watson, you are coming along wonderfully. You have really done very well indeed. It is true that you have missed everything of importance, but you have hit upon the method, and you have a quick eye for colour. Never trust to general impressions, my boy, but concentrate yourself upon details. My first glance is always at a woman's sleeve. In a man it is perhaps better first to take the knee of the trouser. As you observe, this woman had plush upon her sleeves, which is a most useful material for showing traces. The double line a little above the wrist, where the typewritress presses against the table, was beautifully defined. The sewing-machine, of the hand type, leaves a similar mark, but only on the left arm, and on the side of it farthest from the thumb, instead of being right across the broadest part, as this was. I then glanced at her face, and, observing the dint of a pince-nez at either side of her nose, I ventured a remark upon short sight and typewriting, which seemed to surprise her."
>
> "It surprised me."
>
> "But, surely, it was obvious. I was then much surprised and interested on glancing down to observe that, though the boots which she was wearing were not unlike each other, they were really odd ones; the one having a

slightly decorated toe-cap, the other a plain one. One was buttoned only in the two lower buttons out of five, and the other at the first, third, and fifth. Now, when you see that a young lady, otherwise neatly dressed, has come away from home with odd boots, half-buttoned, it is no great deduction to say that she came away in a hurry."

"And what else?" I asked. . . .

"I noticed, in passing, that she had written a note before leaving home but after being fully dressed. You observed that her right glove was torn at the forefinger, but you did not apparently see that both glove and finger were stained with violet ink. She had written in a hurry and dipped her pen too deep. It must have been this morning, or the mark would not remain clear upon the finger. All this is amusing, though rather elementary. . . ."

What makes Sherlock Holmes so successful at detection is not that he never guesses but that he guesses so well. In fact, he unwittingly follows Peirce's advice for selecting the best hypothesis (see 7.220-320). "It is an old maxim of mine," states Holmes, "that when you have excluded the impossible, whatever remains, however improbable, must be the truth" (*The Beryl Coronet;* cf. *The Sign of Four, The Blanched Soldier, The Bruce-Partington Plans*). It was Peirce's own maxim that "Facts cannot be explained by a hypothesis more extraordinary than these facts themselves; and of various hypotheses the least extraordinary must be adopted" (Ms. 696).[4] Paraphrasing Peirce's discussion, we might say that the best hypothesis is one that is simplest and most natural, is the easiest and cheapest to test, and yet will contribute to our understanding of the widest possible range of facts. In the episode of the post office, Holmes's guesses about Watson's actions are the most reasonable under the circumstances.

Furthermore, they enable him, with the minimum of logical baggage, to reach a point from which he may, through further observation, test some of the predictions drawn from his hypothesis and thus greatly reduce the number of possible conclusions. In other words, Holmes not only selects the simplest and most natural hypothesis, but also "breaks a hypothesis up into its smallest logical components, and only risks one of them at a time," the latter procedure being what Peirce describes as the secret of the game of Twenty Questions (7.220; cf. 6.529). Taking the hypothesis that Watson entered the post office in order to conduct some postal business, Holmes deduces (in Peirce's sense) that such business would be either to send a letter, purchase stamps and/or postcards, or send a telegram. He then systematically tests each of these possibilities, quickly coming to what turned out to be the correct one. When several explanations are possible, "one tries test after test until one or other of them has a convincing amount of support" (*The Blanched Soldier*).

One of us (Sebeok 1979: chap. 5) has discussed Peirce's reflections about guessing in the context of some children's games, on the one hand, and certain stage illusions, on the other. The game of Twenty Questions is the full verbal equivalent to the game of Hot and Cold, in which verbal cueing is minimal. Averbal cueing, unwittingly emitted, guides the performer in certain types of magic acts, where verbal cues are excluded altogether, to the object sought. This averbal communication, or feedback, also accounts for such seemingly "occult" phenomena as the movement of a Ouija board, table tipping, and automatic writing, and is the basis of several types of mentalists' acts, variously known in the magic business as "muscle reading" or "thought-reading." In acts of this sort "The spectator thinks he is being led by the magician, but actually the performer permits the *spectator to lead him* by unconscious muscular tensions" (Gardner 1957:109). The best mentalists are able to dispense with bodily contact altogether, finding what they are seeking merely by observing the reactions of spectators in the room.[5]

As we have already noted, Peirce maintained that a hypothesis must always be considered as a question, and, while all new knowledge comes from surmises, these are useless without the test of inquiry. Holmes, too, remarks, to Watson in *The Speckled Band,* "how dangerous it always is to reason from insufficient data." The detective also agrees with Peirce (2.635; 6.524; 7.202) that prejudices, or hypotheses which we are reluctant to submit to the test of induction, are a major stumbling block to successful reasoning. Holmes notes, for example, that "I make a point of never having any prejudices" (*The Reigate Puzzle;* cf. *The Abbey Grange, The Naval Treaty*). Peirce's admiration for great figures in the history of science, such as Kepler, stems precisely from their extraordinary capacity for sustaining the guessing-testing-guessing chain.

It is on this point, concerning the maintenance of objectivity toward the facts of a case, that Holmes, much like Peirce in the story that opens this book, finds himself at odds with the official representatives of the police, or, in the case of Peirce, the Pinkerton professionals.[6] In *The Boscombe Valley Mystery,* for example, Holmes attempts to point out some critical clues to the detective from Scotland Yard, Inspector Lestrade, who, as usual, cannot see the relationship between the details unearthed by Holmes and the crime being investigated. When he replies, "I am afraid that I am still a skeptic," Holmes answers calmly, "You work your own method, and I shall work mine." Holmes later describes this conversation to Watson as follows:

> "By an examination of the ground I gained the trifling details which I gave to that imbecile Lestrade, as to the personality of the criminal."
> "But how did you gain them?"
> "You know my method. It is founded upon the observation of trifles."

What so often leads the police astray in the Holmes stories is that, early in the investigation of a crime, they tend to adopt the hypothesis which is most likely to account for a few outstanding facts, ignoring "trifles" and thereafter refusing to consider data that do not support their position.

"There is nothing more deceptive than an obvious fact," says Holmes in *The Boscombe Valley Mystery.* The police also make the "capital mistake" of theorizing before they have all the evidence (*A Study in Scarlet*). The result is that, "insensibly," they begin "to twist facts to suit theories, instead of theories to suit facts" (*A Scandal in Bohemia*). The mutual distrust that results from this major difference in methodology pervades the Holmes stories. In *The Reigate Puzzle,* Watson remarks to a country official, Inspector Forrester, that "I have usually found that there was method in his [Holmes's] madness," to which the inspector replies, "Some folk might say there was madness in his method."[7]

We are not the first to point out the importance of guessing in Sherlock Holmes's method of detection. Régis Messac, for example, speaking of Holmes's reading of Watson's mind in *The Cardboard Box* (cf. the almost identical scene in some editions of *The Resident Patient*), notes that there are a million things that Watson might be thinking about when he is looking at the portrait of General Gordon or that of Henry Ward Beecher, and that Holmes is in fact guessing (1929:599). Messac is correct in pointing out that, although Holmes occasionally admits that a kind of instinct for guessing is involved in his work (e.g., he admits, in *A Study in Scarlet,* that his "curious gifts of instinct and observation" are due to a "kind of intuition"—a sentiment he echoes in *The Sign of Four* and *The Problem of Thor Bridge*), he nevertheless "affirms the reality of 'deduction'" (1929:601). Messac also argues that Holmes's deductions are not true deductions at all, nor are they inductions properly speaking, "but rather reasonings founded upon the observation of one particular fact and leading, through more or less complex circumventions, to another particular fact" (1929:602). And Nordon concludes that "it must be said that in practice he [Holmes] gets much more conclusive results from observation than from logical processes" (1966:245).

Marcello Truzzi, in a searching article on Holmes's method (1973: 93-126), anticipated our present work by pointing to the similarities between the detective's so-called deductions, or inductions, and Peirce's abductions, or conjectures. According to Peirce's system of logic, furthermore, Holmes's observations are themselves a form of abduction, and abduction is as legitimate a type of logical inference as either induction or deduction (Peirce 8.228). In fact, Peirce maintains that:

> Nothing has so much contributed to present chaotic or erroneous ideas of the logic of science as failure to distinguish the essentially different characters of different elements of scientific reasoning; and one of the worst of these confusions, as well as one of the commonest, consists in regarding abduction and induction taken together (often mixed also with deduction) as a simple argument. [8.228]

Peirce admits that he himself, "in almost everything [he] printed before the beginning of this century . . . more or less mixed up Hypothesis and Induction" (8.227), and he traces the confusion of these two types of

reasoning to logicians' too "narrow and formalistic a conception of inference (as necessarily having formulated judgments from its premises)"
(2.228; cf. 5.590-604; Ms. 475; Ms. 1146).

Abduction and induction do, of course, "both lead to the acceptance
of a hypothesis because observed facts are such as would necessarily
or probably result as consequences of that hypothesis." But:

> Abduction makes its start from the facts, without, at the outset, having
> any particular theory in view, though it is motivated by the feeling that
> a theory is needed to explain the surprising facts. Induction makes its
> start from a hypothesis which seems to recommend itself, without at the
> outset having any particular facts in view, though it feels the need of facts
> to support the theory. Abduction seeks a theory. Induction seeks for facts.
> In abduction the consideration of the facts suggests the hypothesis. In
> induction the study of the hypothesis suggests the experiments which
> bring to light the very facts to which the hypothesis had pointed. [7.218]

Taking an example which could have been drawn from one of Holmes's
cases, Peirce provides the following demonstration of the difference between these two types of reasoning:

> A certain anonymous writing is upon a torn piece of paper. It is suspected
> that the author is a certain person. His desk, to which only he has had ac-
> cess, is searched, and in it is found a piece of paper, the torn edge of which
> exactly fits, in all its irregularities, that of the paper in question. It is a
> fair hypothetic inference that the suspected man was actually the author.
> The ground of this inference evidently is that two torn pieces of paper are
> extremely unlikely to fit together by accident. Therefore, of a great number
> of inferences of this sort, but a very small proportion would be deceptive.
> The analogy of hypothesis with induction is so strong that some logicians
> have confounded them. Hypothesis has been called an induction of char-
> acters. A number of characters belonging to a certain class are found in a
> certain object; whence it is inferred that all the characters of that class
> belong to the object in question. This certainly involves the same principle
> as induction; yet in a modified form. In the first place, characters are not
> susceptible of simple enumeration like objects; in the next place, char-
> acters run in categories. When we make an hypothesis like that about the
> piece of paper, we only examine a single line of characters, or perhaps
> two or three, and we take no specimen at all of others. If the hypothesis
> were nothing but an induction, all that we should be justified in con-
> cluding, in the example above, would be that the two pieces of paper
> which matched in such irregularities as have been examined would be
> found to match in other, say slighter, irregularities. The inference from
> the shape of the paper to its ownership is precisely what distinguishes
> hypothesis from induction, and makes it a bolder and more perilous
> step. [2.632]

Holmes indirectly acknowledges the more dangerous nature of hypothesis
when he advocates the use of "imagination" (*The Retired Colourman,*

Silver Blaze), "intuition" (*The Sign of Four*), and "speculation" (*The Hound of the Baskervilles*). One must be willing to imagine what happened and act upon such surmise, and this takes one "into the region where we balance probabilities and choose the most likely" (*The Hound of the Baskervilles*).

Holmes was known to oscillate between the almost frenzied single-mindedness of the fox-hound on the trail of his quarry and a sort of lethargic reverie, a combination John G. Cawelti calls "stereotype vitalization" (1976:11,58), an imaginative synthesis of figure types I. I. Revzin dubbed "fusion," also with specific reference to detective fiction (1978: 385-388). The device, in this context, of course, derives from Poe's ambiguous Dupin. Watson points out, in the following passage from *The Red-Headed League*, that the latter type of activity was also important to Holmes's detection:

> My friend was an enthusiastic musician, being himself not only a very capable performer but a composer of no ordinary merit. All the afternoon he sat in the stalls wrapped in the most perfect happiness, gently waving his long, thin fingers in time to the music, while his gently smiling face and his languid, dreamy eyes were as unlike those of Holmes, the sleuth-hound, Holmes the relentless, keen-witted, ready-handed criminal agent, as it was possible to conceive. In his singular character the dual nature alternately asserted itself, and his extreme exactness and astuteness represented, as I have often thought, the reaction against the poetic and contemplative mood which occasionally predominated in him. The swing of his nature took him from extreme languor to devouring energy; and, as I knew well, he was never so truly formidable as when, for days on end, he had been lounging in his armchair amid his improvisations and his blackletter editions. Then it was that the lust of the chase would suddenly come upon him, and that his brilliant reasoning power would rise to the level of intuition, until those who were unacquainted with his methods would look askance at him as on a man whose knowledge was not that of other mortals. When I saw him that afternoon so enwrapped in the music at St. James's Hall I felt that an evil time might be coming upon those whom he set himself to hunt down.

Peirce has also commented on the relationship between such mental activities and more mundane practices. "There is," he writes, "a certain agreeable occupation of mind which . . . involves no purpose save that of casting aside all serious purpose" and which "I have sometimes been half-inclined to call . . . reverie with some qualification; but for a frame of mind so antipodal to vacancy and dreaminess such a designation would be too excruciating a misfit. In fact, it is Pure Play" (6.458). One type of Pure Play, "a lively exercise of one's powers" with "no rules, except this very law of liberty," he names Musement, and defines as a process by which the mind searches for "some connection" between two of the three Universes of Experience (*viz.*, of Ideas, of Brute Actuality, and of Signs [6.455]), "with speculation concerning its cause" (6.458). Musement begins passively enough with drinking in the impression of some nook in one of the three Universes. But impression soon passes into attentive observation, observation into musing, musing into a lively give and take of communion between self and self. If one's observations and reflections are allowed to specialize themselves too much, the Play will be converted into scientific study. . . . [6.459]

Crime, Peirce notes, is particularly suited to the application of Musement. Citing Dupin's remarks in Poe's "The Murders in the Rue Morgue" (to wit: "It appears to me that this mystery is considered insoluble for the very reason which should cause it to be regarded as easy of solution. I mean the outré character of its features"), Peirce remarks that "those problems that at first blush appear utterly insoluble receive, in that very circumstance . . . [t]heir smoothly-fitting keys. This particularly adapts them to the Play of Musement" (6.460). Compare Holmes's remarks: "I have already explained to you that what is out of the common is usually a guide rather than a hindrance" (A Study in Scarlet); "Singularity is almost invariably a clue" (The Boscombe Valley Mystery); "The more outré and grotesque an incident is the more carefully it deserves to be examined, and the very point which appears to complicate a case is, when duly considered and scientifically handled, the one which is most likely to elucidate it" (The Hound of the Baskervilles); and, "It is only the colourless, uneventful case which is hopeless" (Shoscombe Old Place).

We agree, but for different reasons, then, with Nordon's opinion that "As the creation of a doctor who had been soaked in the rationalist thought of the period, the Holmesian cycle offers us for the first time the spectacle of a hero triumphing again and again by means of logic and scientific method. And the hero's prowess is as marvelous as the power of science, which many people hoped would lead to a material and spiritual improvement of the human condition, and Conan Doyle first among them" (1966:247).

DISEASE, CRIME, AND SEMIOTICS

The roots of semiotics are grounded in ancient medical treatises (Sebeok 1976:4,125f., 181f.; 1979: chap. 1), illustrating Peirce's contention that "Speaking in a broad, rough way, it may be said that the sciences have grown out of the useful arts, or out of arts supposed to be useful." As astronomy has evolved out of astrology, and chemistry out of alchemy, so, too, "physiology, taking medicine as a halfway out of magic" (1.226). Peirce appears to have been well versed in the history and theory of medicine. His family considered him headed toward a career in chemistry and made available to him the medical library of his late Uncle Charles, who had been a physician (Fisch: personal communication). In at least one place (2.11n1), Peirce lists some of the books on the history of medicine which he had consulted. In 1933, in an interview with Henry S. Leonard (a graduate student in philosophy at Harvard who had been sent to Peirce's home in Milford, Pennsylvania, following the death of his widow, Juliette Peirce, to collect any remaining manuscripts), Peirce's last attending physician, G. Alto Pobe, claimed that

> Peirce knew more about medicine than I did. When I went to see him I would stay with him a half-hour to an hour at a time. It did you good to talk to him. When I arrived he would often tell me all of his symptoms and diagnose his illness. Then he would tell me the whole history of the medical treatment for this illness. Then he would tell me what should be prescribed for him now. He was never wrong. He said he had to ask me to write out the prescriptions since he did not have an M.D. degree. [In the notes of Max H. Fisch]

Peirce acknowledges that, concerning statistical problems relating to sampling and induction, "The medical men . . . deserve special mention for the reason that they have had since Galen a logical tradition of their own," and, "in their working against reasoning '*post hoc, ergo propter hoc*'," recognize, "however dimly," the rule of induction that states that "we must first decide for what character we propose to examine the sample, and only after that decision examine the sample" (1.95-97). Peirce recognizes, on the other hand, that medicine, that "materialistic profession" (8.58), has difficulty adhering to another maxim of induction, which requires that samples not be small ones:

> It is by violating this maxim that figures are made to lie. Medical statistics in particular are usually contemptibly small, as well as open to the suspicion of being picked. I am speaking now of the statistics of reputable physicians. It is extremely difficult to collect numerous facts relating to any obscure point in medicine, and it is still more difficult to make it evident that those facts are a fair representation of the general run of events. This accounts for the slow progress of medical science notwithstanding the immense study which has been bestowed upon it and for the great errors which will often be received for centuries by physicians. Probably there is no branch of science which is so difficult in every point of view. It requires a really great mind to make a medical induction. This is too obvious to require proof. There are so many disturbing influences—personal idiosyncrasies, mixture of treatment, accidental and unknown influences, peculiarities of climate, race, and season,—that it is particularly essential that the facts should be very numerous and should be scrutinized with the eye of a lynx to detect deceptions. And yet it is peculiarly difficult to collect facts in medicine. One man's experience can seldom be of decisive weight, and no man can judge of matters beyond his personal knowledge in medicine, he must trust to the judgment of others. So that while a sample requires to be more extensive and more carefully taken in this science than in any other, in this more than in any other these requisites are difficult to fulfill.
>
> Nothing, therefore, more pitiably manifests the looseness with which people in general reason than the readiness of nine persons out of ten to pronounce upon the merits of a medicine upon the most limited, the

most incxact, and the most prejudiced experience which it is possible to call experience at all. Any old woman who has seen any amelioration of symptoms follow after the administration of a medicine in a dozen cases at all resembling one another, will not hesitate to pronounce it an infallible cure for any case resembling at all any one of the dozen. This is shocking. But what is worse still, treatment will be recommended even upon a hearsay acquaintance with one or two cases.

Observe, I pray you, the combination of fallacies involved in such a procedure. In the first place, no induction can, with propriety, be drawn unless a sample has been taken of some definite class. But these foolish creatures—who think that merely spending time in a sick-room has made Galens of them—are utterly unable to define the disease in question. Suppose it to be *diptheria* [sic] for instance. How do they know diptheria [sic] from sore throat? Their samples are in reality samples of no definite class at all.

In the second place, the number of their instances is scarcely sufficient for the simplest induction. In the third place the instances are very likely derived from hearsay. Now in addition to the inaccuracy which attaches to this kind of evidence, we are more likely to hear of extraordinary things relatively to their frequency than we are of ordinary ones. So that to take into account such instances is to take picked samples. In the fourth place, the predicate which belongs to all the instances in common is usually utterly vague. In the fifth place, a deduction is usually made respecting a case in hand without carefully considering whether it really comes under the class from which the sample was drawn. In the sixth place more is apt to be predicated of the case in hand than has been found of the previous instances. All these fallacies are combined in a sort of argument which one can scarcely go a week without hearing an instance of. [Ms. 696][8]

Reviewing the large number of examples of medical diagnosis in the Holmes stories (diseases of the heart and tropical diseases especially), Maurice Campbell, himself a heart specialist, concludes that, medically speaking, "Watson seems to have been excellently informed" (1935:13). It is interesting to note that while Watson successfully follows the logical method of diagnosis with regard to pathology of the body, he is singularly inept in transferring this method to the detection of crime, and provides an example of someone who is only incompletely versed in what Peirce termed *logica docens* (see p. 46, below).

To the extent that the character Sherlock Holmes himself practices the methods of medicine, an element of art and magic is blended into the logic of scientific discovery that he pursues. In our opinion, this is what sets Holmes apart as a character from the more purely logical method of Edgar Allan Poe's detective Dupin.[9]

It is by now well recognized that Conan Doyle, a practicing physician himself until the Holmes stories made him rich enough to give up his practice, patterned the character of Sherlock Holmes after his professor, Dr. Joseph Bell, of the Royal Infirmary of Edinburgh. Conan Doyle's partial use of a doctor as a model was, however, a conscious attempt to introduce a more rigorous scientific method into criminal detection than was used theretofore. Messac correctly notes that Doyle followed Bell regarding diagnosis extended to the entire personality and life of the patient, and that diagnosis "is never absolutely rigorous; it involves irresolutions, errors." Detection of crime, like medicine, is a sort of "pseudoscience" (1929:617). Writing of the birth of A *Study in Scarlet,* Doyle wrote:

> Gaboriau had rather attracted me by the neat dovetailing of his plots, and Poe's masterful detective, Chevalier Dupin, had from boyhood been one of my heroes. But could I bring an addition of my own? I thought of my old teacher Joe Bell, of his eagle face, of his curious ways, of his eerie trick of spotting details. If he were a detective he would surely reduce this fascinating but unorganized business to something near to an exact science. [1924:69]

Doyle was impressed by Bell's exceptional ability at diagnosis, "not only of disease, but of occupation and character." He was Bell's outpatient clerk, which meant that he had to "array his out-patients, make simple notes of their cases, and then show them in, one by one, to the large room in which Bell sat in state surrounded by his dressers and students" (1924:20). The young medical student then "had ample chance of studying his [Bell's] methods and of noticing that he often learned more of the patient by a few glances" (ibid.) than by Doyle's own series of questions preceding the interview with the doctor.

> Occasionally the results were very dramatic, though there were times when he blundered. In one of his best cases he said to a civilian patient:
>> "Well, my man, you've served in the army."
>> "Aye, sir."
>> "Not long discharged?"
>> "No, sir."
>> "A highland regiment?"
>> "Aye, sir."
>> "A non-com. officer?"
>> "Aye, sir."
>> "Stationed at Barbados?"
>> "Aye, sir."
> "You see, gentlemen," he would explain, "the man was a respectful man, but did not remove his hat. They do not in the army, but he would have learned civilian ways had he been long discharged. He has an air of authority and he is obviously Scottish. As to Barbados, his complaint is elephantiasis, which is West Indian and not British."

To his audience of Watsons it all seemed quite miraculous until it was explained, and then it became simple enough. It is no wonder that after the study of such a character I used and amplified his methods when in later life I tried to build up a scientific detective who solved cases on his own merits and not through the folly of the criminal. [1924:20-21]

While the Barbados dialogue was the only example of Bell's skill in observation and deduction recorded by Doyle himself, several other accounts of Bell's remarkable performances, noted down by physicians who were medical students with Doyle at Edinburgh or friends of Dr. and Mrs. Bell, have been published and are reviewed by Trevor Hall (1978:80-83). William S. Baring-Gould has reproduced one of the lesser-known anecdotes (from the *Lancet*, of August 1, 1956):

> A woman with a small child was shown in. Joe Bell said good morning to her and she said good morning in reply.
>
> > "What sort of crossing di' ye have fra' Burntisland?"
> > "It was guid."
> > "And had ye a guid walk up Inverleith Row?"
> > "Yes."
> > "And what did ye do with th' other wain?"
> > "I left him with my sister in Leith."
> > "And would ye still be working at the linoleum factory?"
> > "Yes, I am."
>
> "You see, gentlemen, when she said good morning to me I noted her Fife accent, and, as you know, the nearest town in Fife is Burntisland. You notice the red clay on the edges of the soles of her shoes, and the only such clay within twenty miles of Edinburgh is the Botanical Gardens. Inverleith Row borders the gardens and is her nearest way here from Leith. You observed that the coat she carried over her arm is too big for the child who is with her, and therefore she set out from home with two children. Finally she has dermatitis on the fingers of the right hand which is peculiar to workers in the linoleum factory at Burntisland." [1967:vol.I,7]

Or consider the following report of an interview with Doyle, in June 1892, originally published in an article by a Mr. Harry How entitled "A Day with Dr. Conan Doyle," which appeared in the *Strand Magazine* in August of the same year, and was reprinted by Hall (1978:82-83):

> [At Edinburgh] I met the man who suggested Sherlock Holmes to me . . . his intuitive powers were simply marvelous. Case No. 1 would step up. "I see," said Mr. Bell, "You're suffering from drink. You even carry a flask in the inside breast pocket of your coat." Another case would come forward. "Cobbler, I see." Then he would turn to the students, and point out to them that the inside of the knee of the man's trousers was worn. That was where the man had rested the lapstone—a peculiarity only found in cobblers.

Hall (1978:78) also notes that Doyle acknowledged his debt to Bell on the verso of the title page of *The Adventures of Sherlock Holmes* (1892), where he dedicates the book to his former teacher. Hall further reports that, in a letter of May 4, 1892, to Bell, Doyle explained:

It is most certainly to you that I owe Sherlock Holmes, and though in the stories I have the advantage of being able to place [the detective] in all sorts of dramatic positions, I do not think that his analytical work is in the least an exaggeration of some effects which I have seen you produce in the outpatient ward. Round the centre of deduction and inference and observation which I have heard you inculcate, I have tried to build up a man who pushed the thing as far as it would go—further occasionally— and I am so glad that the results satisfied you, who are the critic with the most right to be severe. [1978:78]

Certainly the following passage from *The Greek Interpreter* echoes to a startling degree some of the anecdotes involving Joseph Bell. Holmes and his brother Mycroft are seated together in the bow window[10] of the Diogenes Club, when Mycroft says:

"To anyone who wishes to study mankind this is the spot. . . . Look at the magnificent types! Look at these two men who are coming towards us, for example."

"The billiard-marker and the other?"

"Precisely. What do you make of the other?"

The two men had stopped opposite the window. Some chalk marks over the waistcoat pocket were the only signs of billiards which I [Watson] could see in one of them. The other was a very small, dark fellow, with his hat pushed back and several packages under his arm.

"An old soldier, I perceive," said Sherlock.

"And very recently discharged," remarked the brother.

"Served in India, I see."

"And a non-commissioned officer."

"Royal Artillery, I fancy," said Sherlock.

"And a widower."

"But with a child."

"Children, my dear boy, children."

"Come," said I [i.e., Watson], laughing, "this is a little too much."

"Surely," answered Holmes, "it is not hard to see that a man with that bearing, expression of authority, and sun-baked skin is a soldier, is more than a private, and is not long from India."

"That he has not left the service long is shown by his still wearing his ammunition boots, as they are called," observed Mycroft.

"He had not the cavalry stride, yet he wore his hat on one side, as is shown by the lighter skin on that side of his brow. His weight is against his being a sapper. He is in the artillery."

"Then, of course, his complete mourning shows that he has lost someone very dear. The fact that he is doing his own shopping looks as though it were his wife. He has been buying things for children, you perceive. There is a rattle, which shows that one of them is very young. The wife probably died in childbed. The fact that he has a picture-book under his arm shows that there is another child to be thought of."

Bell himself brings out the similarity between crime and disease in the following passage, written in 1893 and cited by Starrett (1971:25-26):

> Try to learn the features of a disease or injury, gentlemen, as precisely as you know the features, the gait, the tricks of manner of your most intimate friend. Him, even in a crowd, you can recognize at once. It may be a crowd of men dressed all alike, and each having his full complement of eyes, nose, hair and limbs. In every essential they resemble one another; only in trifles do they differ—and yet, by knowing these trifles well, you make your recognition or your diagnosis with ease. *So it is with disease of mind or body or morals.* Racial peculiarities, hereditary tricks of manner, accent, occupation or the want of it, education, environment of every kind, by their little trivial impressions gradually mould or carve the individual, and leave finger marks or chisel scores which the expert can detect. The great broad characteristics which at a glance can be recognized as indicative of heart disease or consumption, chronic drunkenness or long-continued loss of blood, are the common property of the veriest tyro in medicine, while to masters of their art there are myriads of signs eloquent and instructive, but which need the educated eye to discover. . . . *The importance of the infinitely little is incalculable.* Poison a well at Mecca with the cholera bacillus and the holy water which the pilgrims carry off in bottles will infect a continent. The rags of a victim of a plague will terrify every seaport in Christendom. [Emphasis ours]

This manner of viewing symptoms as distinctive features of the identity of a disease, which is then treated as a concrete entity, brings to mind a passage in one of Peirce's unpublished manuscripts (Ms. 316), where, explaining that "our knowledge of the majority of general conceptions comes about in a manner altogether analogous to our knowledge of an individual person," he criticizes the dictum of French physiologist Claude Bernard (1813-1878) that "Disease is not an entity; it is nothing but an assemblage of symptoms." Peirce maintains that, rather than a physiological doctrine, it is one of false logic. "But in the light of the positive discoveries of Pasteur and Koch, considered in connection with the theories of Weissmann [*sic*], we see that, as far as zymotic [i.e., infectious] diseases are concerned, they are just as much a thing as the ocean is a thing . . . [An] assemblage of symptoms [is] not only an entity but necessarily a concrete thing. . . ." Had Bernard understood this, Peirce goes on to say, "he might have set himself to work very usefully to obtain some further acquaintance with that thing."

Sherlock Holmes does indeed practice what Bell preaches. He builds up to a "diagnosis," that is, an identification of a criminal pathology, through a series of minute perceptions, linked together by hypothesis, and he furthermore usually ends by treating a former case like an old familiar friend. Consider, for example, the following often-cited account of Holmes reading Watson's mind, from *The Cardboard Box:*

> Finding that Holmes was too absorbed for conversation, I had tossed aside the barren paper, and, leaning back in my chair, I fell into a brown study. Suddenly my companion's voice broke in upon my thoughts.
> "You are right, Watson," said he. "It does seem a very preposterous way of settling a dispute."

"Most preposterous!" I exclaimed, and then, suddenly realizing how he had echoed the inmost thought of my soul, I sat up in my chair and stared at him in blank amazement.

"What is this, Holmes?" I cried. "This is beyond anything which I could have imagined. . . . I have been seated quietly in my chair, and what clues can I have given you?"

"You do yourself an injustice. The features are given to man as the means of which he shall express his emotions, and yours are faithful servants."

"Do you mean to say that you read my train of thoughts from my features?"

"Your features, and especially your eyes. Perhaps you cannot yourself recall how your reverie commenced?"

"No, I cannot."

"Then I will tell you. After throwing down your paper, which was the action which drew my attention to you, you sat for half a minute with a vacant expression. Then your eyes fixed themselves upon your newly framed picture of General Gordon, and I saw by the alteration in your face that a train of thought had been started. But it did not lead very far. Your eyes turned across to the unframed portrait of Henry Ward Beecher, which stands up upon the top of your books. You then glanced up at the wall, and of course your meaning was obvious. You were thinking that if the portrait were framed it would just cover that bare space and correspond with Gordon's picture over there."

"You have followed me wonderfully!" I exclaimed.

"So far I could hardly have gone astray. But now your thoughts went back to Beecher, and you looked hard across as if you were studying the character in his features. Then your eyes ceased to pucker, but you continued to look across, and your face was thoughtful. You were recalling the incidents of Beecher's career. I was well aware that you could not do this without thinking of the mission which he undertook on behalf of the North at the time of the Civil War, for I remember you expressing your passionate indignation at the way in which he was received by the more turbulent of our people. You felt so strongly about it that I knew you could not think of Beecher without thinking of that also. When a moment later I saw your eyes wander away from the picture, I suspected that your mind had now turned to the Civil War, and when I observed that your lips set, your eyes sparkled, and your hands clinched, I was positive that you were indeed thinking of the gallantry which was shown by both sides in that desperate struggle. But then, again, your face grew sadder; you shook your head. You were dwelling upon the sadness and horror and useless waste of life. Your hand stole toward your own old wound, and a smile quivered on your lips, which showed me that the ridiculous side of this method of settling international questions had forced itself upon your mind. At this point I agreed with you that it was preposterous, and was glad to find that all my deductions had been correct."

"Absolutely!" said I. "And now that you have explained it, I confess that I am as amazed as before."

Testing a hypothesis as to the identity of a person through the collection of clues from that individual's physical appearance, speech patterns, and

the like always involves a certain amount of guessing, for which reason
Peirce calls it *abductory induction:*

> But suppose that, while I am travelling upon a railway, somebody draws
> my attention to a man near us, and asks me whether he is not something
> allied to a catholic priest. I thereupon begin to run over in my mind the
> observable characteristics of ordinary catholic priests, in order to see what
> proportion of them this man displays. Characteristics are not capable of
> being counted or measured; their relative significance in reference to the
> question put can only be vaguely estimated. Indeed, the question itself
> admits of no precise answer. Nevertheless, if the man's style of dress,—
> boots, trousers, coat, and hat,—are such that are seen on the majority of
> American catholic priests, if his movements are such as are characteristic
> of them, betraying a similar state of nerves, and if the expression of
> countenance, which results from a certain long discipline, is also charac-
> teristic of a priest, while there is a single circumstance very unlike a
> Roman priest, such as his wearing a masonic emblem, I may say he is not
> a priest, but he has been, or has been near becoming, a catholic priest.
> This sort of vague induction, I term an *abductory induction*. [Ms. 692;cf.
> 6.526]

In the preceding example, the question put to Peirce is itself an hypothesis,
similar in some respects to the inference noted in an autobiographical
passage from another Peirce paper, where he writes:

> I once landed at a seaport in a Turkish province; and, as I was walking
> up to the house which I was to visit, I met a man upon horseback, sur-
> rounded by four horsemen holding a canopy over his head. As the
> governor of the province was the only personage I could think of who
> could be so greatly honored, I inferred that this was he. This was an hy-
> pothesis. [2.625]

The above examples illustrate what Sherlock Holmes refers to as "reasoning backward" (cf. Peirce's *retro-duction*), a skill which, while similar
in many respects to the type of thinking in which the common man
engages in his everyday life, nevertheless requires a certain amount of
specialized training:

> "In solving a problem of this sort, the grand thing is to be able to reason
> backward. That is a very useful accomplishment, and a very easy one,
> but people do not practice it much. In the everyday affairs of life it is
> more useful to reason forward, and so the other comes to be neglected.
> There are fifty who can reason synthetically for one who can reason
> analytically."
> "I confess," said I [Watson], "that I do not quite follow you."
> "I hardly expected that you would. Let me see if I can make it clearer.
> Most people, if you describe a train of events to them, will tell you what
> the result would be. They can put those events together in their minds, and
> argue from them that something will come to pass. There are few people,

however, who, if you told them a result, would be able to evolve from their own inner consciousness what the steps were which led up to that result. This power is what I mean when I talk of reasoning backward, or analytically." [*A Study in Scarlet*]

Holmes, in fact, frequently remarks to Watson that he sees just what everyone else sees, only he has trained himself to apply his method in order to determine the full significance of his perceptions. In *The Blue Carbuncle*, for example, Watson is asked by Holmes to examine a hat in order to find a clue as to the identity of the gentleman who had worn it. "I can see nothing," is Watson's reply, to which Holmes responds, "On the contrary, Watson, you see everything. You fail, however, to reason from what you see. You are too timid in drawing your inferences." Or, again, in *The Speckled Band*, when Watson says, "You have evidently seen more in these rooms than was visible to me," Holmes replies, "No, but I fancy that I may have deduced a little more. I imagine that you saw all that I did."

Holmes, then, like Peirce, is more interested in his method than in the particular subject matter to which it is applied. In *The Copper Beeches*, for example, Holmes and Watson discuss the way in which the latter has reported the cases of the former, and Holmes criticizes Watson, saying, "You have erred perhaps in attempting to put colour and life into each of your statements instead of confining yourself to the task of placing upon record that severe reasoning from cause to effect which is really the only notable feature about the thing." When, in response, Watson implies that Holmes's criticism is based on egotism, Holmes answers, "No, it is not selfishness or conceit. . . . If I claim full justice for my art, it is because it is an impersonal thing—a thing beyond myself. Crime is common. Logic is rare. Therefore it is upon the logic rather than upon the crime that you should dwell. You have degraded what should have been a course of lectures into a series of tales."

Peirce himself distinguished between what he called *logica utens*, or a rudimentary sense of logic-in-use, which is a certain general method by which everyone acquires truth, without, however, being aware of doing so and without being able to specify in what that method consists, and a more sophisticated sense of logic, or *logica docens*, practiced by logicians and scientists (but also certain detectives and medical doctors), which is a logic which may be self-consciously taught and is therefore a theoretically developed method of discovering truth (Ms. 692; cf. Ransdell 1977:165). The scientist or logician does not, however, invent his *logica docens*, but rather studies and develops the natural logic he and everyone else already use in daily life. Sherlock Holmes would appear to share this view, judging from his speech to Watson, at the opening of *A Case of Identity*, in which he remarks: "We would not dare to conceive the things which are really mere commonplaces of existence. . . . Depend upon it, there is nothing so unnatural as the commonplace." Holmes asserts, furthermore, that his methods are "but systematized common sense" (*The Blanched Soldier*).

> The ideal reasoner . . . would, when he had once been shown a single fact in all its bearings, deduce from it not only the chain of events which led up to it but also the results which would follow from it. As Cuvier could correctly describe a whole animal by the contemplation of a single bone, so the observer who has thoroughly understood one link in a series of incidents should be able to accurately state all the other ones, both before and after. [*The Five Orange Pips*]

There seems to be little doubt that the *logica docens* of Sherlock Holmes stems in large part from the scientific training of his creator, Conan Doyle. Doyle's teacher, Bell, in fact, had written that "Dr. Conan Doyle's education as a student of medicine taught him to observe, and his practise, both as a general practitioner and a specialist, has been a splendid training for a man such as he is, gifted with eyes, memory and imagination" (Bell 1893, cited in Nordon 1966:213). In particular, the controlling awareness exhibited by Holmes would appear to owe much to his dedication to chemistry.[11] While "the façade of chemical research, never very strong, became less and less well-maintained as time went on, until it collapsed entirely," Holmes's chemical corner served "to keep him in practical touch with an exact science where cause and effect, action and reaction, followed each other with a predictability beyond the power of the less precise 'science of detection' to achieve, however hard he might strive toward exactitude in his chosen profession" (Trevor Hall 1978:36-37). As Holmes proclaimed in *A Study in Scarlet*: "Like all other Arts, the Science of Deduction and Analysis is one which can only be acquired by long and patient study, nor is life long enough to allow any mortal to attain the highest possible perfection in it."

Peirce himself had a life-long devotion to chemistry. In 1909, he wrote:

> I early became interested in a childish way in dynamics and physics and my father's brother being a chemist, I must have been about twelve years when I set up a chemical laboratory of my own and began to work through Liebig's hundred bottles of qualitative analysis and to make such things as vermillion both in the dry and in the wet way and to repeat a great many well-known processes of chemistry. [Ms. 619]

Chemistry was the profession for which Peirce was specially educated, and it was "the science in which [he had] worked the most" and "whose reasoning [he] most admire[d]" (Ms. 453; cf. Hardwick 1977:114).

For the person unschooled in theoretical logic, an exhibition of the reasoning skills of an expert will, if he is unenlightened by the latter as to the logical steps which he followed, appear to be very much like magic. Nordon points out that "His deductions lead Holmes to make revelations which appear almost magical" (1966:222). Dr. Watson is, as every-

one knows, constantly overwhelmed by the deductions of Holmes. This
effect is heightened by Holmes's "notable taste . . . for theatrical arrangement and dramatic effects" (Starrett 1971:29), an inclination that he
shares with Peirce, judging from the dramatic way in which the latter
related the story of the missing watch, as well as from the fact that he
was reputed to have shown quite an interest in and talent for drama
from boyhood on.

The Peirce family had for generations displayed an interest in
theater and opera, even entertaining performers in their home. While
still a boy, Peirce is reported to have distinguished himself as an orator,
both through the reading of such works as Poe's "The Raven" and as a
member of his high school debating society (Fisch: personal communication). As an undergraduate at Harvard, Peirce continued to cultivate
an interest in elocution, rhetoric, and theatrical performance. He became
a member, in his junior year, of the W.T.K. (Wen Tchang Koun, Chinese
for "hall of literary exercise"), which specialized in debates, orations,
mock trials, and the reading of essays, poems, and plays. During his
senior year, in 1858, he was a founding member of the O.K. Society of
Harvard College, which pursued the elocutionary and oratorical arts
in relation to literary works (Kloesel: personal communication; cf. Kloesel 1979). As an adult, Peirce was known to have given readings of
Shakespeare's *King Lear* to friends, at his older brother "Jem's" house
in Cambridge, and to fellow members of the Century Club, in New York.
Peirce attended the theater and the opera when in Paris, and his second
wife, Juliette, was an actress. He and Juliette remained in contact with
theatrical friends, such as Steele and Mary MacKaye, and even occasionally took part in amateur theatrical events, such as a performance
of Legouvé's *Medea,* which Peirce had translated into English (Fisch:
personal communication).

"The stage lost a fine actor," writes Watson of Holmes, in *A Scandal
in Bohemia,* "even as science lost an acute reasoner, when he became a
specialist in crime." To some extent, the dramatic way in which Holmes
displays his logical operations is akin to the manner in which some physicians seek to impress their patients as to their seemingly magical powers
of diagnosis, thereby developing a feeling of confidence on the part of
the patient that will contribute to the healing process.

Ritual trappings in clinical practice constitute the essential ingredient
of the placebo effect (see Sebeok 1979: chaps. 5 and 10). The placebo
is thought to be efficacious because the patient believes that it will be,
a belief that is bolstered by appropriate cueing on the part of the
physician and other attendant personnel, as well as shaped by the context in which the placebo is administered.[12] Some psychologists, such as
Karl Scheibe, employ the term *acumen* for a mode of prediction exhibited
by Holmes, constituting "an emphatic skill combined with analytic precision." Scheibe observes:

If one believes oneself to be at a disadvantage vis-à-vis the terrible but well-controlled powers of observation and inference of the . . . detective . . . then one has in effect granted authority to a superior and has no hope of mastering events. . . . To the extent that the . . . detective is considered by the public at large to possess special powers of penetration, the powers of acumen of these practitioners will be enhanced. Also, to the extent that any player is able to exploit the naiveté or credulity of the other player about innocence of intent, the second player is effectively under control of the first. This is the basic principle for the confidence game. [1978: 872-875]

A similar con game is played out between the author of a detective story and his audience, of course. Conan Doyle acknowledged this both indirectly, through the character of Sherlock Holmes, and directly, in his autobiography. In *The Crooked Man,* for instance, Holmes tells Watson:

It is one of those instances where the reasoner can produce an effect which seems remarkable to his neighbour, because the latter has missed the one little point which is the basis of the deduction. The same may be said, my dear fellow, for the effect of some of these little sketches of yours, which is entirely meretricious, depending as it does upon your retaining in your own hands some factors in the problem which are never imparted to the reader.

In his autobiography, Conan Doyle, discussing the composition of a detective story, writes: "The first thing is to get your idea. Having got that key one's next task is to conceal it and lay emphasis upon everything which can make for a different explanation" (1924:101). Holmes himself enjoyed taunting official detectives by deliberately pointing out clues without indicating their significance (*The Boscombe Valley Mystery, The Cardboard Box, The Sign of Four, Silver Blaze*).

Joseph Bell himself refers to this type of psychological manipulation as follows:

The recognition [of disease] depends in great measure on the accurate and rapid appreciation of small points in which the disease differs from the healthy state. In fact, the student must be taught to observe. To interest him in this kind of work we teachers find it useful to show the student how much a trained use of observation can discover in ordinary matters such as the previous history, nationality and occupation of a patient. *The patient, too, is likely to be impressed by your ability to cure him in the future if he sees that you, at a glance, know much of his past. And the whole trick is much easier than it appears at first.* [Trevor Hall 1978:83; emphasis ours]

Holmes frequently opens his initial interview with a prospective client with a stunning series of "deductions," much as Bell describes, and these "clever little deductions . . . often have nothing to do with the matter in hand, but impress the reader with a general sense of power. The same effect is gained by his offhand allusion to other cases" (1924:101-102).

And who among us has not been intimidated by a related interview technique used on us by our own doctor, when he asks us a series of seemingly unrelated questions (e.g., Have you been smoking heavily lately? Does it hurt only at night? Has your mother ever suffered from headaches?), upon the termination of which he may suddenly announce his diagnosis, a pronouncement that appears to us, being unable to judge the significance of each separate clue, and hence the logicality of the sequence of questioning, as nothing short of numinous. If the physician has already guessed at a diagnosis, but has not announced it to the patient, the questions which he uses to test his hypothesis will appear to the patient almost as an exercise in extrasensory perception (e.g., You have this sensation only one and a half hours after eating, and it is accompanied by a throbbing pain in your right arm? Why yes, how did you know?).

While guessing is an important part of all logical operations, as Peirce taught us, the typical patient might be expected to lose confidence in his doctor were he to learn the amount of guesswork that goes into medical diagnosis and treatment, so that physicians are more or less obliged to cover up this aspect of their practice, much as Sherlock Holmes is in order to build up his reputation as a master detective. As in the example just discussed, physicians do so by so-to-speak mystifying the client through the intentional obfuscation of the reasoning process, making questions appear as deductions, by simply acting as if a diagnosis had been arrived at through deduction and induction, without a preceding abduction, or by appearing to understand our innermost thoughts and feelings without the intermediary of signs given off by the patient.

The importance of such tricks for Holmes's reputation is brought out in the following passage from *The Red-Headed League*, where the detective is interviewing a Mr. Jabez Wilson. Holmes announces his startlingly accurate conclusion as to Mr. Wilson's background and lifestyle, at which point Mr. Wilson "started up in his chair" and asked "How, in the name of good fortune, did you know all that Mr. Holmes?"

> "How did you know for example, that I did manual labour? It's as true as gospel, for I began as a ship's carpenter."
>
> "Your hands, my dear sir. Your right hand is quite a size larger than your left. You have worked with it, and the muscles are more developed."
>
> "Well, the snuff, then, and the Freemasonry?"
>
> "I won't insult your intelligence by telling you how I read that, especially as, rather against the strict rules of your order, you use an arc-and-compass breast pin."
>
> "Ah, of course, I forgot that. But the writing?"
>
> "What else can be indicated by that right cuff so very shiny for five inches, and the left one with the smooth patch near the elbow where you rest it upon the desk?"

"Well, but China?"

"The fish that you have tattooed immediately above your right wrist could only have been done in China. I have made a small study of tattoo marks and even contributed to the literature of the subject. That trick of staining the fishes' scales of a delicate pink is quite peculiar to China. When, in addition, I see a Chinese coin hanging from your watch-chain, the matter becomes even more simple."

Mr. Jabez Wilson laughed heavily. "Well, I never!" said he. "I thought at first that you had done something clever, but I see that there was nothing in it, after all."

"I begin to think, Watson," said Holmes, "that I made a mistake in explaining. 'Omne ignotum pro magnifico,' you know, and my poor little reputation, such as it is, will suffer shipwreck if I am so candid."

Or again, in *The Stock-broker's Clerk*, Holmes remarks that "I am afraid that I rather give myself away when I explain. . . . Results without causes are much more impressive." Holmes is less than completely candid when he says to a client, in *The Reigate Puzzle*, "I am afraid that my explanation may disillusion you, but it has always been my habit to hide none of my methods, either from my friend Watson or from anyone who might take an intelligent interest in them."

THAUMATURGY IN FACT AND FICTION

The juxtaposition of the method of Charles Peirce, detective, with the method of Sherlock Holmes, semiotician, which began as a *jeu d'esprit*, ends by shedding unexpected light on both the historical figure and the fictional one. From the perspective of the great logician and polymath, Holmes's Science of Deduction and Analysis, set forth comprehensively in his "The Book of Life" (*A Study in Scarlet*), where the "writer claimed by a momentary expression, a twitch of a muscle or glance of an eye, to fathom a man's inmost thoughts," are seen as far from the "ineffable twaddle" or "rubbish" that Watson at first thought they were. The theories that Holmes expressed in the article, which appeared to his Boswell "so chimerical, are really extremely practical," and his projected one-volume textbook on the "whole art of detection" (*The Abbey Grange*), to which he had planned to "devote [his] declining years," assumes a contextual rationale in the history of ideas, based, partly as it is, partly as it might have been, on a "mixture of imagination and reality" (*The Problem of Thor Bridge*) and the judicious exercise of speculation as "the scientific use of imagination" (*The Hound of the Baskervilles*).

Holmes was a brilliant physician to the body politic, the disease of which is crime. As in the adventure of *The Creeping Man*, he speaks of his cases "with the air of a pathologist who presents a rare specimen." Holmes was pleased that Watson had chosen to chronicle those incidents that gave room for deduction and logical synthesis. While he maintained, in *A Study in Scarlet*, that "all life is a great chain, the nature of which is known whenever we are shown a single link of it," he also held that his conclusions from one to the other "were as infallible as so many propositions of Euclid. So startling would his results appear to the uninitiated that until they learned the processes by which he had arrived at them they might well consider him as a necromancer."

Peirce was, in his way, as great a necromancer as Holmes, and that is why his writings and the details of his biography keep us all spellbound. He was, according to Charles Morris's both weighty and accurate characterization (1971:337), "heir of the whole historical philosophical analysis of signs. . . ." Peirce represents the tallest peak so far in the mountain range that begins to rise in ancient Greece with the clinical semiotics of Hippocrates, is more fully as well as more explicitly developed by Galen (Sebeok 1979: chap. 1), and continues with the physician Locke, whose *semiotiké* Peirce "distinctly weighed, and duly considered" and which surely afforded "another sort of Logick and Critick, than what we have been hitherto acquainted with" (Locke 1975:721).

It is one thing to proclaim—as we do—the continuity and cumulative effect of this panorama, extending from archaic medical diagnosis and prognostics to the modern expressions of a doctrine of signs by Peirce and beyond, on the part of such modern virtuosos as the Baltic biologist Jakob von Uexküll (1864-1944), and the French mathematician René Thom (born 1923). To document it is quite another. The proof will take at least one more generation of concentrated effort by teams of knowledgeable specialists in the labyrinthine history of the sign science (cf. Pelc 1977), only the barest outlines of which have hitherto been delineated by those few explorers who are equipped to follow upon the clues laid bare by Peirce, so far the boldest pioneer, or backwoodsman, in this high adventure.[13]

NOTES

1. ". . . Abduction is, after all, nothing but guessing," he wrote elsewhere (*Collected Papers* 7.219; cf. Ms. 692). Compare Noam Chomsky's explicatory remarks, in relation to abduction, concerning "the philosopher to whom [he feels] closest": "Peirce argued that to account for the growth of knowledge, one must assume that 'man's mind has a natural adaptation to imagining correct theories of some kinds,' some principle of 'abduction' which 'puts a limit on admissible hypothesis,' a kind of 'instinct,' developed in the course of evolution. Peirce's ideas on abduction were rather vague, and his suggestion that biologically given structure plays a basic role in the selection of scientific hypotheses seems to have had very little influence. To my knowledge, almost no one has tried to develop these ideas further, although similar notions have been developed independently on various occasions" (Chomsky 1979:71).

2. On the notion of *"lumière naturelle"* see Ayim 1974:43n4.

3. Holmes, alas, never said that. He never said "Elementary, my dear Watson" either.

4. Martin Gardner describes this process as follows: "Like the scientist trying to solve a mystery of nature, Holmes first gathered all the evidence he could that was relevant to his problem. At times, he performed experiments to obtain fresh data. He then surveyed the total evidence in the light of his vast knowledge of crime, and/or sciences relevant to crime, to arrive at the most probable hypothesis. Deductions were made from the hypothesis; then the theory was further tested against new evidence, revised if need be, until finally the truth emerged with a probability close to certainty" (Gardner 1976:125).

5. Examples of this from Persi Diaconis and a performer who goes under the name of Kreskin (George Kresge, Jr.) are cited by Sebeok (1979:93). These cases bear an uncanny resemblance to Peirce's story of his watch. Diaconis, besides being one of the most talented of contemporary magicians, is also among the foremost experts in the sophisticated statistical analysis of guessing and gambling strategies, and in applying novel techniques in parapsychological research—with hitherto totally negative results (see Diaconis 1978:136). Yuri K. Scheglov's observation about the growth of tension and excitement as Holmes's logical reasoning gradually "creeps up on the criminal and lifts a corner of the curtain (we have here much the same effect as in the children's game 'Cold or hot' in which the area for hunting narrows down and gets 'hotter and hotter')" should also be mentioned in this connection (Scheglov 1975:63).

6. Two Holmes stories, by the way, feature detectives from the Pinkerton National Detective Agency: Young Leverton, who has a minor role in *The Red Circle,* and Birdy Edwards, alias John ("Jack") McMurdo, alias John ("Jack") Douglas, who was probably tossed overboard off St. Helena by the Moriarty gang at the conclusion of *The Valley of Fear.*

7. An interesting parallel is found in Voltaire's *Zadig* (chap. 3), where Zadig's clever reading of clues causes him to be arrested, tried, and fined. There is a considerable body of secondary literature on Holmes and Zadig.

8. As Stephen Jay Gould recently confirmed, in reference to the academic world in general, "unconscious or dimly perceived finagling, doctoring, and massaging [of data] are rampant, endemic, and unavoidable in a profession that awards status and power for clean and unambiguous discovery" (1978:504). In brief, such manipulation of data may be a scientific norm.

9. On this point, see also Messac, as well as Hitchings.

10. On the significance of windows in the Sherlock Holmes stories and the works of Jules Verne, see chapter 3 of this volume.

11. Describing Holmes's knowledge of various subject matters, Watson lists only one—chemistry—as "profound" (*A Study in Scarlet*). On Holmes as "a frustrated chemist," see Cooper (1976:67-73).

12. For a sound, popular account by a surgeon of the workings of the placebo effect by "healers," and the power of suggestion, including sometimes hypnosis, see Nolen 1974.

13. Advances are being made, however. See the collaborative *Encyclopedic Dictionary of Semiotics,* being prepared under the guidance of a multinational editorial board (Bloomington: Indiana University Press, forthcoming).

Chapter 3

Captain Nemo's Porthole[1]

> Whoever wants to describe a
> window will do it well only if he
> also describes the view beyond, the
> view of which that window is, as
> it were, a framework.
>
> —Kotarbinski 1966:514

NORDON (1966:22-23), in his standard biography of Conan Doyle, reports that in the summer of 1873 the fourteen-year-old boy, who was to become the creator of Sherlock Holmes and of Professor George Edward Challenger, became "possessed of a sudden passion for the French language, which he studied by reading Jules Verne." He read *Vingt mille lieues sous les mers* (1870), *Cinq semaines en ballon* (1863), *De la terre à la lune* (1865), and *Aventures de trois Russes et de trois Anglais* (1872), and, according to his biographer, he "soon began to find it easy to slip from one language into the other." As Doyle wrote to his mother in June of that year: "I am getting to relish [the Verne novels] quite as well as English books" (Nordon 1966:21f.). It was also about this time that he began to realize that he had certain literary gifts of his own. Nordon (ibid.:82) confirms that, except for works by Jean Froissart, the fourteenth-century chronicler, those of Verne "were among the first [French] books Conan Doyle read," although he later read a great many others throughout his life.

In *Through the Magic Door* (1923:118, 255), Doyle refers twice to Verne. He remarks that "all pseudo-scientific Verne-and-Wells stories have their prototypes in 'Voyage to the Moon,' . . ." and that Verne, like Poe, "also produces a charmingly credible effect for the most incredible things by an adept use of a considerable amount of real knowledge of nature." Not until 1912, says Nordon (1966:328), does "Conan Doyle emerge as one of Jules Verne's most talented disciples," referring, of course, to the publication of *The Lost World*, a detective story of sorts, which Higham (1978:109, 210) called "a masterpiece of imaginative fiction, reminiscent of Jules Verne but not suffering from the comparison."

This article, written in collaboration with Harriet Margolis, is also slated to appear, with some modifications, in *Poetics Today* 3 (1981-82). That publication will include six tables summarizing information about the use of windows throughout the entire canon.

53

Echoes of Verne, one of Doyle's "idols" (ibid.:55), also turn up earlier, however, in the Sherlock Holmes stories. For instance, in NORW,[2] Dr. Watson's benefactor, a distant relative of Holmes himself, is named Dr. Verner. Furthermore, in GREE, we learn that Holmes's grandmother "was the sister of Vernet, the French artist." Professor Maracot is clearly a composite of various characters, among whom Captain Nemo surely figures as one important source, Professor Challenger another.

Less specific echoes of Verne also appear in the Holmes stories. Scheglov has observed that Verne preceded Doyle in "creating a genre of 'scientific journeys,'" and that the Holmesian cycle is not, in fact, pure detective fiction, "but a combination of the detective genre and that of 'scientific expeditions'" à la Verne (1975:60). He further emphasized that the imposition of the theme of "comfort," whether personal and altruistic or other-directed (that is, the possession of comfort vs. the provision of comfort), on any set scene "is especially typical of Verne" (ibid.:63), as when the protagonists build a tree house during the flood in *Les enfants du Capitaine Grant* (1867-68), to say nothing of the furnishings of the *Nautilus*, with its 12,000-volume library and its drawing room containing "all the marvels accumulated in this museum" (Verne 1870, Part I, chaps. 10-11). In Doyle's work we vicariously experience an application of this

FIG. 3.1. Captain Nemo's porthole.

"imposition of comfort" motif, for example, when Holmes brings a deck of cards (though it remains unused) to the cellar segment of REDH, or a stack of newspapers into his train carriage (as in SILV and COPP).

In his perceptive, although characteristically laconic, essay on "The *Nautilus* and the Drunken Boat," Roland Barthes (1957:90-92) speculates that Verne's work is likely to lend itself with special force to structural study because of its highly thematic organization: "Verne a construit une sorte de cosmogonie fermée sur elle-même, qui a ses catégories propres, son temps, son espace, sa plénitude, et même son principe existentiel" (ibid.:90).[3] Closely kindred features can be said to characterize and define the individual stories of the Holmesian canon in its entirety, in which Scheglov claimed to uncloak an overarching opposition between "security complex" features and "adventure" features.

Barthes's remark (1957) about the archetypal location, "où l'homme-enfant ré-invente le monde, l'emplit, l'enclôt, s'y enferme, et couronne cet effort encyclopédique par la posture bourgeoise de l'appropriation," applies, *mutatis mutandis*, with fascinating variations, to Sherlock Holmes no less than to Captain Nemo. This principle of self-seclusion, involving the appropriation of the world and the heaping up of its pieces in a confined space (a literary device that Barthes contends Verne invented, in addition to his use of the innumerable resources of science), applies as well to 221b Baker Street as to what Barthes calls the "almost perfect novel" of Verne, *L'Ile mystérieuse* (1874). Indeed, in certain of the detective's cases, there may even appear a surrogate human universe that tends to be constructed in an almost claustrophobic manner, as when Holmes takes up a temporary residence among the ancient stone huts on the moor in HOUN, or, to a lesser degree, in the aforementioned cellar in REDH. Doyle, however, carried the attendant sets of images vividly and imaginatively in further directions, as he transferred them from a context of general scientific inquiry into the context of scientific detection. If the emblem of closure, of cherished seclusion (a bundle that Scheglov breaks down into such elementary features as safety, comfort, domesticity, tranquility, satisfaction, intimacy, warmth, congenial company, and so forth), of "la caverne adorable," as Barthes (1957:92) depicts the *Nautilus*, is to be used as a productive narrative maneuver, it must attain its full and proper function in terms of its opposite: adventure (another bundle, composed of such distinctive features as chance, dangers, reversals of fortune, drama, vicissitudes, discomforts, struggle, and the like).

The dialectic movement, which impels man's encapsulated habitat constantly to beget departures into the infinite,[4] requires channels, portals, or other loopholes through which such passage (of sound, of sight, of objects) is possible from the inside to the outside or from the outside to the inside, between order and chaos—in short, in terms of the classical antithesis between Nature and Culture accentuated and amplified in manifold ways by Lévi-Strauss (e.g., 1958:389), to assure "une poétique

véritable de l'exploration" (Barthes 1957:92). The *Nautilus* contains a
pilot's cage, constructed so as to allow the man at the wheel—often Nemo
himself—to see in all directions through four light-ports with lenticular
glasses (Verne 1870, Part 2, chap 5).[5] This paper focuses on only one
such conduit, which is a most important and pervasive trope, and perhaps
the key figure, used by Conan Doyle: the window.

In pictorial art, windows often indicate an attention to formal aspects
of painting centered around lighting. There is, in fact, a whole genre of
window-centered paintings, in modern times perhaps most stupefyingly
represented by the Belgian Surrealist master of menace, René Magritte.
He has, for instance, given us streets of houses at night, with their windows illuminated but with a daytime sky beyond. The multiply equivocal
The Domain of Arnheim (1949) shows a mountain view through a shattered window, and scattered on the floor are fragments of the mountain
itself. Eitner, in discussing the connection between early nineteenth-
century images in both paintings and literature, comments that "The
window image . . . illustrates perfectly the themes of frustrated longing,
of lust for travel or escape which run through romantic literature" (1955:
286). In terms of signification, windows in painting may serve much the
same multitude of purposes as in literature.

Earlier studies on the role of windows in literature appear mainly
within the tradition of French literary criticism, especially in connection
with certain works of Mallarmé, Zola, and Proust. Mallarmé's *Les fenêtres*
has generated a small body of critical writings. Mallarmé was a leader of
the Symbolist school, which, as Hamon (1968) remarks at the beginning
of an article on Zola, encouraged approaching the literary text as a crypto-
gram that must be deciphered. Symbolist works tend to incorporate
private symbols or even systems of symbols, which, in turn, tend to
instigate an analysis of the author along with his work. Cohn points
out that in *Les fenêtres* "There is a clear progression in the series door-
window-mirror, a growing arrestation. The window is midway between
the door and the mirror. With the full mirror there is a blockage, a reflexion, a return upon the self" (1977:29). While both doors and windows figure prominently in the Holmes stories and their illustrations,
there are very few mirrors, and in only one case, suss, does a window
double as a mirror. In that instance, Holmes uses the mirror to look not
at himself but at the "villain" of the case. Watson is interested in Holmes,
and Holmes is not unaware of his own nature, but Holmes is hardly a
character who returns "upon the self." Nor was Doyle a Symbolist, and
he did not write windows into his stories in order to provide a key to
either his literary puzzles or himself.

Commenting generally on windows, Cohn (ibid.) remarks that

> We note in passing that the window is a small theater—the place of en-
> counter of all outdoors and the most intimate interior life, of the high
> and the low, and so forth—and that the curtains are easily assimilated to

this image. An actor, dramatically emerges from between theater curtains as if born: He *appears,* a phenomenon.

There are occasions in the Holmes stories (COPP, SIGN, and VALL, to name three), when a character (or characters) watches the action within a window, much as an audience watches actors on a stage. Characters also look out windows to watch the passing scene, as when Mycroft and Holmes gaze through the window of the Diogenes Club (GREE) or Watson sees the client arrive in BERY. In the latter example, a relatively rare one, the client is obviously integrated into the plot of the story, while the passersby whom Mycroft and Holmes observe figure in the story (as is more common in such circumstances) merely to motivate dynamically the presentation of certain information about the two brothers. Since Holmes uses a Baker Street window shade as a projection screen in EMPT, we should perhaps also consider the window as a small cinema theater, though Watson sees the effect as "that of one of those black silhouettes which our grandparents loved to frame."

There are, of course, differences for the audience between watching a film and a live presentation, primarily because of the greater passivity and suspension of disbelief involved in watching a film. In fact, making these comparisons between Doyle's windows and the stage or screen requires a fairly active reader, for neither Doyle himself nor Watson (the character in the Holmes stories who stands in for Doyle, among other ways, as artist) ever overtly discusses this particular similarity. Though we find Holmes stories in which windows as a formal device may be said to substitute for an unnatural situation in which the audience passively observes characters in motion, these examples are relatively few and not of great importance either within the plot or the thematic structure in Doyle.

In light of this, then what of Hamon's comment (1968:388) that "La fenêtre, à la limite, remplace, justifie et symbolise l'oeil du romancier"? If the window is not a surrogate stage through which the reader views the action, then is it a surrogate eye through which the novelist views the material of his work? Schor, in an article that surveys the multifaceted role of windows within the works of the prolific French novelist who was Verne's contemporary, quotes both Zola and Henry James as using a window metaphor in an attempt to define art, and fiction in particular. In Schor's words (1968:39), James speaks of "the multiplicity of windows, each corresponding to an individual artist's vision and consciousness." According to Zola,

> all works of art are like a window open on creation. A kind of transparent Screen is mounted in the window frame. Through this Screen objects appear more or less distorted, as they undergo greater or lesser changes in their lines and colors. These changes depend on the nature of the Screen. Thus, one no longer sees creation exactly and realistically, but creation transformed by the medium through which the image passes. [Ibid.:38]

Doyle is hardly the literary theorist that James or Zola was, and neither he nor Watson ever mentions windows in connection with any sort of theory of literature. Holmes, in fact, chides Watson for the literary qualities of a report that should have been written "in the same cold and unemotional manner" (SIGN) of the science it was meant to depict. Notwithstanding the fact that these stories are not "scientific" enough for Holmes's tastes, there is no sense in which windows function within them as either a "medium through which the image" is "transformed," as Zola would have it, or, in a Symbolist fashion, as something that must itself be interpreted.

Walker (1969), referring to Zola's "realism," notes that windows, among other paths of vision, serve as a device for the transition between subjective and objective modes. In addition, windows, mirrors, and eyes, as a sort of prism, give us a multiple perspective on the characters and events of Zola's novels. The tie between windows and subjective moods is the primary topic for Lapp (1975) in his study of two important and similar scenes in Zola and Proust, in which windows are associated with sexual frustration and jealousy.

In another article, Lapp writes that:

> Recent semiological studies of the realist novel—I am thinking in particular of those of Philippe Hamon—have emphasized the outward gaze, treating the novelist's windows primarily as *transparent,* an accessory of description, and one of those constraints that the nineteenth-century postulates of objectivity and impersonality imposed upon the author. According to this view, a novelist uses windows, open doors, transoms, and similar vehicles of a character's glance, as a hinge between the narrative and the insertions of descriptive material gleaned from his notebooks. Thus Zola's windows, which provide the bulk of Hamon's examples, are shown as necessarily and immediately transparent, permitting a "libre circulation infinie des regards" and serving primarily to authorize description. The window and the observer at this vantage point would thereby constitute a fairly obvious tool, a *thématique vide,* as Hamon puts it, and a difficult problem for the novelist is to make it play an actual role in the narrative. Hamon completely neglects the window seen from without. [1976:39]

While Lapp does not entirely agree with Hamon's conclusions, the concept of windows "as a hinge" applies quite well to the Holmes stories. On some occasions in the canon the appearance of a window may be better motivated and integrated into a given story than on others. However, taking the stories collectively, it is difficult to write off Doyle's use of windows as a *thématique vide.*

Of the 56 canonical short stories and the four novellas by Conan Doyle in which Sherlock Holmes appears,[6] there are only two, SHOS and LION, in which windows play no role at all. In Schor's survey we find a veritable catalog of uses Zola finds for windows, many of which also appear in the Holmes canon. Schor observes that Zola's windows act most often as barriers, though they occasionally are the means for uniting people; that a light in a window signals the presence of one character to some other character (in much the same way as Doyle uses lights in windows, as in YELL, for example); that windows sometimes look onto or into other windows; and that windows may separate an enclosed inner space from an expansive outer space. Interestingly, Schor mentions that Zola's windows do not provide exits of any sort.[7] More often than not, windows in the Holmes stories have a manifold purpose, since Doyle frequently uses windows actively to work out his plots.

The Holmes stories usually take the form of a story within a story, as Scheglov has proposed in his structural sketch. The client's or victim's story normally fits within a framing narrative that presents two English gentlemen who leave the security of their Victorian homes in search of adventure. The Holmes stories as a whole break down into a typical structure characterized by a prologue, often set in Baker Street and narrated by Watson, which leads to the introduction of the client. After an initial period of probing, Holmes and Watson embark on an investigative and analytic quest that may lead to the solution of their client's problem and the case. If it does not, they may return to some earlier phase, such as another session with the client or to a ratiocinative approach,[8] often centered in Baker Street. Frequently, but not always, the story concludes with a summation and perhaps an epilogue again set in Baker Street.

Even such a simple thematic outline helps categorize Doyle's use of windows, for within each segment of the story windows appear relatively predictably. For instance, if a window is featured in the prologue, we may characteristically associate it with Watson's comments on the weather (FIVE), or with Holmes's remarkable abilities to deduce information about people from close observation (IDEN). During journeys that involve trains, Holmes often stares out the window, signaling to Watson an end to their conversation (STOC). In the client's story and the investigative sequence, windows are not strictly associated with any particular function, but serve, instead, a wide variety of other purposes, ranging from the grotesque image of Duncan Ross waving away a sea of red-headed men in REDH, through the misleading clue the villain of DEVI provides, to the face the client sees in YELL.

Windows rarely appear in the epilogue, except as part of the explanation given while recapitulating the problem and its solution, as in NAVA. The two exceptions to this rule involve a revelation of identity, as when Holmes and Watson learn the name of the woman who unexpectedly murders the villain before their very eyes in CHAS. In ILLU, Watson catches a glimpse of the coat of arms on their lofty client's carriage through a window, thus learning what Holmes already knew—who their client was.

Of course, Doyle varies his use of the window so that one rarely appears in every segment of a given story, nor does it function in any given segment in every way that it might. However, there would be little purpose in studying one particular element of a literary work if no recurring characteristics of that element could be determined, so let us now examine the Holmesian canon as a whole in an effort to isolate recurrent features of windows to be found there.

A framework for our study can be constructed by asking a few obvious questions. Where are windows located? At Baker Street? At the client's quarters? A place of abode or of work? Who is associated with them? A major character in the story, such as Holmes (the protagonist), the villain (the antagonist), or perhaps the client—or a surrogate for any one or combination of these characters? Surrogates usually act as temporary stand-ins rather than as actual replacements (as when the female victim of WIST is rescued and the villain is sighted by a servant following Holmes's orders), although there is one example (in COPP) when one character (the client) serves quite literally as a replacement for another (the victim). Are windows related to the temporal sequence of events? Can we say that the appearance of windows in a story follows from some structural aspect of the story, i.e., do windows appear in the prologue only after Watson comments on Holmes's cocaine habit,

FIG. 3.2. A window *en route* in ABBE. From *Strand Magazine* 28: 249 (1904).

FIG. 3.3. Holmes ends a conversation, in BOSC. From *Strand Magazine* 2:401 (1891).

perhaps, or does the appearance of a window signal the close of a particular sequence of events, and so forth?

Is the window significant in itself, as when Holmes examines it (as in SIGN and SPEC); for its accoutrements (as in STUD and DEVI), such as curtains and sills; because it serves as a vehicle of passage for something (as in BLAN and DEVI); or, to the contrary, because it constitutes a barrier (as in CREE and GOLD), serving to block the passage of something (usually the weather)? Windows are significant for their own sake in two cases: when their shape deviates from the standard rectangle of medium size (which is more the rule than the exception), and when they are the subject of a specific examination. When they serve as a vehicle for the passage of something, the situation becomes more complicated. A window might be open or shut, acting as a barrier or as a conduit, enabling something or someone to enter or exit through it.

The first question, about location, can be readily answered. We find windows where Holmes and Watson live, where the victim/client and/or villain live and work, and in transit to or from these locations. Quite often, the victim and villain both live or work in the same place, a coincidence Holmes usually deems consequential.

FIG. 3.4. A rare appearance in the epilogue, in CHAS. From *Strand Magazine* 27:383 (1904).

The windows at Baker Street figure in the stories less often than we might expect. As we have seen, these windows are most significant at the beginning of the story, as Watson sets the mood with meteorological observations, among other details, or Holmes, exhibiting his own talents, introduces the client to Watson and to the reader from afar. After the prologue, the Baker Street windows tend to disappear from the narrative, with the marginal exception of those few stories in which Holmes and Watson return from the journey to begin the process of dealing with the client and investigating the case again, and the more consequential exception of those stories (primarily EMPT, and DYIN, though here Holmes is a "victim" rather than an actual victim) in which Holmes, through the device of fusion,[9] or combination in Scheglov and Zholkovskii's (1971) terms, doubles as the intended victim.

The victim's living quarters or working places are, not surprisingly, the most heavily visited, not just by the villain but also by the detective team. Watson rarely omits a mention or description of the windows at any new location, just as Holmes rarely omits his scrutiny of them. It is interesting to note that when the victim and the client are not one and the same character, the client often comes to Holmes because of some

Fig. 3.5. Client "acting" as victim, in COPP. From *Strand Magazine* 3:621 (1892).

untoward event related to a victim who lives in the same house with him or her.

The villain's quarters usually appear in the stories because they are also the client's or the victim's. However, when the villain has some document that Holmes needs, or when a kidnapping may be involved, Holmes does not hesitate to break in, often necessitating his illicit intrusion through a window. In one exceptional story, RETI, the client turns out to be the villain.

The category in which windows are perceived while one of the characters is in transit includes not only the windows of actual vehicles that figure in the journeys but also windows located at places Holmes may be investigating, even though these locations are not specifically attached to the victim, the client, or the villain. In effect, this becomes an omnibus grouping, and thus our second largest category.

Naturally, Watson is the person most often associated with windows, for he is Doyle's normal point-of-view character through whose sense organs the reader's perceptions are channeled. Holmes and Watson together are the characters most often watching others through windows, sending or receiving auditory and/or visual messages through windows, and in general being the characters with the most active role in the drama. Occasionally, however, one or both of them are the ones who are under surveillance, and it is important to remember that with all characters associated with windows, the conjunction may be either active or passive. In the category that includes Holmes and Watson, we also find the police, the Baker Street irregulars, and other assistants who can act as surrogate figures for Holmes or Watson. In the same way, the victim/ client category and the villain category include family members, servants, and others who could serve as surrogates for these figures.

While windows figure importantly as a source of light in painting, the appearance of light in a window, or passing through it, serves as an index in the Holmes stories for the presence or absence of some party on either side (as it did on occasion for characters in the novels of Proust and Zola). Though references to moonlight or sunlight abound, their presence in connection with a window does not play a large role in orienting the reader as to the time of day. Without a doubt, most references to light in a window center around the presence of a candle, a gas lamp, or other sorts of artificial light.

There are four stories in which the windows are blocked, causing a non-natural darkness that prevents a character from looking out the

FIG. 3.6. In HOUN. From *Strand Magazine* 23:250 (1902).

window or the passage of light into a room. In GREE and ENGR, the windows of the villain's carriage are darkened to prevent the client/victim from following the route that leads to the villain, while in CHAS and SPEC, the curtains and shutters create a darkness in rooms that would otherwise be light.

"HE DREW UP THE WINDOWS."

FIG. 3.7. Villain "drew up the windows," in GREE. From *Strand Magazine* 6:299 (1893).

In DANC, a table faces "an ordinary window," but this "ordinary" window seems exceptional, given the number of gabled, bay, bow, latticed, mullioned, high, low, deep-set, thin, and broad windows that make their appearance in the other stories.[10] French windows and other windows reaching the floor figure in quite a few stories (as in CROO and SCAN), while tiny windows too narrow for someone to pass through understandably complicate only a small number of stories (such as MUSG and SPEC). This great variety and inconsistency minimizes the symbolic import of the window shapes that appear in the Holmes stories. Even the description of the Baker Street windows changes somewhat over time, for Watson describes the apartment he and Holmes rent in STUD as having two broad windows, though we hear of bow windows at Baker Street in BERY.

Holmes often examines pertinent windows, and occasionally we learn of the police or even the client/victim examining one. Most often this results in the discovery of a smudge or print on a sill. Occasionally, the curtains reveal hidden clues (VALL, CROO), or Holmes and Watson hide behind a curtain (in CHAS). Quite often when Watson or the client describes a room, he will orient the furnishings relative to the windows, as with the cupboard between windows in ILLU.

Windows most often serve in the stories as entrances and exits for a multitude of people and objects. In many stories, such as DEVI, windows may be opened to allow fresh air in and/or to disperse noxious fumes. However, windows may still be penetrated in certain ways even when they are shut. Moonlight and sunlight often pass through, and Doyle often creates atmosphere by describing the quality of such light, as in STUD, where a dirty window lets in gray sunlight. Characters constantly look in and out of windows, noting the presence of other characters. An example intermingling these activities appears in HOUN, in which Holmes and Watson discover the presence of a criminal on the moor when Barrymore, the family servant, flashes a message, using a candle in the window, to his brother-in-law, an escapee from prison.

Fig. 3.8. Signaling through a window, in HOUN. From *Strand Magazine* 22:506 (1901). Illustration by Sidney Paget.

Occasionally, as with the "to let" sign in STUD, a sign may appear in a window. Two windows may form the beginning and end of a communication network, as in REDC, where the victim and his wife communicate with each other by means of a candle lit in one window and visible in another located across the street. Holmes and Watson, in one instance, even look out or at the same window but see different things. This happens in SUSS, when Watson looks out the client's window at a "melancholy, dripping" garden. Holmes interests himself in a different form of nature, using the window as a mirror in which he watches the client's eldest son display his hatred for a younger child. This window, in effect, reflects the contrasting personalities of Holmes and Watson.

Watson begins several stories with a comment on the noise of the wind and rain as they beat against the Baker Street windows. While this particular way in which a window forms a barrier protecting the person inside from something outside is connected almost entirely with Watson and Baker Street, there are instances in which the person inside may be protected from something outside that he or she sees rather than hears. In CREE, for example, a father frightens his daughter when his face appears unexpectedly at her second-floor window.

FIG. 3.9. Holmes in a communication network, in REDC. From *Strand Magazine* 41:429 (1911). Illustration by H. M. Brock.

On several occasions, guns and bullets penetrate the flimsy barrier of the window. Holmes, in EMPT and MAZA, actually sets up his bust in the Baker Street windows as bait for the villain's bullets. In addition, there is the dramatic scene in VALL in which the police put their guns through the Pinkerton agent's window when they capture the leaders of the Molly Maguires.

FIG. 3.10. Watson viewing a "projection screen," in EMPT. From *Strand Magazine* 26:369 (1903). Illustration by Sidney Paget.

According to Plischke (1914:76), closing the doors and windows at midnight (and not looking out the windows) to guard against evil spirits is common practice in many folktales. Though this condition is a positive element in folktales, closed windows and/or blinds are often an unfavorable omen in the Holmes canon. While the villain may open a window in order to do harm to someone inside, windows are most often opened to clear the air. Though Holmes does open windows during the course of his investigation, in the two main examples, BRUC and DEVI, his action is important primarily for what it reveals of the sills and the terrain below. However, in a majority of situations involving shut windows, either Holmes or the villain is responsible or concerned. In HOUN, Holmes and Watson differ over the air quality in their Baker Street rooms because Holmes likes the stuffy atmosphere his pipe smoke creates as he works on the solution to a problem, while Watson thinks Holmes has carried the point too far in this particularly difficult case. The villain, though, is usually the one to shut a window, or to draw a curtain, in an effort to conceal his secrets or to carry out his nefarious activities. This association with shut windows links Holmes with the villain, and Holmes's complex character and surplus of talent supports this bond, as we learn in CHAS, when Holmes opens the safe with the skill of "a surgeon" or "a trained mechanic."

FIG. 3.11. In BRUC. From Smith (1952 [1908]:opp. 1274). Illustration by Frederic Dorr Steele.

In several cases, the open or shut state of the windows remains ambiguous. The blinds may be half drawn or the shutters may not quite meet.

If we return to *Vingt mille lieues sous les mers,* we find the portholes of the *Nautilus* mentioned most often in connection with M. Aronnax's delight at the opportunity to study and observe the sea life passing before him. On one occasion, Captain Nemo communicates through the porthole with a Greek diver about the former's gift of gold, and there is the time when Conseil spots the threatening "giant squid" just as Aronnax describes it. The most striking exception to Aronnax's generally passive delight in front of the porthole is his experience of burning his hand on the glass as the ship passes through boiling water in the vicinity of an underwater volcano. By and large, though, there is a constant situation in which Aronnax and his companions passively sit within the luxurious *Nautilus* watching what passes by outside the porthole. The porthole itself becomes in effect a movie screen, but also a screen that shields the passengers of the *Nautilus* from the dangers of the sea.

Fig. 3.12. The giant squid. See note 1.

When Holmes projects the shadow of his bust on the window shade for the benefit of outside observers, he also uses a window as a sort of movie screen. His role in connection with windows, however, is obviously more active than that of the passengers on the *Nautilus*. As we have seen with the penetration of guns and bullets, the windows of the Holmes stories also form a less protective screen for Holmes from outside dangers than does Captain Nemo's window. Indeed, in FIVE, the window may keep out the rain of the storm raging outside, but the client, synecdochically, as it were, still brings some of it inside to perturb Holmes and Watson within their safe moistureless retreat.

If, after this intensive scrutiny of the appearance of windows in the Holmes stories, we return to the theoretical comments presented at the opening of this paper, it is readily apparent that, indeed, windows are associated with the theme of comfort and security in both Verne and Doyle, as Scheglov suggests. While windows serve to protect the comfort and security of Holmes and Watson, though, they also provide an outlet in the "self-enclosed cosmogony," enabling our detective pair to enjoy the exterior danger and the interior comfort simultaneously.

While we have argued against the idea that Doyle used windows as a symbolic eye for the purpose of obtaining either his own or the reader's view of reality, we do agree with that school of thought, exemplified by Lapp, which views windows as "transparent" and as "a hinge." In other words, Doyle did use windows as a device for the presentation of some descriptive information whose inclusion in the "scientific" annals of Holmes's exploits might otherwise have been difficult. Doyle, however, besides motivating the descriptive function of his window, goes on to incorporate windows into the Holmes canon in other active ways.

Having reached the conclusion of this paper, the reader may recall that the epigraph calls for a description of the view beyond the window if the description of the window itself is to be valid. While this may be true, such a task lies outside the scope of this paper, which endeavored, somewhat more simply, to study the multitudinous functions of windows in Doyle's classic stories.

NOTES

1. The title of our paper—which, notwithstanding that its substance is devoted to Arthur Conan Doyle's Sherlock Holmes stories, names solely Captain Nemo, Jules Verne's unforgettable *genius marum*—requires an explanation, which must be couched in terms that reflect certain distant autobiographical circumstances of the senior author of this paper. These can most conveniently be recalled by him in the first person singular:

My father's private library, in the Budapest of my childhood, was particularly well stocked with nineteenth- and twentieth-century French fiction, and contained, as I can still vividly visualize, volume upon volume of the books of Jules Verne, many in the first French edition by Hetzel & Co. Most of them were graced by sensational engraved pictorial representations on the part of a stable of superlative artists in Hetzel's employ, in particular Leon Bennett (sometimes Benett), George S. Roux (not to be confused, as he often is, with Edouard Riou), and Alphonse Marie de Neuville. De Neuville had prepared (with Riou) the superb illustrations for Hetzel's original publication of *Vingt mille lieues sous les mers*, including the first illustration of this article. It was then engraved by "Hildibrand," whose prestigious pen name alone appears in the lower left-hand corner, but whose real name was Henri Theophile Hildebrand. (On pictorial presentations in the 65 volumes of Verne's *Les voyages extraordinaires*, see Haining 1978, where more than 180 illustrations are reproduced. Some are from the original French editions, others are from English and American translations, and still more are from serializations, films, and comic strips.)

De Neuville and his fellow artists, in effect, achieved for the *Strange Journeys* what the painter Sidney Paget—selected by W. H. J. Boot—accomplished so wonderfully for Doyle's stories in issue after issue of *The Strand*. Ironically, Doyle is said to have thought little of Paget's drawings (Higham 1976:73); nonetheless, the shapes of Holmes and company imprinted upon his readers' memory are those envisaged by Paget rather than those initially described by Doyle. When William Gillette came to portray Holmes on the stage, the great American actor modeled his characterization on the Holmes the public already knew from Paget's creations, and he embellished upon them: for instance, it was Gillette who invented such props as the deerstalker's cap and Inverness cape. Later illustrators, such as Frederic Dorr Steele, and generations of movie actors, notably Basil Rathbone, tended, in turn, to base *their* portrayals on Gillette's face and figure.

My initial encounter with the Verne *opera* antedated by many years my acquisition of French; therefore, the germ for this paper can be said to have been planted before I turned a teenager, yet I am able to revive the exact incident: it dates from my first glimpse of "Hildibrand's" engraving (now our Fig. 1), which thereafter continued to haunt my childhood with a *frisson* inconceivable to adults. The contrast between my impregnable and, I had confidently hoped, inviolable, home and the monstrous perils of the world—"It was an immense cuttlefish"—that kept floating by outside, was, it seems indelibly, etched upon my sensibility by this single picture.

By 1934, having returned to Hungary from an extended period in Lausanne, I had learned to read French, and proceeded to race through all of Verne's *Strange Voyages*, commencing this exercise at exactly Doyle's age of fourteen (see below), even starting with the very same submarine epic, *Twenty Thousand Leagues under the Sea*. My reading, of course, powerfully reinforced the picture show that had already been long flickering in my imagination.

While I am reminiscing, I should like also to record that I can date with absolute, though perhaps unbelievable, accuracy (for reasons which are neither here nor there) my first confrontation with Sherlock Holmes. This momentous event took place throughout the afternoon and evening of April 30, 1927. The novella was a luridly illustrated Hungarian edition of *The Hound of the Baskervilles*, that impressed my immature fancy with Dr. Watson's forebodingly evocative vision from his bedroom window at Baskerville Hall:

> I drew aside my curtains before I went to bed and looked out from my window. It opened upon the grassy space which lay in front of the hall door. Beyond, two copses of trees moaned and swung in the rising wind. A half moon broke through the rifts of racing clouds. In its cold light I saw beyond the trees a broken fringe of rocks and the long, low curve of the melancholy moor. I closed the curtain, feeling that my last impression was in keeping with the rest.

At the risk of being thought afflicted with total recall, I should add that, while reading this chronicle, at the age of seven, I was snugly, if feverishly, ensconced in my mother's bed.

These remarks are meant to establish that the dramatic contrast between the inside and the outside, and the mediating window in between, aspects of which are catalogued and discussed in our text, is a leitmotif that goes back a long, long way in my mind's eye, with, moreover, quite special application to the Sacred Writings of Verne and Doyle.

In sum: the idea for this article and the assessment of its principal literary ramifications are mainly mine. Harriet Margolis, a doctoral candidate in Indiana University's Comparative Literature Program, worked closely with the pertinent primary and secondary sources.

2. The Sherlock Holmes story titles are abbreviated according to a key given in Tracy 1977:xix:

ABBE	The Abbey Grange	LAST	His Last Bow
BERY	The Beryl Coronet	LION	The Lion's Mane
BLAN	The Blanched Soldier	MAZA	The Mazarin Stone
BOSC	The Boscombe Valley Mystery	MUSG	The Musgrave Ritual
		NAVA	The Naval Treaty
BRUC	The Bruce-Partington Plans	NORW	The Norwood Builder
		REDC	The Red Circle
CHAS	Charles Augustus Milverton	REDH	The Red-Headed League
COPP	The Copper Beeches	RETI	The Retired Colourman
CREE	The Creeping Man	SCAN	A Scandal in Bohemia
CROO	The Crooked Man	SHOS	Shoscombe Old Place
DANC	The Dancing Men	SIGN	The Sign of Four
DEVI	The Devil's Root	SILV	Silver Blaze
DYIN	The Dying Detective	SPEC	The Speckled Band
EMPT	The Empty House	STOC	The Stockbroker's Clerk
ENGR	The Engineer's Thumb	STUD	A Study in Scarlet
FIVE	The Five Orange Pips	SUSS	The Sussex Vampire
GOLD	The Golden Pince-Nez	3GAB	The Three Gables
GREE	The Greek Interpreter	3STU	The Three Students
HOUN	The Hound of the Baskervilles	VALL	The Valley of Fear
		WIST	Wisteria Lodge
IDEN	A Case of Identity	YELL	The Yellow Face
ILLU	The Illustrious Client		

3. It is interesting to note that Verne wrote most of *Vingt mille lieues sous les mers* on board his yacht while crossing and recrossing the English Channel.

4. Recall the motto engraved on Captain Nemo's every utensil: *Mobilis in Mobili*, or "Mobile within the mobile element."

5. Verne compares the view from the *Nautilus* to a diorama, on which Miller (Verne 1976:277) comments in a lengthy note:

> To Verne's nineteenth-century reader, this comparison was dramatic and suggestive. Before the age of the cinema, *diorama* (like panorama and cyclorama) gave the visual artist and his audience golden opportunities to enjoy illusions and changing effects.
>
> A *simple diorama* could be a three-dimensional scene with painted models standing in the foreground against an opaque painted background. An *elaborate diorama* could be painted on transparent hangings on which lights could be played to vary the effects. The audience would view a diorama either out in the open or through a peephole.
>
> Early *peep-shows* certainly included dioramas, but credit for their development belongs to Louis Jacques Mandé Daguerre (1789-1851), French painter and physicist best known for his invention of the daguerreotype. In his Diorama, which opened in Paris in 1822 and later in London, he uses translucent curtains and wings and he played with perspective as well as with lights.
>
> Aronnax's simile—*altered the whole landscape like a diorama*—is therefore perfectly appropriate. He is talking of labyrinthine ice masses, some translucent, some mirrorlike, which refract and reflect daylight with great variety as the viewers on the *Nautilus* move by.

6. On what precisely constitutes the "canon" or the Holmesian Sacred Writings, see Truzzi (1973:118n1).

7. A glance at Thompson's *Motif-Index of Folk Literature* (1955-58) reveals an entirely different list of appearances that windows make, in yet another sort of literature, though it is not a list that transfers readily to Doyle.

8. The logic of which is discussed in chapter 2 of this volume; see also Truzzi (1973:97-110).

FIG. 3.13. The bay window, in 3STU. From *Strand Magazine* 27: 604 (1904). Illustration by Sidney Paget.

FIG. 3.14. The latticed window, in YELL. From *Strand Magazine* 5:167 (1893). Illustration by Sidney Paget.

9. On the uses of fusion in detective novels, particularly Agatha Christie's, see further Revzin 1978.

10. According to the *Oxford English Dictionary,* a bay window consists of "a window forming a bay or recess in a room and projecting outwards from the wall, either in a rectangular, polygonal, or semicircular form; often called a *bow*-window." The bow window itself is defined as "a bay-window segmentally curved on plan." In 3GAB, we meet Langdale Pike, who "spent his waking hours in the bow window of a St. James's Street Club"; and in GREE, Mycroft and Holmes sit down in the bow window of the Diogenes Club for their friendly duel testing their abilities to identify strangers. Latticed windows, found in LAST, HOUN, and 3STU, contain a "structure made of laths, or of wood or metal, crossed and fastened together with open spaces left between." Screens, gates, or anything else using such a framework may be called latticed. Mullioned windows, which appear in HOUN and MUSG, simply have a "vertical bar dividing the lights in a window." The porthole, so integral a part of the *Nautilus,* is "an aperture in a ship's side," used now for the passage of light and air, though it formerly served as an opening for a ship's cannon.

For additional information on these specific types of windows as they appear in the Holmes stories, see Tracy 1977.

Chapter 4

The Image of Charles Morris

IN 1970, Charles Morris published, under the imprint of George Braziller, what was to become his last book-length prose contribution to the history of ideas and their interrelationships, *The Pragmatic Movement in American Philosophy*. Four years earlier, Braziller laid before the public Morris's slender collection of poems, *Festival*, which had been, in quick succession, turned down by Norton (January 19, 1965), next by Pantheon (February 10). Although Morris informed Braziller, ten days later, that he "would not expect *Festival* to have a large number of readers (at least at once) . . . ," the canny publisher proposed to him (April 2) a *quid pro quo*, to wit: that his house would be inclined to put *Festival* on its list "if we could be assured of having the book [he was then] working on, *The Pragmatic Movement*, when it is ready." On April 10, Morris accepted the proffered trade gladly, and, in due course, kept his bargain, submitting his work about—and, what is more important, still within—American pragmatic philosophy. The essence of his book, however, was divined in quite another mode as far back as September 11, 1954, in two banausic stanzas of Whitmanesque catalogue verse preserved only in Morris's handwriting:

Pragmatists

We have worked with Mead,
Moore, Tufts, and Ames;
And long known Dewey, Lewis,
Kallen; and are well versed
in Nietzsche, Peirce, and James.

These are to us mammoth names,[1]
Diverse to be sure, but all freed
And utterly pure, all universal
for human destiny, all concerned
that man be as fertile see'd.

From the parochial viewpoint of the professional "semiotician"—a term thought to have been coined by Morris himself (1971:81), later

---

This article has not previously appeared in English. It was written in response to an invitation by Achim Eschbach, who translated the manuscript into German and intends to publish it in a book, edited by himself, entitled *Zeichen über Zeichen: Studien zu Charles W. Morris* (Tübingen: Narr, 1981). (His book will also constitute a Supplement to the journal *Kodikas/Code*.)

encased and ennobled in the title of eight of his most cunningly wrought
lines, his epitaphic "Death of a Semiotician" (1976:86)—Morris looms as
a towering coeval figure of the sign theory, who must "zweifellos als einer
der Begründer und Klassiker dieses Forschungsprogramms im 20. Jahr-
hundert angesehen werden" (Apel 1973:9). This judgment is widely
shared by, among others, Rossi-Landi (1975:155), who held that "Morris' place as the most important representative of twentieth century
semiotics has been generally recognized. . . ." For Wendy Steiner (1978:
105f.), Morris's contribution "prefigures the eruption in the 1960's and
1970's of disciplines concerned with nonverbal sign-systems," and she
perceives "the seeds of kinesics, paralinguistics, proxemics, and so much
more of contemporary sign theory" to have germinated from his writings.
For Posner (1979:70), "keine all-umfassende Perspektive gibt" in semiotics after Morris, and it may therefore be appropriate here to recall again
his own characteristically modest *hic jacet* (Morris 1976:86):

Death of a Semiotician

He revered signs, reared them,
loved them; yet still sought
to be above them... But they thought
otherwise. He was so besieged,
drenched, smothered, wrenched,
mothered, mogrified by the violence
of the signs, that he, ungrieved,
in silence simply died—re-signed.

The implacable fallibilism (cf. Zeman 1980) intimated in this perspi-
cacious, if melancholy, octonary is certainly consonant with Morris's un-
presumptuous self-assessment, which envisaged the progressive advance
of "a comprehensive and fruitful science of signs" to be the task for
"many investigators working in many fields for many generations" and
his semiotic "as something to be modified, amplified, rectified, super-
seded" (Morris 1971:434f.). More interestingly, the central conception
of Morris, startlingly sounded beginning with the fourth line of this
poem, is tantamount to an oft-quoted declaration by Lévi-Strauss (1964:
20): "Nous ne pretendons donc pas montrer comment les hommes pensent
dans les mythes, mais comment les mythes se pensent dans les hommes,
et à leur insu." Morris's intuitive reversal of the vulgarly held view—
including, seemingly, by himself, throughout his sober expository prose—
according to which "Signs are invented, tested, and controlled by individuals" (1971:323), was, in fact, the more profoundly veridical, as I
have briefly argued elsewhere (Sebeok 1979:xiii), and conforms, moreover, to the great modern semiotic tradition bracketed by Peirce and
Thom (ibid:62).[2]

Most practitioners of semiotics "are likely to think of Morris as the
author of the classic works, from 1938 to 1964, which were reassembled
in his *Writings on the General Theory of Signs*" (1971), as Fisch noted

FIG. 4.1. Portrait of Charles Morris

in his brief necrology (1979:159). But Fisch also reminds us of Morris's role in philosophy more generally, as well as of "the youthful magician, the psychologist and intending psychiatrist, the lifelong aesthetician, the student of Oriental religion and philosophy, the lover of dogs, and, above all, the poet. . . ." In addition to *Festival*, Morris published a second selection of his poems, just a decade later, with the final title *Image* (1976). It is chiefly this collection that I would like to feature in the foreground here, as well as to adumbrate certain attributes of the author, my teacher (Sebeok 1976:xii-xiii, 155), not so much as an explicit semiotician (for I have done that at length in a book I have dedicated to him, ibid.: *passim* [see the Index, p. 264]), but rather as a simulacrum for each of us to imitate as best we are able.

The point I wish to make, to begin with, is that I do not mean my essay to be skimmed for mere intellectual amusement. Morris's bookplate read, "Only with the whole of man are we wholly free." Having listened to Morris many times, and having perused his writings over 35 years or more, I am satisfied that there is no way to grasp the great questions he persevered in addressing except through his poetry. Let me, with Morris's hand, rephrase and clarify this stricture. As he reiterated to Robert Y. Zachary of the University of California Press on September 4, 1974:

> It might help to point out that it is misleading to regard *Icon*[3] as a whole as "poetry." It is "poetic" in tone and contains some pieces which anyone would call poetry. But the book as a whole is a form of *wisdom literature* —like Laotze's *The Way*, Heraclitus' *Fragments*, Nietzsche's *Zarathustra*, or even Whitman's *Leaves of Grass*. . . . *Icon* is an image of my work as a whole, and of the decades of social history which it spans. But it is written in a specific idiom of wisdom literature. I regard it as a completion of my life and work.

In an earlier letter to Zachary (July 30, 1973), he characterized *Icon* more concisely thus: "Some of it is clearly poetry, some poetic prose, and some a kind of 'wisdom literature.'" He wrote to Zachary (in a letter dated as far back as April 26, 1971) that he preferred to characterize his contributions to "wisdom literature," the purpose of which was to portray or exemplify the orientation of life he has called *Maitreyan* (see below), "as important as my technical work in science and philosophy." He saw no contradiction whatever, adding: "Nor did Carnap" (whom he first met during a stay in Prague back in 1934, and who sent him some interesting and sympathetic letters about *Festival*).[4]

Morris's "wisdom literature" was his best effort to distill his deepest insights and sapience—the ones he felt himself incapable of articulating in "the colder account appropriate to a science of signs," as he put it in his neglected "A Primer of Semantics" (Morris 1948: chap. III, 51f.). He emphasized the multiplicity of the ways signs can be used. When "Ways of Talking" emerged in the evolution of mankind, they included the talk of artists and the talk of religious men, and

> the high mission of the artist is to explore novel ways of being for or against, and to let us share his explorations through the specialized language which he has created. In this way, we live vicariously, seeing things as others have seen them, standing as they stood before things, and falling as they fell. And in so living vicariously, we enjoy our characteristic appraisals, test them, gain material for their transformation, perhaps repudiate them. This is why we honor the artist for his work as we honor the scientist for his. We do not choose between them because we need them both. [Ibid.:61]

Such was Morris's creed. For his rhapsody on Art as "celebration," see 1976:27.

In a different, more technical, context that we all know, his persuasion led him to a discussion of a sign he came to call an "appraisor," the signification of which is a "valuation." He eventually restated his feelings (in an undated communication, but probably completed in late 1975, to the Editorial Department of his publisher-to-be) thus:

Charles Morris believes that poetry is the highest form of human symbols, utilizing in itself all the resources of the specialized forms of human symbolization such as occur in science, philosophy, the special arts, and in human life. It refers to things and yet expresses human goals and aspirations as to the ideal forms of human relationships. It reflects both human thought and human values. *Image* in particular testifies to the ideas and to the goals of the lifelong work of its author, Charles Morris.

In sum, the scientist informs (1976:26); the artist informs as well as appraises (ibid.:27); the religious man appraises as well as prescribes (ibid.:28). Morris was possessed by a fierce and at times desperate urge to fulfill his triple mission: "It is very important for me psychologically," he pleaded, in declining health in his 74th year, with Zachary, "to have *Icon* (or part of it) published in 1976, for this is in a sense my major completing volume." The University of California Press rejected the book on August 20, the very date Morris put this despondent letter of entreaty in the mail.

At this point, Morris had practically no other option out of this somber cul-de-sac but to approach a "vanity publisher."[5] He chose one of the most renowned, the Vantage Press, for an obvious reason: The previous year, that is, in 1974, this house had brought out *The White Dog*, by Ruth Ellen Allen Morris, his former wife, and Charles considered that to have been a "fine publication." On September 25, 1975 he wrote to Martin Littlefield, Vice President of Vantage, submitting for his consideration "one of my own books, called *Image*," inquiring about the financial terms, specifying further that he "would like the book published in 1976 (on May 23 of 1976 I will be 75)." His manuscript was accepted on October 10, contingent on an initial subsidy of $4,450, later increased to $4,800 (or, roughly, $44 per poem). As he informed members of his family ten days later:

> The big event: I have signed a contract for the publication of a poetry volume, which I am now calling *Image* instead of *Icon*. I paid a good subsidy—so the book is now completely paid for. . . . All this greatly relieves me, especially the completion of my arrangements for the poetry book. You have now all the material I included in it—*Cycles* and the *Turn of the Wheel*. More would have made it too expensive. So there are three other poetry books which I may or may not try to publish.

The titular change was foreshadowed at least as early as 1973, when Morris explained to Zachary (July 30) that

> the name "Maitreya" is not the basic thing in *Icon. Icon* is an "image" of the way that the last 40 or so years have expressed themselves in me. It "reflects" me and the world I have encountered. I regard it as one of my main achievements and am very anxious to have it published. So anxious, in fact, that I am willing to contribute $4,000 to that end.

This open offer was not countenanced by the University of California Press.

Image did not enjoy any sort of public critical reaction; I doubt if the collection was ever even reviewed.[6] As his contract with Vantage specified, Morris was given one hundred copies to distribute as he pleased, and he sent out a limited number to those he counted among his familiars. He had, in fact, stated in the letter to Littlefield that he was anxious to get *Image* published "essentially to get copies to my friends here and abroad." He regarded this "a continuation in spirit of *Festival* and . . . in effect [his] last major book." He well knew that it was not "a book that can expect a large general sale." Such small correspondence as his gift generated is preserved in the most comprehensive collection of Morris's papers, at the Peirce Edition Project at Indiana University–Purdue University at Indianapolis.[7] Perhaps a typical comment was Charles Hartshorne's empathetic: "You have to an amazing extent internalized the Buddhist ideal. And you have poetic gifts" (December 23, 1976).

Morris's gnomic utterances raise a host of intriguing questions about the author's personality and the total character of his work—a bewildering blend of bedrock behaviorist empiricism and vaporous telesthetic superstructure. I have already alluded to his modesty about his achievements in semiotic; and, among all who knew him personally, his unpretentiousness was indeed legendary. His cosmic self-evaluation may therefore discomfit those few who read his autobiographical remarks set forth for the unrestricted use of his publisher—but printed only in a drastically abridged form on the back page of the jacket of *Image*—in which he described himself not merely "as one of the important thinkers of our time," but further thus: "His thought and experience is . . . both Asiatic and Western. Comprehensiveness of outlook and deep concern for intellectual and human activities all over the earth has [sic] been his guiding principle. He is genuinely a planetary personality, a world-citizen."

Then there is the issue of the relation between Morris's prosaic theory of signs and his visceral semiotic wisdom literature. As I have already illustrated, these were sometimes contradictory, with his poetic statement usually the more profound (or, at least, more congenial to me). This seeming discrepancy deserves further investigation. For this occasion, I would merely like to reproduce for the convenience of readers one of Morris's best published poems, and then to publish here, for the first time, his most comprehensive free-rhythmic literary piece devoted to the topic in general (to analyze these in a careful, critical perspective would require a separate article).[8] First, from Morris 1976:39:

Animal Symbolicum

What a remarkable animal: physiological and symbolical.
Kin of every other animal, but symbol-haunted and
dramatical.[9]

It took incessant killing and insistent genitality to carry
man through the long historical ordeal. Plus a fantastic
and fabulous brain to support visions to plot his way.

Becoming man was a tortuous trial. The enemies were
cold and storm, bigger and smaller animals, and alien
other men.

Man is a plucky, chancy, lucky symbolizing thing. His
symbols are his essential glory and his burden. His
dreams came from them, his proximate goals, his sustaining incentives to action, and his delusions.

Symbols are in truth man's heaviest burden, the per-
petuating devices of his perpetual anxiousness, the
armor of his arrogance, the shield which hides him from
himself and from what is other than himself.

Yet symbols are the source of man's fantasies, the bells
of his triumphs in his glance outward, the cries of his
consummations and his defeats, the torch of his joys,
and the light unto his death.

Next, new-sprung:

Semiotic

Those old worshippers of silence, are they indeed so difficult
to understand? Is it really violent to demand that initiates
forbear speech? We who are pressed by the multitudinous signs
of things that would reach us, do we not of necessity comprehend
that ancient stand that for a long time talking cease?

For the body says and says its weakness and its strength. The
small hand talks to us daily, and weaker legs confront the
stronger arms; there is a peripheral limit with which our central
strength cannot be rhymed. You are weak or strong the body says,
and we acquiesce or revolt by speaking other signs.

Our life is verily a long talk with ourselves, a confirmation
and rebuttal of the body's voices, a confirmation and rebuttal
of what other bodies tell us of our vices and our virtues,
of what we are and what we ought to be.

Yes, our affirmations are schooled in our distress. We are
indeed deep enough in signified sin to warrant doubt and seek
for silence. Yet our evil we accept our evil to transmute.
Look! Beyond our tell-tale superficial signs lies a mightier
self that from its well of good and evil yet will write
a praiseful book!

This cadenced essay articulates more insightfully and elegantly the notion I have been calling "The Semiotic Self" (Sebeok 1979:263-267), and
much besides, than does any comparable attempt I am conversant with.

On July 30, 1973, Morris had written to Zachary:

You will note that I make great use of the symbol Maitreya in [*Icon*]—
which in Buddhist lore is the name of the next Enlightened One to come.
. . . The term "Maitreya" is coming again into use. There is a journal by
that name in California (I wrote the first article to appear but have no
further connection with it), the International Council of Cooperation . . .
has made extensive use of my ideas, and several groups around the country
call themselves Maitreyan Centers.

The entire second section of *Image*—fourteen pieces—came to be titled
Maitreya or the "Buddhist ideal" Hartshorne mentioned in his letter of
acknowledgment. Can this "overflowing" (Morris 1976:62) Maitreyan
Wisdom be reconciled with Morris's simultaneous development of semiotic? He boiled the matter down into a dainty tetrametric nutshell (ibid.:
103):

Graph Reading

Everywhere there is lawfulness,
and everywhere there is chance.

Everywhere there is awesomeness,
and everywhere there is dance.

Anticipating McLuhan's overburdened temperature metaphor (1965:
chap. II, "Media Hot and Cold") by a decade and a half, Morris (1948:
51) remarked of "the study of signs" that "[s]ome like it hot and some
like it cold." Instead of confronting the major choice implied by the opposition, however, Morris allowed himself the wide latitude of utilizing all
instruments at his command, no matter what the temperature of the
agency, with the fascinating consequence so well put by Kenneth Boulding
(in his comparably titled *The Image* [1961:7]) by saying: "The meaning
of a message is the change which it produces in the image." The three
temperature ranges Morris undulated among—although, to be sure, with
unequal dexterity—were the cold accounts represented by his specialized semiotic treatises, his searing poetry, and, between these two polar
extremes, the comfortably warm chronicles embodied in such prosaic
works as *The Open Self* and the *Paths of Life*. Like an accomplished juggler alternately tossing a multitude of objects in the air and catching them
one or more at a time, Morris projected an image that metamorphosed, as
if by sorcery, in a rapid kaleidoscopic manner. But the underlying meaning
shifted only to the extent compelled by the medium he employed.

A juggler is a species of entertainer who performs illusions by means
of "whiffs of wizardry," and Morris fancied he was an archimage. Is
this simile strained? A seldom espied letter, typed by a callow Morris, is
reproduced here.[10]

Very few people know that Morris resolved, in 1911, to "adopt" conjury as a career, and started a magic scrapbook in October 1915, which

CHARLES W. MORRIS
ENTERTAINER

WHIFFS OF WIZARDY   5452 MAGNOLIA AVENUE
THE ACT ARTISTIC   PHONE: EDGEWATER 6861

                                              CHICAGO.   6-7-19.

Rogers Park Woman's Club,
Chicago, Ill.

Dear Madam:

        The music plays - the curtain rises - the
onlookers are desiring something new, novel, and
entertaining. Why not give it to them?

        Certainly you have often desired some real
novelty - a novelty combining artistic presentation,
clean showmanship, and uniqueness - an act that
features any occasion. Well, I can offer you just
such an act in my WHIFFS OF WIZARDRY, the most subtle,
baffling, magical entertainment procurable - combining
sleight-of-hand, mind-reading, and spectacular magic.
I am not offering an in-the-rut show, but a distinctive
attraction, appealing to the eye and to the ear.

        You will have need of a well-dressed, finished
performance this summer. I can give it to you. With
several years' experience in society at clubs, cafes,
resorts and hotels, I have handled all types of entertainments - from the smallest to the most extravagant.

        WHIFFS OF WIZARDRY will mystify Chicago between
July 1st and October 1st this summer, and on week ends
next fall and winter. Let me hear from you or talk
with you.

        I take pride in giving you the best. Why not
let me handle an entertainment unique for you? The
price is reasonable - depending on the affair itself.

        Make that dinner dance of yours an enjoyable
success. Liven up that evening with mystery art.
Enhance any occasion in a way you believed impossible.
Ring up the curtain on WHIFFS OF WIZARDRY.

            Yours for an artistic entertainment,

FIG. 4.2. Letter to Rogers Park Woman's Club

he kept up until January 1918. His idol was Howard Franklin Thurston, who was born in Columbus, Ohio, in 1869, and whose "The Wonder Show of the Universe" became internationally famous. He "maintained his position as America's greatest illusionist for 28 years" (Christopher 1973: 240; Thurston died in 1936) and had the reputation of being "[u]nfailingly kind to small boys who were interested in becoming magicians" (ibid.:232). Even after the 1929 stock market crash, Thurston's best mysteries "set new box-office records at the . . . Chicago Theatre in Chicago," among others (ibid.:236), where Morris, it is reasonable to assume, went to see him. His picture graced the front cover of Morris's scrapbook, which was filled with clippings about Thurston's most wondrous tricks, many of them with a distinctly Oriental flavor. In Morris 1966:43 we have his last-known statement, after he has assimilated magic with Magic:

Magic

Rabbits from a hat, doves caught
by a net in free space, the fair girl
that floats in free air and vanishes
there without leaving a trace of herself

anywhere—there are the pantomimes,
the gestures, the replicas of the greater magic,
mimes of the Great Magician
that makes a seed of grass a blade,
that pulls the stars apart without trepidation,
and makes them contract again; that can send
a thought through a millennium of greed
to mate it with a verse; that in the tragic,
joy can still contact; and that from the adverse
and the perverse can mix sweet lemonade.

It is important not to lose sight of the larger questions implied in the foregoing paragraphs, even though this may not be the occasion for providing full answers. For one, we must ask what is the relationship between semiotic on the one hand, thaumaturgy on the other? Just what is it that illusionists do? Simply put, they maneuver signs by misdirection, "the stuff of which illusion is made," as Leech—another contemporary native of Chicago—emphasized in his admirably clever yet concise booklet (1948:6).

Essentially, there are only three forms of semiosic kernel procedures involved in all of stage magic (although the number of innovative permutations may be limitless), whether they involve easy tricks or intricate slight-of-hand effects, and whether they depend on sizable pieces of apparatus, human beings, or animals of whatever size. Secret sign tokens are called "gimmicks" in the business, and it is through such signs that the conjurer, Apollo-like, and in apparent defiance of the laws of physics, or other allegedly binding rules of nature more generally, indicates (*semainei*). Magic, in the last analysis, is thus a metaphysical gag.

1. A sign token, such as a coin, abruptly disappears, or

This operation is usually called "Vanish," or nothing out of anything.

2. A sign token, such as a cage full of canaries, abruptly appears from seemingly nowhere, or

This operation is usually called "Production" and is, of course, the inverse counterpart of the first: the performer creates something out of nothing.

3. A sign token, such as a statue, changes into a living woman (which, by the way, was one of Thurston's finest dazzlers), or, as in "The Lady and the Lion," two huge empty cabinets are set several yards apart from the stage. In Thurston's version, "[a] girl entered one; curtains were dropped around both. The girl vanished; in her place was a

lion in a cage. She reappeared in the second cabinet, perched like a canary in an oversized, suspended bird cage" (Christopher 1973:238). This operation is usually called "Transposition" and may be represented as follows:

The illusion may involve shape-shifting, or teletransportation of the same shape, or—as in the protean Leopoldo Fregoli's uncanny quick-change skits—both sorts of transformation. The process is often reversible or might constitute just one link in a change of further conversions.

As the experienced Morris summed it up (1971:221): "What is often called 'magic' is the persistence of techniques when there is evidence that the practices do not in fact influence attainment of the goal, especially when these practices are symbolic in nature." Yet Morris realized at once that even here caution is needed, for, in a wider context, "the symbolic action may be technically relevant and the technological discourse which prescribes it be adequate. Such complications," Morris warned, "are not to be forgotten in assessing the adequacy of technological discourse for moral and religious ends" (ibid.:222).[11] As Morris grew up, his commonplace juvenile fantasy of magical omnipotence became transubstantiated into Magic, in the twin shapes of poetry and religion—both powerfully imbued by Maitreyism—while, at the same time, his initial preoccupation with the most elementary sign processes underlying magic "routining" (Leech 1948:16-18) blossomed into a scientifically sophisticated Theory of Signs. "As a religion setting high value on scientific intelligence, Maitreyism will be sympathetic to a scientifically oriented philosophy concerned with the integration of knowledge, and including the relation of such knowledge to other human activities," Morris (1956: 177) believed. Nearly a quarter of a century later (1976:61), he recast an identical expression of faith in poetic form:

Union

Science wedded now to Maitreya's vision—
this is man's out to greatness,
this is the next embedded human way.

This is Westness linked with Eastness
in a new day; this is the next elateness,
renewal's shout, heal of irresoluteness.

Selflessness needs support of cosmic grandeur.
Little and large can we only dare to be
if what we envisage can satiate our wonder.

What Morris called the Maitreyan Path was one of seven alternative ways contemporary man could, he thought, align himself *vis-à-vis* himself and in relation to the world surrounding him. In the *Paths of Life* he examines each of them (in later works, he expanded this list to 13 types). Although, following Nietzsche, Morris professedly rejects the notion of *"the Way,"* the mode of orientation he embraces is clearly the Maitreyan (1948:84ff.; 1956: chap. VII), as its centrality in the following diagram (ibid.:167) reflects.

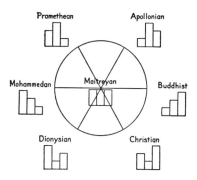

FIG. 4.3. Chart depicting Maitreyan personality

The Maitreyan personality is depicted as integrative, "at once strongly promethean, dionysian, and buddhistic" (ibid.:153), yet he "will often seem to himself, as well as to others, to be simply the chameleonlike Proteus—one type of person at one moment and another type at another moment" (ibid.:155). Witness the legendary quick-change artist, Fregoli, referred to above, whose fantastic act is described by Christopher (1973:282):

> The versatile Italian appeared first as an old man singing in court costume, then as a woman, and finally as a girl soprano, he bowed off at the wings. Before the applause had ended, he was back, dressed as an elderly music teacher. He sat at the piano and began to play. The spotlight moved to the wings as a buxom woman in an evening gown walked out. Suddenly the audience realized this was Fregoli; a dummy was now in its place at the piano. The woman trilled a few notes, left the stage. Fregoli strolled out from the far side, dressed as a conjurer, wearing a beard and a mustache . . . he produced flowers from an empty paper cornucopia, exited at the left, came on from the right dancing—in a wig and ballerina's tutu.

It seems to me that Morris himself best exemplified Maitreya's Way: "the dynamic integration of enjoyment, action, and contemplation" (1948:77). It was his self-chosen fate that his distinctive feature became "flexibility" and provided "a perspective by which the chasms which divide various types of personalities could be bridged." He strove to make himself, as emblematized by his choice of bookplate, "the guardian of the complexity of the full human self" (1956:155).

As a philosophical stance, Morris's concept of the Maitreyan path is frustratingly flawed and addled (as he was not altogether unaware; cf. 1948:119; 1956:154ff.), but as a delineation of his personal guide to a state of spiritual enlightenment it spendiferously irradiates for us his image (1966:73):

Satori

How blind, how complexly dumb we are!
And how simple, inevitable, it is!

Here at the void's unspeaking center
worlds are forever made from nothing's bliss.

From here is forever tossed the outermost star.
Relinquish fear! Go on! Dare enter!

The image of Charles Morris is permanently incarnate in the Image of the compassionate Buddha, who, according to an Oriental legend, "descends again and again to this earth." Morris supposes (1976:57): "You may have seen him even in a bar." Why not in Chicago? Why not in Gainesville?

NOTES

1. George Herbert Mead, Addison Webster Moore, James H. Tufts, Edward Scribner Ames, John Dewey, Clarence I. Lewis, Horace M. Kallen. The evident poetic significance of this chaotic type of enumerative style employed by Whitman and his twentieth-century epigones was to suggest the writer's awareness of the essential unity of the universe, or at least to demonstrate his own connection with the aspect of it that is of concern to him in the microcosm circumscribed by the long lists (cf. Spitzer 1945). Whitman's cardinal influence on Morris's verse is evident: for example, the "Invocation" section of his 1956 book, which consists of two dozen or so poems, takes its epigraph from *Leaves of Grass;* likewise, his *The Open Self* (1948) opens with a quotation from *Democratic Vistas.* He also felt that Whitman's "words from the East and the West serve at least to show that the Maitreyan attitude finds an echo in the long history of man's attempt to weave together the cool amplitude of detached vision with the warmth and insistency of his momentary urgencies and activities" (1948:164). Other writers who, by his own accounts, inspired Morris included Chuangtze, Tagore, Rilke, Nietzsche, Melville (February 6, 1965, letter to Pantheon), as well as Gibran, of *The Prophet* (May 26, 1962, letter to Braziller). For Morris's separate poem on Mead, "linking in oneness othered diversity:/this his direction, bliss, and bestowing," see 1976:78. As Zeman (1980) points out, "The relationship of Morris' thought to that of Mead could itself be a topic of a lengthy essay."

2. Each of these statements thus overturns a dogma, expressed, for example, in the formulation "man makes religion, religion does not make man" and all that this Marxist dictum implies.

Maitreya Buddha. Courtesy of the Antoinette K. Gordon Collection
of Tibetan Art, Indiana University Bloomington.[12] (See p.88.)

Maitreya Buddha. Courtesy of the Antoinette K. Gordon Collection
of Tibetan Art, Indiana University Bloomington.[12] (See p.88.)

3. *Icon,* as such, never appeared. On April 26, 1971, Morris wrote further to Zachary:

> One of the major enterprises which now concerns me is a volume of "poetry" to be called *Icon,* which will include *Festival* (and perhaps *Cycles*) as a center portion, preceded by a part called *White Fire* and terminated by a part called *Turn of the Wheel.* The material for these parts is already written and reflects my entire life from youth until the present. The problem now is merely a selection out of a great bulk of material, and this selection is largely done, I could complete it in 1971 (my 70th year). *White Fire* would consist of about 60 poems, *Turn of the Wheel* of about 97.

Image, as ultimately printed, successively incorporated 34 items under *Cycles,* 14 under *Maitreya,* 32 under *Encounters,* and 30 under *Friendship*—or 110 texts in all, out of a vastly greater manuscript stock.

4. On March 13, 1966, Carnap thanked Morris for having sent him a copy and went on to observe: "I had always thought, that a non-conceptual expression was required, to touch the heart of people. Now you did it with poetry, maybe you or somebody else will try it in music." Although Morris "paid attention to contemporary painting," as Hartshorne recently confirmed (1979: 194), I never knew him to be particularly interested in music (but cf. Morris 1971:274-276). In "Imaginary Meeting" (Morris 1976:79), he asks: "Remember when we heard Scriabin's/*Poem of Ecstasy* in Chicago long/long ago, and celebrated creation?" If this incident really happened, Morris must have been five or six years old, for the years of Aleksandr Nikolayevich Scriabin's American tour were 1906-07; alternatively, of course, some performing artist other than the composer himself might have been involved.

5. A "vanity publisher" is a firm that publishes a book at the expense and thus the sole risk of the author. I should like here to acknowledge the courtesy of William Finnegan, of Vantage Press, in making available for my use original materials from that firm's Morris files, including especially the author's questionnaire, containing his own outline of the theme of the book, with his autobiographical sketch.

6. The book contains very few misprints. Two that I am able to confirm are: on p.85, last line, for "or" read "on"; and, on p.100, last line, for "Mafnificence" read "Magnificence." Contrary to his fears, it turned out that Morris was able to read his own proofs. On January 20, 1976 he had drafted a forethoughtful letter to a Mr. Zimmerman, of Vantage, which I found preserved only in a cramped handwritten scribble, and which reads, in part:

> You may remember that when I submitted *Image* to you, I wrote that I was not feeling well. This illness has increased and may present some serious problems. So merely out of some prudence I wrote this letter.
> In the event that I should be unable to read proof on this book, will you please send the proofs to my daughter. . . .
> It is very important to me that the book be published, hence this precautionary letter. I feel at the moment quite sure that I will myself be able to read the proofs, and receive the final copies.

7. I am much obliged to the staff of the Peirce Edition Project for its assistance in orienting me among the Morris papers, as yet catalogued only in a preliminary way.

8. The starting point for this sort of analysis still remains Hrushovski (1960), who defined free rhythms as poems "which (1) have no consistent metrical scheme . . . ; but (2) do have a poetic language organized so as to create impressions and fulfill functions of poetic rhythm" (p. 183).

9. I first read this composition in manuscript during one of my periodic visits (I think in 1974) at Morris's home, in Gainesville, and commented that

the word *grammatical* would seem to me more felicitous here. Morris smiled, apparently in agreement, but obviously preferred to cling to *dramatical*. I do not know the date of *Semiotic,* or why Morris chose not to disseminate it, or, on the other hand, not to destroy it. He habitually marked some of his poems "I like this very much," but one of his folders bears the legend: ". . . kept from a much larger number (the others now being destroyed)." *Semiotic* ostensibly fell in an intermediate group.

10. The printer's forte was not spelling, and Morris apparently likewise overlooked the embarrassing typo in the subheading.

11. I intend to return to a consideration of magic as a branch of semiotics in a chapter of my forthcoming book, *Clever Hans,* in preparation for the Indiana University Press.

It should also be mentioned, before leaving this topic here, that Martin Gardner, a participant in one of Morris's Chicago seminars on semiotic, is, among his other distinguished accomplishments, one of the world's foremost connoisseurs and authoritative writers about magic (cf. Braun 1978). For Gardner and Morris, see further Sebeok 1978b, where Gardner's 1937 caption read in part: "Few people know that Charles W. Morris was once a professional prestidigitator. There came a time in his young life, however, when he found himself forced to choose between magic and philosophy. He chose the latter as the lesser of two evils. . . ."

12. I am much obliged to my colleague Thubten Jigme Norbu for making available for my use in this study a picture of this beautiful piece of sculpture. For Morris's adept transmutation of "Maitreya Sculpture" into verbal shape, see 1976:55.

Chapter 5

Karl Bühler: A Neglected Figure in the History of Semiotic Inquiry

PEOPLE WHO undertake to reassess the diacritic flavor and scholarly quality of great figures of the past soon find themselves engaged in a free-for-all from which they are more likely than not to emerge by delineating the distinctive features of merely their own contributions. This process of self-definition may apply with special force when we attempt to reinterpret personalities who flourished in the decades following the political and cultural wreckage of the Habsburg *Hausmacht*—an epoch of imperial decay that has justly been described as "always desperate, but never serious"—because some of us were ourselves saturated in that selfsame ambience throughout our formative years. The ensuing era was one of infinite possibilities for the building of novel institutions and social practices, in brief, the new Austrian Republic. In this modern Austria, plenty of opportunities existed for intellectuals to put an effective system of social democracy in working order, none of which was attainable during the times of Habsburg ultraconservatism. It was in this unprecedented atmosphere of social crisis that Bühler's ideas, germinated a decade or so earlier, about "imageless thought" and "rule awareness," began to play the role of chief theoretician in the movement underlying curricular reform in Austria (Bartley 1973:144). Karl Popper and Ludwig Wittgenstein were among the budding giants who enrolled in the resulting teacher-training courses (Janik and Toulmin 1973:288). Much of this constructive development was, of course, poignantly swept away with the coming of the Second World War. Still, the exercise of looking back on the intervening decades is salubrious, for it at least reduces our complacency and melts away the comforting fat of self-delusion about the total innovativeness of our surviving contemporary heroes. As we thus

Key passages from this article, composed in English, were delivered at the 2nd Congress of the International Association for Semiotic Studies, in Vienna, on July 5, 1979. The paper was written as an invited contribution tailored for the week-long special series, "Wiener Erbe," arranged for by the Congress Program Committee. A version of the English text appeared in the *Canadian Journal of Research in Semiotics/Le Journal Canadien de Recherche Sémiotique* 7:3:5-22 (1980), and another is slated eventually to appear as a part of the *Proceedings* of this Congress, to be published by Mouton (The Hague). A German translation was published as a chapter in a book, co-edited by Martin Krampen, Klaus Oehler, Roland Posner, and Thure von Uexküll, under the title, *Die Welt als Zeichen. Klassiker der Modernen Semiotik* (Berlin: Severin und Siedler, 1981:205–32).

FIG. 5.1. Portrait of Karl Bühler

casually journey back to the Vienna of the interwar period, we must, withal, be mindful of two basic facts: first, that we cannot escape the tendency of all travelers, whether in space or in time, to seize upon a dramatic moment here and there and to generalize from it by the imposition of our own prejudices on each such vivid flash; and, second, to paraphrase the extraordinary satirist Karl Kraus about his contemporary bourgeois Vienna, that this city was, during the time of Bühler's residence, already a proving ground for world destruction. George Steiner (1979: 101) summed it up well: "As the waltz tune has it, *Wien, Wien, nur du allein.* Vienna was the capital of the age of anxiety, the hub of Jewish genius, and the city from which the Holocaust would seep." All this was foreshadowed in the scientific arena, with rare subtlety, in Bühler's *Die Krise der Psychologie,* first published in book form two years before the global economic catastrophe of 1929 (see also Wellek 1959).

    The objective of the lecture series on the "Viennese Heritage" was to commemorate and celebrate Austria's multiform yet distinctive role in the development of modern semiotic inquiry. My particular assignment was to observe the contribution of Karl Bühler, who was neither born nor educated in Austria, and who—although he was of small peasant stock and profited from a religiously broad-minded upbringing (his father, Ludwig, being a Protestant, his mother, Berta, in whose faith the young Karl followed, a Catholic)—was forced to flee Austria and settle down uneasily in America after 1938. He nevertheless achieved his international reputation in Vienna, where he chiefly functioned during sixteen of his most maturely productive years, beginning in 1922 (Lebzeltern 1969:25).

Bühler was born on May 27, 1879, in Meckesheim, in the vicinity of Heidelberg, and matriculated at the University of Freiburg/i.Br. In 1903, he was awarded an M.D. under the famous physiologist Johannes von Kries, with a dissertation dealing with theories of color vision, experimentally researched, namely, the question of the limits of the eye's adaptability for light and darkness. His lifelong interest in psychology was also nourished at Freiburg, although it was eventually crowned with a Ph.D. at the University of Strassburg. There, in 1904, he presented to Clemens Bläumker a second dissertation, on the physiological prolegomena that Lord Kames (Henry Home), the eighteenth-century thinker, believed aesthetics required. It is interesting to speculate, at least in passing, about the influence on Bühler of Kames, with specific regard to the Scottish moral philosopher's arguments about the laws of association and the relational qualities that he was concerned with, such as contiguity in time and space (the domain that some of us now call indexicality), and resemblance and dissimilitude (or iconicity), as well as classic notions of signification based on cause and effect (Eugene Miller 1979) and of surface variation against a background of global uniformity.

For a short time, Bühler then seems to have practiced medicine in Strassburg, specializing in ophthalmology (Lebzeltern 1969:13).

Bühler next became an assistant to Kries, in Freiburg, then went on to Berlin to study under Benno Erdmann and to work under Carl Stumpf. Erdmann was a logician and psychologist remembered chiefly for his work in respect to Kant and for his view (1907) of judgment at the core of which is a predicative relationship—a prototype illocutionary act, as it were, performed *in* the uttering of a sentence—a formulation, moreover, critically influenced by semiotic considerations. Carl Stumpf, who brought experimental phenomenology into psychology, is often considered one of the most important precursors of Gestalt psychology. He was also co-founder, in 1900, of Berlin's Verein für Kinderpsychologie, a field in which Karl became active eight years afterward, although not as much so as Charlotte Bühler.

In 1906 Bühler moved on to an assistantship and close collaboration, in Würzburg, with Oswald Külpe (who had himself served as Wilhelm Wundt's second assistant) and obtained his habilitation as a *dozent* in philosophy. This monograph, published as a series of three consecutive articles in the *Archiv für die gesamte Psychologie*, in 1907-1908, was based on Bühler's experimental studies on the psychology of thought processes, and bore the overall title "Tatsachen und Probleme zu einer Psychologie der Denkvorgänge." Bühler's analysis of "what is thought" was strongly influenced by Külpe's original concepts pertaining to imageless knowledge (or, in Bühler's terminology, "thought"), determining tendency (Narziss Ach's 1905 coinage to describe the unconscious process, hidden from introspection, that guides thinking along its proper course; cf. Rapaport 1951, *passim*), awareness, task set (*Aufgabe*), set (*Einstellung*), and the technique of systematic experimental introspection. A substantial section of Part II (excerpts from which were—although not until 43 years later—published in English as well [Rapaport 1951:39-57]) was devoted to the apprehension (*Auffassen*) of thought and the comprehension (*Verstehen*) of sentences, a function semioticians might well translate either as "understanding" or as "interpretation." One of Bühler's important conclusions was that *Verstehen* takes place between integral wholes. He immediately recognized that this experience is the inverse of a problem encountered in the psychology of language, to wit: How does the unitary thought differentiate into the meanings of the concatenation of words whereby it is expressed, or, to reverse this again, how do word-meanings build up to a totality the thought to be grasped? To put it in yet another way, the question—which Bühler's data were insufficient to resolve—brings up the wider issue of the genesis of Gestalt, a lengthy and complex chapter in the history of ideas that can barely even be touched on here (cf. the extended treatment by the man he considered his "Hauptschüler," Egon Brunswik 1929). This and kindred matters concerning "a rich scale of tensions between wholes and parts" involved in the constitution of language and other varieties of semiotic strings were unerringly identified by Jakobson (1963), who alludes (1971b:715) to Bühler's seminal ideas in this connection, while more prominently adducing those of Peirce, Frege, Husserl, and, of course, Sapir. Bühler afterward—in the late 1920s and early 1930s—returned (on at least four separate occasions) to the characteristic experience of sentence comprehension as a consummatory operation climaxing the emergence of conscious relationships.

Külpe's own experiments eventually moved him from the elements of Wundt toward the acts of Brentano, but it was Bühler's study that gave impetus to a far-reaching controversy with Wundt, focusing on the methodological legitimacy of nonexact experiments and retrospective introspection, arguments about the empirical value of which and, more generally, about introspection and the mind are still very much alive (e.g., Lieberman 1979). According to Lebzeltern (1969:15), it was Bühler's prolonged discord with Wundt that made the junior scholar "in der Fachwelt gleichsam über Nacht berühmt." The main points of their argument were clearly summarized by Blumenthal (1974:1114-1116), and need not be recounted here. Bühler's views, that thoughts seem to be independent of the verbal manifestations in which they are cast and that sentence-meaning hierarchically outranks word-meaning (a principle on which, by the way, he and Wundt thoroughly agreed), eventually matured, after 1919, into his brand of a semiotically tinged theory of speech.

When Külpe progressed to Bonn, in 1909, and, in 1913, on to Munich, Bühler followed him; there, he obtained an untenured appointment as an Associate Professor. In 1916, the 37-year-old Karl married Charlotte Malachowski, then 22, a fellow student of his and a former disciple of Husserl's, who herself eventually became a famous psychologist. After the First World War was over, Bühler accepted an appointment as a full Professor at the Dresden Institute of Technology, and, four years later, the couple—lured by Otto Glöckel and his colleagues—moved to Vienna, where Karl became Professor, with Charlotte his assistant. The Institute of Psychology he established in this city—incidentally, with a supplemental ten-year grant from The Rockefeller Foundation—and directed, with his wife's support, until 1938, quickly gained worldwide recognition. He concurrently held a post as Adjunct Professor at the Pedagogical Institute of the City of Vienna. The Bühlers' salon, at Weimarer Strasse 100, soon became a mecca of social and intellectual life for visitors to Vienna from the world over; thus, by 1937, Bühler had attracted doctoral candidates from eighteen countries.

On March 23, 1938, he was arrested by the Nazis, but released on May 7 upon the intervention of influential friends, with whose help he emigrated the next year, via Oslo, to the United States. He had previously taught there in 1927-28 (at Stanford, Johns Hopkins, and Harvard) and in 1929 (at Chicago); in 1930, he had held the MacDougall Professorship at Harvard and simultaneously served in Radcliffe. However, as Charlotte Bühler (1965:187) explicitly related years afterward, "Da wir beide Wien sehr liebten, zogen wir es vor, in Wien zu bleiben." This decision proved, in retrospect, to have been a costly mistake, for, after his exile of a quarter of a century, which, as fate decreed, became irreversible after his sixtieth year, Bühler was unable to secure a post suitable to his eminence and was obliged to teach psychology in a succession of small Catholic undergraduate colleges, in Duluth and St. Paul, Minnesota. When the Second World War came to an end, in 1945, the Bühlers settled in Los Angeles for good, where Karl served, until 1955, as an Assistant Clinical Professor of psychiatry in the Medical School of the University of Southern California, and, at last, as a consulting psychologist at the Cedars of Lebanon Hospital. The harried refugee died in California in 1963. "Wir waren politisch so naiv," Charlotte wistfully added after Karl's death, "dass wir Österreich für sicher hielten." Unfortunately, even his relatively brief, six-week incarceration in the hands of the Gestapo had, it seemed, incurably shattered his personality: realization that his own people would mistreat him in this way wounded him for life. He became withdrawn and suffered from such an abiding depression that the rich wellsprings of his creativity were effectively consumed. I believe that the sole reason for his persecution by the Nazis was that Charlotte—although raised a Protestant—came from a predominantly Jewish ancestry and that, had he consented to divorce her, he could have kept his academic posts and social position.[1]

In tracing the postwar diaspora of Bühler's "school," Charlotte (1965: 193) makes the interesting, startling, and, I fear, exaggerated observation that "er keinen bedeutenden Wiener Schüler auf dem Gebiete der Sprachpsychologie hatte. . . . Es ist wahrhaft tragisch, dass er den allmählichen Triumph seiner Sprachtheorie nicht mehr erlebte." The widow then follows up on her assessment with a shockingly ungracious, petulant, and certainly counterfactual remark, that Roman Jakobsen [sic], "der in seinen Werken sich weitgehend auf Karl stützte, erwies ihm nicht die gebührende Anerkennung für das, was er Karl dankte." As a matter of fact, in Jakobson's Selected Writings I-II (1971a, 1971b) alone, Bühler is cited—almost always with approbation and, what is more interesting for us, almost invariably in a semiotic context—no fewer than twenty times. The opening sentence of Jakobson's celebrated Kindersprache (1971a:328) is a direct quotation from a 1935 paper of Bühler's, and, as late as 1967 (1971b:671), Jakobson still characterized Bühler's Sprachtheorie as being "for linguists probably the most inspiring among all the contributions to the psychology of language." It is certainly no secret that Jakobson's initial exploration of the functions of language, the essence of which lay in the distinction between everyday parlance (both practical and emotive, but always oriented toward the signified) and poetic language (manifested in the set toward the sign as such), a distinction that dates back to 1921, was much later conflated with Bühler's frequently cited triadic organon model of 1934 (as explicitly credited in Sebeok 1960:355), but which Jakobson, in turn, creatively expanded by three further factors of the speech event, each corresponding to a specific communicative function.

Charlotte, curiously, charges a student of Jakobson's, Paul L. Garvin, whom she mischaracterizes as "ein junger Semantiker," with responsibility for the posthumous publication of Bühler's Sprachtheorie in English, as a matter of fact, via the facilities of the Indiana University Research Center for Language and Semiotic Studies. However, no such manuscript was ever received by me, nor, so far as I am aware, has ever appeared anywhere else. Garvin did write a brief necrology, in which he stressed that Bühler's "field-theory of language is an adaptation of the Gestalt-theoretical ideas of figure and ground to the psychology of language" (1964:633). He suggestively rendered organon—the term is heavily laden with Aristotelian connotations and, of course, echoes Bacon—as "tool"—a tool composed of signs, operating deictically (in a Zeigfeld) or symbolically (*Symbolfeld*), the two surrounds bearing the cover-term *Umfeld*. This word instantly evokes Jakob von Uexküll's terminology (Sebeok 1979: chap. 10), and what is especially interesting is that Bühler explicitly recognized its semiotic import. In 1934 (Bühler 1965:27), for example, he remarked that Uexküll's thesis "vornherein in seinen Grundbegriffen 'Merkzeichen' und 'Wirkzeichen' sematologisch orientiert ist."

It should now be noted, as a terminological aside, that Bühler most frequently used Benjamin H. Smart's coinage, launched in an anonymous work of his, entitled *Outline of Sematology* (1831:1), for what we call semiotics. Smart, following Locke's tripartite division of the entirety of knowledge, suggested that "all instruction for the use of *tà sematà*, or the signs of our knowledge, might be called *Sematology*," amplifying this (ibid.:2n): "As to Sematology, the third division, it is the *doctrine of signs*, showing how the mind operates by their means in obtaining the knowledge comprehended in the other divisions." Smart continued to use this terminology in later books, notably in his *Sequel to Sematology* (1837); it was picked up by Archibald H. Sayce and then propagated by the most influential English lexicographer of all, James A. H. Murray, both via the OED and an article he published in the early 1880s. Smart was widely read in his time by, among others, Charles Darwin, whose philosophical views on language were compatible with Smart's (as well as with other authors such as Dugald Stewart). However, *sematology* has all but vanished in the present century, save for Bühler's idiosyncratic Teutonization. I find it particularly strange that he did not favor the competing term of his Viennese colleague Heinrich Gomperz, *Semasiologie* (1908)—originally believed to have been created by Christian Karl Reisig, in Halle, to rhyme with *Etymologie*—because many of Bühler's semiotic notions closely resemble Gomperz's, as traced in some detail in an unpublished Master's thesis by Günther (1968); but Bühler continued habitually, if not exclusively, to favor *Sematologie*, while only sporadically employing *Semiotik* (e.g., 1968:16, 18, 19, 162), usually in a classical context.

It is true, as Charlotte (1965:195) remarked of her late husband, that "Karl ist ein Enzyklopäde, den man nicht rubrizieren kann." He touched on so many areas of psychology that, indeed, he stood tall as "einer der umfassendsten Forscher seiner Zeit." One could, for instance, devote a treatise to an assessment of Bühler's work in the field of child psychology—which influenced the school-reform movement from the outset (Bartley 1973:146), including particularly his pioneering observations on the ontogenesis of verbal signs, notably in his daughter, Inge (1918: 224). According to his wife's hardly unbiased survey of the field of child psychology (Charlotte Bühler and Hetzer 1929:221), its development reached "ihre prinzipiellste und umfassendste Ausgestaltung bei Karl Bühler," but the radically different approach—combining structure with genesis, or a model of rationalism with a role for experience—of Piaget, of the early 1920s, had already had its impact on the German investigators of that decade.

It must be remembered too that Bühler's Vienna was simultaneously the city of Freud and of Adler, rampant with psychoanalytic theories and deeply engrossed in bitter internecine doctrinal imbroglios. Bühler himself had close ties, given his medical training, with the University's Institute of Psychiatry, where many analysts attended his lectures and seminars. As Charlotte (1965:196) perceived it, "Im Unterschied zu Freud hielt ich es für grundlegend wichtig, die Interpretation menschlicher Strebungen von seelisch gesunden statt von seelisch kranken Entwicklungen abzuleiten," and, in this, she shared her husband's point of departure. Lebzeltern's (1969:39) perspective seems also to have been generally correct, that Bühler "stand in der gesellschaftlichen Achtung und wissenschaftlichen Anerkennung turmhoch über Freud." Their relative contemporary positions and seemingly unbridgeable apartheid notwithstanding—in the light of Freud's peripheral position vis-à-vis academic psychology, in contrast to Bühler's own centrality—Bühler generously characterized Freud as a "grosse[r] Zauberer, der alle seine 'legitimen' Schüler in einen Bannkreis gefangenhält" (1927:178). My personal opinion is that the formidably entangled relationships between this outstanding pair of residents of two quite different Viennese worlds have not yet begun to be unravelled in other than superficial attempts.

In what follows, I prefer not to scrutinize anew ground sure to be amply familiar to all who have read Bühler's Sprachtheorie (1934), which is considered by many his single most enduring contribution. Having been well analyzed by Krug (1929) in its historical setting, this field-theory of language was further thoroughly probed in Kamp's recent (1977) remarkably helpful monograph. Bühler's reputed chef d'oeuvre was meant to be read along with, or to amplify, his brilliant anticipatory essay, purporting to constitute an axiomatization of linguistic inquiry (1933) in terms of four Grundsätze, i.e., rudimentary principles. (This monograph was republished 36 years later, in somewhat abridged form but with an extensive new introduction and commentary by Elisabeth Ströker, all lately rendered into English by Robert E. Innis.) Both works revolve around the polestar of Bühler's semiotically based "organic" model of language, but I would rather focus my observations on some more-neglected aspects of Bühler's notions about Zeichenverkehr, or the exchange of messages, which I myself find most arresting and are also of abiding interest to the field. It will be appreciated that even this topic cannot be presented exhaustively here; Bühler's semiotic, in all its implications, and particularly in the context of his work as a whole, awaits extended treatment much more detailed than accorded in Günther's (1968) aforementioned thesis, which is creditable but hardly analytic and fabricated to compare Bühler's Zeichenbegriff specifically with that of George H. Mead.

In Bühler's view, as is generally known, it was the representative function that distinguished language from semiotic processes in the speechless creatures. Taking his point of departure from the speech act, he defined the criterial attributes of language as the combined realization of *Kundgabe,* announcing, or the expressive function, which correlates the sign with the message source, *Appell,* eliciting, or the appeal function, which correlates the sign with the message destination, and *Darstellung,* or the representing function, which correlates the sign with its context (or, to repeat, *Zeigfeld* and *Symbolfeld* combined). Object-relationships are, in other words, represented as a result of the speaker's declaration of what goes on in him, which evokes a psychological process in the listener. It was apropos these three aspects of each linguistic utterance that Trubetzkoy (1939:17-18)—Bühler's close associate at the University of Vienna, who himself died some months before the westward exodus of his psychologist friend—observed: "Es ist das grosse Verdienst Karl Bühlers, diese scheinbar einfache und trotzdem so lange übersehene Tatsache ins richtige Licht gestellt zu haben." It is amply clear by now to most linguists that to make sense of an utterance implies taking into account the cognitive structures in terms of which the addresser's and the addressee's worlds are organized, and how language maps into those structures. (Bühler's theory on the functions of language as an attempt toward a psychological solution of linguistic problems is interestingly discussed by Pazuchin 1963.)

This tripartite scheme, or one very much like it, was already present in the works of Husserl and Porzig, but Bühler connected it further with the principle of "abstractive relevance," which implies that only certain features of the total situation (*Gegenstände und Sachverhalte*) participate in semiosis (this distinction is akin, *mutatis mutandis,* to that which Peirce sometimes drew between "object" and "ground"). Bühler attributes representing function to the verbal sign as the direct consequence of this relevance, a conclusion that he no doubt elaborated from Gomperz's reinterpretation of the scholastic formulation *aliquid stat pro aliquo.* The abstractiveness of the relevance is a consequence of the fact that the verbal sign can simultaneously serve the three functions enumerated, although it is assumed that in any given message one of the factors will be predominant while the other two, depending on the total envelope of the goal-directed speech act (*la parole*), are hierarchically subordinate. *La parole* is also tripartite, consisting of the actor, the field of action, and the needs and opportunities of the actor. It is in this emphasis on the strong social moment of the speech act that Bühler departs from Husserl's subjectivistic act theses, although the influence of the *Logische Untersuchungen*—to say nothing of the philosophical writings of Alexius Meinong (especially 1977)—is palpable throughout Bühler's works. Bühler, directly following Husserl, distinguished between meaning and reference. An expression with its meaning unaltered may refer to various objects, and vice versa: expressions with divergent meanings (e.g., *George Washington* and *The First President of the United States*) may refer to the identical object. To restate this in another way—and here I follow an exposition and critique by Laziczius (1942:22-23)—behind Bühler's argument lurks another divergency, that between "meaning" and "the intention to mean," which implies the four-way matrix below.

	I.	II.
1.	Sprechhandlung (*parole*)	Sprachwerk (*ergon*)
2.	Sprechakt (*energeon*)	Sprachgebilde (*langue*)

The entries under I—that is, the concrete verbal messages and the "speech act"—are both *subjektsbezogen;* those under II—that is, the product of the sender and the linguistic structure—are both *subjektsentbunden.* Those under 2 comprise hierarchically superior manifestations in opposition to those under 1. Laziczius (1939) was first to show, in a careful analysis of this, Bühler's so-called Third Axiom, that what he presented here was, in the form of a vicious circle, a thesis "deren Unhaltbarkeit ganz offenbar ist," a telling criticism one is compelled to uphold (although other readers may disagree with this reading).

Bühler's implied distinction between "meaning" and "the intention to mean" goes to the heart of homonymy. When I utter the isolated English vocable /baer/, whether I use it as a synonym for "to support," "naked," or a mammal of the family *Ursidae,* depends on my "intention," which the addressee can only guess at with a certain probability, depending on how much verbal and/or nonverbal context is supplied. For me, as a speaker, homonymy does not exist, since I already know what I mean; but for my interlocutor intention comes into play, more accurately called by Jakobson (1971b:575) "the conditional probabilities of the context."

It is equally well known that Bühler's consequent classification of sign functions yields the symptom, which is dependent on the source whose introspection it expresses on the surface; the signal, constituting a guide for the destination's inner and outer behavior; and the symbol, which is contingent on contextual circumstances. No doubt, it should be underlined, before leaving this subject, that the list of functions postulated by Bühler, and hence his classification of signs, is considered by modern scholarship as very far from comprehensive; this was realized, as long ago as 1937, by Petr N. Bogatyrev (1971: chap. 19), in his discussion of "the function of the structure of functions," meaning by this awkward phrasing to call attention to a semiotic function of a higher order, to wit, the concerted operation of the whole complex knot of functions—in short, a metafunction. This fruitful notion was eventually and variously extended to other domains, by the linguist Karel Horálek (1948), for instance, and eventually by others.

In Bühler's conception, language is an epiphenomenon to the phenomena of activity and, more specifically, expression. Accordingly, in several interesting respects, his book on expressive behavior—originally published in 1934 and reprinted unchanged in 1968—can be read as his quintessential contribution to semiotics. Yet it is hardly ever cited in either the immense, sprawling Anglo-American literature on the subject or, more surprisingly, in West European works on nonverbal communication—including particularly German—which, in this respect, appear to ignore their autochthonous heritage.

The study of expressive behavior has a composite, essentially dual, origin in psychodiagnostics and in rhetoric—quite specifically, that of Quintilian (Bühler 1968:227-235). The point ("tragende Behauptung") of Bühler's book is to demonstrate that the history of those aspects of behavior that manifest motivational states—emotional attitudes and moods; cognitive states, such as attention and concentration; activation states, such as arousal and fatigue; and quasi-personal attributes; in other words, matters that are functionally quite different—do nevertheless constitute, by and large, a "sachgerechtes System." They are all commonly classed together by the misleading term "expressive behavior"; thus, for example, verbal behavior and expressive movement, which, however, involve multiple categories of enormous complexity, as Ekman and his collaborators have shown (1969), following David Efrón's scintillating and, in many ways, pioneering work (1972). The link between the two is on a quite abstract level, which is precisely semiotic. Thus, for instance, Bühler, in discussing the ancient art of physiognomy—the art of judging human character from facial features (including as a means of divination)—tries to disentangle the distinctive characteristics of this art and finds, among half a dozen contributory impulses, Aristotelian semiotics, as this had actually been denominated in and after the eighteenth century (1968:16n2). As "eine durchsichtige Anwendung antiker Semiotik," Bühler cites (1968:18) a striking judgment by Saint Gregory against the Emperor Julian. In *Adversus Julianum*, Gregory anticipated from Julian's physiognomy, based on the following theatrical depiction, his animosity toward Christians:

> Er hatte einen geraden, steifen Kopf, der fest auf den Schultern sass, sein Blick war unstät, wild und umherirrend; sein Gang unsicher, seine Füsse immer in Bewegung; auf seiner Nase sass Verachtung, Frechheit und Hohn; sein Lachen war lärmend; er war unruhig, ausgelassen; sprach immer Ja und Nein; tat immer überlästige Fragen, und antwortete selten bestimmt oder zu rechter Zeit.

Gregory constructs Julian's character out of seemingly random but distinctive chunks—signifiers, if you like—to form a sort of personal mosaic, the tacit inference being that his accretive procedure will correspond to a unitary "Bezeichnetes," i.e., that the traits will signify the Emperor's inner coherence. Bühler correctly contends that the charge leveled against Classical semiotics as being "atomisierend," as against structural, is more often than not inaccurate, and lucidly explains what is actually involved in the course of its history. For instance, he makes highly interesting observations about insights gained, especially by Johann Jakob Engel, from the theater (1968: chap. 3), and notably goes on to develop, with much understanding and sympathy, Charles Darwin's special frame of reference fusing "Gesamtausdrücke an Tieren und Mensch" (ibid.: chap. 6), general ethology with human ethology, or, in other words, the integration of zoosemiotics into a comprehensive sign science. It was Engel who grounded the basic distinction between representation and expression in semiotic concepts, and Bühler (1968:40) praises this procedure as the "axiomatische Angelpunkt" in the apprehension of mimicry. He insistently calls for an "umfassend neuer Plan in diesen Dingen beherrscht und getragen sein müssen von einer vertieften sematologischen Axiomatik" (ibid.:88).

In reviewing the "Ausdruckslehre" of Ludwig Klages (ibid.: chap. 9), he brings up the seldom discussed teleological question of the relationship of expressive behavior to free will. The argument—anticipated to a degree by Martinak (1901:27, 80-83)—is as intricate as it is erudite, but what attracted me to it was Bühler's recognition of "ein altes Deutungsproblem der Semiotik." Furthermore, not only did this issue engage the so-called Aristotelian *physiognomonica*, but it was newly and vigorously embodied in Wundt's experimental analyses of curves displaying pulse and breathing rates, in short, components of polygraphic "lie detector" tests (the juridical admissibility of which is still being debated; cf. Lykken 1974).

Bühler's summative chapter (1968: chap. 10) about the "present" state-of-the-art and particularly his vision of future researches in the area of *der Ausdrucksforschung* clearly anticipate a unitary semiotic blueprint:

> Was der Ausdruckstheorie heute am dringendsten nötig wäre, um dabei ein klares Wort mitsprechen zu können, wäre der Ausbau einer wohlfundierten *Synsemantik*. Die im Ausdruckslexikon isoliert, wie die Wissenschaft es tun muss, kodifizierten fruchtbaren Momente des mimischen Geschehens stehen, wo immer sie das Leben erzeugt, in einem semantischen Umfeld; ihre pathognomische und physiognomische Valenz ist kontextgetragen. Es ist sematologisch gesehen mit den Ausdruckssymptomen wie mit den Wörtern der Lautsprache oder wie mit den Bildwerten der Farbflecken auf einem Gemälde. [1968:213-214]

It is therefore very much to be regretted that, on the one hand, what little Bühler scholarship exists has tended either to discount or, more

often, to disregard entirely Bühler's masterful chronicle, which is embedded in a theory that is at once consequential and fertile; and, on the
other, a multitude of investigators of this area, whether toiling in American or European workshops, are scarcely aware that they are standing
on Bühler's broad shoulders. I am not exaggerating when I assert that I
have never met a single student of nonverbal communication who confessed to even a passing acquaintance with the *Ausdruckstheorie,* itself
a milestone whose antecedents go back at least as far as Quintilian. While
the book is listed, and exceptionally, in the Bibliography by Desmond
Morris and his collaborators (1979:278) *pro forma,* there is no evidence
in their text that any of the authors have actually consulted it. This
neglect is an especial embarrassment for German-language scholarship,
and it should be promptly remedied.

Another facet of Bühler's concerns with the theory of signs consists
of its foundations in corrective change, homeostasis, or cybernetics
avant la lettre. Problems of control, recursiveness, and information pervade his writings, with consequences that were examined by Ungeheuer
(1967) with respect to the *Sprachtheorie,* but that could be usefully extended to his *Zeichentheorie,* as a whole, as well. Bühler was certainly
familiar with the ideas of Eduard Pflüger and Claude Bernard, developed
virtually at the same time in the late 1870s, with the latter's key observation that any animal's *milieu interne* was balanced, or self-correcting;
but the homeostatic concept, later elaborated by Cannon, seemed to Bühler ultimately insufficient to describe human psychic life fully. All the
same, I call attention to a remark of Bühler's that came to light only ten
years after his death:

> Nach einer Belehrung aus der Geschichte wird das eigene konstruktive
> Denken den *Milieubegriff* erörtern und über ihn hinweg zu der entschei-
> denden Idee fortschreiten, die ich den Sachverständigen vorlege. Es ist die
> Annahme, dass ein echtes *Signalwesen* im Bereich der innerkörperlichen
> Regulationen enthalten ist. Die Frage, was das heisst, wird aber erst im
> erweiterten Rahmen des letzten biologischen Modellgedankens, den wir
> formulieren und durchsprechen, wieder aufgenommen und, soweit wir es
> vermögen, zu Ende gedacht. [1969:188]

As Bühler himself was very much aware (1968), the decisive elements
for the semiotic alterity that he drew between representation and expression were emphasized by certain English classical logicians and advanced
substantially by Frege and, following him, Marty, Martinak, Husserl,
Gomperz, and especially Meinong (see, in particular, his theory of suppo-
sitions [1977], written in reaction to a pair of Brentano's theses). Bühler
deemed all these predecessors to have been in such agreement with
himself "that I scarcely need to add anything to what I have myself written on the subject since 1918." (Meinong's *Über Annahmen,* by the way,
was itself an important statement about communication and about other

semiotic topics such as the nature of play and of games, and the conformation of inference; to grasp Bühler's thought, you must understand
Meinong's!) To the listing of these primary sources, one may well add
Plato's *Kratylos*, Aristotle, Quintilian, and, above all, Kant, whose semiotic
ideas are still consistently misunderstood and certainly underestimated,
as well as Humboldt, Cassirer, and Saussure (Haller 1959:154). In turn,
Bühler's influence on Trubetzkoy, which began as far back as 1931, and
the continuing "fruitful discussions" (Jakobson 1971b:715) between the
two, the results of which diffused among other members of the Prague
School generally, are common knowledge. Bühler's Second Axiom, which
asserted that verbal phenomena are to be subsumed under the vaster
domain of semiotic phenomena, was widely accepted by linguists of the
time. The sign function was subsumed by Bühler under his notion of
representation, giving rise to yet another triad: objective meaning, the
phonemic mark (or *Mal*), which is but a "relevant" component of the
sign, and the "field signs" that emerge in and from the context (a notion
elaborated, e.g., by Jost Trier). Representation is, of course, opposed
by Bühler to expression, which, in the guise of the "indexical function,"
persistently reappears in the *Funktionslust* (as Bühler called it) of
Prague School linguists and with particular force after Jakobson's "discovery" of Peirce.

In passing, it should also be noted that Bartley (1973:148) was of the
opinion that although Wittgenstein does not appear in any list of Bühler's
students, it seems that he was "the most eminent of those who learned
from" Bühler (although, from time to time, Wittgenstein would also
denounce him as a charlatan). This notwithstanding, there are "striking
similarities between some of Bühler's leading ideas and those of the later
Wittgenstein" (ibid.:149).

Bühler's writings are characterized by a pedantic density that requires a modicum of familiarity on the part of the modern reader not
merely with the history of modern psychology but with the entire stream
of its philosophical pedigree. The dialectic movement underlying all of
his work can, however, be reduced to rather simple terms. It was his
cardinal thesis, rather facile but nonetheless subtly argued, that a correspondence exists between certain well-defined states—*Regelbewusstsein*,
or "consciousness of rules"—and given logical structures. Bühler failed,
of course, to prove the existence of such an isomorphism, even partially,
between the subject's logic (the business of the psychologist) and that of
the logician (who casts his net far beyond the former). This idea, in
turn, rested on two radically antithetical terms: the inanimate, that is,
mindless, *pleroma* (Plenitude)—as Jung, following the Gnostics, called
it—vs. the animate, or *creatura*, with its inherent tension between two
polarities: the creative nature of human thought, the spark (*pneuma*)
emerging from and operating atop a biologically governed foundation.
In the last analysis, the latter two belong in essence together, for the

creative nature of life follows from the creative nature of the mind, and vice versa, and both are in fact separated from the ordinary material universe. In the summative words of Wellek, "His final conclusion was that what is essentially human—thought and reason, gestaltic and holistic experience—is independent of the machine, or the mechanical principle, and also independent to some extent of what is merely biological in the animal kingdom" (1968:201).

In view of this judgment, it may perhaps appear surprising that, toward the end of his career, Bühler wrote a posthumously published (1969) study on spatial orientation, or steering, in man and animals, under the main title *Die Uhren der Lebewesen*. This little monograph deals with the problem of biological clocks and "cognitive maps," which Bühler always had assumed his fellow men and animals—whether a navigating Lindbergh or a bee flying long-distance—to experience alike. As his student Konrad Lorenz testified (1971:324), this assumption is not at all based on "analogization." In fact, he regarded it among Bühler's greatest achievements to have realized that this train of reflection is "a genuine *a priori* necessity of thought and experience," in brief, has the evidentiary force of a Bühlerian axiom. Bühler dubbed this the *Du-Evidenz*, the attestation adduced from the addressee. Lorenz (ibid.:268) is led by his teacher's arguments to opt, among several alternative approaches toward a resolution of the body-soul dichotomy, for the postulate of indubitable identity. While for the practical purposes of psychophysiological researches, it may indeed be irrelevant which position one takes in regard to this apparent partition, our view of the relationship between the observer and the thing observed has, as I have tried to show elsewhere (Sebeok 1979: chap. 5), very far-reaching consequences for the kind of semiotic researches we engage in. To paraphrase one of Bühler's very last antemortem paragraphs (1969:157), such inquiries are "reizvoll und brennend," and certainly once again exceedingly timely.

I want finally to return to Egon Brunswik, whom, as I have already noted, Bühler at one time considered as his *Hauptschüler*. Brunswik contributed a remarkable tract on "The Conceptual Framework of Psychology" to the *International Encyclopedia of Unified Science*. Substantial portions of his discourse were devoted to an objective functional approach to psychology, cybernetics, and communication theory. Brunswik was, moreover, thoroughly familiar with Charles Morris's work on semiotics as well. The only two references to Bühler that I was able to detect in his piece are one in connection with the picture he presents of "nineteenth-century psychology as an intersection of introspectionistic, elementaristic, sensationistic, and associationistic tendencies" and another concerning Bühler's early studies in color consistency (Brunswik 1955: 711, 728). It remains to be determined whether Bühler—certainly a transitional figure in the history of semiotic studies, although, to be sure, a scholar richly endowed with technical virtuosity—will be promoted to more than an outstanding footnote when the annals of this wide-ranging field are at last set forth.

APPENDIX

A slightly emended transcript of Bühler's autobiographical sketch.

LEBENSLAUF

Karl Bühler ist am 27. Mai 1879 in Merkesheim bei Heidelberg geboren. Vater: der Eisenbahnarbeiter (später Eisenbahnbeamter) Ludwig B. Mutter: Berta geb.Emmerich. Die Bühlers dürften letzten Endes aus der Schweiz stammen, wo die Baseler und Züricher Träger dieses Namens einen kontinuierlichen Stammbaum derer aus "Bühel" bis auf einen See Seevogt B., weöcher eine Rolle in der Schlacht bei Sempach (1389) spielte, nachgewiesen haben.—Die Emmerich waren in der Nähe von Karlsruhe ansässige Bauern und dürften vom Niedersheim dorthin gekommen sein. Ich hatte einen jüngeren Bruder, der im Krieg gefallen ist, und habe noch zwei Schwestern, die in Baden leben.

Mir war nach sonnoger Kindheit eineherbe Lehrzeit beschieden; nach humanistischem Gymnasium (Tauberbischofsheim) studierte ich grösstenteils mit selbstverdienten Groschen Medizin und Philosophie, promovierte in Medizin 1903 (Freiburg i.Br.) und in Philosophie 1904 (Strassburg). Zwei Jahre später wurde ich Assistent am psychologischen Institut in Würzburg, 1907 Privatdozent dort. Es folgte 1909-13 meine Dozentenzeit in Bonn, 1913-1918 in München (seit 16 a.o.Prof. dort).—August 14 Kriegsfreiwilliger, dann Truppenarzt (Ingolstädter Pioniere); ich blieb es auch, als ich nach dem Tode Külpes 1916 nach München zurüvkberufen wurde. Kraftfahrer München) und hatte neben meinem Lehramt die psychologische Prüfungsstelle der Kraftfahrer zu leiten; später war ich auch beauftragt die psychologische Prüfstelle für Flieger in Schliessheim vorzubereiten.—1918 Ordinarius in Dresden seit 1922 in Wien. Gastprofessor in Amerika 1927/28.

Als ich nach Wien kam, war die Psychologie seit langen verwaist; ich hatte anfangs 20 Hörer in der Hauptvorlesung; zehn Jahre später waren es über 1.000, und ich musste im kleinen Festsaal, später im Auditorium maximum lesen. Das Institut blühte auf und zog eine grosse Zahl ausländischer Studenten besonders aus England und Amerika neben den österreichischen und Reichsdeutschen an.—Die gedruckten Arbeiten aus dem Institut sind in einem Katalog, der vorliegt verzeichnet, es sind (bis zur Gegenwart geführt) 319 Nummern. Wir hatten 1929 den deutschen Kongress für Psychologie in Wien und sind für 19140 beauftragt, den Weltkongress für Psychologie hier vorzubereiten; zum Präsident dieses Weltkongresses bin ich gewählt.

Diesem Aufriss möchte ich noch folgendes hinzufügen:

1.) Ich war unpolitisch und habe mich politisch nicht betätigt. Unter meinen Mitarbeitern waren eine Reihe von aktiven Nationalsozialistaen, die ich nicht gehindert, sondern, wo es not tat, geschützt habe; ich nenne z.B.K.Mohrmann aus Dresden, der nach meinem Wissen als Parteimitglied einen politischen Auftrag in Wien hatte und durch mehrere Semester Bibliothekar in meinem Institut war. Ebenso arbeitete Herr Jos. Grohmann, der Nachfolger Mohrmann's als Bibliothekar bei mir. Weiter wurde Dr. Bruno Sonneck mein Mitarbeiter in der Sprachtheorie und 1934 in meinem Buch "Sprachtheorie" als solcher lobens erwähnt, als man ihm politische Schwierigkeiten bereitete, von mir geschützt (1934). Ein wertvoller Mitarbeiter des Institutes auf seinem Gebiet ist seit Jahren Herr Kollege Dr. Hugo Bernatzik, Pd.in Graz. Ich darf sowohl auch in diesem Zusammenhang Konrad *Lorenz,* dessen Habilitation in Tierpsychologie ich förderte, und Herrn Norbert Thumb, der seit Jahren die Statistik in meinem Institut verantwortlich und mit grossem Erfolg geleitet hat, erwähnen. Ebenso den Prinzen Auersperg, der die von Pötzl und mir veranstalteten Seminarabende seit Weihnachten leitet.

2.) Ich habe ein Programm für die Zukunft meiner Wissenschaft entworfen und hoffe es durchzuführen. Im Mittelpunkt dieses Programmes steht ein Charakterologie, wie sie z.B. in der Militärpsychologie erforderlich geworden ist. Dies Zukunftsprogramm vor Augen habe ich meinen Beamteneid abgelegt und hoffte sofort an seine Ausführung schreiten zu können, als ich am 23.März überraschend in Schutzhaft genommen wurde. Sie muss auch irrtümlicher Anzeige beruhen, denn ich bin ohne Protokoll aus ihr entlassen worden. Das Programm für die Zukunft ist wesentlich gefördert und ausgebaut worden in den Wochen, die ich in Schutzhaft verbrachte.

Wien,am 21. Mai 1938.

Heil Hitler!
Karl Bühler eh.

NOTES

I gratefully acknowledge the advice and assistance of Daniela G. Camhy, of the University of Graz, received after I had completed the reading draft of my remembrance but before the preparation of this final draft. Miss Camhy's forthcoming assessment of Bühler's work in its totality promises to be definitive. Responsibility for any errors of fact or lapses of judgment in this article are mine alone.

1. Exactly a fortnight after his release from detention, that is, on May 21, Bühler, by his own hand, typed out a painfully craven document, entitled "Lebenslauf." For obvious reasons, it has remained buried in a Viennese archive until now, but I think that it is important that it should at last be published, and I therefore do so as an Appendix following this article. This soul-sick sketch

goes a long way toward explaining Bühler's subsequent discomposure and haunting melancholy, besides illuminating other personalities and the infectious madness of the times. An expert in analyzing the character of an author by means of the study of his typewriting—presumably a would-be special branch of the very "Charakterologie" Bühler mentions in his program—could draw voluminous inferences from the eerie subliminal facts of this text, particularly from Bühler's type-overs and marks of emphasis. The reader is invited to draw his own conclusions.

Chapter 6

"Talking" with Animals: Zoosemiotics Explained

SEMIOTICS IS, quite simply, the exchange of messages. A message consists of a sign or a string of signs. "Zoosemiotics" is a term coined in 1963 to delimit that segment of the field which focuses on messages given off and received by animals, including important components of human non-verbal communication, but excluding man's language and his second-ary, language-derived semiotic systems, such as sign language or Morse code.

Biologists define life as a system capable of evolution by natural selection. This genetic definition, which places great emphasis on the importance of replication, is entirely compatible with the modern semiotic point of view, which asserts that all communication is a manifestation of life, and that it is the capacity to communicate that distinguishes living beings from inanimate substances. Reproduction is itself a matter of communication, the molecular code being one of the two master sign-systems on earth. The other one is the verbal code—our language. The molecular code is apparently the same in all terrestrial organisms; the verbal code is fundamentally the same—with superficial variations—in all the peoples of the globe.

Scholars distinguish two varieties of animal communication: intra-specific and interspecific. Intraspecific communication refers to all the de-vices at the disposal of an animal that link it to every other member of its own species, and all others to it. Territory delineation, and the location of kin, competitors, and prospective mates, are among these de-vices. Examples of intraspecific messages are the bright flashes of light used in the dialogue among fireflies, an exchange of coded information about species identity, sex, and location. The flash code used varies from species to species within the family of beetles to which fireflies belong. Certain fishes communicate with their own kind by broadcasting differ-ent patterns of electric pulses to threaten, indicate submission, carry on courtship, or even, by discharging a particular set of signs, insure indi-vidual recognition from a mate, companion, or rival and thus help pro-mote cohesiveness within its social group.

This article, prepared at the initiative of Susan Burns, then the magazine's managing editor, first appeared in *Animals* 111:6:20-23, 36 (December 1978), with original illustrations by Plunkett Dodge.

Although "flehmen," or lip-curl, which involves the closure of nasal openings when the head is jerked back, is a widely distributed behavioral trait in mammals, this facial expression has evolved into a particular sign in horses which elicits particular responses on the part of other horses. A fearful rhesus monkey carries its tail stuck stiffly out behind, while a baboon will convey the same emotion to its fellows by holding its tail vertically.

In brief, each kind of animal has at its command a repertoire of signs that forms a system unique to it or is, in biological parlance, species-specific. Language is a species-specific trait of man; it is therefore counterproductive and misleading to ascribe language to any other animal, except, perhaps, metaphorically. Some features of tail signaling, as of any other kind of communicative device, may vary geographically; linguistic diversity in space may produce dialects, a term that is also used in zoosemiotics to characterize behavioral differences in populations of the same species occupying different areas. Thus langur monkeys in northern India carry their tails up and arched over the back, while the same species in the south carry them up and then looping backward to signify an individual's degree of "confidence."

No species, however, can survive in isolation from other sorts of animals. Each species must live in a vast ecosystem which requires its members to coexist with a variety of neighbors on certain terms. In order to avoid predators, capture prey, or in other ways further the mutual advantage of two or more species, animals must have additional code-switching capabilities, an *interspecific* communication system. In parts of India, for example in Kanha Park, some half a dozen hoofed animals occupy a range which they must share with the tiger and lesser carnivores, like the leopard and jungle cat, sloth bear, striped hyena, jackal, and an occasional python—to say nothing of man. Each prey and each predator species must communicate with every other within range to enhance the survival of its own kind.

A number of marine fishes specialize in eliminating parasites that plague another species of fish. The "cleaner" fish entices its hosts by means of a sign—the "cleaner dance" or nod swim—which the hosts acknowledge by permitting themselves to be cleansed. The hosts, in turn, know how to invite the cleaners to perform their lustral chores.

The saber-toothed blenny is, by contrast, a fake and a natural opportunist: it mimics the communicative behavior of the harmless cleaner fish in order to deceive the hosts, enabling the impostor to bite chunks off their fins and gills and get away with it. Such deception by mimicry is a common perversion of interspecific communicative processes throughout the animal kingdom.

A famous example of interspecific communication to mutual advantage is found in the savannahs of Africa south of the Sahara, where a bird, called the honey guide, indicates to man the location of beehives that the bird cannot open but on whose honeycombs it likes to feed. This bird produces conspicuous beckoning calls, followed by certain optical signs, until a willing human being finds the hive, feeds the wax to the bird, and consumes the honey himself.

How man and animals communicate with one another poses all sorts of interesting problems that require a great deal more study. Man may encounter animals under a wide variety of circumstances that make it necessary for each party to learn—even if never entirely master—the essential elements of the other's code.

Here are some possibilities for contact:

1. Man is an animal's despoiler (e.g., potential exterminator, such as of the starling); or

2. Man is an animal's victim (e.g., of our most devastating killer, the mosquito).

3. Man is an animal's (unequal) partner or symbiont (say, a human host and his household pet guest, like his goldfish or canary).

4. Man is a parasite on an animal (e.g., the reindeer) or the other way around (e.g., the flea and the louse); or the two exist in a state of commensalism (like seagulls following the plow or robins perched on a spade).

5. The animal accepts a human as its conspecific, even to the extent of attempting to mate (as a panda tried with her keeper in London, or a male dolphin with his female trainer in St. Thomas).

6. The animal defines humans as inanimate objects (e.g., when men are in a vehicle driving through a wildlife park).

7. Man subjects an animal to scientific testing and experimentation (*apprentissage*) in the laboratory or to performing in exhibitions (*dressage*), as in the circus.

8. Man tames animals and continues to breed them selectively (domestication).

Each of these situations—and others—involves a crucial understanding on our part of the animals' biologically given communicative capacity. The success of processes like taming and training depends on our having mastered relevant elements of animals' codes. In order to flourish in our company, each animal must be able to discern man's verbal and/or nonverbal behavior.

All communication systems, especially those of animals, are studied under six major rubrics. I have already mentioned that messages, or strings of signs, are a chief focus of attention, but all messages have to be generated by an emitting organism (source or addresser) and interpreted by one or more receiving organisms (destination or addressee). The kind of messages emitted is dictated by the biological makeup of the source, particularly its sensory apparatus, and the environmental conditions, or context, to which the species has adapted. A message can but rarely be transmitted directly in the shape in which it was generated (quite probably, electrochemically). Messages have to be encoded in a form that the channel connecting the communicants can accommodate. For the message to have an impact the receiving animal must have the key for decoding it back into a shape (also electrochemical) that its biological makeup enables it to interpret. This is the reason why messages appear in coded form and why the source and the destination must (at least partially) share either an inherited or a learned code, or, commonly, some mixture of both.

Picture, then, an organism that formulates a message—say, "I want you!"—directed at another individual, a very special one, of the opposite sex within its own species, as a gannet calling out to its mate after prolonged separation at sea during the winter, so that each member of the pair can recognize the other again as they both return to their nesting cliffs. This message is encoded in acoustic form, and the sound waves travel through the medium of air from the vocal organs of one gannet across to the auditory apparatus of the other. Contrast this with the promiscuous scented advertisement of a flightless female silk moth to any male flying by within a radius of a few miles: Her glands emit a sex-attractant pheromone (or message-bearing chemical released to the exterior) called bombykol which is transported through the air surrounding her, eventually to be picked up by certain receptor organs on the male antennae. Bombykol molecules are absorbed by the hair surface and diffuse to and through the pores and tubules into a fluid, where they hit the membrane, eliciting a cell response which sets the male off traveling to and, perhaps, mating with the stationary female. A single odor molecule (or very few) can apparently trigger an explosive series of events. Among other things, this chain of happenings illustrates an important principle of animal communication: signing behavior often releases far more energy than is used for the act of launching a message.

All messages are encoded to suit the medium and can, accordingly, be conveniently classified in terms of the channel or combination of channels employed by the animal in question. Understandably, human beings, in whose daily lives speech plays such a prominent part, tend to think of the vocal-auditory link as the paramount channel. Actually, the use of sound in the wider scheme of biological existence is rather uncommon: the overwhelming majority of animals are both deaf and dumb. Of the dozen or so phyla of animals, only two contain creatures that can hear and produce functional sound: the arthropods and the chordates. Of the latter, the upper three and a half classes of vertebrates are unique in having all their members capable of sound production as well as—excepting only snakes—of hearing. The methods of sound production vary enormously, of course, from group to group. Our own method seems not only to be unusual but, to all appearances, to have evolved only once in the stream of life. The vocal mechanism that works by means of a current of air passing over the cords and setting them into vibrations is confined to ourselves and, with distinctions, to our nearest relatives—the other mammals—the birds, reptiles, and amphibians. (Although some fish use wind instruments as well, they do so without the reed constituted by our vocal cords.) So far as we know, no true vocal performances are found outside the land vertebrates or their marine descendants, the whales. Acoustic communication may take place in air or in water and it varies in range. The human ear can register only a narrow portion of that range. In that respect, we are overshadowed by the smallest bat, by every dog, as well as by many rodents and, no doubt, countless other animals hitherto not investigated.

Optical communication is, similarly, much more extensive than the limits of the human eye might indicate. Our eyes can register only visible light, whereas bees and some other insects are able to communicate in the ultraviolet range. Nocturnal mammals, possessing a "tapetum lucidum" (an irridescent pigment choroid coat causing reflected night eye-shine), are able to "see in the dark," a feat man can accomplish only with the aid of specially constructed infrared equipment. The sensitivity of our sense organs tends to vary from those of other species: the auditory reaction time of the avian ear has been estimated, for instance, to be ten times that of a human ear. African vultures were shown to be capable of distinguishing, from a height of about 13,000 feet, whether a gazelle lying on the ground is dead or only sleeping; we, even using field binoculars, are unable even to identify the bird soaring at such a height.

Besides the acoustic and the optical channels, animals may rely on chemical signs through their sense of smell, for example, as do many carnivores and ungulates. The dog's superior sense of smell is legendary. I have mentioned pheromones previously; more and more of them are being isolated and analyzed. The "flehmen" of horses, as well as that of bats and a variety of other predators and prey, is also a specialized device for closing the nostrils to rechannel such olfactory substances as female urine to the so-called vomeronasal organ, located on the roof of the palate of the male, where the chemical message is decoded for ultimate interpretation in the hypothalamus. In snakes and lizards, the vomeronasal organ simply registers olfactory substances, but in such animals as antelopes it enables bucks to know the state of a doe—whether, for example, she is in heat.

Advances are rapidly being made in our understanding of communication by means of electrically coded messages in both marine and freshwater environments. In certain animals, notably such reptiles as rattlesnakes and pit vipers, slight changes in temperature can have significance. Tactile communication—by direct contact or through physical conduits as different as the spider's web and tracks of silk or the slime trails of snails and slugs—is practiced in various corners of the animal world.

The integration of a species may be achieved via a hierarchical combination of channels: the social dynamics of a wolf pack depend, for example, on (a) visual signs, especially the subtle repertoire of tail and body displays and facial expressions; (b) vocal signs, including collective "singing"; (c) tactile signs, such as grooming, nibbling, licking, or just lying together in rest and sleep; and (d) olfactory signs, involving scent marking and rolling. These four channels are used either in alternation, according to certain rules (for instance, when a member has lost visual contact with the pack, it may continue to track, at high speed, following a scent) or to reinforce one another. Such supplementation, called redundancy, becomes necessary under certain unfavorable environmental conditions that introduce noise—unwanted signs—into the stream of communication.

People who want to understand how animals communicate must abandon the layman's traditional notion of the "five senses." Many more than five are already known to science, and many others undoubtedly remain to be discovered. Equally important, humans tend to underestimate many animals' sensorial efficiency. Such misestimates, based on ignorance, sometimes lead to ludicrous pronouncements claiming "extrasensory perception" on the part of certain animals, for example, horses. It has been known, however, since 1926, that horses are capable of detecting movements in the human face of less than one-fifth of a millimeter. A sign consisting of a movement so minute simply escapes the ken of human onlookers. There are assuredly many such phenomena that should be checked and checked repeatedly in every species of animal.

Specialists in zoosemiotics concentrate on one topic, or a combination of topics, among the following:

1. How does the source animal successively formulate and encode its messages? Squids and octopuses, which are mollusks with a truly extraordinary control of color and pattern, have, for instance, arranged their comportment so as to respect the demands of gravity; to be able to achieve this, they have evolved parts which by their physical structure symbolize gravity and movement. The English anatomist, J. Z. Young (1977), has shown in detail how these internal structures are, as it were, miniature models of the universe, and how these features, among others, guide these cephalopods—whose social existence is confined largely to combat and copulation—in their communicative behaviors, or in other words, how the signs they use signify some change in their inner or outer world or embody some instructions for action.

2. Once encoded, how is the message transmitted—through what channel(s), operating under what conditions? If a multichannel system is involved, as with wolves, what rules determine how channels are to be combined or when an animal is to switch from one to another?

3. How does the receiving animal successively decode and interpret the incoming message? What is its sensory capacity like; what are its limitations? Cicadas are interesting in this respect. While calling to the female, the male abruptly turns deaf to his own raucous song; the female, however, perceives pulses (which, to us, sound like a mere rattle) from

the time patterns of which she is able to sort out her species and fly to the correct type of male.

4. What is the total message repertoire in a given species? (Some investigators maintain that each species of birds and mammals has only about fifteen to forty-five display messages, classifiable into a dozen or so categories.) What form does each sign take? How are signs arranged into strings and what does each concatenation signify—what information is embodied by each complex sign, and how can this be decomposed into smaller meaningful units?

5. What are the properties of the code used by each species? (A code is a transformation, or a set of rules, whereby messages are converted from one representation to another; an animal either inherits or learns its code, or both.) Thus, insects, which do not have a constant temperature, face a problem created by fluctuations in the environment: male grasshoppers are known to double their rates of singing for every $10°C$ rise in outside temperature. If the female recognizes the species solely on the basis of the number of pulses per unit of time, the code, inherent in her nervous system, must allow for temperature differences to enable her to locate the male. Such must indeed be the case, for females at $25°C$, for example, fail to respond to calls of males at $15°C$.

6. An animal always interprets messages it receives in the light of two different variables: the incoming signal itself; and the specific qualities of the context in which the message was delivered—such as whether the water was quiet or turbulent; whether the display was performed in the emitter's territory or the receiver's, near a cover or in the open; or whether, during the act of communicating, the animals were approaching one another, withdrawing, or still. Every previous message, moreover, provides contextual information for the interpretation of every succeeding message. Very little is known about the way animals or, indeed, people utilize contextual information, but there is no doubt as to its critical importance in every communicative transaction.

There are two fields of complex research that can only be touched on in this brief survey. One focuses on the question: how have sign systems evolved—that is, changed into communicatory devices from some segment of behavior that previously fulfilled a different function—in one species or another (the study of what ethologists refer to as "ritualization")? For instance, the evolution of human laughter, which also occurs in monkeys and the chimpanzee as the "relaxed open-mouth display," interpreted as a friendly sign of play, has been traced to a movement that was originally associated, as far back as primitive insectivores, with grooming and respiration.

The other field attempts to deal with the development (or ontogeny) of sign systems in the life of a given individual, from its birth or hatching to maturity. Much fascinating and useful information has come to light, for example, from longitudinal studies of the vocal development of a variety of songbirds, and the crystallization—the reaching of the final adult pattern—of this manner of territorial assertion.

There are many reasons for encouraging the serious study of zoo-semiotics. Let me conclude by mentioning only two. We are as yet far from understanding the pathways along which our own nonverbal and verbal communicative abilities have evolved. Zoosemiotics searchingly illuminates both the commonalities and the distinctions between human and animal communication.

Second, we share our globe with a great many fellow-creatures but are totally ignorant of—or worse, entertain childlike ideas about—most of them. Sentimental or outright mistaken notions must be replaced by sound knowledge. Therein lies our only hope for establishing realistic, workable communication links with the host of the speechless creatures that form a vital part of our environment.

Chapter 7

Close Encounters with Canid
Communication of the Third Kind

Why should a dog, a horse,
a rat, have life . . . ?
—SHAKESPEARE

They are a higher form of life,
My dog, my daughter, and my wife,
Inhabitants of a fourth dimension
Too mystic for my comprehension.
—OGDEN NASH

ETHOLOGISTS CUSTOMARILY distinguish between two sorts of communication systems in the domestic dog (*Canis lupus familiaris*): intraspecific— that is, concerning the semiosic comportment of the dog, via a combination of acoustic, chemical, optical, and tactile means, *vis-à-vis* other dogs (Fox and Cohen 1977; Fox 1978:24-26); and interspecific—that is, having to do with the semiosic repertory used by the dog when interacting with other species of animals (Fox 1971, chap. 9), say, when working with sheep, or when in social contact with human beings in a large variety of situations, such as training, hunting, guarding, rescuing, guiding, tracking, hauling, entertaining, and providing companionship (Lorenz 1954; Scott and Fuller 1965:175-180; Dale-Green 1966, Part II; Fox 1978, chap. 3). This is not the place to discuss either of the two sorts of codes alluded to, which might, respectively, be dubbed canid communication of the first kind and of the second kind. The topic of this paper will be commerce of a third kind, involving a very special kind of canid interlocutor: the anthropocentric phenomenon of the talking dog.

Reports about talking dogs fall into several distinct categories. The most ancient among them are clearly identified as belonging to folklore or mythology (Dale-Green 1966). In Stith Thompson's *Motif-Index of Folk-Literature*, the prevalence of such dogs in folktales and fairy tales

This article is an amalgam of three earlier treatments of the same theme: one version appeared in *Studies in Diachronic, Synchronic, and Typological Linguistics: Festschrift for Oswald Szemerényi on the Occasion of his 65th Birthday*, edited by Bela Brogyanyi (Amsterdam: John Benjamins, 1974), 2:809-828; another in the *Zetetic Scholar: An Independent Scientific Review of Claims of Anomalies and the Paranormal* 3/4:3-20 (1979) (supplemented by *corrigenda, idem* 5:2-3); and a third, with illustrations added, in *Animals* 113:1:6-10 (February 1980).

is evidenced under his classification B211.1.7., where he cites American, Arabic, Breton, Jewish, Polynesian, and South American Indian references, among others. There are also countless North American Indian tales in which the talking dog appears as truth teller (B134), for instance, or as a tattler (B134.1). In Ireland, if the dog talks, that is a sign of impending disaster, as it is among the Hupa and Yurok Indians of California, and elsewhere (Leach 1961:279-280). In contrast to the worldwide etiological tales explaining why dogs do not talk, Leach relates (ibid.:281) that "in the great body of African folktale it is *taken for granted*" that they do talk, specifically to men. She also records that, during the reign of the English King Charles I, there were many rumors about Prince Rupert's pet poodle, Boye: some said it was a scandal that Boye should be "allowed to converse so much with the king's children, lest he taught them to swear" (ibid.; cf. Dale-Green 1966:81-83).

The second category features talking dogs in a quasi-literary setting, which may range from serious philosophical works to comic strips. It

FIG. 7.1. Literate literary dog. Ponto the "sagacious" pointer graced the pages of Charles Dickens's *The Posthumous Papers of the Pickwick Club*. Author's collection.

was Plato who, in *The Republic*, characterized the dog as the "philosophical" animal *par excellence;* the most celebrated contemporary avatar of the philosophical dog is undoubtedly Charles Schulz's creation, Snoopy. There are many novels, short stories, and fictive memoirs where all the action is narrated from the viewpoint of a dog hero: one thinks of Buck, in Jack London's *The Call of the Wild,* who converses with his fellows in "dog language," but is represented as thinking and dreaming in human terms; Virginia Woolf's *Flush,* who overhears "snatches of talk held in passing with the dogs of Wimpole Street" (1933:39), and could "read signs that nobody else could even see" (ibid.:59); and, above all, of Berganza and Cipión, the principal speakers in Miguel de Cervantes' delightful and widely imitated novella, amounting to an indictment of human conduct, *El coloquio de los perros.*

Nikolai Gogol, in his 1835 story, "The Diary of a Madman," introduced two dogs who not only talked but also exchanged letters. Gogol's narrator says:

> With my own eyes I saw Madgie forming the words, "I was, bow-wow, I was, bow-ow-ow, very sick." Talk about a lap dog! I must say I was quite surprised to hear her talking. Later, however, when I had properly sized up the situation, I was no longer surprised. As a matter of fact, the world has seen many similar occurrences before. I've heard that, in England, a fish broke surface and uttered a couple of words in such an outlandish language that scholars have been trying to work out their meaning for three years—so far in vain. Then, too, I read in the newspapers about two cows who went into a store and asked for a pound of tea. But I'll confess that I was much more bewildered when Madgie said: "I *did* write you Fidele. Perhaps Fido didn't give you my letter." Now, I'd be willing to forfeit a month's pay if I've ever heard of a dog that could write. [Gogol 1960:9]

The last story Franz Kafka ever wrote, his serene and tender "Investigations of a Dog" (1936), is a perfect manifestation of this genre in the twentieth century. The dog informs the reader: "Apart from us dogs there are all sorts of creatures in the world, wretched, limited, dumb creatures who have no language but mechanical cries; many of us dogs study them, have given them names, tried to help them, educate them, uplift them, and so on" (ibid.:5). In this tale, dogs perform toward the dumb creatures the very part the human race ordinarily fulfils toward the dog world, while men are elevated into invisible though still operatively present entities, a role we customarily ascribe to the incomprehensible powers of the divine.

One of the most remarkable examples of this fictional genre was Olaf Stapledon's fantastic novel about Sirius, a super-sheepdog created by a scientist by means of certain hormones introduced into the fetus through the mother's bloodstream. This scientist, Thomas Trelone, had originally planned to work with apes, because they offered the hope of more spectacular success. They were by nature better equipped than dogs. Their brains were bigger, their sight was more developed, and they had hands. Nevertheless from Trelone's point of view dogs had one overwhelming advantage. They were capable of a much greater freedom of movement in our society. [1944:15]

Sirius is brought up as a member of the family, along with a little girl, Plaxy, and achieves "true speech," which is "a sure sign of the fully human degree of intelligence. The baby chimpanzee that was brought up with a human baby kept level with his foster-sister until the little girl began to talk, but then dropped behind; for the ape never showed any sign of using words" (1944:26). Sirius far outstrips the Kelloggs' Gua, to whom this indirect reference is made. We are further told that Sirius was so sensitive "to odour and to sound, that he found human speech quite inadequate to express the richness of these two universes" (1944:36). Eventually, he was also taught to sing. His adventures at Cambridge were especially noteworthy, even though the famous academics he would converse with there suspected that Trelone "was playing a trick on them" (1944:103). Sirius ultimately reverts to wolfhood and comes to a tragic end.

A special case allied to the foregoing category is Dog Toby, of the *Punch and Judy* show, a live dog trained to perform with the puppets in the booth. This dog was sometimes expected to vocalize, even to sing.

Another special case is the use of a dog in lieu of a hand puppet, a shadowgraph, or especially a doll-dummy, in staging a "near" ventriloquist act. In such entertainments, the dog must, of course, be trained to move its jaws in coordination with his master's ventriloqual voice.

Yet a third, quaint category was recently fabricated by the dogfood industry, which, in a blatant attempt to sell more of its product, "has populated our television screens with so many loquacious dogs" (Ziolkowski 1977:22).

In a fourth category belong reports dealing with real dogs that are reputed to actually talk (or, in some instances, sing, as a dog named Zopicus, referred to by Plutarch, and many others, mentioned with increasing frequency since 1650), and it is with these humanized creatures, belonging to the curious intermediate world Horace Walpole designated "dogmanity" (which is not the same as, but probably has common roots with, a more brutal transformation, lycanthropy), that this paper is chiefly concerned. Talking dogs in general exemplify the Clever Hans experimenter expectancy effects, which were most thoroughly explored in horses, although many other so-called clever animals are mentioned in the literature, such as mice and rats; bears; cats; "learned pigs"; a "goat of knowledge"; sea lions and even a walrus; innumerable birds, including geese and woodpeckers; the dolphins of the 1960s; and three species of African apes in the 1970s. After all, as Emily, "his monkey wife," descries about her relationship with Mr. Fatigay (Collier 1969:14), the chimp is "Something better than his dog, a little dearer than his horse!" Now all talking dog cases of this kind fall into two broad classes: those involving intentional deception (hoax, fraud) and those affected by self-deception in varying degree, exemplifying the Clever Hans fallacy proper. Those of the second class are much more instructive from a semiotic point of view, but those of the first are not without points of interest (cf. Sebeok 1979: chap. 5).

Dogs can readily be trained to bark in response to cues, imperceptible to other human bystanders, emitted by their operators. Bernard Grzimek (1975:12:225-226)—no mean observer of the nuances of animal behavior—witnessed one such performing dog barking "answers" to questions addressed to it by its master:

> The dog carried out its routine several times without Grzimek noticing any cues being given by the dog's master. Afterward, the trainer told Grzimek that his dog began to bark when the man shifted his weight from one foot to the other, and the dog ceased barking when weight was shifted back to the original foot. The beginning and ending of barking series could be accurately controlled in this way. The trainer had also taught the dog other signs used to communicate commands.[1]

The condensed transaction related by Grzimek suggests a series of questions of capital interest to the semiotician. Among them are:

1. What is the function of the *source* of the message, the man, as against the function of its *destination,* the dog? The answer, which comes from stage magic, stems from the principle of misdirection, the basis of which is that the audience will look wherever you artfully direct its attention. In performing a trick, beginners in magic are enjoined never to look at the opposite end of their effect. If you want to know how the illusion of the talking dog is created, keep a sharp eye on the operator, not, as he wants you to, on his subject alone.

2. What *channel* links the message source (the master) with its twofold destination: the subject (dog) and the audience (Grzimek)? The answer is by no means self-evident, and needs to be broken down into several parts.

Of course, Grzimek was told that the cue the trainer had purposefully emitted consisted of a slight deflection in his own posture. The dog was thus supposedly informed via the optical channel either to commence or to cease vocalizing. A whole series of subsidiary questions is immediately spawned: Was the optical channel the only one engaged in triggering the dog's response? If not, what other, secondary channels came into play—the acoustic perhaps, e.g., activated by an alteration in the operator's breathing rate (Johnson 1912:9)? Changes in the operator's muscle tension can likewise be detected by other than the visual avenue, as Johnson's tests with blind dogs has proved; both normal and blind dogs "in ordinary situations rely greatly on kinaesthetic and muscular sense-processes in making their adjustments" (ibid.:78), and consideration of the experimental literature on the visual capacity of dogs indicates that "the average dog has far more faulty vision than most dog-lovers suppose" (Warden and Warner 1928:2). If a galaxy of channels was indeed involved, which of the strands were indispensable, which redundant? Was the operator fully aware of what he was doing and, if so, was his explication veridical? Which channel was under his voluntary control, or employed wittingly, which was not, or out-of-awareness?

Le chien calculateur.

FIG. 7.2. The dog that talks. From Hachet-Souplet 1897.

If the dog perceived its master's sign behavior, why was the self-same display imperceptible to an expert human spectator? The last question at least is easily answered by invoking Carl Stumpf's principle of *minimale unabsichtliche Bewegungen,* enunciated by that eminent scholar, in 1907, in his capacity as chairman of the *Wissenschaftliche Kommission* set up to investigate the horse now known as Clever Hans (Sebeok 1977a:1068). Hediger (1974:27-28), in his fascinating excursus into the field of sense organs in the animal kingdom, rightly emphasizes that, as between animals and men, "the animal is frequently the considerably better observer of the two, or is more sensitive than man; it can evaluate signals that remain hidden to man." The range of the channels utilized is still unknown, as is the degree of deliberation the trainer may have exercised. Startling as these assertions must seem, they are true even in very thorough experiments conducted by eminent psychologists in which no other animal was implicated, but only "The Control of Another Person by Obscure Signs" (Stratton 1921; this refers to the case of Eugen de Rubini, which is discussed in more detail in Sebeok 1979: chap. 4).

3. The account cited leaves no doubt that the dog *barked*. Why, then, was this animal designated a "talking" dog? The answer is both complicated and intriguing. I propose to return to it at the end of this paper, after some observations about *dressage* of dogs to perform in the circus and a brief historical digression about talking dogs in general.

The most perceptive and useful exposition of the techniques for training dogs to perform in the circus—best understood when reread in the light of Bouissac's insightful semiotic approach (1976)—is still the manual by Hachet-Souplet (1897:35-77). This shrewd observer of circus life, especially of animal acts, describes various types of Clever Dogs, including Munito, the "plus connu de tous les chiens savants," who flourished during "la grande vogue des chiens calculateurs . . . ," i.e., the early nineteenth century (ibid.:36). Munito answered questions pertaining to botany, natural history, and geography, and, at the urging of his master, a certain Signor Castelli, would pick up lettered cards between his teeth to spell out the answers. In 1750, the craft of one Clever Bitch was billed thus:

> Chienne savante. L'on espère que les curieux voudront bien honorer par leur présence une chienne qui sait lire et compter par le moyen de cartes topographiques, et qui répond par le même moyen aux demandes que l'on lui fait sur les métamorphoses d'Ovide, la géographie, l'histoire romaine. . . . Elle compte les personnes qui sont dans une assemblée, elle écrit tous les noms propres. Elle démontre les quatre règles de l'arithmétique. Elle désigne l'heure, les couleurs, etc. . . ." [Ibid.:36-37]

Hachet-Souplet (ibid.:43) quickly disposes of the legend of the Clever Dog, represented as "pouvant tout faire de lui-même, raisonnant comme une personne." The *dressage* of the performing dog is in fact accomplished by a compromise between persuasion ("par la parole et le geste") and coercion ("par la ficelle et tels carcans appropriés") (ibid.: 47), according to instructions he sets forth in ample detail, explaining, among many others, the stunts of the great Munito; the likes of his distinguished predecessor, Don Carlos, "The Double-Sighted Dog," who gave a command performance before King William and the royal family at Brighton during the 1830s; and of his many epigones who followed.

Especially noteworthy is Hachet-Souplet's instructive explication of the accomplishments of Singing Dogs, which goes as follows (ibid.:74-75): Imagine playing a tune on a piano placed side by side with another piano, which is shut and from which the dampers have been removed. A person who puts his ear against the closed piano will hear the vibration of certain chords whenever the corresponding chords are activated on piano No. 1. A comparable resonance is set off in the vocal cords of the dog whenever the trainer articulates sounds;

> et, *s'il se trouve que la bête est extrêmement nerveuse*, elle perçoit, au gosier, des espèces de petits chatouillements qui la forcent pour ainsi dire

à articuler des mots à son tour. Elle a d'abord l'air de s'étrangler, puis se met à hurler en proférant des sons variés se rapprochant de la voix humaine; on peut alors diriger ses lèvres avec les doigts, pour l'habituer à perfectionner son jeu." [Ibid.:74][2]

Here Hachet-Souplet properly underlines that it is understood that the vocalizations emitted by the dog "n'ont pour elle *aucune signification,*" although by further patient education, if correctly carried out, he thinks it may be possible to forge in the dog's central nervous system a bond linking the sign to the object—feasible in theory perhaps, but in practice very difficult to achieve.

Thirty years later, Warden and Warner (1928) have explored, with an attitude of healthy skepticism, this very proposition in great detail with Fellow, a canine star of stage and screen. Was this dog's éclat for understanding human language justly warranted? The investigators concluded that "there would seem to be no doubt that scores of associations between verbal stimuli and definite responses have been well fixated" (ibid.: 26) by the patient teaching, over several years, of Mr. Jacob Herbert, this dog's operator. The evidence, on the other hand, for associations between verbal stimuli (signs) and objects or places could never be determined because of the uncertainty, due to the meagerness and inconclusiveness of the data, with respect to the dog's capacity for making a delayed reaction, that is, to disengage from the immediate context. As Bronowski (1974:2548) convincingly argued many years afterward, the time-lag is precisely the most important and basic among the four behavioral criteria postulated by him for distinguishing speech from other animal communication systems.

It is of more than passing interest to note that the dog's intelligence—including "the arithmetical condition of the dog's mind"—was scientifically studied, as early as the 1880s, by Lord Avebury (Lubbock 1866), who experimented with his black poodle, Van. Avebury was among the first to suggest "that some such system as that followed with deaf mutes" be adapted to further two-way communication with animals (a technique many people imagine was first invented by psychologists barely in this decade to enable them to communicate with the apes). Avebury was also keenly aware of what came decades later to be called the Clever Hans Fallacy, which he further, quickly and correctly, connected with the mentalist illusion commonly dubbed "thought-reading." In discussing how a dog may learn to count, he relates an episode in which the operator, a Mr. Huggins, "did not *consciously* give the dog any sign, yet so quick was the dog in seizing the slightest indication, that he was able to give the correct answer" by barking when he came to the card on the ground with the correct number.

In view of Avebury's prescient sagacity, it is disheartening to read about Chris, the pet dog who flourished in the 1950s in the home of G. H. Wood, in Warwick, Rhode Island, and who "was reported to be able to answer any kind of question put to him" (Pratt 1977:223). Chris made remarkable scores at symbol-card guessing. He indicated his choice by pawing once for a circle, twice for a cross, three times for wavy lines, four times for a square, and five times for a star. Pratt, one of the two associates of J. B. Rhine who observed Chris, although never under proper laboratory conditions—the dog died in 1963, just when "the trained psi research worker" was about to find the opportunity "to investigate further along similar lines" (ibid.:235)—offered three possible explanations for Chris's extraordinary performance. The first, which he favored, was the exercise of the dog's own ESP. The second was "the possibility that the successful agents were unconsciously giving sensory information of what the cards were to the person [*viz.*, Mr. Wood himself] working with Chris" (ibid.:234). The third was the intrusion of "some honest mistake in interpreting the rules they were supposed to follow," thus nullifying the safeguards (ibid.). The latter two, Pratt concluded however, "are hardly within the bounds of reason" (ibid.). The fourth possibility, the one foreseen and incisively delineated by Avebury, and amply proved by others, seems not to have occurred to the committed parapsychologist.

Gould (1978:504) has recently referred to "finagling, doctoring, and massaging"—that is, the unconscious manipulation of data by professionals or, *a fortiori*, by the laity, innocent marks that they mostly are. Consider Leibniz (Ritter 1911:1). In a letter to Grimarest, he wrote:

> Ich habe soeben einen Brief des Kaiserlichen Prinz-Regenten empfangen, wo Se. Hoheit mir bemerkt, dass er in diesem Frühjahr zweimal auf der letzten Leipsiger Messe einen Hund, der spricht, gesehen und sorgfältig geprüft habe. Dieser Hund hat deutlich *mehr als 30 Worte* ausgesprochen, sogar *ziemlich sinngemäss seinem Herrn geantwortet.* Er hat auch *das ganze Alphabet ausgesprochen,* mit Ausnahme der Buchstaben m, n, x.

Leibniz also sent a letter, through the intermediary of the mathematician Pierre Varignon, in 1715, to the Abbé de St. Pierre, where the report caused a sensation at the Académie Royale des Sciences (Observations 1718:3-4). As Varignon had already written to Leibniz (1962:194) on August 9, 1713,

> L'histoire du chien parlant a causé ici [Paris] d'autant plus de surprise qu'elle seroit incroyable si vous n'asseuriez l'avoir aprise d'un Prince qui l'a entendu parler dans une Foire, où une infinité d'autres personnes en doivent avoir été temoins: sans doute que le maître de ce chien ne manquera pas de le promener par toute l'Europe: s'il vient ici, il en remportera seurement beaucoup d'argent, quoyque ce chien ne parle qu'Allemand que peu de gens de ce pais-ci entendent, lui suffisant pour la curiosité dont on est ici, que son chien y prononce les lettres de l'Alphabet que vous me dites qu'il scait prononcer.

Leibniz (ibid.:199), in an undated missive, then amplified further: "Je suis maintenant témoin oculaire et auriculaire du chien parlant; entre autres mots il a bien prononcé Thé, Caffé, Chocolat. . . ."

FIG. 7.3. "Ja." Don would answer questions in spoken German when tempted with a tasty reward. Author's collection.

It was naturally very convenient that this native German-speaking dog could scarcely commune with a Francophone audience; Varignon's stricture prompts me, however, to repeat my wonderment already expressed in another place (Sebeok 1979: chap. 4): How was the con perpetrated on an intellectual eminence of the stature of Leibniz? Before I attempt to explain this, I might adduce the case of Rolf, the astounding Airedale terrier of Mannheim (Larguier des Bancels and Claparède 1915; MacKenzie 1913), whose wondrous reputation persists to this very day (e.g., Jutzler-Kindermann 1954:39-53; Borgese 1968:9; Rowdon 1978: *passim*). Probably the most telling incident about Rolf was that he suddenly became ill shortly after the arrival of the Swiss psychologist Professor Claparède, the scientist who was to have subjected his ability to a series of critical tests (Warden and Warner 1928:14). This little detail is almost never mentioned in the many colorful yarns about Rolf. (It reminds me of nothing so much as the authenticated [Randi 1978:28] refusal of the Israeli "psychic," Uri Geller, to perform in Birmingham after receiving word backstage that the front row was packed with magicians. Instead, he made up a story about a bomb threat, thus forcing the cancellation of his show.)

The Clever Hans affair gave renewed impetus to a dialectic launched by Descartes and others in the seventeenth century, then carried far forward by Julien Offray de la Mettrie, the eighteenth-century physician and forerunner of the behaviorist position, with his sharp rejection of Cartesian dualism. The issue centered on the question whether language and the cognitive structure assumed to underlie it was *the* critical feature of *Homo sapiens* that separated him from the speechless creatures. The thorough but amateurish book of Krall (1912) and the equally thorough but far more expert response of Máday (1914) well represented opposing points of view on this topic, respectively. Griffin's recent (1976) monograph is a most important contribution to this protracted argument, which shows no signs of abating (Shepard 1978). The center ring of contention has shifted (at least in the United States) from horses to marine mammals in the 1960s (Wood 1973: chap. 5), but is now solidly occupied by chimpanzees (*Pan troglodytes* and an occasional *Pan paniscus*), along with a handful of Bay Area gorillas (Sebeok and Umiker-Sebeok 1980). The sideshows continue to feature the most varied sorts of animal species, among which "educated horses" (Bouissac 1976:52) still appear with reliable regularity (Blake 1975, 1977), while birds such as the Gallic Greater Spotted Woodpecker, whose communicative bond with man is alleged to be "analogous to that found by the Gardners and Premack" in apes in America (Chauvin-Muckensturm 1974:185) and whose *"bec est au moins l'égal de la main du chimpanzé"* (ibid.:207), remain perennial favorites.

Amid the long but inconclusive disputation, always emotionally charged and often acrimonious, about the uniqueness of language and/or mind and the attendant literature dealing with language learning in infrahumans, dogs are continually being brought forth for incidental consideration. On occasion, talking dogs are exalted to the front of the stage. Thus Krall (1912:211-224) describes in some detail (and with photographic illustrations) the conversational ability of Don, a German setter belonging to the royal game warden, Hermann Ebers, at Theerhutte, in Gardelegen—"Ich hatte wiederholt Gelegenheit, *Don*, den berühmten Hund . . . 'sprechen' zu hören," he records (ibid.:215); I shall return to this case below (see also Sebeok 1979: chap. 4). He gives quite a few other instances, concluding: "Aus all diesen Veröffentlichungen durfte wohl zur Genuge hervorgehen, dass die Sprechbegabung des Hundes nicht gar so selten auftritt, wie wir bisher annehmen mussten . . ." (Krall 1912:220). His acute critic Máday (1914:228-229) refers to talking dogs only in passing. He correctly refocuses the problem on two more specific questions: Does the dog speak imitatively; and does the dog conjoin a string of sounds, or signifiers, with a particular object or goal? He points out that experts, like Oskar Pfungst—the solver of a Clever Hans conundrum—and Paul Kammerer (whose own troubles with allegations of scientific fraud lay far in the future—see Koestler 1973; Sebeok 1979: chaps. 4, 5), both answered the first question decidedly in the negative, but held that, even if the answer turned out to be in the affirmative, dogs would merely have achieved the level of what parrots do. The second question, Máday acknowledges, is "zumeist zugegeben," but we have already seen that Warden and Warner remained dubious about this concession even a decade and half later.

In the interwar period, some four score and more dogs were "educated," and the interest of scientists, writers (such as Maurice Maeterlinck), animal trainers and circus folk, as well as numberless dilettantes, converged on thinking, talking, counting canines. (Inexplicably, it turns out that 66 percent of these anthropoid dogs were instructed by women!) In 1954, Henny Jutzler-Kindermann, who identified herself as an agronomist, brought together experiences and observations, ranging from 1890 to 1953, about sixteen horses, one cat, and no fewer than 88 dogs. Her sedulous collection—obviously a labor of love—accentuates the positive. Actually, it is a gallimaufry of unreliable lore in which rare nuggets of useful information are embedded here and there. Graham Greene, in his amusing essay, "Great Dog of Weimar," poked gentle fun at "Lola Kindermann, the airedale, and her father Rolph Meokel [read Rolf Moeckel], of Mannheim." (For the case history of Lola, see Jutzler-Kindermann 1954:56-76. When Lola was asked to explain how dogs knew so much, she replied that all dogs have taken an oath—like honorable stage magicians—not to reveal this secret [cf. Jastrow's devastating, if short, analysis of this case, 1935:213-214].) Greene remarks (1969:323) that he has "always suspected dogs: solid, well-meaning, reliable, they seem to possess all the least attractive human virtues. What bores, I have sometimes thought, if they could speak, and now my most appalling conjectures have been confirmed." A more sinister concern with Kindermann's Clever Dogs was evinced by Hermann Goering, who proposed that their talents for communication be put to serve the State's interest, but there is no indication that they were thus actually used by the Nazis. (A similar role was later envisioned for the possible naval utilization of small whales; this program is discussed, under the heading "Kamikaze Porpoises," by Wood [1973:209-220].)

The Jutzler-Kindermann omnibus by no means satisfied the specialized clientele attracted to this sort of Museum of Canine Wonders. There followed the book of Borgese (1968: chap. 2), with her saga of some English setters, notably one Arli, whom she claimed to have taught to read, as well as, beginning in 1963, to type—including spontaneous "concretist" poetry—on an electric Olivetti. Borgese believed that, at least in instances where his motivation was high, Arli did associate a string of letters with a particular signified (ibid.:53). Since typing is almost always an automatic process—for human secretaries as much as for dogs—the implied resemblance is discomposing. Emily Hahn (1978:35) noted, not altogether reassuringly, "Sometimes Mrs. Borgese forgot . . . that Arli couldn't really read or write. . . . She found it necessary now and then

to remind herself of this, otherwise she would be getting false notions."
In fact, Borgese's style of writing is so effusive that her interpretations of
her dogs' feats are, to put it in the kindest way, ambiguous.

The latest—but doubtless not the last—contribution to this flourishing
genre is by Rowdon (1978). His book, which reads rather like artless
fiction, reveals a naiveté about unconscious sensory cueing that is hard
to endure and is embogged in every imaginable trap in which the Clever
Hans Fallacy can inveigle an unwary mark, as well as implicated in a
few novel perversions. The operator Hilde Heilmaier, of Berchtesgaden,
and Dorothy Meyer, a teacher in her employ, seemingly convinced this
writer that, in witnessing two dogs tapping à la Hans, he was privileged
to be in the presence of what he repeatedly refers to by a catch phrase,
once suggested by Krall, as "a second Copernican revolution" (e.g., in
the title of chap. 2). Not only were these dogs, Belam, a saluki, and Elke,
a poodle, language-endowed but they also became bilingual. Since they
were slated to appear on television in Anglophone areas, "Mr. Heilmaier
now felt that the dogs should learn a little English" (ibid.:156). It apparently never entered Rowdon's mind that any tapping dog "knows"
every natural language equally well, since the gesture is initiated and
terminated by averbal messages—*minimale Bewegungen*—wittingly given
(as in a con) or unwittingly given off (as in instances of self-delusion)
by the operator. Rowdon ends his book, speculating about "our future,"
on a note of unkempt Oriental mysticism that will do the dog family
no good at all. (It is instructive to contrast his treatment in this respect
with the splendid study by Rensberger [1977], especially as to the wisdom
of the new conservation ethic that the latter calls for.)

"Talking dogs" is a popular cover term for a variety of inculcated
canid semiosic comportments, tapping being one prominent form that
such transmissions take. The tapping behavior of dogs and, of course,
of horses, is analogous to the drumming out of messages by a woodpecker
to its human feeder (Chauvin-Muckensturm 1974); to the transfer of
information by means of certain noises from dolphins to their handlers
(*nota bene*, there being "little reason to believe that they have a means
of communication that can be considered a true language" [Wood 1973:
118]); as well as, in some of its most salient aspects, to silent gestural
message transmittance between literally enthralled apes and their otherwise enthralled trainers (Sebeok and Umiker-Sebeok 1980). Space limitations do not permit me to pursue the ins and outs of this postulated semblance here. I should like, instead, to take a closer look at another sort
of "talking dog." Don, the dog that by all objective accounts barks, yet
is widely avouched to have spoken, will serve as the prototype.

First, it is appropriate to call attention in this connection to the admittedly fuzzy notion of "presupposition," in the extended, pragmatic
sense. Karttunen (1973:169) says that "To presuppose something as a
speaker is to take its truth for granted and to assume that the audience

does the same." In other words, according to this conception, presuppositions inhere in communicating organisms; they are not a property of the messages flowing between interlocutors. In the framework of the case under discussion, and all others like it, three or four parties are assumed to be co-present: 1. the barking dog (or message source), 2. the listening and often eliciting human (or message destination), 3. the operator, and 4. the optional but customary accomplice. For brevity, as well as to properly frame the situation, I rename 1. the subject, 2. the mark, 3. the con, and 4. the shill.

The con must see to it, to begin with, that the wanted presuppositions get planted in the mark, or, according to another terminology, that an appropriate "semiotic key" (Bouissac 1976:190) is turned on. This is usually accomplished with the assistance of a shill, who is, in an ordinary confidence game, the decoy whom the mark sees winning—the "fourth business" (to introduce a theatrical figure), who lurks, so to speak, in the wings. The shill is used to impart an aura of legitimacy to the proceedings, increasing the probability that the mark's expectations will be fulfilled. Shill-induced presuppositions work much in the manner of medical ritual trappings that tend to assure that the placebo being administered will effectively relieve some complaint, or as does the Cyrano-like audience perspective that furthers the enactment of the dramatic episode commonly known as the hypnotic scene (as is evident from Theodore R. Sarbin's beautiful dramaturgical metaphor of hypnosis, also supported by Ernest R. Hilgard's allied concept of the "hidden observer"—see also Sebeok 1979: chaps. 10 and 5).

In the circus world, the keying begins with carefully planted advance publicity, reinforced by the circus poster, the unique semiotic status of which Bouissac (1976: chap. 10) has described so elegantly. The media, as it were, are placed in the role of a shill. In the matter of Don, for instance, the press served as a quasi-metonymic shill, much as the semi-private epistles of Leibniz to Paris did two centuries earlier: Their function was to create the atmosphere of confidence, or the felicitous sincerity conditions (Karttunen 1973:170), initially required for playing the illusion out. It could not help affecting Leibniz's own sensibility that no less a personage than the Imperial Prince Regent himself had told him that he had twice seen and scrupulously tested the dog at the Leipzig fair. Just so, the French recipients of Leibniz's letters in turn placed their full reliance on the distinguished philosopher's report, even though, up to that time, Leibniz had not yet himself witnessed the dog's act. It is no coincidence that "Extensive comment has been made in the German and even in the American daily press on the reported conversational ability of 'Don,'" and that "Numerous observers reported that he had a vocabulary consisting of eight words . . ." (Johnson 1912:749). The requisite presuppositions had thus been put in place by the journalists, and the rumor mill ground out its curtain-raising work of metasignification. This sour view of publicity is in line with previous research suggesting "that the impact of newspaper stories may be at once more general and more grave than was previously suspected" (Phillips 1978: 749). The show could now begin.

What the main act consisted of was Don speaking (not tapping or typing),

> if food were held before him and the following questions propounded: "Was heisst du?" "*Don.*" "Was hast du?" "*Hunger.*" "Was willst du?" "*Haben haben.*" "Was ist das?" "*Kuchen.*" "Was bittest du dir aus?" "*Ruhe.*" Moreover, he was set to answer categorical questions by "*Ja*" and "*Nein*"; and in reply to another question to speak the name, "*Haberland.*" [Johnson 1978]

Like the horse Hans, Don could be questioned in any language. Unlike Hans, however, he replied not in a sign language but in spoken German. One of Don's interlocutors chanced to be Oskar Pfungst, the same gifted psychologist who had figured out the correct solution to the Clever Hans problem, and who, of course, by no means shared the presuppositions of the general public. Pfungst thoroughly investigated the dog's behavior, in part on the basis of a number of phonographic documents that he had recorded. His conclusions, first briefly published in a newspaper supplement, on April 27, 1911, were subsequently summarized in *Science* by Johnson (1912), himself an expert on the acoustic behavior of dogs.

In the process of recording, a curious acoustic transformation occurred—or so it seemed. In place of the real Don's spoken German, the recorded Don produced only disyllabic and monosyllabic noises that, to disinterested hearers, i.e., those whose presumptions had not been doctored, sounded like nothing so much as ordinary barking. Pfungst quickly established two facts: that the dog invariably answered all questions with answers, from "*Don*" to "*Ruhe,*" ordered in the same sequence—if the arrangement of the elements in the questioning changed, his responses turned out to be inappropriate or "ungrammatical"; and that Don learned nothing by observation and imitation.

Pfungst then decided, correctly, "that the speech of Don is therefore to be regarded properly as the production of vocal sounds which produce illusions in the hearer" (ibid.:750). The explanation for this susceptibility derives from the circumstance that

> the uncritical do not make the effort to discriminate between what is actually given in perception and what is merely associated imagery, which otherwise gives to the perception a meaning wholly unwarranted; and they habitually ignore the important part which suggestion always plays in ordinary situations. [Ibid.:751]

The riddle of the talking dog thus stands fully elucidated: When the effect is not altogether chimerical, the underlying mechanism must either be intentional cueing (deception) or unintentional cueing (self-deception). Perhaps it is as well to recall here a story told of Dr. Samuel Johnson, in whose presence a fatuous lady made her dog perform tricks. The Doctor was unimpressed. The lady exclaimed, "But, Dr. Johnson, you don't know how difficult it is for the dog!" Dr. Johnson replied, "Difficult, Madam? Would it were impossible."[3]

A singular feature of quantum mechanics that has emerged from a recent series of experiments appears to be the possibility that the observer's knowledge or ignorance has some influence on the state of the particle observed. In semiotics, it is an established fact that, in searching for an understanding of the nature of dyadic communication, we have often been misled to search in the message destination for what should have been sought in the source (Sebeok 1979: chap. 5). Our brief but close encounters with canid communication of the third kind have once again underscored this common error: the secret is concealed not in the dog but in the man. Accordingly, this essay is meant as a reminder that the actor's influence is decisive, and of the correlated fact that presuppositions (or, more generally, context) are ignored at one's peril.[4]

NOTES

1. Martin Gardner (personal communication) recently wrote me:

Years ago a magician told me he once worked a show with a mind-reading dog act, and the owner had a "stooge" in the audience who did all the cueing simply by moving a thumbnail to make a slight snap sound. I can't vouch for the truth of this, but the fingernail method seems to be a simple way to cue a dog. Even the trainer, on the stage, could do it with his hands behind his back.

2. Heini Hediger (personal communication) calls my attention to Caro, a "singing" fox, who could range over almost two octaves; see also Schmid 1938:108-109.

3. Gardner's favorite talking dog joke, and mine as well, is the oldie about the man who showed a booking agent his dog act. One dog sang while another played the piano. The agent, much impressed, wanted to know how he ever trained the dog to sing so well. "Confidentially," said the trainer, "he can't sing a note. The dog at the piano is a ventriloquist."

4. Sebeok 1979 (especially chap. 10) discusses in detail Jakob von Uexküll's semiotic concept of "Umwelt-Forschung." The talking-dog phenomenon was disposed of, in this particular framework, thirty years ago, by the Menzels, the most knowledgeable specialists of their day as concerns various facets of the social relations prevailing between dog and man, and the designers of many fine experiments with dogs (see, for example, Katz 1937:10, 40, 41, 46, 66, 87, and 88). Since their article (1948) appeared in an obscure and inaccessible magazine, I would like to quote their pertinent paragraph in full:

Der Fehler liegt in der Annahme, die voraussetzt, dass der Hund mit dem Menschen die gleiche Gegenstands- und Tätigkeitswelt gemeinsam hat, dass die gleichen Interessen ihn bewegen. Die heutige Wissenschaft weiss, dass der

Hund, wie jedes andere Tier, auf Grund seiner biologischen Andersartigkeit in einer anderen Umwelt lebt als z. B. der Mensch oder die Maus, d. h., dass der Ausschnitt der Welt, den er erfasst, eben ein hundlicher und kein menschlicher ist. Es ist ein krasser Anthropormorphismus, anzunehmen, dass Hunde sich für Literatur oder Kunst, für Politik und *Weltanschauungsfragen* interessieren, sie interessieren sich für ihre "hundlichen" Dinge, für Futter und Lager, für vierbeinige Gefahrten oder Feinde, für Geschlechtspartner, für Spiel and Kampf, für Geruche, die biologische Bedeutung für sie haben usw. Ihre und unsere Interessen treffen sich nur auf einem kleinen Ausschnitt der beiderseitigen Umwelten; es ist die Kunst der Abrichtung, diesen Ausschnitt etwas zu vergrössern und den Hund ausserdem dazu zu bringen, in diesem Bereich

  1. zu verstehen, was wir von ihm wollen,

  2. das Verlangte auch auszuführen.

Chapter 8

Smart Simians: The Self-Fulfilling Prophecy and Kindred Methodological Pitfalls

> The peculiarity of the case is just that there are so many sources of possible deception in most of the observations that the whole lot of them *may* be worthless. . . . I am also constantly baffled as to what to think of this or that particular story, for the sources of error in any one observation are seldom fully knowable.
>
> —WILLIAM JAMES

INTRODUCTION: MORALITY PLAY OR COMEDY OF MANNERS?

IT HAS BEEN justly observed, most recently by the prominent historian Lynn White, Jr. (1979:74), that "Scientists focus so sharply on objects that they forget to think critically about subjects, that is, themselves." When scientists edit themselves out of their own internal representations of their work, or out of those fashioned for communication with colleagues and laypersons, they become the perpetrators of both self-deception and the deception of others. Left unchecked, years, even decades of human effort—and public funds—can be wasted before a more accurate conception of investigations can be constructed, usually with devastating consequences for those who were the victims of self-inflicted blindness. The turn of the decade witnessed a tidal wave of revelations about the methodological shortcomings of widely praised, long-term projects—one now in progress almost a decade and a half—designed to teach apes language-like skills. Some attacks came from "insiders," or members of competing experimental teams (e.g., Petitto and Seidenberg 1979; San-

---

This article, written in collaboration with Jean Umiker-Sebeok, is the fourth, substantially expanded and continually updated, version of, successively: "Performing Animals: Secrets of the Trade," *Psychology Today* 13(6):78-91 (1979); "Questioning Apes," in *Speaking of Apes*, edited by Thomas A. Sebeok and Jean Umiker-Sebeok (New York: Plenum Press, 1980), pp.1-59; and "Clever Hans and Smart Simians: The Self-Fulfilling Prophecy and Kindred Methodological Pitfalls," *Anthropos* 76(1-2) (1981).

ders and Terrace 1979; Seidenberg and Petitto 1979; Terrace 1979, 1980a, 1980b; Terrace et al. 1979, 1980) and constitute the latest in a long line of expressions of inter-experimenter hostility[1] that led to Griffin to comment:

> The leading groups of experimenters training apes to use symbolic communication share a general faith in the significance of the endeavor, but they are often critical of each other's specific experimental procedures. If one accepts the sharpest of these mutual criticisms, it is tempting to dismiss all of the results as inconclusive. [1978a:555]

In their recent attack on the entire group of projects, including their own, Savage-Rumbaugh et al. do, in fact, dismiss all work prior to 1980, save, needless to say, their current experiments with Austin and Sherman.

> To date, there is no evidence that Washoe, Sarah, Lana, Koko, or Nim achieved symbolization proper. . . . In fact, most ape-language studies have not really gone beyond the basic communicative level of the chimpanzee. [1980a:60]

"Outsiders" have also contributed to the debate (e.g., Desmond 1979; Gardner 1980; Hediger 1980; Ristau and Robbins 1979; Sebeok and Umiker-Sebeok 1980; Thompson and Church 1979; Umiker-Sebeok and Sebeok 1980a), the cumulative effect of which has been to shift some attention away from earlier questions about the nonlinguistic character of the data published by ape "language" researchers and onto the dubious nature of the very procedures employed in training and testing the experimental animals and the interpretations of the results of those procedures.

Throughout a number of critical assessments (especially in the popular press), as well as in defensive counterattacks, animals and humans involved are assigned, either openly or by implication, roles appropriate to a degenerate form of morality play, individual apes and experimenters serving as personifications of Good and Evil, Beast and Humankind. The allegorization of ape "language" projects stems in large part from two facts: First, the research is still being discussed without the benefit of the branches of zoosemiotics that deal with human and ape nonverbal communication, whether intra- or interspecific, in scientific or nonscientific settings. Second, despite the considerable variety and number of methodological shortcomings so far uncovered, with more sure to come, little attention has been paid either the vast literature on sources of deception in behavioral research in general or the wealth of information about deceptive communication available in the oral and written statements of animal trainers, stage magicians, and other performers. Drawing from these varied and underutilized sources, this chapter will demonstrate, through the critical evaluation of the self-fulfilling prophecy— particularly the Clever Hans Effect—and kindred methodological pitfalls at play in attempts to teach language skills to apes, that such projects, far from being morality plays, are rather a kind of comedy of manners, additional entries in an already thick catalogue of fads and fallacies in the name of science (Gardner 1957). Investigators and experimenters, outwardly absorbed by the pursuit of the idealized abstractions that inform their investigations, but driven by somewhat ruthless, down-to-earth aims, have generally failed to check their own personal attitudes, feelings, and expectations and the role that these play in their interactions with specific experimental animals. Thus we find the ape "language" researches replete with personalities who believe themselves to be acting according to the most exalted motivations and sophisticated manners, but who in reality have involved themselves in the most rudimentary circuslike performances.

VARIETIES OF INTERSPECIFIC COMMUNICATION

A common definition of communication involves nothing more than the moving of information in time from one place to another. From this point of view, it is of little consequence whether the trafficked ware consists of random noise, the 10^{10} bits of information inherent in a strand of DNA programmed to rebuild itself, or some configuration of signs, like a sonata by Mozart, charged with high aesthetic value. If information is available, it can be communicated.

Semiosis, or a triadic cooperative production involving a sign, its object, and its interpretant (Peirce 1935-66:5.484), is as much a criterial attribute of all life as is the ability to metabolize. Whatever form life may assume, two basic activities that sustain interaction with its environment are the packing and discharging of nutrients and gases in order to grow or derive energy, and the processing of signs in order to maneuver and operate information so as to maximize the chances of the survival of its kind.

Just as there are different sorts of strategies for metabolic activity, there are also various kinds of communication devices. Plants, for example, are characterized by an autotrophic reaction: the organism derives energy from sunlight. Animals employ heterotrophic reaction: they usually receive nourishment from organic compounds outside their own bodies. Phytosemiosic techniques have hardly begun to be scientifically explored, so our knowledge of them is still very much at a rudimentary level. The investigation of the enormous variety of zoosemiotic systems, on the other hand, has long interested humanity, and, during the last quarter of the century, has emerged as the cardinal area of concentration in the biological study of animal behavior (see chap. 6 of this volume).

Broadly speaking, two principal modes of communicative behavior can be demarcated in animals for purposes of research: intraspecific and interspecific. Each species of animal possesses a unique code. By adverting to this code, an amalgam of partially inherited and partially learned components, the conspecific membership can exchange messages that tend biologically and/or socially to promote the welfare of that population. This vast heterogeneous category of substratal communicative events (Sebeok 1977a) will concern us hereafter only incidentally.

Interspecific communication, by contrast, always entails more than one specific code, the number depending on the complexity of the ecosystem occupied by animals belonging to different species that congregate there to their mutual advantage (see p. 112 above). In mixed populations, where members of every participant species necessarily co-exist in some sort of affiliation with individuals of another—relationships such as parasitism, commensalism, mutualism, or, more generally, symbiosis—some messages flowing to and fro are registered against a higher-order, as it were, xenogeneic code. A quantum of knowledge of that code is necessarily shared by concerned communicants belonging to separate but allied species, say, the oxpecker (*Buphagus africanus*) calling out to the rhinoceros prior to alighting on its skin, or to the zebra signifying by its posture (legs spread, tail raised, ears drooping) its own readiness to be cleansed. The insects, ticks, or other parasites infesting the quadruped also constitute an essential part of this particular communicative network. The permutation in mutually modifying response patterns of this second kind can become very elaborate indeed when the members of one species are barraged by the displays of one or more others that, in turn, react to displays of *theirs*.

The intricacy of the animal's environment may be heightened still further in the interesting special case when one of the participating species in the system chances to be man. It is on some varieties of this type of communicative dyad that we shall focus in what follows.

The circumstances under which man may encounter animals, necessitating that each party learn—even if never entirely master—the essential elements of the reciprocal's own code, are many and varied. A few of the most common situations in which man/animal interactions take place (cf. Hediger 1969: chap. 4) can be identified and briefly exemplified:

1. Man preys upon, even annihilates, an animal species for different reasons—some, like antelopes, may be hunted down as game; certain carnivores (such as the East African crocodile) are condemned as "vermin"; primates are overused in medical research; marsupials are killed for their hides; and cetaceans are exploited for their oil (cf. Ehrenfeld 1972). In effect, every time a population of animals is exterminated, a unique communicative code is concurrently and irreversibly eliminated.

2. Man becomes the casualty of an animal's depredations; individuals of the Southeast Asian *Anopheles balabacensis*, one of perhaps fifty species of this genus, may come into noisome taction with man (even now, more people die each year of mosquito-borne disease than from any other single cause; see Gillett 1973).

3. Man co-exists with an animal in some sort of partnership, for example, in a purely guest/host relationship (as aquarium fishes with their master) or in a nexus of mutual dependency (such as a Seeing Eye dog working in the service of a blind person, or a cormorant catching fish for a Japanese fisherman and being rewarded with food according to the size of the catch).

4. Parasitism may work in either direction.

a. The activities of man in relation to the reindeer (Zeuner 1963: 46-48), for instance, can be described as those of a social parasite. We are the exploiting species, taking advantage of its greed, sated only when the reindeer licks up salty matter (like human urine) that attracts and binds the animal to human camps. The Masai custom of drinking the blood of cattle without killing them is another example of parasitism in which the human guest lives, especially in times of famine, on body fluids of the host.

b. Each of us has about as many organisms on the surface of our skin as there are people on earth. The mite *Demodex*, crab lice, fleas, and bedbugs are but a few samples of the teeming miniature parasitic population sharing our ecology (see, e.g., Rosebury 1969).

5. An animal may accept a human as a conspecific. As early as 1910, Heinroth described the attachment of incubator-hatched greylag goslings to human beings. These goslings reject any goose and gander as parent objects, opting instead to look upon humans as their exclusive parents. Many other hand-reared birds were later found to have transferred their adult sexual behavior toward their human caretakers. Morris and Morris (1966a:182; see also Morris 1979:271) have recounted attempts by a "fully humanized" female panda, Chi-Chi, to mate with her keepers (including Desmond Morris); and the ardent sexual advances of a male dolphin, Peter, toward his female trainer, Margaret Howe, were recorded in her published protocol (Lilly 1967:274f.).

6. An animal may define a human as a part of its inanimate environment,[2] as when men are driving through a wildlife park in a closed vehicle. In certain circumstances, small mammals (such as bats, house-mice) and even some larger ones (e.g., koala bears) will grasp a human limb and, mistaking it for an insensate substrate, climb it.

7. Taming, defined as the reduction, or possibly total elimination, of an animal's flight reaction from man, may be deliberately induced. This precondition is indispensable for both training and domestication. In the latter not only the care and feeding but most particularly the breeding of the animal—or communication of genetic information from one generation to the next—have to some degree come under human control. (When the biologically altered domesticated animal breaks out of control, it is referred to as "feral," as opposed to "wild.")

8. Man trains an animal. Such management may take one of two counterpolar forms:

a. A rat forced to swim under water to escape drowning is taught to take the alley in a submerged Y-maze when the correct decision is indicated by the brighter of the two alleys; a porpoise is brought under behavioral control to locate and retrieve underwater objects. Such efforts are called *apprentissage,* loosely rendered as "scientific training," or in German, "wissenschaftliche Dressur."

b. A horse is taught to perform a comedy act for purposes of exhibition (Bouissac 1976: chap. 8); a porpoise is taught to play basketball. Such efforts are called *dressage,* or circus (*viz.,* oceanarium) training, or "höhere Dressur."

Apprentissage and *dressage* are fundamentally distinct ways of shaping behavior, although from a semiotic point of view they constitute complementary measures, in particular as regards their pragmatic import. This variance was intuitively appreciated by Hediger as early as 1935 in his dissertation and was later substantially advanced in several of his published writings (e.g., 1968:120f.; 1974). For instance, Hediger insightfully emphasized that *apprentissage* entails a reduction of the animal-man nexus to as close to zero as feasible. *Dressage,* on the other hand, requires a maximum intensification of the ligature, with the richest possible emotional involvement. This is one dimension along which the signs employed fluctuate. Apropos *dressage,* Breland and Breland (1966:108) related an interesting informal observation concerning the emotional component of a parrot's vocalization: in the exhibition in question, the bird picks up a toy telephone, holds it up to his ear, and says "Hello!" Afterwards he receives a peanut. It was noted that every time the bird said "Hello," "the pupils of his eyes contracted and dilated remarkably." This sign is emitted solely in an emotionally charged situation, for the pupil-size cue may not occur if the bird is talking merely for peanuts (for kindred observations in domestic cats, see Hess 1975:116f.). The second dimension oscillates, in Hediger's words (1938:243), between "Dressur ohne Affektaufwand" and "Dressur mit bedeutendem Affektaufwand."

TWO MODES OF ANIMAL TRAINING: APPRENTISSAGE VERSUS DRESSAGE

Some of the searches for primate language capacity clearly constitute strivings toward pure *apprentissage;* others can more readily be characterized as leaning toward *dressage.* But most of these projects fall somewhere between these two ideal types of semiosic construction because of both the practical and the theoretical constraints on such investigations. On the practical side, it was found that experimental ape subjects perform poorly if they are deprived of a congenial social environment. Gill and Rumbaugh report, for example:

> During early training we maintained that Lana should have little interaction with the experimenter so that her strict training schedule would not be disputed. We soon found, however, that the social aspect of lan-

guage training was of great importance. Accordingly, we modified our
initial decision and began allowing increased social contact between Lana
and the experimenters. Lana did much better in an informal social setting
with the training procedures modified as needed. [Rumbaugh 1977:161]

Premack, too, describes the "most efficacious training phase" as the
one in which Sarah's trainer worked inside her cage, sitting on one side
of the table with Sarah on an adjacent side (1976:24). "The whole arrangement was intimate," he writes. "Sarah's hand could be guided when
needed and her head turned gently in a desired direction to assure attention. Astute cajoling often served to stretch out the lesson. Trainers
held her hand, patting and encouraging her with affectionate tones.
Sometimes she reciprocated, gently chucking the trainer under the chin"
(ibid.:25). Sarah was rewarded with tidbits. Although Premack, so far
as we know, did not test to see whether Sarah would have performed
as well without such material reinforcements, he emphasizes the importance of the rapport between trainer and chimpanzee by supposing that
"social approval . . . would have proved to be a more potent reward"
than the food (ibid.:27).

Trainers, even those educated in the tradition of the experimental
technique of *apprentissage,* also appear to derive a great deal of satisfaction from a close, emotional involvement with their ape charges. It is
not uncommon for young apes to elicit parental feelings of attachment
in their caretakers, as evidenced in the following passage by Ann Premack,
who played an active role in training Sarah as well as in planning the
chimpanzee's overall teaching program:

> People who raise chimps have high expectations for them as they have for
> their own children, and when the chimps don't perform at these levels,
> the "parents" are often bitter. . . . Aside from a human baby, I can think
> of no creature which can arouse stronger feelings of tenderness than an
> infant chimpanzee. It has huge round eyes and a delicate head and is far
> more alert than a human infant of the same age. When you pick up a
> young chimp, it encircles your body with its long, trembling arms and
> legs, and the effect is devastating—you want to take it home! [1976:16-17][3]

In contrast to experiments in which a chimpanzee being given linguistic training is raised as much as possible as a regular member of a
human family (e.g., Hayes 1951; Kellogg and Kellogg 1933; Temerlin
1975), reports of a trainer's subjective reactions to his or her ape subject
in more recent ape language projects are rare, probably because they are
thought to be irrelevant to the scientific aims of training and testing.
Since every trainer, even one brought in from the outside for purposes
of blind testing, must go through several "get acquainted" sessions in
order to work directly with the animal subject, it would appear that the
reluctance to allude to, let alone analyze, such encounters, which seem
to be in some ways as fundamental a part of *apprentissage* as of the more

explicitly emotive technique of *dressage,* is due more to received notions concerning scientific method and *apprentissage* in general than to the actuality of each case. A more candid expression of these human affective responses, such as Ann Premack's early associations of the relationship between herself and Sarah with memories of her childhood experiences with a retarded sister, and the slow process of accommodation between herself and the chimpanzee, would no doubt furnish a richer picture of the actual circumstances in which humans are pursuing their overt stated goal of *apprentissage.*

Tradition dictates that the ape's "learning" begins only during the next stage—during the first actual training sessions—and that this type of encounter warrants a fuller description than the preceding one, in which trainer and subject first strive to establish a social rapport, i.e., they learn to interpret and respond to one another's signs—come to share, in sum, a common semiosic code—in such a way that mutual understanding will thereafter become possible. As alluded to above, even scholars such as Premack and Rumbaugh, who are careful to achieve as emotion-free a context as possible for their work, admit that "interpersonal" communication of affect is a *sine qua non* of a successful training or testing session, and yet, strangely, they are quick to deny that the exchange of such information interferes with the attainment of more or less pure *apprentissage.* The implication is, of course, that communication may be neatly divided into two types—affective and symbolic—and that the two are independent and may be separated one from the other at will. However, speaking of ape communication in general (and this would presumably apply as well to intraspecific communication among humans), Marler notes that "[i]t is important not to underestimate the potential richness of the information content of affective signalling" and, further, citing Premack himself, "as long as there is some concordance between the preferences and aversions of communicants then a remarkable amount of information can be transmitted by an affective system" (1980:226).

It is ironic that David Premack should defend the affective communication system of apes (and presumably humans) and then proceed more or less to ignore the importance of the affective communication taking place between his experimental chimpanzees and their trainers. This is especially puzzling because, in his descriptions of interactions between Sarah and her trainers, there is frequent allusion to the human's emission of nonverbal signs. Describing Sarah's extralinguistic antics, for example, he writes that "[W]hen she miscalculated in her gymnastics and fell 6-8 feet to a concrete floor, she rose without a whimper, often to come over to investigate *the grimacing trainer whose face was wreathed in emphatic pain*" (Premack 1976:27; our emphasis). After sixteen months of training in the intimate conditions described above, Sarah became sexually mature and sometimes dangerous, so that training had to be carried on through a small door in her cage, human and chimpanzee on opposite sides. This arrangement proved less successful than the preceding one. "It was now difficult to pat Sarah and hold her hand, and she rejected far more lessons than she had in the first phase" (ibid.:28).

The emotional commitment of Sarah's trainers to her success is even palpable in the following passage, where Premack is denying that the Clever Hans Phenomenon played a part in his project: "There were numerous informal contraindications of social clues, the most vital of which were the clever innovations made by the subjects themselves. *These innovations delighted and surprised the trainers, for they were in no way traceable to the training*" (ibid.:29; our emphasis). It is reasonable to assume that the emotions of delight and surprise were expressed at least nonverbally in the presence of the chimpanzees, and could in fact have served as added reinforcing cues. Savage-Rumbaugh et al. (1980a: 54) comment on this source of cuing:

> When one is trying very hard to teach a chimpanzee a symbol it is quite difficult not to show displeasure or pleasure as it starts to fail or succeed. One may thus cue a chimpanzee by showing approval as it starts to make the correct sign or select the correct symbol. Because the chimpanzee does not have an inherent predisposition toward referential learning, it readily becomes dependent upon the experimenter's help, and as the experimenter tries to give the chimpanzee less help, the chimpanzee looks for more minimal cues.

In the Premack project and in other similar ones, this sort of personal involvement in the outcome of training and testing could be due to the trainer's relationship to the project itself as well as to the appealing chimpanzee or gorilla subjects. A graduate student, for example, may strive for successful performances as a way of pleasing his employer, the principal investigator, or both himself and his professor, should he be developing a doctoral thesis from his work with the ape. The principal investigators themselves, of course, require success in order to obtain continued financial support for the project, as well as personal recognition and career advancement. Such behavior is far from uncommon in the academic world, of course. Barber (1976:36-44, 60-63) has reviewed a large number of studies documenting cases of intentional fudging of data both by principal investigators, who are often in intense competition for funds and prestige, and by experimenters, who, if they do not have a stake in the research itself, may fail to follow required procedures or "improve" data in order to carry out assigned tasks and hand in materials that will be acceptable to the investigator.

Whatever the reason, it is immediately clear to an outside visitor to any of the ape "language" projects, or to anyone who talks at length with those involved in them, that the animals are surrounded by a dedicated group of enthusiastic workers, one that constitutes a tightly knit social community with a solid core of shared beliefs and goals in opposition to outside visitors, as well as against groups elsewhere that are competing for scarce research resources. In fact, it is difficult to imagine a skeptic being taken on as a member of such a "team." The fervor of the team members increases with the amount of time that individuals have spent on the project, which, in some cases, now exceeds ten years. The total dedication required for projects of this sort may partially explain why it seems to be the rule rather than the exception that the work becomes a family affair, the principal investigators—husband and wife (e.g., the Gardners, the Premacks, and the Rumbaughs)—both becoming deeply involved. Often graduate students, younger colleagues, and even, as in one case, relatives of the principal investigators serve as the subjects' uncles and aunts, or members of an extended family.

No matter what the sociological and psychological context of the different ape "language" projects, or the degree to which each approaches *apprentissage* as opposed to *dressage,* those involved are for the most part unaware of the literature on *dressage.* How many psychologists, we wonder, have ever even glanced at Hachet-Souplet's eye-opening chapters (1897:79-91) on "le dressage du singe," reporting training procedures traceable back to at least the thirteenth century and reaching a stage of modern sophistication by the eighteenth?[4] This knowledgeable circus buff and observer of its world of wonders puts in doubt even educated monkeys' supposed ability to imitate human movements, and tells us how that illusion is built up by dint of their quadrumanous configuration. Part of the difficulty in properly assessing attempts at *apprentissage,* such as in the ape "language" projects, or apparently miraculous performances, such as talking animals (Sebeok 1979: chap. 5; chap. 7 of this volume), is that the experts called in to judge such events are usually trained only in *apprentissage.* It is precisely the person who is thoroughly familiar with *dressage* (e.g., Hediger, the world's leading expert on the psychology of animals in captivity, especially man-animal communication in zoos and circuses—see 1968, 1969, 1974) or other performance-oriented activities, such as conjury (e.g., Christopher 1970; Randi 1975), or a combination of scientific methodology and conjury (e.g., Diaconis 1978; Gardner 1957, 1966) who is best able to detect the operation of subtle affective cues—whether unwitting and therefore self-deceptive, or aimed at misleading others—in a supposedly "controlled," emotion-free laboratory experiment.

GREAT EXPECTATIONS

All the ape "language" studies fall into the eighth category of man-animal interactions, or man training animal, in which further far-reaching distinctions must now be introduced. Two variables of direct concern in the present context are: the performance intended to be induced and the organism selected for the training. As for the former, the class of behaviors most pertinent are those involving attempts to *humanize* an animal, that is, to attribute to it hominine traits, indeed, "to endow the animal with psychical capabilities like those of men, and to say that it acts from similar motives" (Katz 1937:19). This anthropomorphism is associated with the romantic indulgences of the school of Romanes. Griffin (1976:68-71), particularly in reference to nonverbal communication, suggests "that it is more likely than not that thoughts or mental experiences in people and animals share important properties without being completely identical" (1976:70). He cautions "that enthusiastic observers of animals are constantly in danger of interpreting their behavior in more complex terms than is necessary or correct" (ibid.:72), and proffers the Clever Hans effect as "an outstanding example" (ibid.). More recently, the special issue of *The Behavioral and Brain Sciences* devoted to "Cognition and Consciousness in Nonhuman Species" and featuring articles by Griffin (1978a), Premack and Woodruff (1978), and Savage-Rumbaugh, Rumbaugh, and Boysen (the last reprinted as 1980b), plus a lengthy section of commentaries by a wide range of discussants, brings this problem sharply into focus, especially from the perspective of input from projects designed to teach apes language-like skills to the establishment of a cognitive ethology. Nowhere is the matter of anthropomorphic tendencies among ape "language" researchers more thoroughly or more cogently discussed than in Desmond (1979), where the problem is traced back to the earlier primate experiments and observations that gave rise to modern approaches.

Several separate but intertwined issues appear to be at stake here—namely, the risk that the beliefs, aspirations, and expectations of investigators and experimenters will lead to (1) inaccurate observations and/or recordings of ape behaviors; (2) the overinterpretation of ape performances; or (3) the unintended modification of an animal's behavior in the direction of the desired results. It is to these subjects that the following sections of this chapter are devoted.

OBSERVATIONAL AND RECORDING ERRORS

The first of these issues is especially important for the analysis of projects attempting to teach apes the American Sign Language of the deaf (ASL), since in the methods of observation and informal testing it was unclear exactly what should be counted and recorded. As several studies have shown (see Barber 1976:74-75), the expectations of the experimenters can affect how they interpret or score responses of their subjects. But this issue is certainly relevant as well to researches using artificial symbol systems. Barber (ibid.:57-59), in fact, reviews studies showing that experimenters not infrequently make errors in recording events, and that these mistakes are generally in the direction of the experimenters' expectations or desires, and illustrates the relevance of this particular type of pitfall to any experimental procedure (cf. Rosenthal 1978).

Beginning with the seminal work of the Gardners with the chimpanzee Washoe, all subsequent ASL research with either chimpanzees (that led by Fouts, late of Oklahoma, and by Terrace and Bever, in New York) or gorillas (by Patterson, formerly at Stanford) has been open to question as to the accuracy of the observations of spontaneous signing by ape subjects in more or less informal, conversational settings. The Gardners report (1980a:300) that in their original work with Washoe as well as with later subjects (Moja, Pili, Tatu, and Dar), the criterion of reliability of reporting sign acquisition was that a sign be reported on three independent occasions by three different observers, at which point it is listed as an acquired sign. Such a sign was counted as a "reliable item of vocabulary" only when, in addition, it had been noted to occur "spontaneously" and "appropriately" at least once on each of fifteen consecutive days.

The Gardners claim that these are much more stringent criteria than those used by students of language acquisition by children, e.g., by asking the parent to list new words—a technique, by the way, no longer favored in modern child language studies—or by taking random samples of a child's speech on different occasions. However, such comparisons are not altogether appropriate. In contrast with the situation of a parent and a language-learning child, for example, the assistants teaching the chimpanzees are brought into contact with the animals for the sole purpose of inculcating in them certain carefully programmed communication skills. They are thus more narrowly and intensely focused on a restricted range of the learner's behavior than is a mother or father in a home setting. In addition, they have frequent discussions with one another and with project leaders about signs they believe they have seen, doubtless even reading one another's notes and research diaries. Utilizing such a method—and this procedure was followed also by Fouts, Patterson, and Terrace—one observer may prime another to create inadvertently situations in which a newly reported sign is likely to recur; for example, by using a certain tool when the sign for that object has been reported by another observer. This outcome is especially likely since the trainers were instructed by the Gardners to record the context in which a new sign was observed as well as the sign itself. Should the ape actually produce a sign in this sort of context, it would not be considered the result of outright prompting, molding, or the Clever Hans Effect, all of which the Gardners deny played a role in the reporting of new signs, and yet such innocent provision of opportunities for corroboration of other observers' records would certainly influence the overall course of the study.

Other methods employed in the ape ASL projects make such distortions even more likely. To take the Gardners' project as an example, "old" signs were, first of all, continually reassessed to see if they had become a permanent part of the chimpanzee's repertory. Reassessment consisted of deliberately introducing the appropriate context for such signs if they had not yet appeared spontaneously during the day. New signs that had not yet met the criterion were elicited, for example, by presenting a picture of a cow, since it would be unlikely that the chimpanzees would see a real one fifteen days in a row, and, finally, new signs were taught through prompting and molding.

A second weakness in the reporting procedures in this type of enterprise is that after conferring with one's colleagues about new signs, one may be more inclined to interpret a certain gesture on the part of the ape as the new sign reported yesterday by someone else. If a sign has come up in conversation, it is only to be expected that this knowledge will predispose observers to interpret any gesture that remotely resembles that sign configuration as the sign itself, in the manner of a *pars pro toto*. Thus Clifford and Bull (1978:161) have shown that when a group of witnesses gets together to reconstruct an event, it may produce a more complete account of details, but "at the cost of increased inaccuracy with groups obtaining 40 per cent more errors of commission than individuals. . . . Group interactions may pressure witnesses into offering inferences rather than perceptions, or even into prefabrications." It is thus misleading to emphasize either the independence of observations or the spontaneity of the apes' performances, since the actual working conditions of such projects considerably reduce both elements.[5]

That reports of ape signs may be incorrect is even more likely when one considers that trainers were commonly asked to keep daily diaries, for which they had to rely on their memory of sign exchanges that occurred while many other events were competing for their attention. Anyone who has ever attempted to reconstruct a dialogue that took place even a few minutes earlier knows how difficult a task this is, even if one only tries to capture the basic form of each utterance, ignoring all the paralinguistic and nonverbal elements that infused and surrounded it.[6]

There are several other methodological considerations that cast doubt on the objectivity of the record-keeping procedures involving signing apes. The Gardners report that as their subjects matured and the frequency of signs increased, maintaining a complete inventory of signs and contextual descriptions became impossible. "Often the brisk pace of an extended conversational interchange precludes verbatim recording." It thus became necessary to employ a different method of recording: during a specified period, "everything signed by the chimpanzee," as well as contextual descriptions, was recorded. These sign protocols required a team of two persons, one whispering an immediate spoken transcription of signing, together with notes about context, into a tape recorder, the other "performing the usual role of teacher, caretaker, playmate, and interlocutor" (1980a:311). The Gardners patterned this method after the work of Roger Brown and his colleagues with language-learning children, but in so doing overlooked the critical difference between the medium of communication being studied in each case. The majority of the assistants working with signing apes are native speakers of English, having learned ASL only for limited use during their participation in the project. These observers are thus placed in a situation where they must transform one sign system, ASL, which is for them a secondary form of communication, into another, speech, which requires not a simple translation within a single channel, but an entire transmutation from the visual to the acoustic mode. It seems reasonable to conclude that there would be a far greater rate of misinterpretation in this type of situation than in one where a speaker of, say, English, were called upon to make a simultaneous translation of the utterances made by a language-learning child in a spoken language—say, Hungarian—in which that observer is not fluent!

The simultaneous recording of children's speech, even when in one's own native linguistic code, is itself difficult, especially when undertaken within the rapid, noise-filled context of a young child's living quarters. Errors are easily introduced at every stage of the process—from the original observations to the final transcription of the tape itself. It is puzzling that critics of the ASL ape projects have overlooked this fundamental shortcoming of this method of data collection. Despite the not inconsiderable number of sources of misjudgment, they seem to take for granted the reliability of observers, based largely, one would assume, on their trust in the spot checks made by so-called expert witnesses who are proficient in ASL and who testify that they have in fact observed the apes making what they took to be genuine ASL signs. We shall return to the question of the reliability of such expert testimony.

Further possible sources of error can be uncovered if one imagines what kind of communication could be taking place between the pair of humans involved in the team recording sessions described above. Reports indicate that trainers and observers enter these situations with the tacit understanding that it is the chimpanzee's, not one another's, behavior that is of interest. But surely at least some of the comments of the recorder will be heard by the ape's interlocutor, thus inevitably altering the latter's own interpretations of the ape's signs and in this way influencing the direction the human-ape conversation may take. If the session is to yield usable data, the ape's interlocutor must make sure that the signs are visible to the recorder, and this, coupled with the feedback produced by overhearing a slightly delayed interpretation of the ongoing interaction, and the knowledge that one is performing for an audience, cannot help but make sign exchanges less than completely spontaneous. The construction of reality in such situations would involve communication among all three of the participants, in complex two-directional forms between the two humans and between each human and the ape. By observing the human interlocutor's reactions to the ape's behavior, the reporter is as much cued to the meaning of the exchange as by watching the chimpanzee's performance, just as the human interlocutor is influenced by the spoken interpretation of the interaction by the reporter.[7]

This is not to say that some researchers have not been aware of the springes mentioned above. Terrace and his colleagues, for example, have attempted to check the reliability of their trainers' observations of Nim's signs by having outside observers, some of them, unlike the students, fluent in ASL, witness sessions between the chimpanzee and one of his trainers, and then comparing the two accounts. They state (n.d.:13) that agreement between the teachers' reports and the transcripts of independent observers was between 77 and 94 percent. This figure sounds impressive until one reads, in a footnote, that these levels of agreement were attained only following discussions between the teacher and "independent" observer, during which they attempted to determine whether particular hand movements of Nim's were in fact ASL signs, as against gestures or approximations of signs. The two human participants, in other words, renegotiated the reality of the events in question, leaving us to wonder how much the figures quoted represent what communication took place between the chimpanzee and the teacher, as opposed to what transpired between the two observers. This sort of communication might be compared with discussions between a mother and a stranger concerning the meaning of the utterance of the former's child. The influence of linguistic interpretations over perceptions works in both directions, especially if the stranger is an "authority" on language acquisition, child psychology, or the like. The extent to which students of language acquisition bias a mother regarding her own child's linguistic performances remains unexplored. Terrace and his colleagues are to be applauded for their honesty in reporting this and other procedural steps that others, we suspect, omit from their accounts. It makes it possible for the reader to assess more accurately the reliability and import of the data presented. (See, however, Terrace et al. 1979:901n25.)

To continue with the example of the use of independent observers of Nim's sign behavior, other questions come to mind concerning the collection of data itself, prior to their evaluation. Nim's classroom consisted of a bare, 8'-square room, one wall of which contained a large one-way mirror, beneath which there was a portal used for photographing and videotaping the chimpanzee's behavior. The independent observer sat in an adjacent room, viewing the chimpanzee and the teacher through the one-way mirror. This situation did not preclude the possibility that the observer, who we assume was not deaf (although we are not informed about that), could hear the teacher's spoken account of the interaction and thus receive acoustic as well as visual cues from the teacher concerning the meaning of Nim's gestures. We are not told that sound could *not* transude from the classroom to the observation room, although this seems all the more probable in view of the existence of the portal and the fact that, in order to assure proper recordings of the teacher's and observer's spoken commentaries, all possible sources of noise in the acoustic channel had probably been eliminated. In any case, this one example exposes a few among the many conceivable flaws in the laudable plan to introduce "independent" observers to check the reliability of project personnel.

In a pair of articles published in 1979, Petitto and Seidenberg, members of the Columbia Project Nim, headed by Terrace, trace observational and recording errors in the Fouts, Patterson, and Gardner projects to investigators' and experimenters' ignorance of three crucial things: the natural gestures of apes, the structure of ASL, and the methodology of studies of first language acquisition. Ape researchers, they point out, have not distinguished between the natural nonverbal signs common to apes, both wild and tame, and those that are learned in the course of specific training procedures. Instead,

> all of the apes' communicative behaviors (and some non-communicative ones as well, e.g., scratching) are together classified as "signs." This generic use of the term "sign" with reference to a diverse group of behaviors contributes to uncertainty over the interpretation of their activities. [Seidenberg and Petitto 1979:195]

> Each ape's vocabulary includes signs such as *pick* (signed by picking a part of their anatomy), *hug* (signed by hugging), *tickle* (signed by *tickling*), *kiss* (signed by kissing), *scratch* (signed by scratching), and others. The term "sign" is, in fact, inappropriate since, in contrast to signs, these behaviors do not stand for or represent any referent; they are simply activities exhibited by wild apes. . . . In the sign language projects . . . they are glossed as lexical items, with attendant linguistic implications. Estimates of the size of the apes' vocabularies are inflated when such activities are glossed as 'signs'. These behaviors can be termed 'linguistic' only under a definition so broad it would fail to distinguish between human language and the behaviors of many lower animals. [Petitto and Seidenberg 1979: 170-171]

Once again, we see the results of scientific investigators' failing to take into account the natural behavior of their experimental animals, mistaking species-typical reactions to humans for learned responses. Another example of this fundamental error so common to research in instrumental conditioning is provided by Moore and Stuttard (1979), who demonstrate that "the principal reactions [of domestic cats] described in Guthrie and Horton's classic learning monograph [1946] appear to have been caused by the mere presence of the experimenters" (1979: 1031). Contrary to the claims of Guthrie and Horton, "neither escape nor food reinforcement is necessary for the establishment of such responses. They are species-typical 'greeting' reactions, readily elicited by the sight of human observers" (ibid.).[8]

The apes' natural behaviors, glossed by experimenters as ASL signs, did not resemble the highly stylized ASL signs, according to Seidenberg and Petitto, and "the exact configurations of elements which characterize ASL signs are not observed in the gestures of apes" (1979:196; cf. Petitto and Seidenberg 1979:171). "Evidence concerning the structures and/or expressive devices common to the apes' behavior and to signing in ASL is superficial at best," and it is, in fact, "highly questionable whether Washoe or Koko were taught ASL at all" (Seidenberg and Petitto 1979:208).

> Rather, the apes were taught individual vocabulary signs, some taken directly from ASL, some reduced from ASL signs, and some invented for the ape; these were signed largely in English word order. Since neither the apes nor their teachers used the appropriate grammatical structure or expressive devices, their signing was not ASL; since they did not use grammatical morphemes (e.g., -ing, -ed, -ly) or function words (e.g., a, the, are) they were not following Signed English. The language model in each project was a pidgin sign. In light of these facts, it is misleading to term their behavior signing in ASL. [Ibid.]

The apes' behaviors were described exclusively in terms of hand configurations, while in true ASL, signs are defined along several dimensions simultaneously. The apes failed to learn to use these other expressive devices even after years of training, while deaf children pick them up easily, as a matter of course, and use them even in their early utterances. Other primary signaling devices of ASL, such as eye gaze and facial expressions, were also not employed by the apes (ibid.:209).

A number of techniques developed by students of language acquisition in hearing and deaf children could have been employed by the ape language researchers working with ASL but were not. In fact, many of the methods of observing and testing ape sign acquisition fall prey to precisely those problems of interpretation that stimulated the creation of new methods for studying human language development. "The ape researchers," Seidenberg and Pettito show, "frequently demonstrate unfamiliarity with the basic methodology of language acquisition research" (1979:206). We have, one must conclude, teams of researchers trying to teach animals, whose natural behavior they do not understand except in a very restricted context, a sign system they themselves know very little about, using methods that are not suited to the task. This is, however, only the beginning of the story.

OCKHAM'S RAZOR

The second issue at stake here is the methodological principle of economy of explanation, commonly known as "Ockham's razor": "What can be done with fewer assumptions is done in vain with more." The principal justification for parsimony is the elimination of pseudoexplanatory entities. Criteria for judgment in accounting for any fact, according to Ockham, must derive either from manifest experience (the empiricist criterion of evidence) or from compelling reasoning.

Probably the commonest form of criticism leveled by one ape "language" investigator against another is that simpler, more parsimonious explanations are available to account for a rival's data, whether or not they were gathered through a participant observation method or forced-choice testing. Commenting on the Gardners' use of spontaneous productions to judge knowledge of language, Lenneberg (1980a:81) warns that all of Washoe's spontaneous signs should be disregarded for purposes of assessing her linguistic competence, not only because of the peril of the Clever Hans Effect, but also because, in our attempts to determine the appropriateness of such messages, "we are simply testing our own ingenuity to assign interpretations to productions that might, for all we know, have been emitted randomly. It would always be possible to claim that the ape had 'intended' to tell us something. . . ." Illustrating the principle that the simple concatenation of signs by an animal may be the result of random generation rather than the early application of rules of syntax, Lenneberg provides the following amusing thought experiment:

> Suppose a mathematician wishes to teach an animal a simple arithmetic language consisting of four symbols only. He finds that if he says "three," the animal responds "one, two." He interprets this as a primitive but essentially appropriate and correct *combination of words* by imputing to the animal the intention of wanting to say "one and two (is three)." Soon he discovers that when he says "two" the animal again says "one, two," which delights him; now he has proved that the animal has learned multiplication. When the animal hears "one," it again says "one, two," which, of course, can mean nothing else but that it has caught on to subtraction. And when it says "one, two" upon presentation of "zero" his trainer finally has evidence that the animal has spontaneously learned to do addition with the residue class modulo three! The mathematician may, of course, be correct; but then again, the animal may be responding randomly. The combining of words is of interest only if we can demonstrate the particular type of relationship upon which the combination is based. [1980b: 128]

Overly rich interpretations of chimpanzee and gorilla gestures abound in the published reports. Savage-Rumbaugh and her colleagues (1980b: 375) have repeatedly argued that, given the weak acquisition criteria employed by those working with signing apes—namely, the ability to name pictures or to produce an iconic gesture repeatedly, under the same or similar circumstances—"it is impossible to tell whether the chimpanzee is simply imitating or echoing, in a performative sense, the action or object, or whether the animal is indeed attempting to relay a message." Since, as they further allege, ASL is a highly iconic system of communication, they conclude that there is nothing to prevent us saying parsimoniously that the apes are merely producing "short-circuited iconic sequences." Unless it can be shown, they go on to say, that the ape could competently use a sign apart from the original context in which it was acquired (i.e., in a situation where the actions and signs of the trainer cannot remind the animal of the hand movements used in the sign), the mere announcement that signs occurred in "new contexts" is not sufficient to rule out the possibility that the animal's behavior can be accounted for by the simpler explanations of deferred imitation or error interpreted in a novel manner by the experimenters. The records kept on Washoe, according to Premack, were meant to preserve sense or meaning rather than word order, and, as such, "reflect dispositions of the recording organisms no less than of the organism recorded" (David Premack 1976: 331).[9]

Seidenberg and Petitto (1979:195-200) note that a large proportion of ape "signing" behavior involves indexical and iconic—that is, nonarbitrary—elements. Some of these motivated gestures are, it is true, a part of the ASL used by human signers, but, in contrast with humans, the apes fail to utilize such information within the larger complex, conventional system of ASL.

> If, in fact, a large proportion of the signs are gestural, possibly modifying or extending the apes' natural system of gestures, then the possibility that the remaining signs were learned in a rote fashion and signed using non-linguistic responding strategies increases. We should note that if our interpretations are correct, it is misleading to describe this behavior as "signing," since this term suggests a level of abstraction that is largely absent. Nor is pantomime the correct term, since the apes' behaviors are time-locked to on-going activities, unlike true pantomime. . . . Nim, Washoe, Koko, and other signing pongids show evidence of having learned a "standardized system of gestures." Although modern language may have evolved from such gestural systems . . . , these gestures do not exhibit critical features of human languages. [Ibid.:200]

Much has been made of various experimental apes' so-called innovations, several examples of which—including generalizations of signs and construction of new lexical items—are provided by Gardner (1980), Hill (1980), and others. Unfortunately, the reporting of these instances does not usually provide enough of the context of the occurrence to enable us to rule out the possibility of either trainer suggestion or over-interpretation. Terrace and his associates (1979:895; cf. Terrace 1979; Sebeok and Umiker-Sebeok 1980), for example, note that there is available a more parsimonious explanation for Fouts's report that Washoe was creating a new compound lexical item when she produced *water* plus *bird* in the presence of a swan when asked *what that?* Since Fouts provides no evidence that Washoe characterized the swan as a "bird that inhabits water," we may just as well assume that the chimpanzee, who was very familiar with the question form *what that?*, was merely responding by first identifying a body of water, then a bird (cf. Martin Gardner's comment on this example, 1980:4).

Seidenberg and Petitto (1979:181-183), in discussing the sampling problems of the Gardner, Fouts, and Patterson projects, conclude that without the publication of large corpora of ape utterances, there is no solid evidence in support of interpreting anecdotal reports of behaviors, such as Patterson's description (1978b:88) of Koko's signing *cookie rock* for a stale sweet roll, as proof of an ape's ability to create novel sign forms.

This problem is seen most clearly with respect to the anecdotes that are frequently cited (e.g., *water bird*). In the absence of a corpus, one cannot determine whether such sequences were synthesized through the application of linguistic rules, or merely the result of the ape acting as a random sign generator which happened to emit some interesting-looking strings. The *water bird* example loses much of its force if the ape also combined each of these signs with a large number of other signs (e.g., *water shoe, water banana, cookie bird*, etc.). This alternative is not implausible. As the Terrace et al. (1980) corpus indicates, their subject . . . combined signs into a very large number of permutations, most of which occurred with low frequency. Some of the resulting combinations are fortuitous, others are not. While even the most bizarre combinations could . . . be interpreted metaphorically, it is simpler to assume that they occurred as the result of random pairings of signs or other non-linguistic combinatorial processes. . . . [Seidenberg and Petitto 1979:182; cf. Petitto and Seidenberg 1979:163-164]

When Savage-Rumbaugh et al. looked closely at the novel combinations of signs produced by Lana over a period of two months in 1979 and compared them with the stock phrases used during the same period, they found that, contrary to their earlier, more impressionistic interpretations of such combinations,

many of Lana's novel combinations fell within one or more stock formats, and a few novel combinations of 5-8 words apparently reflected no semantic comprehension of various individual elements in the chain or of the significance of their location with respect to the rest of the chain. Placing the novel utterances within the entire corpus partly removes the problems of the anecdotal and isolated descriptions characteristic of many ape-language reports. [1980a:55]

If a sign or other response produced by an ape appears to be inappropriate, to take a second type of example, human trainers appear all too willing to stretch their imagination in order to make the animal's performance "fit" conversationally. This reminds us of the clever interpretations of the so-called telepathically communicated images drawn by such allegedly psychic persons as Uri Geller. Gullible observers, wishing to believe in the performer's extraordinary powers, eagerly project their own concept onto his sometimes amazingly crude but suggestive scribbles (Randi 1975; cf. Randi 1978). Thus anomalous chimpanzee or gorilla signs may be read as jokes, insults, metaphors, or the like, much as the "not infrequent offenses against the very elements of counting and the fundamental arithmetical processes" made by Clever Hans "were regarded in part as intentional jokes and by an authority in pedagogy as a 'sign of independence and stubbornness which might also be called humor'" (Pfungst 1965:145). Patterson (1978a:456) reports that Koko "seems to relish the effects of her practical jokes, often responding exactly opposite to what I ask her to do. One day, during a videotaping session, I asked

Koko to place a toy animal under a bag, and she responded by taking the toy and stretching to hold it up to the ceiling." Or, to take another example from the same source, it was interpreted as a deliberate joke (the gorilla was "grinning") when Koko, in response to persistent attempts to get her to sign *drink*, made "a perfect drink sign—in her ear." Assuming that, as Patterson reports, the trainer had been trying for some time to persuade Koko to make this sign, we may guess that the ape in fact moved her hands in various directions during the session, with various accompanying facial expressions. As we have asked elsewhere (Umiker-Sebeok and Sebeok 1980b), how were all of these other "signs" and expressions interpreted? If Koko happened to place her hand above her head, thumb down, could she have been said to be creating a ludic sign for *shower* or *shampoo*? The possibilities, given the lack of the kind of information any thoughtful person would demand, are limitless (see Sebeok 1979: chap. 5). Examples of such overinterpretation—for perhaps the most endearingly preposterous instances, see Hiller (1980)—are found scattered throughout the literature on signing apes, in both laudatory (e.g., Linden 1980) and critical articles (e.g., Gardner 1980).

While accepting that the sign play of apes is genuine, Hill nevertheless comments (1980:341) that "there remain serious questions about whether their [the apes'] metaphorical abilities are truly linguistic. . . . No matter how suggestive is the circumstantial evidence, the semantics of the chimpanzees' symbol systems cannot be said to be the same as the semantics of the signs into which they 'translate,' since the system is so truncated."[10] David Premack (1976:29) claims that Sarah's symbolic innovations were the "most vital" type of informal evidence that the animal's performances in general were not the result of social cuing. However, the examples he provides (ibid.:30) are all ambiguous, being based on a trainer's hunch about what the chimpanzee meant by a deviation from the regular trained responses.

The determination of trainers to show their animals in the best light has even led to the denial that errors are mistakes, again bringing to mind one of the assumptions that sets research on psychic phenomena apart from normal scientific procedures. The mistakes of a so-called psychic in tests of his powers are frequently used to prove that those powers are real, using the argument that, if the performer were using mere tricks, he would be correct every time, while his occasional mistakes prove that his correct responses are based not on conjury but on a special yet unpredictable "force." "Thus," as Randi (1975:11) points out, "the performer who can consistently turn out effects that defy explanation by ordinary means is considered a fraud, and the one who 'hits and misses' or who has periods of impotency is judged to be the real goods." Turning to the chimpanzee experiments, we find Premack (1976:30-31) using Sarah's mistakes on matching sets with more than five items as proof that Sarah was not responding to social cues. He argues that since the chimpanzee had done well on matching sets that did not involve numerosity, the trainer would expect her to do as well on those that did, and thus would be likely to cue her toward success. This is a mighty assumption. It is at least as likely that the trainer would reasonably doubt that a chimpanzee could handle so many items at once, despite her earlier performances. As far as we can tell, Premack never tried to determine what the trainer actually expected or did in the training situation.

Ristau and Robbins have noted that examples of gratuitous interpretations of conversational exchanges with Lana are also common.

> [A]t times the interpretations of Lana's productions [Rumbaugh 1977: chaps. 9 and 12] involve assumptions about reasons for her errors that either the authors cannot possibly know or that rely on information that the authors have not offered the reader. For example, they cite an error as the "result of Lana not attending to the question posed," giving no indication of what clues led them to this conclusion (p.243). [Ristau and Robbins 1979:270]

In another example (Rumbaugh 1977:243-244), of two seemingly irrelevant contributions by Lana to a conversation, one is simply ignored and the other is excused, without evidence, as a "typing error" (Ristau and Robbins 1979:271).

Another instance of a chimpanzee in a "no-forfeit" situation is provided by Premack (1976:31-32). He notes that Sarah had difficulty learning the concepts "is" and "if–then," and the quantifiers "all," "none," "one," etc. He assumes that, "If social cues were the basis of Sarah's learning, she should have had no more difficulty learning complex predicates than simple ones" (1976:31). The logic of this argument is difficult to follow. According to his training procedures, complex predicates were broken down into simpler parts, so that Sarah had to go through more preliminary training sets to reach the full form. Yet, he says, because the difficulty of each step is about the same (his reason for breaking difficult patterns down), the animal should not make any more errors learning a complex pattern than a simple one! But it would seem that the very fact that there were more steps involved would mean more errors, even if the chimpanzee performed about as reliably on each step as when learning a simple predicate. Premack further confuses the issue by saying that Sarah's difficulty on some of the complex forms was *his* fault, not hers, since he did not break down the form properly. Is he saying, then, that Sarah did *not* make more mistakes on complex forms?

The danger of overinterpretation of an ape's signing or use of artificial symbols is thus present even when the method of testing controls the input to the animal. On the level of the single lexical item, Premack (1976:36) claims that the Gardners' double-blind vocabulary tests—also employed by Fouts and Patterson—have shown only that Washoe "learned to associate different responses with different objects." He asks, "In view of the chimpanzee's capacity . . . is there any serious reason to doubt that it can learn to associate different responses with different objects?"

Likewise, Rumbaugh (1980:242) criticizes the Gardners' testing procedure:

> [It] did not provide for a way to determine the degree to which Washoe's signs were essentially generalized responses to stimuli similar to those used in prior training. Her competence in the use of her signs syntactically in order to generate and transmit truly novel messages, information, or requests was not tapped by this or any other test. Instances of her using signs in these ways were reported separately; however, they may have been fortuitous productions.

The execution of a specific behavior, such as a hand sign, in the presence of particular objects is not adequate evidence of naming ability.

> It is quite plausible to assume that even pigeons have this ability. Herrnstein, Loveland, and Cable (1977) have shown that pigeons can give the appearance of having learned simple concepts (e.g., discriminate pictures of trees from pictures of other objects). It would be trivial to teach them to pair the pecking of a particular colored light with the presentation of a picture of a tree. They would then be said to "name" the picture. . . . Furthermore, the ability of Herrnstein et al.'s pigeons to discriminate trees from other objects extended to literally thousands of exemplars. Hence, they possess the capacity to "name" a potentially infinite class of objects. [Petitto and Seidenberg 1979:169]

Savage-Rumbaugh et al. dismiss all ape "language" studies prior to their own work with Austin and Sherman by stating that they all made the mistake of taking the production of a sign (or use of a token or computer symbol) by an ape as indication of comprehension of that sign, and by erroneously assuming that the process of labeling implies symbolization (1980a:52). They argue that, to the contrary, "representation or symbolization is not inherent in the chimpanzee's capacity to select a symbol when presented with an object, action, or state" (ibid.).

Tests of Washoe's comprehension of multisign sequences have also been criticized from the point of view that in most cases nonsyntactic or nonlinguistic explanations are readily available to account for the chimpanzee's responses. Terrace et al. (n.d.:62), for example, note that the Gardners accepted as correct any response to a wh-question that they thought lexically appropriate. For example, if Washoe signed *blue* in response to the question *what color?* when the object being used was a red ball, her answer was counted as correct because it was a color. Washoe clearly learned to respond to such category questions by producing a response that fell within the correct category, but many of her specific responses were inappropriate.

> Washoe's response to a question was scored as correct if it contained a sign from a predesignated target category. For example, the question *what's that?* took a noun response; the question *where's that?* took a locative, etc. Washoe's vocabulary signs were grouped into grammatical

categories for scoring purposes; the sign glossed as *listen,* for example, was scored as a noun. The presumed meanings of her signs were ignored. Thus, if the Gardners held a ball in front of Washoe and asked her *what's that?* the response *listen come* would be scored as correct because it contains *listen.* [Seidenberg and Petitto 1979:204]

Washoe could have answered a question simply "by learning to associate a single target sign with a wh-sign; since meaning was irrelevant, she could use this sign in any context where the discriminative stimulus (wh-sign) occurred" (ibid.). Certainly, as Terrace and his collaborators maintain, such responses cannot be used to show, as the Gardners claim, that Washoe's performance at the time was comparable to that of the human child at Stage III in Brown's scheme of language development (see Brown 1968).

Even when Washoe's responses to wh-questions were appropriate, Rumbaugh (1980:244) wonders

whether this level of mastery constitutes "grammatical" control, for grammar subsumes word-order effects. The constituents of Washoe's responses to the wh-questions (e.g., Q. "Who you?" A. "Linn"; Q. "Whose that?" A. "Shoes you"; Q. "Where we go?" A. "You me out") were by and large appropriate, but the report [Gardner and Gardner 1975] and its analyses did not address questions regarding the logic inherent in the organization of responses that entailed *more* than one word—a relevant issue in the evaluation of "grammatical control."

For one reason or another, investigators find it difficult to avoid the use of tests in which the animal subject can rely on nonlinguistic strategies to accomplish a task in a way that is considered correct. Take, for example, the experiment designed by Fouts and his colleagues to test the ability of Ally, a young male chimpanzee, to comprehend novel commands. "Ally was first taught to pick, on command, one of five objects out of a box to put it in one of three locations (i.e., *put the baby in the purse*). After Ally had learned the procedure, new items were placed in the box, and in addition, a new location was added in which to place the items" (see Fouts et al. 1979:301). To prevent cuing, a screen was placed between the experimenter and the locations in which the item was to be placed. Ally scored 40 percent correct for total commands, with a chance level of responding being approximately 7 percent.

At closer look, however, one wonders what such results actually mean. Since the sentence frame, "Put x in y," did not vary, only the object (slot x filler) and the location (slot y filler) elements were not redundant. All Ally had to do was to recall his prior associations between a restricted number of signs and their objects and perform the general task, which had been learned in the training phase of the experiment, of placing the object in the designated place. The order object-plus-place was maintained throughout the test, so that Ally would know from this nonlinguistic cue that (1) the first nonredundant element was something in the box, and (2) it was to be moved toward the second nonredundant element in the string of signs. At most, then, this test was one of Ally's ability to name, not his knowledge of sentence structure. Compare the similar analysis, made by Terrace and Bever (1980:183-184), of Sarah's alleged sensitivity to the sentence structure of apparently more complex sequences such as *Sarah insert banana pail apple dish*.

A number of kindred attacks have been made on Premack's interpretations of Sarah's use of language tokens in forced-choice tests. After analyzing his treatment of Sarah's training with "name of" concept, for example, Gardner and Gardner (1980a:316) conclude that "Since Sarah's program of training and testing concentrated on each 'linguistic concept' for days and weeks at a time, she could have solved Premack's entire battery of problems by rote memory alone." Savage-Rumbaugh and her associates (1980b:379) also affirm that some of Sarah's performances—notably the match-to-sample paradigm tests designed to demonstrate Sarah's symbolic representational capacity—could be accounted for on the basis of simple recall, their own experimental chimpanzee, Lana, having performed much more difficult recall problems. "Questions as to whether or not such a [symbolic] capacity is necessary to solve the various problems could and should be raised for the entire gamut of tests presented to Sarah," they write (ibid.; cf. Savage-Rumbaugh et al. 1980a:52). They agree with Mounin (1980:174) that "the suspicion lingers" that only an illusion of language is created by the translation of Sarah's token sequences into English, while, stripped of this linguistic surface, the animal's behavior could reasonably be explained in terms of simple response-reward associations that have little to do with linguistic competence. One of the reasons Pfungst (1965:227) concluded that Mr. von Osten, the owner of Clever Hans, was not deceiving the public was that von Osten's training technique, which the horse's master thought of as "instruction," took much longer to accomplish than would a straight-forward stimulus-response training, without the illusion of intervening mathematical or linguistic concepts. For years, Mr. von Osten "taught" Hans as one might a high school student, and it was this aspect of the Clever Hans story that both sets it apart from earlier examples of counting pigs, dogs, horses, and other animals—going back to at least the time of Justinian (Timaeus 1974:146-147)—and makes it particularly relevant to modern ape sign language studies. Pfungst recognized that Mr. von Osten's training procedures were not what was then known as classical conditioning, but rather came only much later (1928) to be called instrumental conditioning (ibid.).

Terrace has, in fact, applied the law of parsimony to a large number of David Premack's testing procedures, and, in each case, "The homogeneous nature of the questions posed during any one session, along with the restricted range of possible answers, increases the likelihood that nonlinguistic contextual cues contributed to the performance of Premack's subjects" (1980b:392). Sometimes, as Terrace shows, it was even possible for the experimental animals to solve a problem without knowing the critical word involved. Simple discrimination learning and memory could account for many of Sarah's responses that hitherto have been cited by Premack as examples of knowledge of sentence structure, communicative intent, pronouns, prepositions, and predicates. For example, Premack (1976:32) argues that Sarah was responding to sentential complexity rather than nonlinguistic factors of a certain test because, for one thing, she took longer to handle the complex sentences than the simple ones presented (although length of time was not recorded—this was just Premack's impression, it seems), and she would do fewer of the former in any given training session. This might be said to prove, rather, that Sarah was solving problems on the basis of memory and that it took her longer to remember the more numerous training associations for tests involving complex sentences, since she had to go through a greater number of training steps for them.

Terrace and Bever (1980:185) note that the Lana project's use of a computer provided Lana with access to a much larger set of alternative symbols than did Premack's. Nevertheless they point out that Lana was also trained in long sessions devoted to a single type of problem, requiring constant primary reinforcement in such a way that a sequence, glossed by Rumbaugh and his associates as *Please machine give Lana M & M* or *Please machine give Lana piece of raisin*, "can be analyzed as a complex X-R chain." Such two-step, chained associations would be the equivalent, they say, of the learning of a rat in a double-T maze. Gardner and Gardner (1980a:317) have also criticized the interpretations made of Lana's performances, claiming that all Lana had to do to get a reward was to produce one of a very small number of correct color sequences on her computer console. "There is no reason to suppose," therefore, "that Lana's productions have any semantic content." The large number of drill sessions with the same small set of keys and stimulus arrays, they add, would not "have placed any great strain on the rote memory of a chimpanzee" (cf. Fouts and Rigby 1980). Moreover, several commentators have suggested simpler explanations of the tool use and exchange by the chimpanzees, Austin and Sherman, described by Savage-Rumbaugh et al. (1980b). Jolly (1978:580), for example, remarks that "the cleverness . . . is the experimenters' not the chimps'. At the circus we applaud with awe as the human acrobat brachiates above ground. Then we chortle when bediapered chimps waddle in on their hind legs and sit down to tea. Could the authors now devise an intellectual equivalent of letting the chimpanzees loose on the trapeze?" (cf. Lockard 1978; Mellgren and Fouts 1978).

Harlow (cited in Hill 1980:337) concluded his review of the Premack project by describing it as "a series of learned tasks ranging in difficulty from simple discrimination to relatively simple matching-from-sample problems." While Harlow compares Sarah's performances with "more complex learning accomplished by macaques," Terrace et al. compare

(1979:899-900) the multisign utterances of both Sarah and Lana with the problem-solving of pigeons trained by Straub and others to respond to nonsense symbols in a fixed order (see also Chomsky 1980; Ristau and Robbins 1979:272). Apparently, pigeons can learn to peck arrays of four colors in a particular sequence, irrespective of the physical position of the colors. If, as seems likely, they say, pigeons can also be trained to respond to ABCX problems, where X could refer to a variety of objects or actions, such performances could be compared with the chimpanzees' *Mary give Sarah apple* or *Please machine give apple*. But why should one refer to the sequence green, white, red, blue as *Trainer give R-42 grain?* Schubert also questions the assignment of English labels by Rumbaugh and his collaborators to the computer lexigrams manipulated by their subjects, Lana, Austin, Sherman, and Ally. He argues that, in the case of some of these translations, such as *straw* in the tool exchange experiment described in Savage-Rumbaugh et al. (1980b), the experimenters "cash in on the overtones of the word" (1978:598) in an unintentionally misleading way. Epstein et al. recreated, with some modifications, the experiment by Savage-Rumbaugh et al. (1978), using pigeons instead of primates. Their subjects, Jack and Jill, demonstrated an ability to "engage in a sustained and natural conversation without human intervention," showing as well that "one pigeon can transmit information to another entirely through the use of symbols" (Epstein et al. 1980:545), according to one possible interpretation. A more parsimonious explanation, the authors maintain, would be that "The performances were established through standard fading, shaping, chaining, and discrimination procedures. . . . A similar account may be given of the Rumbaugh procedure" (ibid.). On the basis of a rigorous analysis of the manipulation of the Yerkish computerized symbols by the chimpanzee Lana, which was designed to examine the extent to which simple reinforcement principles can explain her reactions, Thompson and Church conclude that most of the animal's performances can be attributed to two basic processes: conditional discrimination learning, where situational cues determine the selection of one sentence from a small set of six stock sentences; and paired-associate learning, or the coupling of a lexigram with an object, person, or event (1979:17-18).

The comparison of apes with pigeons and Brown's (1973) discussion of Premack's work and the "pigeon ping-pong problem" (i.e., you can teach two pigeons to bat a ball, but is it ping-pong?) points up the degree to which the selection of apes for this type of research introduces substantial distortion of perspective. We are much more likely to anthropomorphize an ape's performance, accepting English glosses as appropriate, than that of a pigeon, rat, tortoise, or woodpecker (see below). Certainly our tendency to perceive apes as either humans who have not had the benefit of enculturation (much as the so-called wolf children or as mentally retarded children—both documented by Desmond 1979) accounts in large measure for the numerous instances of completely spurious attributions of understanding of complex social and emotive terms, such as *sorry, please, happy, sad, good, bad, funny,* and various expletives, to chimpanzees and gorillas (Petitto and Seidenberg 1979).

It is up to those doing this sort of work to prove that the sequences of symbols produced by an ape are evidence of linguistic relationships. Simply assigning English glosses is appealing, but insufficient as well as misleading. Lenneberg (1975), using normal high school students, replicated Premack's study as closely as possible. He found that human subjects quickly outperformed Premack's chimpanzees, but they could not correctly translate into English any of the sentences they themselves had completed. Thinking that they were merely solving puzzles, the subjects failed to connect the plastic tokens with language.

It is also misleading to assume, as do Fouts, the Gardners, and Patterson, that, because a chimpanzee or gorilla produces hand configurations similar to those used by deaf users of ASL, the animal is employing signs in the same way as its human counterpart. Even if we overlook the fact that "at the level of hand shapes, the degree of correspondence [with human ASL] is questionable" (Petitto and Seidenberg 1979:165), the form of a behavior cannot determine its status as a linguistic unit—much as the vocal imitations of psittacine birds—and, in the absence of detailed descriptions of the contexts of the apes' performances, it is impossible to tell to what extent the form-function association approximates that of a human ASL user (ibid.:166).

> Although some of the apes' behaviors may be similar to some of the formational components of ASL signs . . . , there is no indication that any of their gestures show the exact configurations of hand shape, movement, orientation, and location which characterize signs in ASL. . . . The differences between the apes' behaviors and signing in ASL are profound. [Ibid.:175]

In what is certainly the most skeptical approach yet made to this type of data, Terrace and his associates (1979; Sanders and Terrace 1979; Terrace 1979, 1980a) analyzed over 19,000 combinations of two or more signs produced by the chimpanzee Nim and reached the conclusion that each instance of what appeared to be grammatical competence on the animal's part could be adequately explained by simpler, nonlinguistic processes. The examination of videotaped records of dialogues between Nim and his human trainers indicated "a strong tendency for the chimpanzee to sign only when the teacher signs to him," that "60% of the chimpanzee's signed utterances imitated one or more signs from the teacher's prior utterances" (Sanders and Terrace 1979), and that non-imitative utterances tended to be stock expressions used repeatedly to obtain rewards from the teacher. Nim was transformed not so much into a Pygmalion in the classroom as into a circus chimp in human "disguise."

Applying the same rules that they followed in analyzing Nim's transcripts, Terrace et al. (1981) performed a discourse analysis of the five one-hour transcripts of Koko's signing found in Patterson's dissertation (1979b). They estimate that only 28 percent of Koko's signed utterances were spontaneous (Terrace et al. 1981:88). Their transcription of a portion of a NOVA film that showed Koko signing led them to assert that all of Koko's signs in the film were produced by her human interlocutor prior to Koko's use of them (Terrace et al. 1979, 1981). Patterson's outrage (1981:86-87) at the suggestion that Koko's "signs" are by and large simply trained responses to human prompting is contradicted by her assertion, in her thesis (1979b:153), that "The majority of Koko's utterances were not spontaneous, but elicited by questions from her teachers and companions. My interactions with Koko were often characterized by frequent questions such as *What's this?*"

Clever Hans Effect

This brings us to the third issue at stake here, that is, the possibility of the human observer's unintentionally modifying the animal's behavior to produce the desired results. It may never be feasible to exclude the fallible human half of the dyad under conditions of *apprentissage*, let alone the looser protocols of *dressage*. Hediger deems the task of elimination of the Clever Hans Effect analogous to squaring the circle, "if only for the reason that every experimental method is necessarily a human method and must thus *per se* constitute a human influence on the animal. . . . The concept of an experiment with animals—be it psychological, physiological or pharmacological—without some direct or indirect contact between human being and animals is basically untenable" (1974: 29). When this statement is considered in the light of Niels Bohr's complementarity principle, the unavoidable interaction between the observer and the system observed is seen to impose the ultimate limitation on the knowability of the "real" state of affairs. The quantum of action couples the observer with the system observed, such that an observation necessarily changes the observed system.

If Hediger is right, as we believe he is, then the door always remains wide open, as well, to the subtle intrusion of a host of experimenter effects (Barber 1976) in the course of participant observation as a method to decipher animal behavior, for the technique necessarily hinges on a particular hermeneutic: the interpenetration of signs by and of actors in the game. This holds *a fortiori* for animals, such as all apes, which can scarcely survive in the absence of an intense level of social intercourse with their handler before they are capable of undergoing the rigors of training for any task. We have already noted the often profound emotional, even quasi-familial ties that exist between the apes learning ASL or an artificial language and their trainers, to the extent that the apes' performances uniformly declined—or the animals refused to cooperate altogether—when the animals were faced with a novel interlocutor in a double-blind testing situation. The temperamental response of a subject has been an all too convenient excuse used by investigators for not relying more heavily on outside experimenters in direct tests of ape language capacities. As in some parapsychological research, the basic rule that subjects

FIG. 8.1. Portrait of Oskar Pfungst

do not select their own experimenter is broken when chimpanzees or gorillas are allowed to exclude certain individuals or classes of persons from testing situations. Randi (1975) has shown how important it is to Uri Geller and other so-called psychics that skeptical observers be excluded from tests of their special powers. He also demonstrated how the extraordinary personal control Geller has over the perceptions and expressions of sympathetic observers makes it possible for him to appear to them as a true psychic. Kreskin (1973:26-27), in his discussion of ESP as entertainment, explains how he goes about capturing an audience:

Rapport with the audience is built up through verbal contact, and to a lesser extent, body movement. The latter is not studied but does coordinate with patter to command attention. I attempt to keep all eyes on me. I then go about creating a climate for suggestible responses, literally playing it by ear and "feel" until I can sense that the audience is ready for communication and response. The main task is to instill faith, establish a "faith-prestige" relationship early. It may take fifteen or twenty minutes but the audience is seldom aware that the program is rapidly changing from the establishment of rapport and the conditioning of conjuring to an area far removed from magic. When volunteers come up onstage, they are unknowingly ready for response.

In any case, it would be interesting to know precisely *why* the animals in the ape "language" researches have such difficulty performing for strangers.

A related issue concerns the personal preferences exhibited by the apes for certain project members. All the animals used so far in the ape "language" projects have shown some preference for certain trainers, performing better for these "favorites" than for the rest, but there has been no systematic attempt to account for these differential responses on the part of the animals. As Hill (1980:348) has pointed out, project reports have not "attended to the possibility that the chimpanzees have input into the communication dynamics, and hence into the society being constructed. The chimpanzees have often been seen as exclusively receptive; the interest in their output has been in its structural complexity and lexical variety." But, as Hill has noted, it is clear from many anecdotes, as well as from the very design features of some of the testing and training protocols, that there is a a great deal of input from the animals in these experiments, and this input should be considered seriously as a component of every procedure followed.

The ape subjects are not the only ones to show a preference for certain project personnel, of course. Investigators appear to favor certain subjects—notably such "star" performers as Washoe, Koko, and Sarah—and their reports tend to emphasize the results obtained with these animals over those stemming from the behavior of less-gifted individuals. Thus what Barber calls the "Investigator Data Analysis Effect" (1976: 19ff.)[11] comes into play when, for example, investigators obtain negative results with some animals and fail to report them, excluding from their analysis subjects that do not conform to their predictions and thereby distorting the reliability of their conclusions as to the significance of the data. A particularly disturbing example of this type of pitfall is found in Premack's work. In his book-length report (1976), for example, an early chapter, devoted to a discussion of the experimental subjects used and containing a series of *ad hoc* justifications for the poor performances of several chimpanzee subjects, is followed by others in which not only are the performances of Sarah, his prize pupil, highlighted, but also it is often over-painted exactly which subjects are being discussed. Savage-Rumbaugh and Rumbaugh (1979:293) criticize other ape "language" research projects for not retaining subjects "not particularly adept or behaviorally pleasant to work with."

As in any behavioral research, experimenters in the ape "language" projects differed in their rates of success in teaching the animals. Terrace and his colleagues (n.d.:14-15), for example, report that some of Nim's teachers were much better at their job than others, so much so that they conclude that the rate of learning by the animal could be said to tell as much about the human involved as about the chimpanzee. It is regrettable that, once again, individual differences in success in teaching subjects have received so little attention from investigators in this field, especially since numerous studies have shown that "experimenters differing in such characteristics as sex, age, ethnic identity, prestige, anxiety, friendliness, dominance, and warmth at times obtained divergent results when testing similar [human] subjects," and that such an "Experimenter Personal Attributes Effect has been found on a wide variety of tasks including intelligence tests, projective tests, verbal conditioning tasks, and other physiological and educational measures" (Barber 1976:47). At the very least, investigators who do not use a sample of experimenters should, as Barber suggests, state the conclusions from their studies more cautiously, including a proviso that the results may be restricted to the specific kind of experimenter(s) used.

Pfungst, it may be remembered, also underlined that certain questioners were more successful than others in eliciting correct responses from Hans and that "Hans acquired a reputation for 'Einkennigkeit,' that is, he would accustom himself only to certain persons. . . . Such a reputation was hard to reconcile with his much praised intelligence" (1965:210). Hans preferred, and performed best for, as Pfungst discovered, persons who exhibited (1) an "air of quiet authority," (2) intense concentration, (3) a "facility of motor discharge," and (4) the power to "distribute tension economically" (ibid.). In other words, the successful examiner, focusing intently on the horse's tapping or other responses and on the anticipated perception of a correct movement, was able to sustain a tension and release it at the right moment, in such a way that a detectable movement resulted, a movement used by Hans as a sign to stop performing. In what is still the most thorough examination of minimal, unwitting cues between man and animal, Pfungst succeeded in explaining the bulk of errors made by Hans, not in terms of insufficiencies on the part of the horse but rather as instances where the questioner was inattentive, tired, unaware of the correct answer, or for some other reason incapable of producing the necessary muscular sign. Pfungst was even able to show the relationship between skepticism on the part of the experimenter and the poorer performance of the animal with such an examiner. A skeptical observer, he noted (ibid.:144-145), had a lower degree of concentration than one who expected to see Hans perform correctly. The skeptic thus did not relax at the proper moment, and often Hans tapped too many times. The nonbeliever, it would seem, relaxed after his suspicion that the horse would *not* stop at the correct number had been confirmed. Hans, of course, did not know the difference between this and the correctly timed cue of relaxation given off by less-skeptical observers.

Timaeus (1974:155) has restudied and to a degree refined Pfungst's procedures. His reinvestigation essentially confirmed the accuracy of Pfungst's work, but he did not assign as great a significance to head movements as did Pfungst. His analysis, on the other hand, uncovered eight sources of cuing:

1. *eyes:* blinking, changes in gaze direction
2. *head:* head movements upwards, downwards, and sideways
3. *mouth:* changes in lip configuration
4. *body:* changes in postural tension
5. *hands:* hand movements
6. *jaw:* changes in muscle tension
7. voiceless *counting* along
8. *breathing:* patterns of inhalation

Timaeus further found that all these cues took place in a fixed order, which we interpret as imparting, to the horse, a great deal of redundancy. Timaeus, like Pfungst, confirmed that these types of cues were responsible for incorrect as well as correct responses.[12]

Despite the fact that the issue is still hotly debated among psychologists (see, e.g., Barber's critique [1976:64ff.]), a recent review of 345 studies of "interpersonal expectancy effects" (or "interpersonal self-fulfilling prophecies") by Rosenthal and Rubin suggests that there is ample reason to believe that,

> Effects of interpersonal expectations are pervasive and of special importance, both scientific and social. . . . Apparently, when behavioral researchers, teachers, or supervisors expect a certain level of performance from their subjects, pupils, or subordinates, they somehow unwittingly treat them in such a way as to increase the probability that they will behave as expected. [1978:377]

One of the findings of Rosenthal and Rubin that should serve as a warning to investigators and experimenters involved in ape "language" projects is that this interpersonal expectancy effect was especially large for studies of animal learning, a fact that Ellsworth suggests may be due to a combination of three features of such research: repeated measures are taken on the same subjects (especially when the experimenter is aware of the subject's responses); an experimenter runs subjects in only one condition; and the design of the research or the predicted behavior is simple (Ellsworth 1978:393; see also Carlsmith et al. 1976). Regarding the last of these characteristics, it should be noted that it is still open to question how complex a task has to be to render Clever Hans cuing unlikely. Rosenthal (in Pfungst 1965:xxxviin4) describes the case of Lady, the "talking" horse of Richmond, Virginia, who was reputed to be a good finder of lost objects. When consulted about a missing dog, Lady, operating a special typewriter, spelled out the word "dead."

> In some way, not at all apparent to even a keen observer, the horse's owner [sensing the dog's owner's belief that her pet had been killed] must have communicated to her the sequence of appropriate keyboard responses. It is one thing to find the cues that start and stop a horse's tapping. It is quite another to find the cues that lead a horse to choose one letter out of 26 and then another and another, especially when the "keys" of the typewriter are quite close together. To learn the unintentional (if it was unintentional) signalling system in this case would have provided Pfungst with another worthy challenge. [On Lady, see further Gardner 1957:351-352; Christopher 1970:40-46; and Sebeok 1979:90.]

Each of the ape "language" projects suffers from at least one of these three factors. This makes it all the more important that, in the future, investigators assign a much greater importance to the exploration of both "procedures for minimizing and calibrating the effects of experimenter expectations" (as far as we know, there has been no controlled attempt to ascertain the impact of experimenter expectations on ape performances) and the fundamental semiotic problem of the "role of nonverbal processes of communication mediating interpersonal expectancy effects" (Rosenthal and Rubin 1978:385).

ANTECEDENTS OF APE "LANGUAGE" RESEARCHES

Alternatively, Ockham allows, dogma—*viz.*, the articles of faith—may impose the benchmark. The prevailing Darwinian tenet that fuels or constrains most of the investigations of ape linguistic capacity postulates (as the subtitle of Griffin's 1976 contribution to cognitive ethology also perfectly captures) the "evolutionary continuity of mental experience." The countervailing older type of psychology defines the animal, following Descartes, as a push-pull automaton, and, as an inevitable consequence of that definition, affirms the superiority of man over the brutes. His slogan, which has influenced the thought of all generations that came after, was formulated in quasi-semiotic terms: "instinct and reason, the signs of two natures." The historical roots of the ensuing dialectic are sketched in Limber 1980 (see also Desmond 1979; and Appendix II of this volume), but no doubt take on special evolutionary meaning in the context of the great African apes, notably both varieties of *Pan*.

Current evidence suggests that humans, chimpanzees, and gorillas diverged from some common ancestor between eight and twelve million years ago. On the one hand, as we know since 1975 (King and

Wilson), the difference in structural genes between "us" and "them" is astoundingly small, for the average human polypeptide was reported to be nearly 99 percent identical with its counterpart in chimpanzees, although the data, by the same token, also indicated that one-quarter of the proteins were genetically different (i.e., while the DNA is very similar, the proteins are far less so—cf. Plomin and Kuse 1979:189). We also know now that there is a consequential homology of repeated and unique copy DNA in both *Homo* and *Pan*, and that the amino acid sequence of a large number of proteins studied is similar, because more than twenty genes have been localized to homologous chromosomes and chromosome bands of the two species. (At present no one knows the functions of the "dark material" on the tips of the chimpanzee chromosomes, which do not appear in humans.)

On the other hand, adult chimpanzees do not conspicuously resemble grown-up people, and their respective behavior patterns—most particularly with respect to the semiosic faculty—are separated by a chasm the depth of which remains unplumbed and which therefore persists as a major concern (cf. Ristau and Robbins 1979:295). What we do not know, in other words, is why the genotype maps such seemingly consonant information into two such widely divergent phenotypes; or as Yunis et al. (1980:1148) concluded: "Such a remarkable degree of similarity makes difficult a precise explanation of the large biological differences between two closely related species." The fulcrum of our profound phenotypic and adaptive disunion from the chimpanzees and the gorilla perhaps lies in the differential timing of gene expression during brain development. The regulatory changes have a retarding influence on the pace of our unfolding and, particularly, of our brain. Fetal growth rates eventuate in hypertrophy of the organ-complex controlling (among other effects) human linguistic competence for speaking and in processing the speech of others, in brief, the language-using animal's species-specific behavior. It is difficult to understand why this simple fact of evolution, setting humans apart irreversibly from their closest primate relatives, is so hard to grasp on the part of behaviorists.

As Suzanne Chevalier-Skolnikoff claims to have found (1976; now considerably altered and amplified in her contribution in Sebeok and Rosenthal 1981: chap. 5), baby chimpanzees, gorillas, and orangutans develop behavior patterns during the first 24 months of their lives that closely resemble those of human infants on Piaget's six-stage model of intellectual and motor development. The pivotal difference is that young apes stop advancing in their vocalization at an early age; this lack of development presumably accounts for differential subsequent maturation. While orangutans, too, cry at birth, only human infants go on to more sophisticated vocalizations, successively to cooing, laughing and babbling, combining phonemes, using words instrumentally, and creating two-morpheme phrases. Alloprimates never coo, never babble, and never acquire more-elaborate ways of articulating.

Malmi (1980) has wisely warned against the use of either simple analogies or the design-feature approach to language as arguments for evolutionary continuity in language development. The much more stringent criteria of true homologies—based especially on the examination of neurological substrates—must be met before conclusions about the biological roots of the human semiotic system *par excellence* can be drawn. And "presumed phylogenetic closeness is not sufficient to establish behavioral homology, especially when the behavior does not naturally occur in one of the species but is elicited only through extensive training" (ibid.:192), as is the case with language-like systems of communication.[13] This admonition is of special importance in light of some ape "language" researchers' stubborn insistence (e.g., Fouts et al. 1979) on overlooking the significance of the self-fulfilling prophecy in their work, preferring instead to interpret as homologous with a language-learning child's the behavior of animals masquerading—in the eyes of their trainers—as loquacious little people.

African apes were not always judged the fashionable, or even the ideal, animal models for simulating human linguistic behavior. It is noteworthy that the ape chosen, around 1908, as the first candidate for language training, by Lightner Witmer at the University of Pennsylvania, was the chimpanzee Peter, who had attracted the scientist's attention by his astute stage imitations of humans, most notably as a star roller skater. This performing chimpanzee did not actually undergo long-term language schooling, but the idea of such an undertaking was passed on by Witmer to a Philadelphia physician by the name of William H. Furness, who worked intensively on teaching language to a native-born chimpanzee and two orangutans between 1909 and 1914. Furness eventually admitted that his attempts to train the animals to comprehend or produce speech had failed. He observed that the apes did not act according to an understanding of linguistic signs, but instead used his gestures and facial expressions, either some or all of the time, as unwitting cues to what response was required of them. When Furness was not present, the animals failed their tests of comprehension (Furness 1916; cf. Desmond 1979:61ff.). Curiously, later researchers totally ignored this important discovery, and the chimpanzee series was begun in earnest. The gorilla first entered stage center in the 1970s. Despite Furness's difficulties and Galdikas's remark (1978:291) that "a worse model . . . than wild orangutans could not possibly be imagined," Asia's sole living species of great ape is now also undergoing ASL training, under the supervision of Lyn Miles, in Tennessee, and Gary Shapiro, in the field. (Cf. work with a male infant orangutan by Fouts [1973], and a Premack-inspired experiment with a four-year-old female orangutan by Shapiro [1975].)

In the early 1960s, the mystique of the porpoise (or dolphin) began to captivate the imagination of the public. It was claimed that dolphins were capable of producing sounds like those of human speech and of engaging in audio-mimetic activities. We are told—with undeniable accuracy—by an investigator with medical credentials: "The dolphins may learn English (or Russian) or they may not . . ." (Lilly 1978:188). Recently, their superiority over primates is contrastively insinuated:

> The almost unbelievable ability of the dolphin to match the sounds of human speech can further be appreciated by examining communication with the apes. The human and the dolphin share the capability of communication by means of sounds. The chimpanzee and the gorilla cannot do this with any degree of complexity whatsoever. [Ibid.:78]

The fact is that marine mammals have never been proven to possess the rudiments of language (cf. Wood 1973:118, specifically with respect to porpoises); in Wilson's judgment (1975:474), among others', the communication system and social organization of delphinids generally "appears to be of a conventional mammalian type." This is not surprising, for the outcome of even the best-designed experiment has shown that "dolphin social behavior is much more akin to the example of elephant seal social behavior than it is to human linguistic behavior" (Evans and Bastian 1969:433). William Langbauer's Porpoise Language Acquisition Project, patterned after Premack's experimental design with Sarah, appears, so far, to have made little progress (Linehan 1979:529, 533). The same is true of several other recently initiated projects, in Hawaii and in Florida. As Louis M. Herman, director of a new "language" training project at the Marine Mammal Research Laboratory on the Honolulu waterfront, foresees, "the difficulties will be 'formidable'" (Sullivan 1980:C2). Herman also said that "communication [by means of an artificial language] has never before been achieved by man and another species" (ibid.). (See now Parfit 1980.)

Once again, by the stringent application of Ockham's razor, the dolphins' performance is sufficiently explained by the inadvertent conditioning postulated by Bastian, coupled, probably, with a modicum of trial and success. While it is quite safe now to prognosticate that within the next decade many computers will be able to talk—if not yet necessarily listen—in "human language," it is equally certain, we think, that no porpoise will ever be able either to generate or to understand continuous speech on a remotely comparable level of linguistic and contextual sensitivity. Needless to emphasize, for computers to achieve the implied level of sophistication, vast but justifiable funding will be required; but money spent on chimerical experimentation to hominify speechless creatures of the deep is tantamount to squandering scarce resources.

Apes, Cadillac-like, being also expensive animals to maintain in home or laboratory, it is small wonder that their "linguistic" tutelage has, so far, proceeded exclusively in America, wholly with domestic support. In France, the Renault of animals appears to have been the Greater Spotted Woodpecker (*Dendrocopos major*), the natural drumming behavior of which was molded by Chauvin-Muckensturm (1974) in association with selective food demands. The woodpecker was taught the use of the following code: one tap for a pistachio nut, two taps for a house cricket, three taps for a mealworm, two plus two taps for a May bug, and two plus two plus two taps for a locust. The investigator's conclusion was that this bird's behavior "seems to represent a phenomenon of man-animal communication analogous to that found in monkeys by the Gardners and Premack" (ibid.:185). This seemingly exorbitant comparison is buttressed by a functional equation of the bird's beak with the simian's hand, an identification that may be less shocking if one is prepared to accept a common characterization of some birds (notably the psittacines) as "the monkeys of the bird world" (Breland and Breland 1966:106).

One should by no means neglect to mention, in passing, that Michael J. Babcock, of the University of Wisconsin-Milwaukee, with his wife, Rosemary A. Babcock, seriously claim to have trained their pancake tortoises (*Malacochersus tornieri*), indigenous to East Africa, to "read-talk" English words and to form sentences. One of us (TAS) has witnessed the flow of two-way "communication" between the Babcocks and their tortoises—a classic, blown-in-the-bottle instance of the Clever Hans illusion, differing merely in scope and lack of pretension from the other projects discussed here, and its vulnerable transparency. The tortoises, by the way, also watch television, and "report" that they are (understandably, since their isolated relative *Testudo elephantopus* is so prominently featured) "fascinated by the Darwin series and Jacques Cousteau" (Aschoff 1980).

The code-drumming woodpecker carries us back to code-tapping horses, and thus right to the heart of the prototypal case of Clever Hans, or to similar pseudocommunicative deportment in other domestic species. This effect has been dealt with in a semiotic frame (Sebeok 1979: chaps. 4 and 5; for talking dogs, see chap. 7 this volume), and a book is in preparation (Sebeok, forthcoming) on the broader implications and applications of the compelling principle of ideomotor behavior at work and the interacting fallacies such motor automatism nourishes. It may be worth pointing out here that, in its crudest form, Clever Hans seems to undergo perpetual reincarnation in one guise or another. Thus Blake (1977:40) now claims to have "thirty or forty proven [*sic!*] cases" of telepathic communication in horses; while Rowdon (1978:235) copiously expatiates upon the miracles wrought by a certain Mrs. Heilmaier in displaying the linguistic capacities of her dogs. He depicts her powers over animals in such picturesque statements as: "I saw [a] chimpanzee leap down from his perch to the bars of the cage as if starved for conversation, to greet her and chatter to her with funny little movements of the mouth." Our credulity is no more strained by such anecdotes than by the tale of one Mucianus about the tame elephant that could write Greek (amusingly pictured in Anon. 1891:291).

EXORCISING HANS'S SPIRIT

From the outset, responsible experimenters with anthropoid apes have been wary of the devastating effects of "illicit communication in the laboratory," as Pilisuk and his collaborators (1976) refer to *sub rosa* semiosic activities rampant in research establishments generally. It will be remembered that all the feats of Clever Hans were ultimately uncloaked as having amounted to nothing more than either "go" or "no go" responses to unwitting minimal cues given off by people present in the horse's milieu (for a clear, succinct account, see, e.g., Goldenson 1973: 262-279; for an analytic account, see Sebeok 1979: chaps. 4-5). One of the earliest discussions of the possibility of the Clever Hans Effect in the ape "language" projects (Ploog and Melnechuk [1971:631-634]) suffers from a number of fatal defects. Instead of evidence, heavy reliance was placed on authority, or the observational and rhetorical powers of prominent scientists: "Brown and others vouched for [Washoe's] ability to do what was claimed for her. . . . Ploog visited both [the Gardners' and Premack's] laboratories, and he is personally convinced that no answer 'leakage' à la 'Clever Hans' accounts for the results with either Washoe or Sarah." The epistemological status of such sincere prose calls for the challenge well posed by Ziman (1978:137-142): "*How* much *can be believed?*" It also readily brings to mind the nuptial pads of Paul Kammerer's midwife toads, apropos of which no less an authority than Stanley

FIG. 8.2. Mr. von Osten with Clever Hans

Gardner assured the world that "Kammerer begins where Darwin left off," to which G. H. F. Nuttall added that Kammerer had made "perhaps the greatest biological discovery of the century" (Koestler 1973:91). We must also recollect that the 1911 forgery of "Piltdown Man" was not only maintained, for over forty years, on scarcely more than the testimony of otherwise competent scientists, such as Sollas, but required a thorough reworking of the ancestral tree of humanity to accommodate "the earliest Englishman," which was accordingly gnarled by many eminent anthropologists, such as Arthur Keith and Earnest A. Hooton (cf. Millar 1972). As Sollas (1915:54) asserted when a question was raised about the possibility that the jaw did not belong with the skull, "The chances against this are . . . so overwhelming that the conjecture may be dismissed as unworthy of serious consideration."

USES OF AUTHORITY AND SELF-CONTROL

There have been two main types of expert witnesses cited by researchers as verification of the accuracy of their results with apes learning ASL: those who have special knowledge of ASL; and those whose areas of expertise include not ASL but some discipline relevant to the issues raised by this research, such as linguistics, first-language acquisition by children, or physical anthropology. In either case, however, outsiders are dependent on project members for the bulk of the information they receive during their visits. During our stay in Reno, in 1969, for example, we were, as guests, necessarily at the mercy of our gracious hosts, the Gardners, in terms of where and when we could view Washoe and what additional experiences of the project we were allowed to have—in our case, heavily edited films of the chimpanzee, casual testing of her signs in our presence using a box of well-worn objects, and discussions with some of the animal's trainers. In every case with which we are familiar, site visitors are carefully chaperoned by members of the local research team. Unavoidably, a good deal, if not all, of the visitors' "first-hand" observations are filtered through the commentary provided by their guides, who often furnish the frames of reference within which the observers are more likely to "perceive" what is consistent with the team's findings and expectations. This semiotic keying (Bouissac, cited by Sebeok 1979: chap. 5) is especially important when the visitors, although experts in the field of language acquisition, primatology, or whatever, know little ASL. Do such observers actually see the ape's signs, or do they only think that what they saw corresponds to what the guide has interpreted for them, or what earlier reading of research reports has led them to expect to witness?

Even when the outside observers are fluent in ASL, there may be some question about the reliability of their judgments about the ape's behavior (for an example, see Sebeok 1979: chap. 5). First of all, visitors are unlikely to have had much first-hand or possibly even indirect experience with chimpanzees or gorillas and are thus unable to determine which of the actions they see performed by such an animal are part of its natural repertoire and which are the result of special training. How many of us, one wonders, are truly aware of the extent of the artifice of the Chitas we see in Tarzan movies, the clever chimpanzees on Marlin Perkins's television show, and so forth? Visitors will, furthermore, be distracted by the nonsigning behavior they may be witnessing—and attempting to interpret—very likely for the first time. *All* outside observers will be distracted from the signing behavior of the ape to a certain extent by their need to accommodate themselves to the animal's individual personality—not to mention that of each of their hosts. Not only are the observations of such visitors suspect for this reason, but the written reports of their experiences are often anecdotal and/or based on a reinterpretation of their "first-hand" observations after consideration of the written or film materials made by or about principal investigators and/or their staff.

One serious drawback to using deaf persons as independent judges of signing apes is that they will miss any auditory cues given the subject. This is especially relevant in the case of Koko, Nim, and the Oklahoma subjects, to which trainers were allowed to speak and make other sounds with no control over the flow of auditory signals. The same problem would arise in regard to the paralinguistic signs uttered by humans working with the Gardners' chimpanzees.

Hediger (1980), expressing his misgivings about the legitimacy of claims regarding the linguistic competence of the anthropoid apes, points to a major fallacy underlying all such work: the assumption that scientists, even those unfamiliar with apes, can be counted on to detect social cues and/or other forms of self-deceptive manipulative behavior at play in the interactions between man and ape, while those experienced in the nonscientific training of performing animals in circuses, zoos, and similar installations are not called in to give an account of what is going on. This situation somewhat parallels that described by Randi (1975) for the investigation of Uri Geller's claims to teleport objects or persons, read minds, and the like. Geller prefers scientists as witnesses and will not perform before expert magicians, and for good reason. Scientists, by the very nature of their intellectual and social training, are among the easiest persons for a conjuror to deceive, while a good magician can spot deceptive techniques in a very short time. While what is most likely to be occurring in the ape research is self-deception, in the form of experimental expectancy effects or the "trimming" or "cooking" of data by investigators (Merton 1957), as opposed to outright fraud, one wonders whether it would not be wise for the principal investigators of ape "language" projects—not to mention the funding agencies that support them—at least to seek the advice of persons who are practiced in the art of purposefully manipulating animal behavior to create the illusion of humanlike activities.

At the very least, but preferably in addition, those expert in the microanalysis of human communication—in any modality—should be consulted, and not in a casual manner, but under conditions rigidly controlled by the outsiders themselves rather than by the research team whose work is being investigated. Someone trained in the analysis of the rhythms of dialogue, interaction ritual, or conversational sequencing, for example, would probably have brought to light much sooner the profoundly important effect on the apes of the signs used by their human interlocutors, a form of discursive cuing only now being uncovered. In the past, it was generally only the chimpanzee's or gorilla's utterances that were recorded and studied, the human's input being either summarized or cut out altogether. This trend is being reversed by Terrace and his collaborators, who have recently given this issue the attention it deserves, and with illuminating results (Sanders and Terrace 1979; Terrace 1980a; Terrace et al. 1979, 1980).

Through an analysis of Nim's use of ASL, which related the chimpanzee's utterances to his trainer's earlier signs within the same discourse, these astute researchers found that Nim imitated and interrupted his teacher to a much greater extent than does a language-learning child. The teacher's signing appeared to cue the chimpanzee that it can achieve a reward, a desired object or activity, only if it uses ASL. Since Nim had learned that many of the signs used by the teacher are generally acceptable as responses and therefore useful in obtaining a reward, he imitated some of them together with other generally acceptable signs such as *Nim* or pronouns. The authors explain the chimpanzee's interruptions by pointing out that the more rapidly Nim fulfilled the human's requirements the sooner he would reach his goal.

Analysis by Terrace and his associates of films of other signing apes revealed a similar dependence on the prior utterances of an animal's teachers, even to the point that, in certain exchanges, most of the animal's signs had already been modeled by the human interlocutor before the animal used them. The authors' comparison of unedited with edited film versions of the same sequence of discourse also shows how this crucial aspect of ape signing is unwittingly masked—and the meaning of the interaction thus remarkably altered—by the usual editing of a film or videotape while preparing it for display.[14]

The correlative proverbial formula, "Monkey see, monkey do," is amply supported in the literature of *dressage*, and not only by Hachet-Souplet (1897:79-91), whose testimony we have earlier adduced. Note the following insightful and decisive passage from Burrough's illuminating seventeenth chapter, dealing with performing monkeys:

> In training performing monkeys the instructor is greatly aided by that imitative faculty which is a characteristic of the whole monkey family. The intense passion a monkey has for mimicking the actions of persons is well known, and to such an excessive degree is this passion sometimes possessed that several instances are on record of their cutting their own

throats while attempting to shave themselves, having observed some man performing that operation. It is this imitative instinct which is taken advantage of in preparing monkeys for public exhibition. Indeed, their instruction consists mainly in the teacher performing the act for himself, for the monkey to copy. [1869:157]

In the light of this and other observations, the suggestion that "Nim could have simply imitated what his teachers were signing" (Terrace et al. 1979:72) seems eminently plausible, indeed, the most likely of several alternative explanations.

The startling thing about the study by Terrace and his colleagues is that neither Nim's trainers nor the many "expert" observers who were fluent in ASL were aware of the discursive cuing that was occurring. Human attention was focused instead on the content of the animal's utterances and their nonverbal context. Terrace et al. are convinced that the conspicuous differences between the conclusions they drew about chimpanzee linguistic competence on the basis of a traditional distributional analysis of Nim's signs—a method similar to, but much more thorough than, those employed in other projects—and those that resulted from their careful discourse analysis of a complete and painstakingly transcribed film record of ape-human "conversations," casts doubt on the bulk of previous analyses of the so-called grammaticality of ape sign sequences (n.d.:49).

It is not surprising that trainers are by and large unaware of this sort of interactive modeling, since they—not the apes—are the ones doing most of the work during the training and testing sessions. In his discussion of one of his trainers who was clearly giving social cues to Peony, Premack (1976:29) gives us some idea of the considerable number of tasks that the trainer must perform in such situations (e.g., "setting out the test items, following the data sheet—and doing all of this without being bitten!"), while at the same time trying to gain and maintain the attention of the animal. And yet researchers and experts alike continue to believe that they are in control not only of the verbal signs they emit in such a distracting situation but even of the nonverbal signs they give off. Premack, for example, asserts that his trainers were aware of the fact that if a chimpanzee did not know an answer it would look into the trainer's face for clues, but that the trainers controlled this by "refusing" to give clues and by redirecting the chimpanzee's attention to the task (ibid.:2). The use of self-control as a protection against unintentional cuing is of dubious value. Pfungst (1965), after having decoded the system of minimal cues being given Clever Hans, admits that he was himself unable to keep from cuing the horse, even though he was making a conscious effort not to do so. Rosenthal, in his introduction to Pfungst's account of the investigation of Hans, discusses a number of additional examples of this, in tests of ESP, water witching, muscle readers, and several clever animals, where observers were incapable of controlling their cuing of the subject under examination. (See also note 12, above.)

Premack claims that of the twenty trainers he used over the years, only one was found to be clearly giving social cues. "There is no question but that both chimpanzees and children try to use social cues on occasion. However, I have never seen either do so with sufficient stealth to go undetected by an experienced trainer, and especially not by a second trainer who observes the first trainer and the subject" (1976:29). This summary dismissal of social cues as an influence in the interaction between trainers and apes raises more questions than it answers. First, does Premack restrict "social cues" to such obvious, consciously controlled visual behaviors as direct stares and symbolic gestures? If so, he is omitting from consideration a vast array of semiosic processes in the visual and a host of other channels that have been shown to play an important part in human and animal communication (for numerous references, see Sebeok 1976, 1979) but that operate largely out of the awareness of interactants. Such an underestimation by Premack of the potential of unwitting cues is curious, in light of his earlier criticism, noted above, regarding a general lack of awareness, on the part of scholars, of the power of affective signaling. Marler notes:

> Far from being an impediment that somehow blunts the effectiveness of animal signalling behaviors, I would rather view the affective component as a highly sophisticated overlay that supplements the symbolic function of animal signals. Far from being detrimental, it increases the efficiency of rapid unequivocal communication by creating highly redundant signals whose content is . . . richer than we often suppose. [1980:225]

Indeed, in experiments conducted by Menzel (1975), chimpanzees were able, through nonverbal means, "and without any deliberate training . . . , to convey to each other the presence, direction, probable location, and the relative desirability and undesirability (if not the more precise nature) of a distant, hidden goal which no one had directly seen for himself."[15] Since affective, nonlinguistic communication is just as crucial to effective human communication as it is to animal exchanges, it would seem wise to suppose, at least until concrete evidence to the contrary is available, that it *would* come into play in interactions between man and ape. It is most unfortunate that there is even less known about man-ape communication than about either human or ape intraspecific codes, outside of what understanding comes from a few experiments (e.g., Exline and Yellin 1971) and anecdotes about researcher-ape signaling in the wild (e.g., van Hooff and Goodall, cited in Morris and Morris 1966b) or misunderstandings between captive animals and the untutored public (e.g., Desmond Morris 1979: 155ff.).

The second question that arises is: What does Premack mean by an "experienced" trainer? Nowhere is it specified that Premack himself, or his trainers or outside observers, had received special instruction in any

of the techniques of observation and control of subtle nonverbal signals
—e.g., control over their own individual facial muscles or training in the
recognition of the facial expressions of apes; experience in observing
and understanding ape or human body movements and proxemic behavior; training in the apes' use of odors as telltale signs; experience
in controlling one's own pupil responses (if indeed this is possible[16])
and in noting those of one's ape partner; tutoring in the use of nonlinguistic acoustic signals, such as throat clearing, breathing patterns,
hums, hesitation fillers, and the like—that would make them especially
qualified to perceive unwitting nonverbal cues. Without having some of
this sort of sensitivity training, on what grounds can a trainer or outside
observer deny conclusively that social cues are present? In a revealing
passage based, presumably, on personal communications, Desmond discusses the extent to which Nim excelled, and continually surprised, Laura
Petitto, his trainer for three years, with respect to his ability to detect
subtle nonverbal cues of which she, and apparently other humans with
whom they came in contact, were unaware.

> Nim read Laura Petitto's feelings like an open book, which made life with
> him occasionally precarious. She could even explore hidden aspects of her
> emotional self simply by trusting to Nim's heightened perception rather
> than her own coolly rational judgment: "he made me *wary* of my body,"
> she confides, and relates an incident which explains this cryptic state-
> ment. Laura was angry with someone; it was, of course, bottled up. . . .
> By all human accounts, there was not the slightest sign of anger when she
> next greeted the person who had caused the upset. Yet no sooner were
> pleasantries exchanged than Laura unknowingly triggered Nim's sympa-
> thetic aggression, and with hair erect he flew into an attack on the culprit.
> Laura is first to admit that she learnt more from Nim than he from her. . . .
> If anything, pidgin-signing cramped Nim's style. . . . [1979:231]

The very fact that it was only after painstaking analysis of unedited
film records that verbal cuing was discovered to be operating between
chimpanzees and their trainers, as noted above, not to mention the difficulty with which the Clever Hans and similar cases in the past were
"cracked," should put us all on our guard against facile judgments about
social cues. Witnessing a demonstration of an ape's linguistic capacities
plus having access to an unedited videotape or film of that same performance would seem to provide the only type of data by which truly
qualified observers could reach a conclusion—maybe—about the presence
or absence of subliminal communication between trainer and ape.

However, lacking these, still photographs are themselves enlighten-
ing, despite the fact that, in many cases, either the photographer has
focused exclusively on the ape or the photograph is cropped in such a
way that the human member of the dyad is totally or partially absent.
Nevertheless, when we do catch a glimpse of the trainers in action, they
are anything but detached and stone-faced. In conformity with the

National Geographic's notorious predilection for the beauty-and-the-beast motif, Francine Patterson has been featured in the majority of photographs illustrating her article (1978a). The richness of the non-verbal communication accompanying the signing of Patterson and Koko leaves little doubt that there is ample opportunity for Clever Hans cuing here. To take but two illustrations from this article, there is a series of four photographs showing Koko signing, according to the caption, *you, dirty, bad, toilet*. In each picture, Patterson's head position, facial expression, posture, and gestures change—in response to or in anticipation of Koko's signs it is impossible to tell. (It is also not possible to tell what took place in the time intervals between the four shots.) Nowhere in the text of the article is it mentioned that Patterson was signaling to Koko. Just what was she doing, then? In another, two-page photograph (pp.442-443), Koko is shown signing *teeth*—by grinning and touching her teeth with an index finger. Patterson is beside her, holding a picture of a grinning chimpanzee, and she is shown touching its teeth with her index finger!

Barber (1976: chap. 7) reviews a number of investigations of what he calls the Experimenter Failure to Follow the Procedure Effect. Citing especially Friedman (1967: chap. 5), he notes that "most experimenters have serious difficulties in following the experimental procedures closely even when the experimental protocol is standardized or is not especially 'loose'" (1976:54). In addition to this, "there appear to be wide deviations in kinesic and vocal behavior on the part of the experimenter" (ibid.). Both the "standardized" experiment and the "standardized" experimenter, in other words, are largely an illusion. In a number of cases, photographs of apes with their trainers not only furnish important information not specified in the report but may also contradict assertions made in the text. For example, in Ann Premack's book about her husband's project (1976), three photographs (p.54) reveal that, contrary to the description of working conditions given by Premack in his own book (1976), the chimpanzees—in this case, Elizabeth—could see their trainer not only before and after being given a problem and solving it, but while they were placing the plastic symbols on their display board.

In the first of a sequence of two scenes, Elizabeth reads the instruction on the board, and in the second, she responds by washing an apple in a carton of water. Several things can be said about these two photographs, keeping in mind, of course, that we are not told how much time elapsed between them or what behaviors occurred during that interval. Although the caption of the initial photograph explains that it is Elizabeth who is "reading" the instruction, *both* the trainer and the ape are shown pointing to one of the tokens at the same time, their hands even appearing to touch. The trainer, moreover, is looking at Elizabeth, head tilted slightly to one side, leaning expectantly toward the board and ape. Elizabeth is looking at the board but is in such a position that she could see (and hear) the movements of the trainer. In the second picture, the trainer relaxes against the back of her chair, her shoulders no longer tense but hunched forward, and she is looking down at the carton of water, grinning. Her whole attitude is one of a person who was tense while waiting to see if the animal could make the right response, and now relaxes as it does. Elizabeth, who is either about to place the apple in the water or is removing it, is not only looking directly at the trainer but returning her grin. At which moment, we might ask, did the trainer begin the process of relaxation, which could have served to inform the chimpanzee that it was on the right path? It was, after all, precisely the conversion of experimenters' anticipatory tension, as Clever Hans approached the correct response to a question, into involuntary cues—such as leaning back and relaxing—that permitted the horse to perform what, even to some of the world's then leading psychologists, appeared to be mathematical and linguistic operations (Pfungst 1965). To return to the case of Elizabeth and her experimenter, if so many obvious cues appear in these two photographs, how many more were in evidence during the entire session? In light of these observations, the following statement by Premack (1971: 820-821) takes on portentous significance:

> Was Sarah responding to the plastic language or to nonlinguistic cues arising from the trainer's face and body? In principle, this could be tested by eliminating the nonlinguistic cues. Trainers could wear dark glasses, or, after presenting Sarah with a question, station themselves behind an opaque screen, or simply look away from her. But these measures were practically useless. When the trainer put several questions on Sarah's board and then walked away, leaving her to answer them, Sarah worked erratically or quit altogether. . . . Social contact may be Sarah's primary motivation. In any case, she did not work under these circumstances.

Was it, one wonders, the absence of social reward or the lack of social cues that caused Sarah to fail?

In the third photograph, a different trainer is seen giving off equally obvious signals as Elizabeth, we are told in the caption, "writes" a message to her on the message board. The trainer is leaning forward expectantly, mouth open (whether to emit sounds or not is, of course, impossible to tell),[17] her hand poised in the box of tokens (grasping what one would assume is one of the symbols), eyes focused on Elizabeth. Now, if it is the *ape* who is writing the message, why is the trainer handling the tokens? An obvious clue? Possibly, for Elizabeth is looking directly at the trainer's hand in the box. Elizabeth is facing the trainer and could also conceivably take in the latter's facial expression, posture, and the like. Why, too, is the trainer staring so intently at the ape? It would seem likely that it would not be necessary for the human to look anywhere but at the display board in order to read Elizabeth's message. Could it be that it is as important for the trainer to be cued by her subject as the other way around? To what extent does she rely on nonverbal cues given off by the ape to determine what the latter may "mean" by using a given token, or to learn what Elizabeth is likely to do momentarily, thus making it possible for her to intercede—unintentionally, of course—in order to steer the ape in the proper direction through cues of her own?

In another example of a photograph illustrating the contrary of verbal descriptions, Patterson explains her use of the double-blind box test devised by the Gardners. A plywood box, 12 inches high by 14 inches wide by 14 inches deep, one side of which was a removable Plexiglas window, was baited by one experimenter with a random selection from a pool of objects. "A second experimenter, who did not know the contents of the box, stood behind it, and when Koko started the trial by uncovering the box, asked her what she saw (Figure 4)" (1979a:340). Figure 4 consists of a photograph of Koko, seated in front of the test box, signing, according to the picture's caption, *tiger*, the correct response since the box contained a toy tiger. In the photograph, Patterson is standing to one side of the box, *not* behind it, as the text states, and, in such a position, would have been able to see the contents of the box with little difficulty. Koko is clearly strong enough to move the test box around as she pleases. Under such conditions, the experimenter can hardly be said to be "blind." The photograph also shows Patterson's hand in the same configuration as Koko's signing hand, and she is obviously communicating with the gorilla through facial expression, gaze, and possibly sound.

THE DOUBLE-BLIND STRATEGY

Workers in this field exhibit a touching faith in the so-called double-blind strategy (Ploog and Melnechuk 1971:632-686),[18] borrowed from pharmacology, where it is now all but universally recognized that the method entails a multitude of booby traps on the experimenter's side as well as on the subject's: both "can serve as sources of unintended cues leading to the breakdown of experimenter blindness" (Rosenthal 1976: 372; see especially Tuteur 1957–1958). Constant and Dubois (1975) have shown how improper it is to assume that, in a double-blind study, the only pair of significant variables are the active ingredient and the placebo; they also pointed out how such a study may importantly affect personnel attitudes and their interactions with subjects.

Researchers have uniformly found it more difficult to test their ape subjects under the more stringent conditions of a double-blind situation than in normal, more sociable circumstances, and both chimpanzees and gorillas—whether using ASL or an artificial language—have shown a marked deterioration in their performance in the former, more artificial type of setting. The lack of cooperation on the part of an ape in such situations is usually described in reports in general terms rather than in detail, with frequent allusions to the animal's psychological or emotional attitude toward the "blind" experimenter, reminiscent of Clever Hans's being labeled "distrustful" of questioners who were unaware of the correct answers (Pfungst 1965:201).

The casualness of reports makes it extremely difficult in some cases to determine the significance of the data collected. For example, in the box test Patterson used with Koko—discussed above—the gorilla's reactions were described as follows:

> This test situation required a fair amount of discipline, and curiously enough we found that, like Washoe, Koko's interest and cooperation could be secured for no more than five trials a day and two sessions per week. Her methods of avoiding the task were varied—she would either respond to all objects with the same sign, refuse to respond at all, or regress to an earlier pattern of asking to have the box opened. [Patterson 1979a:340-341]

Koko is said to have scored correctly 60 percent of the time, or above chance, on the series of double-blind tests administered to her. It is reasonable to ask, however, how Koko's instances of avoiding the test— e.g., by responding to all objects with the same sign—were scored. We are not told whether such inappropriate responses were discounted as avoidance measures or counted as errors. Since these types of responses are not included in any of the four categories of errors listed on p.11 of Patterson's report, we may assume that they are, in fact, not represented in the 60 percent score. We can only guess whether Koko's performance would have been below chance if a less-biased accounting had been made.

The problems with this procedure do not end here, of course. As with so many of the double-blind tests administered to the apes, no allowance has been made for the fact that, when working with such a relatively small corpus of signs, the "blind" experimenter, no doubt a clever human, may be applying certain game strategies that enable him or her to guess at what the input to the chimpanzee or gorilla has been. The "random" selection of objects placed in the test box sounds good until one consults the various figures and tables provided by Patterson. When the double-blind tests were administered to Koko in September 1975, she was four and probably had only 107 nouns in her vocabulary for objects appropriate for use in the box. Each trial, then, with thirty objects, would constitute 28 percent of her total inventory of nouns. This would surely allow a good deal of successful guessing to go on by the "blind" experimenter (not to mention Koko), who, as a regular trainer (which we must assume was the case, since Patterson does not say that the person was independent of her project), would surely have a memory sufficient to hold 107 such items.

A second strategy could also have been operating here. It is not specified whether different experimenters were used for each of the double-blind tests. If the same individuals were used, then several questions come to mind: How was the "random" selection of objects made in each trial? If not done by computer but by human, did the person making the selection choose the objects while blindfolded, perhaps pointing to them with a stick, while a third person picked them up and placed them in a box? If not, that is, if the person is aware of which items he has selected, he would surely be tempted, on subsequent trials, to vary the objects presented. The second, "blind" experimenter could also work according to the assumption that the objects used on one trial would not be likely to recur too frequently in subsequent ones.

There is, furthermore, the possibility that the "blind" experimenter, especially if he was familiar with Koko's earlier sign performances, could have been cued by the gorilla's nonlinguistic reactions to the objects, which were, after all, familiar to her. If, for example, Koko were accustomed to smacking her lips when presented with a preferred food, the accustomed response during the double-blind test could furnish the experimenter with valuable information about which class of objects—foods Koko likes—the animal has in view. Judging from our own observations of Koko on television, as well as reports of other apes in similar situations, such nonverbal responses are bound to occur even in the double-blind testing context, and it is difficult both to understand why they are so routinely ignored by researchers and to imagine how to avoid them altogether. Even an observer unfamiliar with Koko, for example, might correctly interpret some of the gorilla's more obvious reactions, especially when the test objects are repeated on subsequent trials with the same person as witness. In the case of the tests with Koko, the ambiguities are many, since we are not told if the blind observer had prior experience with the project or if he was engaged in more than a single trial. Furthermore, only the overall score for the whole series of tests was reported, making it impossible to judge the effects of learning by both Koko and her human experimenters.

The Gardners' description (1980a:318ff.) of their double-blind testing procedure administered to Washoe indicates a more carefully controlled situation than the one just discussed. Washoe was seated in front of a booth, before a sliding door that she could open or close, behind which there was a screen on which slide pictures could be projected. One "blind" observer, called O-1, stood to one side of the box and, when Washoe opened the sliding door and a slide was projected onto the screen, asked the chimpanzee in ASL what she saw. Observer O-1 then wrote down Washoe's signed response to this question and deposited the slip of paper in the message slot (M. S.), where it was retrieved by experimenter E-1, who, seated behind the booth and to the left of the compartment where Washoe viewed the slides, operated the slide projector and recorded the observations of both O-1 and O-2. The second "blind" observer, O-2, sat behind the booth, opposite Washoe, and could view her through a one-way mirror. In one version of the test, all three human participants were project assistants, while in another, control situation, O-2 was a deaf person with no particular association with the Washoe project and O-1 and E-1 were members of the Gardners' staff.

Despite the added precaution of two "blind" observers, some of the above-mentioned problems concerning experimenter learning, guessing

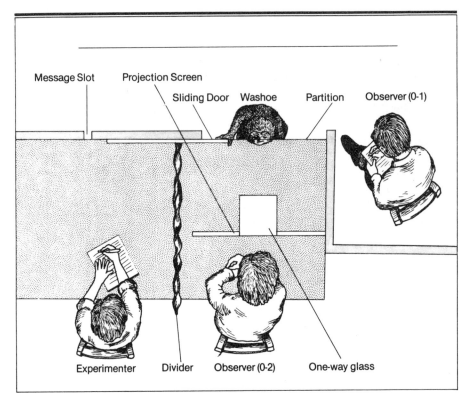

Message Slot   Projection Screen
Sliding Door   Washoe   Partition   Observer (0-1)

Experimenter   Divider   Observer (0-2)   One-way glass

FIG. 8.3. Double-blind testing by the Gardners

strategies, and the presence of nonlinguistic cues could still be operating during the Gardners' procedure. The research assistants could, through their familiarity with Washoe's relatively small vocabulary, stand a good chance of guessing which object was being shown on the screen, even though the particular exemplars exhibited were changed from those used in training and the order of presentation was randomized (how, we do not know). Non-naive observers could also rely to some extent on familiar nonverbal cues given off by the chimpanzee in response to certain objects. That the two observers may have been learning both the kinds of objects likely to be used in the test and Washoe's nonlinguistic cues is shown by the fact that "their agreement increased from one test session to the next" (ibid.:320).

The use of a naive deaf observer in the O-2 position does not necessarily eliminate these problems. For one reason, the Gardners report that this deaf observer was familiarized beforehand with the two vocabulary lists that might be used in the test in which they served as an observer. Why this was thought necessary is not clear, since one would assume that if the chimpanzee's signs are good ASL signs, any native signer would have no difficulty interpreting them at first encounter, without having to study a vocabulary list. This also raises the question of what other types of information were conveyed to the deaf observer during his or her initial training period—e.g., familiar contexts of use of vocabulary items, characteristic nonlinguistic responses of Washoe or E-1 or O-1. (In fact, did either E-1 or O-1 have a hand in training the outside observer?) How "naive," in other words, was this deaf observer when the tests began?

Some of the danger of learning by the deaf observer could have been reduced if the Gardners had used a different deaf person in each trial. As it is, the fact that "The degree of agreement between the deaf observer and the project assistant *during the second test* was well within the range of agreement found between O-1 and O-2, when each was a project assistant thoroughly familiar with Washoe's signing" (ibid.:320; our emphasis), may only indicate that the deaf observer was a fast learner.

Outside of such ambiguities, there exists a whole set of difficulties with the double-blind tests administered to "language-learning" apes. While the double-blind tests were designed especially to eliminate the possibility of illicit communication in either direction between experimenters and their subjects, a close look at those in which enough information about the actual setting and procedures followed is available reveals that in every case leakage is not only possible but probable.

Take, for example, the Gardners' own double-blind test. After O-1 writes down Washoe's response, he must pass in front of the sliding door in order to reach the message slot. If, as seems possible, the door is open as O-1 passes by, he would have visual access to the interior of the viewing box. E-1, who operates the slide projector, may have been instructed to leave the slide on the screen until O-1 has delivered a message, in which case the latter will have an opportunity to see the picture and learn whether Washoe's response was correct and whether the observer's reading of the chimpanzee's signs was accurate. Even assuming that O-1 was not allowed to change his message en route to the message slot, this type of feedback would greatly enhance his ability to predict, in the fashion of a Markov chain (see Cherry 1978), which objects would be projected at a later time, as well as to develop skill in interpreting any idiosyncratic signing behavior by the chimpanzee. Furthermore, what would prevent O-1 from inadvertently indicating to Washoe—and to O-2, who could no doubt see O-1 as he passed behind the chimpanzee—whether her response had been correct? And, in his article on statistical problems in ESP research, Diaconis (1978) has demonstrated how merely knowing whether or not he has made a hit or a miss in guessing ESP cards gives an alleged psychic an advantage and thus influences the outcome of the test.

The Gardners report that O-2 communicated his interpretations of Washoe's signs to E-1 verbally, as they sat side by side. How do we know that O-1 could not hear O-2's spoken observations, which might be expected to influence his own, thus leading to an increased level of agreement between the two? Furthermore, if there is an acoustic channel open between E-1, who knows what the correct responses should be, and

O-2, what evidence is there that auditory cues were not given by E-1 to O-2, signals such as "uh-huh," coughs, the sound of shifting in his seat, and the like, which could have provided O-2 with clues as to the accuracy of his own as well as Washoe's performances? Pilisuk et al. (1976) have described a host of seemingly innocent sounds that, in laboratory experiments, can and often do function as unwitting cues to subjects. Rosenthal (Pfungst 1965:xxi) also mentions an interesting example of auditory cuing in which the experimenter, using a scratchy pen, unintentionally cued a subject by the recording system he was using (long vs. short scratches).

Was the deaf O-2 totally deaf, or could he too have taken advantage of such a channel? If he was totally deaf, to what extent could he control the volume of his verbal report to E-1? And would not E-1, in this case, have a tendency to raise his voice in order to acknowledge O-2's response, thus making it more likely that Washoe and/or O-1 (both of normal hearing) would hear him? If E-1 could not make use of verbal acknowledgments, did he lean back and sign to O-2? Or could O-2 have leaned back, thus catching a glimpse of the written record being made by E-1?

If there was an acoustic channel open between E-1 and O-2, and between O-2 and O-1 (either through the partition or through the one-way glass as O-1 passed in front of the booth), would there not be reason to believe that O-1 could also hear any auditory cues given by E-1?

Furthermore, since one-way glass does not ordinarily impede the passage of sound, we can assume that Washoe could hear O-2's verbal interpretations of her signs, which might lead her to change her answer, which might be picked up by O-1. We are not told whether Washoe was allowed to do so, or whether only her first response was counted. If there is an acoustic channel open between Washoe and O-2, and between O-2 and E-1, would it not seem likely that Washoe could hear any auditory feedback provided by E-1 as well?

Even if we assume that E-1 could not see or hear Washoe or O-1, he would have to wait until both written and oral interpretations were received before projecting a new slide. This means that whichever observer finished last would have an opportunity to witness a larger set of chimpanzee signs, one of which, but not necessarily the first, being correct.

This test could have been improved by the use of deaf persons for O-1 and E-1, with only written responses.[19] The Gardners seem to have thought of that but ruled it out on the grounds that Washoe would not have performed as well with a strange O-1. Since the only interaction *required* between O-1 and Washoe was the execution of simple question-answer adjacency pairs, one wonders why this should be the case. Perhaps because this linguistic exchange was *not* the only behavior required by the chimpanzee?

Premack first attempted to eliminate the Clever Hans Effect by testing Sarah with a "dumb" trainer, i.e., someone unfamiliar with her token language, although it is not clear precisely what type of experience the new trainer had had with Sarah prior to the tests. We are merely told that Sarah was "adapted" to the person, who "engaged in normal social behavior" with her during a preliminary stage, under conditions that "differed from those of testing" (David Premack 1976:821). As Premack describes this double-blind test (1971, 1976), the "dumb" trainer presented Sarah with a problem on the display board, following only a number code. Sarah's response was communicated by the trainer to a project member, stationed in an adjacent room, by microphone, The project member then told the trainer if Sarah's response was correct or not.

Under these conditions, Premack reports, there was a definite "decrement in her accuracy" and a "deterioration in the form of her behavior" (1976:34).

> The most striking aspect of this deterioration was a regression to an earlier form of sentence production that was once her dominant form. Early in training she had not produced sentences in their final order: she put correct words on the board in incorrect orders and then made one or two changes before settling on a final order. Although she had abandoned this mode of production at least ten months earlier, she reverted to it with the "dumb" trainer. [Premack 1971:821]

This is precisely the sort of behavior one might expect the chimpanzee to exhibit if she had been searching for clues from the experimenter. She displays the tokens and then, moving them around, waits for an unintentional sign from the trainer that one arrangement is considered acceptable.

It is not difficult to conjecture how even a "dumb" trainer could inadvertently cue Sarah that a certain sequence of tokens was correct. Since the "dumb" trainer did not understand Sarah's token language, how did he know when she had "settled on" a "final order"? It would seem logical that he would only report her *first* arrangement of tokens—incorrect responses, according to Premack. If the trainer did do so, and, as one must assume from Premack's discussion of this experiment, these responses were not counted as errors, then one may conclude that the project assistant in the adjacent room instructed the experimenter in some way not to go on to the next problem, but to wait for further responses from Sarah. In this way, the chimpanzee could learn which order—relayed indirectly from the person in the next room—was acceptable, since only after that particular attempt would the "dumb" trainer be told to acknowledge her responses.

In addition to this sort of cuing, Sarah may also have been relying on her memory to solve some of the problems in the double-blind test, as Brown (1980) has suggested. Premack (1976:34) denies that this is the case, saying that, by the time the tests were given, Sarah had experienced 2,600 sentences and would have had to memorize that many to do as well as she did in the 58 sentences used in the tests. His explanation is not as compelling as it might appear at first blush, for only 14 of the 58 test sentences were new to Sarah, and we are not told whether the 44 "old" sentences were taken from recently learned sets. As noted above, the manner in which the test frames were set up was such that Sarah did not actually have to take into account all the signs in a sequence in order to respond correctly, so she might have had to memorize far less than Premack alleges in order to do well. In light of these considerations, Premack's estimate (1976:35) that about 10 percent of Sarah's accuracy was due to nonlinguistic cues seems unrealistically low.

Another deficiency noted in Sarah's responses was that the verticality of her sentences suffered. "Ordinarily, words were placed more or less below one another, but with the 'dumb' trainer she failed to maintain this orderliness. The sprawling sentence was another characteristic of her early behavior" (Premack 1971:821). Again, if the symbols were "sprawling," how did the "dumb" trainer know in what order to report them to the project member? Did the latter, perhaps, impose an order on the numbers read to him, possibly also conveying to the trainer some information about proper order through the inadvertent signing of his recognition of a familiar pattern or asking questions about the exact spatial relationship between the tokens on the board?

Premack took into account that the new trainer may have, over a number of trials, learned something of Sarah's code, thereby enabling him to cue her. When he tested the trainer, he found that the latter had in fact guessed some of the rules of the token language, but also that in certain cases his inferences were incorrect, so that in some instances his cues—if responded to by the chimpanzee—would actually have led Sarah to make erroneous responses. Since Sarah did about as well on the first test with the new trainer as on subsequent ones, cuing was not deemed a significant influence on test results. If, however, the new trainer was serving as a *conduit* for cues coming from the person in the next room, a uniform level of performance is precisely what *would* be expected. While, as Ristau and Robbins remark, "the possible role of cues in these chimpanzee projects is far more difficult to imagine and cannot be so simple" (1979:288) as those involved in the Clever Hans case, surely there is ample reason to doubt that Premack's "dumb" trainer experiment "is conclusive in that the accurate aspects of her [Sarah's] performance cannot be attributed to subtle cues given by the dumb trainer" (ibid.:289).

In the double-blind experiment with Ally mentioned above (and in another test of his understanding of *in, on,* and *under*), to take another example, the screen placed between the experimenter and the three possible locations in which the chimpanzee was to place a test item would have allowed the experimenter to hear, if not see, where Ally was putting the object, and to cue him accordingly. Such cuing is all the more likely when one learns that "Ally is a hyperactive chimpanzee and often grabbed the correct item and rushed to the different possible locations before the experimenter had completely finished signing the command" (Fouts et al. 1979:301). Fouts and his colleagues concluded from this that Ally's 40 percent correct score was only a conservative estimate of his ability to comprehend novel commands, since such behavior drastically lowered his overall score. Alternatively, one might take this as evidence that the chimpanzee's basic strategy in this testing situation was to respond not to the ASL command, but to the experimenter's unwitting auditory cues, produced as he rushed toward or away from various target sites.

A more recent attempt by Premack, Woodruff, and Kennel (1978) to devise a test for Sarah that would be free of social cues involved a paper-marking task utilizing pictures of tokens she had been trained with, plus pictures of toys, objects, and foods familiar to her. A project assistant placed in front of the chimpanzee trays containing pairs of pictures of objects and pairs of tokens. Sarah was supposed to mark with tape that member of a pair of tokens that correctly described the relationship between the objects (same vs. different, similar vs. same, and similar vs. different). Sarah was later tested on same vs. different with letters of the alphabet rather than pictures of objects. The trainer was to leave the room after presenting the trays to the chimpanzee and to return only when Sarah rang a bell.

Although over the five tests given, Sarah's overall score, we are told, was above chance, her accuracy for the concept "different" was only at chance level on two of the tests, as was her performance for the concept "similar" on one of them. The materials, furthermore, as Premack himself admits, tested "only rudimentary cognitive and linguistic capacities" (ibid.:905). It is perhaps significant that, as the double-blind controls become more stringent, the tasks required of Sarah become simpler and, from the point of view of linguistic capacity, less interesting. The same may be said of the recent experiment by Savage-Rumbaugh et al. (1980) that purportedly demonstrates Austin's and Sherman's "comprehension" of two (!) lexigrams as "representational labels"; (Lana was incapable of proceeding beyond the early stages of training).

Even in these experiments, however, the controls were not absolute, and the possibility still exists that social cues were operating in them. Despite Premack's claim that "the present results cannot be interpreted in terms of the subject's sensitivity to inadvertent social cues" (ibid.),[20] for instance, it is possible that the trainer unwittingly cued Sarah as he was placing the trays in front of her. He could have inadvertently touched or pointed to a correct response while, perhaps, straightening a paper on a tray, or even merely tensed or in some other way called attention to the hand that was closer to a correct answer. Even a fleeting glimpse at the correct token could serve as a cue, as would the mere positioning of the bell more or less close to a correct response. None of these cues would have been easily visible to the camera or to a second observer stationed opposite the chimpanzee's cage, for the trainer would, for at least part of the time, have had to have his back to both. In addition, it seems unlikely that Sarah would always wait patiently until the trainer had left the room before proceeding to mark the paper, especially since she seemed motivated primarily by a desire for the trainer's presence, praise, or more tangible reward.

Project reports all too frequently give the impression that ape subjects sit quietly through tests, while this is far from what actually happens. As several of the examples noted in this chapter show, experimenters must spend a good part of testing time interacting with the animal just to get it under sufficient control to enable them to administer the test, hardly what one would call ideal experimental conditions. If cuing is feasible even when a subject is sitting still and attentive, it is even more so under the sometimes chaotic circumstances created by an ape's natural responses to such man-made rules.

Alone in a Crowd

Sarah's paper-marking test raises an additional question concerning the double-blind strategy of the ape "language" projects. The trainer was not the only person capable of cuing Sarah in this context. Judging from the photographs used to illustrate the testing situation (Premack et al. 1978:905), there was a photographer present for all or at least some of the test, even when the trainer was not in the room. We are not told in the report if the photographer was familiar with Sarah's token language, but with such a restricted number of tokens as found in this particular test, it would not be difficult for anyone to learn fairly quickly which responses were correct and which ones wrong. Assuming that, if the photographer was in the room when the trainer departed, he would be able to sign to Sarah by optical, acoustic, and/or other means, if only by the timing of his camera shots. Even if they were separated by a one-way mirror, the photographer could inadvertently let Sarah know when she was about to select the correct answer by his choosing that moment to snap a picture, which Sarah could detect. The same would apply as well to any discontinuous videotaping or filming process. This is based on the not unreasonable assumption, supported by a study of photographs and films of several of the chimpanzee and gorilla projects, that if a photographer may select what to record, he is most likely to find photogenic—even dramatic—moments when the animal is doing something significant in terms of the purpose of the occasion: e.g., gesturing distinctly if it is a matter of the use of ASL, or solving a problem with tokens or computer keys if an artificial symbol system is involved.

One can also speculate—and, since very little information is ever given in reports about the procedures followed for recording events, this is all one can do at present—that some sort of communication may take place between the photographer and the experimenter conducting a test. It is certainly not out of the question that a trainer, hearing a camera clicking to a start, could be primed to apply an extra ounce of unintentional pressure on the experimental subject to produce a significant response "for the record." If the photographer were a project assistant and the experimenter an outside observer, the former could actually cue the animal through the latter. Pfungst (1965:210), who seems to have overlooked nothing in his investigation of the Clever Hans case, remarked that, while spectators did not influence Hans, "[t]he effect upon the questioner . . . was unmistakable." Given a calm and confident person, such as Mr. von Osten, "the questioner's zeal was increased and with it the tension of concentration." Less-assured questioners, on the other hand, were distracted by the audience so that, rather than improving, the accuracy of their cuing of Hans suffered.

In general, there is a frustrating lack of agreement between assertions made about a project's "usual" procedures and the reporting of any particular training or testing event, leaving the reader to question whether a given procedure in fact lived up to the claims made for it. One particularly striking example of this is provided in Rumbaugh 1977 (159-160), where Gill and Rumbaugh give the following description of Lana's early training:

> Since Lana seemed to thrive on social contact, the behavioral technicians maintained close contact with her and frequently entered her room to "model" the correct behavior, taking her finger and pressing the correct key with it or pointing to the appropriate key or set of keys. Although these supportive techniques were used in the training sessions . . . the experimenters gave no such assistance during the *test* phases in which proficiency levels . . . were assessed. During the tests every precaution was taken to preclude the possibility that any extraneous cues might aid Lana's performance. Blinds were installed to deny her visual access to the experimenter; the sequence of trials for different tasks was randomized; her responses were automatically recorded by the teleprinter; and, when possible, experimenters not involved in training were used to test Lana.

While it is easy to grasp how cues could have been given during the training sessions (Gill and Rumbaugh mention, for example, that in some cases an experimenter would communicate with Lana by tapping on the walls of her room [ibid.:172]), it is more difficult to assess the degree to which such cues have been eliminated in testing conditions. For example, of the five experiments reported (ibid.: Part III, chaps. 9-13), only one actually lived up to the special "blind" conditions noted above, and this consisted merely of a cardboard screen at the window leading into Lana's room.

In another report by Savage-Rumbaugh et al. (1980b:369) we are told that, in general, "Iconic gestures have been repeatedly devised by the animals, and by the experimenters, as an adjunct to the abstract symbols available on the keyboard," such gestures serving "as an intermediate link between symbol and event." But members of the Lana project seldom discuss such gestures in their reports, rarely mentioning the possibility of acoustic, tactile, or olfactory cues, although some sound was able to pass between the animals' cages and the room in which the experimenter was located. In the test reported in Savage-Rumbaugh et al. (1980b), for example, the subjects, Austin and Sherman, had to hand each other tools from one room to another; sound surely could pass through the opening needed for this, yet the trainers tested only for visual cues, not acoustic ones.[21] Schubert (1978) questions how "blind" the tests with Austin and Sherman really were. On the one hand, the investigators reported that changes in experimenters resulted in performance decrement during all stages of training, suggesting that some information loss must have occurred when one experimenter replaced another. The possibility of Clever Hans cues being given by the experimenters was not completely eliminated in this experiment, according to Schubert, because, for example, in the naming task, the experimenter stood outside the subject's room and held up a tool so that the chimpanzee could see it through a lexan wall. "But if the C[himp] could see the tool well enough to distinguish it, he could also see at least part of E[xperimenter]'s hand, and perhaps part of his arm(s) too. How much more information does a chimp need to identify which human (among the small sample of available alternatives) he was dealing with?" (ibid.:598). In addition, Savage-Rumbaugh reports that the chimpanzees "could come out of the room and seek contact or comfort between trials at any point" (1980: 13), but does not specify how the animals were informed about the definition of "a trial." Can we not imagine Austin and Sherman repeatedly attempting to make contact with the experimenter *during* trials?

During the "blind" tests of the chimpanzees' use of tools to open a container in order to obtain a reward, the experimenter stood outside the subject's room so as not to be visible from the keyboard. He viewed the animal's request for a certain tool on a projector outside the room and then handed the animal the tool. The experimenter knew which tool was the correct one and could have provided the chimpanzee with unwitting auditory cues.

When blind tests of the chimpanzee's ability to understand and comply with a request for a tool were administered, two experimenters were present. The first, E-1, was in the room with the chimpanzee, seated with his back to the projector. E-2 was stationed outside the room and, we are told, out of the view of the subject. E-2 projected a tool lexigram onto the animal's projector, whereupon the subject was to note the lexigram on his projector, choose the tool, and give it to E-1, who then reported his response verbally to E-2, who recorded it. In this situation, communication between E-2 and E-1 was not ruled out, nor was auditory signaling between E-1 and the subject. While it is specified that E-2 could not be seen by the subject, we are not told that the human could not see the animal; it is not too difficult to imagine a situation in which the chimpanzee was visible to E-2, in which case he would be aware of its actions and whether they were appropriate. Pertinent information could then have been communicated from human to human, and ultimately, through a variety of channels, from human back to animal.

Photographs of the Yerkes facilities make it clear that the rooms used for testing contained windows, doors, portals, and transparent walls. It is hardly fair, under these circumstances, to expect that the reader of this project's experimental reports, in which these pictures figure prominently, will conclude that, when the investigators simply claim that an experimenter stood outside the testing chamber, communication (other than by lexigrams) between human and animal was thereby eliminated. In the case of the tool-using experiment, one wonders not only if the human could see the animal but also if—contrary to the description given by the investigators—the chimpanzee could in fact see the experimenter. The naivete of such assertions as "It would seem reasonable to conclude that *if* the chimp could not see the experimenter, then the experimenter also would be unable to see the chimpanzee" (Savage-Rumbaugh 1980:15-16) throws doubt on all those seemingly straightforward claims about an experimenter being "absent" or "outside" the room and outside the view of the subject. How, one might legitimately ask, did the investigators determine that the animal could at no time during trials see the experimenter?

Finally, in the description of the tests of the chimpanzees' ability to perform the naming, receptive, and functional tasks together, several curious elements of the situation further reduce the significance of the experiment as a whole. First, it was only on one of six days of trials that "blind" conditions were imposed on the animals. Why weren't all the trials blind? Second, the blind trials did not take place until the fifth day. The investigators explained that

> Earlier, E's presence had been necessary to help both Cs to coordinate attention and action and to remind them of the task at hand. Without this help and structure they tended to play and to become easily distracted, like preschool children. [Savage-Rumbaugh et al. 1980b:366-367]

What, one wonders, happened between the fourth and fifth days that suddenly enabled the chimpanzees to perform so well on "blind" tests—even *better*, in fact, than on tests that were not blind? Certainly, despite the overly optimistic and unsubstantiated denial by the investigators, this increase in accuracy

> suggested that perhaps the animals had learned nonverbal signals during this period that enabled them to transmit information through a channel other than the symbols on the keyboard. Perhaps their use of the keyboard merely reflected the continuance of behaviors that they had been conditioned to emit by E, although these behaviors were no longer functional in the communication. [Ibid.:367]

Alternatively, it may have been the case that experimenters on that fifth day—and by then they must have been extremely eager to obtain some positive results to reward them for the long training periods that led up to that day—were not as "blind" as one is led to believe by the investigators' report. In fact, we are not given any details at all about the "blind" conditions on the interanimal trials, merely that the experimenter was "blind." However, we have already pointed out how many sources of cuing there were in the blind tests of a single animal; so, without further information, the scores for the interanimal "blind" trials must be considered suspect. The investigators slip in yet another unknown factor here, which is mysteriously left unexplained—namely, that, on the fifth day, some of the trials were conducted with the experimenter "absent." In fact, the scores for both "absent" and "blind" conditions are reported together, making it impossible to determine whether there were any significant differences in performance level in the different situations. Furthermore, we are not told what "absent" means, but from descriptions of other experiments by this team of researchers—and from pictures of this experiment itself, in which a strange, disembodied human hand and arm appear with alarming regularity—it seems highly unlikely that the subjects were in fact completely isolated from humans for entire trials. Someone had to bring them into the room, bait the containers, activate the computer, remove the animals from the room, and so forth. Why are so many of these details omitted from a description that is aimed precisely at proving the absence of cuing?

The investigators ultimately support their claim that the animals were not responding to nonverbal cues by the fact that, when the keyboards were deactivated, the animals failed miserably. To this one might respond that, as in their previous work on interanimal communication (see below), such a testing situation only proves that the animals fail (1) when the experimenters, unable to learn the correct responses by reading the keyboard, are truly "blind"—as they are not in double-blind tests; and (2) when the experimenters, aware of the correct response but *wishing or expecting the animals to fail* in order to prove the validity of their hypothesis, cue the animals in a negative sense, as Pfungst (1965) has shown skeptics to have done for Clever Hans. One must not assume that experimenters want their animals to succeed in all testing situations.

In the majority of photographs of Lana, she is shown alone with her computer console, giving the impression of an interaction completely devoid of human contamination. And yet, as Terrace and Bever (1980:186) have pointed out, "many of her most striking 'utterances' occur with a trainer present," precisely when, as even the project members themselves agree, conditions are anything but free of social cues. When the trainers do not enter her cage or tap on the walls, they nevertheless "can vary the time, rate, and choice of presentation, which leaves open the possibility that Lana's performance is still being shaped by uncontrolled factors (which often appear to be unrecorded), e.g., Lana's cage position, her drive state, the trainer's current assessment of her position and state, and so on" (ibid.:186). Pictures of the more stringently controlled tests raise the question of how "alone" Lana really is even under these less-social conditions. Someone, after all, is taking the picture of her, and presumably can be heard by the chimpanzee while doing so. Furthermore, given the large staff associated with this project, one suspects that there might be other detectable personnel performing their varied chores in the wings.

Reports of studies of apes in their natural habitat are similar in their disregard of the presence of photographers and other project staff members. Pictures of Goodall, Fossey, or Galdikas, for example, tend to delineate the romantic image of a brave, young woman alone with the beasts of the jungle. While this may have much the same appeal as the image of Jane in Tarzan stories or the prototypal beauty in the tale of "Beauty and the Beast," it is hardly an accurate record of the actual, far more complex, conditions of research. Designed to bolster the credibility of the findings presented in the narrative part of the report, these illustrations actually obfuscate rather than clarify, at least for the average viewer, who approaches them expecting to have verbal reports confirmed and even amplified.

In this respect, the Lana enterprise resembles the other ape "language" projects insofar as they attempt to communicate a sense of solitary splendor in which experimental animals operate, while in actual fact it is usually more a question of the subjects being "alone in a crowd." Consider, as a final example, the experiment conducted by Savage-Rumbaugh and her associates (1978) to test the ability of two chimpanzees, Austin and Sherman, to communicate symbolically with one another. Using the same computer language (Yerkish) designed for Lana, the subjects were trained to identify the symbols for eleven types of food and drink. In the first of a series of tests, the animals shared a keyboard. On alternate trials, one of them was taken into an adjacent room, where it watched the experimenter bait and seal a container with one of the foods. On its return to the first room, this chimpanzee, called the "informer," was asked—by computer, we assume—what was in the container. When the informer had pushed the key on which the proper lexigram was embossed, the second chimpanzee, known as the "observer," who had not been allowed to witness the baiting of the box, but was able to watch the informer's "description" of the contents, was then permitted to request the food via the keyboard. If both chimpanzees responded appropriately, the container was opened and the food was given to the subjects. The animals were correct on 33 of 35 trials.

The investigators were aware that in this test, it was particularly likely that the experimenter, who knew what was in the box, could cue the animals, since, as seen in the photograph on p.642 of the report, that person was holding each chimpanzee by a leash.[22] To control for this, in all subsequent tests the experimenter did not accompany the informer into the other room, and the box was baited by another project member. It is not stated, however, that the experimenter was not permitted to see the informer's keyboard description of the contents of the container. That means that the moment a correct response was made by the informer—which could be explained adequately on the basis of a simple X-R association—the experimenter, who knew the meaning of the symbols used, was no longer "blind" and would have therefore been in a position to cue the observer during his subsequent performance. This weakness in the experimental design would occur also in tests in which the animals were not allowed to see one another pushing the single keyboard they shared, with only the lexigram projecting above the keyboard, and those in which they had separate keyboards (in different rooms, separated by glass), on which the lexigrams were arranged in different sequences.

In a final control experiment, the informer was not permitted to use the keyboard but could communicate in any other way with the observer. The latter was, after 30 to 60 seconds, encouraged to use the keyboard to request the contents of the container. As opposed to their high scores on all the earlier tests, Sherman and Austin did only 4 of 26 trials correctly under these conditions; the investigators claim this result shows that it was only through symbolic, not affective, signs that the animals had been communicating when they had been more successful. It is possible, however, that the reason the animals' performance was so poor was that this was the only test in which the experimenter was truly "blind" and therefore unable to provide cues.

Even if the experimenter was not cuing the chimpanzees, another source of information was available to them that should have been taken into account by the investigators, but was not. Since the container itself was within the reach of at least one of the animals in each test situation, it is possible that its contents could have been made known to the observer (and experimenter) by lifting, shaking, or otherwise manipulating it. This trick is well known to alleged clairvoyants; for example, in order to "see" which of a number of sealed, identical cans is filled with water, they may tap their feet, walk around, or in some other unobtrusive way shake the containers in order to observe the different sounds or other sensations given off by the filled can.[23] In the case of Sherman and Austin, simply picking up the can for a second could tell them whether the food inside was liquid or solid, large or small. Identification of the contents could also be made by smell from a distance. Since we are in fact told by the investigators (1978:643) that "attempts to steal the container" were made by the subjects in this experiment, that "they wanted to hold, smell, and bite the container" (Savage-Rumbaugh 1980: 23), such an alternative explanation of the results does not seem too far-fetched.

Additional doubt is thrown on the investigators' interpretations of Sherman and Austin's performances by statements such as "The chimpanzees were mutually attentive and if one appeared to have difficulty finding a key, the other often tried to assist, though restrained from doing so" (Savage-Rumbaugh et al. 1978:643), and "Sherman and Austin were also able to use symbols to request that specific foods be given and to respond appropriately to one another's request. Thus if Sherman has an array of foods in front of him, and Austin asks for an 'orange,' Sherman will look over the food until he finds an orange, then give it to Austin. If he has difficulty sighting the orange, Austin may point to it for him" (Savage-Rumbaugh 1980:7). Beneath the pseudoscientific jargon (e.g., "sighting" instead of "seeing"), one glimpses the complex human-animal and interanimal nonverbal communication taking place, complete with "assisting" (read: "grabbing," "touching," "looking," "pointing") and "restraining" (read: "tugging on leash," "pushing," "pulling," "reprimanding").

THE CLASH OF UMWELTEN IN FACT AND FICTION

Critics, on occasion, have asked why the cognitive behaviors alleged to have been elicited in hand-raised apes have never been observed in the wild. This question is closely paralleled by a second one: Why, if apes have a strong picture-making potential in captivity, have they neither developed nor utilized it in nature (chap. 9, p.236)? The usual rejoinders are sanguine: We don't yet know enough about either the native communication system or artistic tenue of these creatures, but, any day now, someone will catch them at it. However we think yet another fallacy lurks behind this optimism, one that fails to allow for the fact that apes live in a radically different phenomenal world—or what, since Jakob von Uexküll, ethologists call *Umwelt* (Sebeok 1979: chap. 10; J. von Uexküll 1980). An ape is not interested in verbal art, or painting, or the like, but in "apely" objects and relations; in brief, in signs that are functionally meaningful to its species preeminently (cf. Hediger 1980). As Franz Kafka's (1917) ape-man tells the Academy, apes think with their bellies. A narrow segment of their world of signs may, of course, overlap with the modern human *Umwelt*. What the research community is trying to achieve—and, to a limited extent, had succeeded in doing, by means of *apprentissage* or *dressage*—is the widening of this area of overlap; but it by no means follows that the expanded sign repertory will be biologically significant for the trained animal. As Desmond notes, in his discussion of Koko's alleged acquisition of signs such as *cry, damn, sorry,* and other "blatant misnomer[s] listed in ape vocabularies," "a word can only be absorbed if it is relevant; and it can only be made relevant by mapping it on to one's own psychosocial framework" (1979:54). The simple act of imitating a sign, or even using it "appropriately" "may only mean that humans understand both context and sign differently from the ape" (ibid.).

That apes sometimes can be taught large repertoires of gestures or other visual signs—even signs that could be characterized, according to one of Peirce's trichotomies of sign classification (1931-65:2.249) as *symbols,* that is, when the relationship between the sign itself and its object is arbitrary—has been established by the ape "language" projects. While Premack (in Chomsky 1979:8) emphasizes the importance of the finding that "the ape, too, can recognize the relation between an item and an arbitrary representation of an item," this should hardly surprise anyone, since, as has been shown (Sebeok 1976: chap. 8; 1979: chap. 1), examples of true symbols can be found throughout the animal world, including among insects. Furthermore, what has *not* been proven by the ape "language" research is that the symbols used by the animals are any more propositional than the tricks taught apes in circuses (Umiker-Sebeok 1976). And man's ability to make *propositions* and, further, self-consciously arbitrary *arguments,* as Peirce saw, constitutes an essential part of his species-specific ethogram. Time and again, reports indicate that there is only a faint resemblance between the chimpanzee's or gorilla's application of its newly acquired semiotic tools and that of humans'. We have already mentioned that Sarah was primarily motivated, according to Premack, by social needs and food rewards. The same appears to be the case for the other animals involved in learning language-like skills. McNeill (1980:160), for example, has remarked that Washoe's "reorganization of ASL" to express affect and messages related to social relationships while ignoring the human focus on analysis of objects and relationships between them suggests that chimpanzees are simply not interested in what humans are concerned with, and there is no reason to suppose that they would have evolved, in nature, a communication system at all on a par with human language. Premack's failure to teach Sarah the plastic chip language by the observational method used by language-learning children and their parents was partially due, no doubt, to the fact that the chimpanzee simply "did not focus on those aspects of the situation that were of primary interest to the experimenters" (Ristau and Robbins 1979:275).

Rumbaugh (1980:249; cf. Rumbaugh et al. 1975) has admitted that, while his "primary goal was to cultivate in Lana the desire and the skills needed to converse . . . about a wide variety of subjects," Lana in fact used her computer language almost exclusively to solve practical problems with which she was faced, such as getting a trainer to supply her machine with a favorite food. For Lana, in other words, the symbols she had learned were primarily of instrumental value in achieving goals that could not be obtained otherwise. Similarly, the function of Nim's ASL signs was not to identify objects or convey information about the world, but rather to obtain a reward, whether it was the engagement of a human in some desired activity (such as a game of chase or tickle) or some desired object. Patterson does not specifically mention this aspect of Koko's signing, but a glance at the illustrations of a recent article (1978b) reveals that, like the chimpanzees in other projects, the gorilla signs mainly in situations in which a human is holding out the promise of a reward (e.g., a glass of milk, p.81; a stereo viewer, p.82; a game of tickle, pp.84 and 86; a stethoscope, p.85). As Savage-Rumbaugh et al. (1980a:54) have noted, "while it is relatively easy for chimpanzees . . . to achieve skills that bear a superficial similarity to language, it is quite difficult for them to achieve the functional symbolic communicative ability and the reciprocal receptive behaviors that reflect the essence of language."

Investigators have sought to narrow the gap between ape and human uses of language-like symbols by encouraging the intraspecific exchange of messages between trained animals and between trained and untrained animals, in the latter case with the symbol-wise ape serving as teacher. Such attempts have achieved limited success in that the animals do exchange symbolic messages with one another, but there is, as far as we know, no evidence to date that the symbols, in such cases, function in a noninstrumental way (see, e.g., Fouts and Couch 1976; Fouts and Rigby 1980; Fouts et al. 1973, 1978; Savage-Rumbaugh et al. 1978, 1980b). Fouts and his colleagues (1978:178) report, for example, that

> Although chimpanzee-to-chimpanzee signing has been observed . . . , it is difficult to decide if a chimpanzee receiver has comprehended the signs of a chimpanzee sender. Most signed conversations between chimpanzees are one-way, with the signer actively requesting some food item or game and the receiver usually reacting either neutrally or negatively (by ignoring or leaving the dyad).

Terrace (1980c), analyzing transcripts of ASL "conversations" between Ally and Booee reported in Miles 1979, claims that the animals' exchanges were, like Nim's, unspontaneous and concerned primarily with obtaining objects and activities from one another.

Efforts to establish the cultural transmission of ASL signs from one individual to another, and from one generation to another, are made difficult by the gradual fading from view of the "star" performers, Lana, Sarah, and Washoe, which is in itself disturbing. "[O]ne begins to wonder why these performing chimpanzees are no longer the subject of intense study. Haven't they become unmanageable and thus dangerous to their trainers? Have they reached the limits of their abilities and resorting to a variety of learning procedures fails to improve performance?" (Ristau and Robbins 1979:294). Sexual maturity in chimpanzees and gorillas is accompanied by an increase in aggressivity, which should be viewed, according to Hediger (1980), as a normal characteristic of the animal's life-cycle, one that, in the wild, serves an important function in the protection of individual and group territories as well as the safety of offspring.[24] Ape "language" researchers—with the exception of David Premack, who, as we noted above, has described the physical dangers of working with Sarah—have attempted to underplay, or even deny, the aggressive behavior of their subjects, but a number of attacks on trainers or observers have been reported. On November 13, 1979, for example, the *Oklahoma Daily*, a student newspaper of the University of Oklahoma, printed a story about a graduate assistant with the Fouts project, Dave Rowe, whose face and hands required more than fifty stitches after an enraged Washoe bit him in April of that year. In a later article in the *Tulsa Tribune* (November 29, 1979), an enraged Fouts is said to have requested that the reporter of the incident, Judy Gorman, be removed from the staff of the student publication on the grounds that she had promised to let him see the story before it was published, but did not. Gorman, the report continues, denied that such an arrangement had been made, and Fouts's request was denied by the University of Oklahoma Board of Publications. Hediger, furthermore, has remarked that on his visit to the Oklahoma project, he witnessed a cattle prod being used by Washoe's custodians (1980). Our own first-hand experience with Washoe, mentioned above, coincided with the animal's attack on another visitor, whose finger was severely bitten when he did not do as Washoe, then still a subadult, wished. The visitor was rushed to the local hospital for first-aid treatment and a tetanus shot, where he learned that the Gardners were not unknown to the hospital's emergency room staff. In 1980 Washoe mutilated the hand of a world-famous colleague in neuropsychology, and Booee, some time ago, inflicted a similar injury on one of the investigators featured in this chapter. Desmond Morris (1979:114) is surely right: "Never mind the killers, it's the cuddlies that get you."

Certainly the hope that Washoe would one day teach ASL to her offspring has not been realized, for Washoe—who was, in effect, raised as a human daughter—did not show much maternal interest in either of her two babies, both of whom died in infancy (see Fouts et al. 1978). This raises the question of how "natural" the home- or laboratory-raised animals are vis-à-vis their wild conspecifics. Irrespective of any training with language-like symbol systems, the former's rearing in a man-made environment must surely have altered their Umwelt. This alone makes difficult any extrapolations from the ways these symbol-using apes utilize their acquired communication skills, even were there to be significant breakthroughs in the future in this regard, to the potential adaptive significance of such symbols for the species as a whole.

What we have at the moment, with respect to the interspecific communication between ape and human in the ape "language" projects, is both accommodation and conflict between Umwelten. The chimpanzees and gorillas, placed in a totally man-made environment, whether a private home, experimental laboratory, or primate research colony, adapt themselves, somewhat reluctantly, by learning a number of arbitrary signifier-signified associations and by utilizing them in situations where trainers will accept no alternative type of response. They will follow certain elementary prescribed rules of play, in other words, but there is no indication that they are playing the same "game." Investigators and experimenters also accommodate themselves to the expectations of their animal subjects, unwittingly entering into subtle nonverbal communication with them while convincing themselves, on the basis of their own human rules of interpretation, that the apes' reactions are more human-like than direct evidence warrants.

Real breakthroughs in man-ape communication are the stuff of fiction, which usually accompanies—or even anticipates—the stream of scientific research. Morris and Morris (1966b: chap. 2) have surveyed

some early science fiction with a simian character, winding up with
Pierre Boulle's 1963 satirical novel, best known in the United States as
The Planet of the Apes. The plot hinges on the contrast between a language-endowed master-race of anthropoids and the human beings, who,
having regressed into a state of speechlessness, are turned by them into
subjects for laboratory training and worse.

In *The Village in the Treetops* (1901), Jules Verne invented the
device of a German savant who undertook a fantastic scientific journey
to the central African jungle. Eventually he is located by two big-game
hunters—the American, John Cort, and the Frenchman, Max Huber—who,
in the seemingly impenetrable forest, encounter evolution at work. The
most fascinating aspect of this late and seldom-read book of Verne's
about "the so-called language of the monkeys" is that the protagonist
and his peregrinations were made up out of bits and pieces suggested
by the biographical circumstances and quasi-scientific works of Richard
L. Garner, a *bona fide* forerunner of today's primatologists seeking for
the roots of language (Sebeok 1979:268, 291n4). Verne ordered his
bricolage into a fictional maneuver, laced with equal amounts of sympathy
and raillery, and capped by a moral about cooperation in adversity and
its absence when the danger is dissipated.

John Collier's *His Monkey Wife or, Married to a Chimp* (1931), remains possibly the most celebrated spoof in this fictional vein. In the
course of this rich and cunningly crafted novel about erotic and racial
relations, Emily, the heroine, understands both spoken and written
English (she has read, among other classics, *Origin of Species* and
Murders in the Rue Morgue) and types quite proficiently, but never
masters speech. Even at the end of the book, just before the consum-
mation of her miscegenetic marriage, she continues tacitly to gesture
"with one or two of those quiet signs by which she managed to express
to [her husband's] now subtler understanding almost all that she desired to communicate to him (*my gracious silence* he sometimes laugh-
ingly called her). . . ."

An even more thought-provoking novel on this broad theme was
published, in English, in 1953, by Jean Bruller (who used the pen name
Vercors), under the title, *You Shall Know Them*. In a trenchant and
suspenseful fashion, it deals with the question: What is man? It does so
by way of a two-faced contrast, employing an inverted hybrid species
called *Paranthropus*, an intermediate group of creatures familiarly
known as *tropis*. While working out his definition of humanity, the
author has much to say about language in ape, man, and the Janus-
like ape-man in between. One of the characters, Captain Thropp, who
"had read several scientific papers to the Natural History Society on his
studies and tests on Great Apes," begins his testimony with a reference
to (evidently John B.) "Wolfe's experiments. . . . [He] gave his chimpanzees a slot machine," he reports, and they "had reinvented money, and
even avarice! Not abstract thinking, that?" (Cf. Wolfe 1936.) He continues: "Sixty years ago [Richard L.] Garner established that there's

merely a quantitative difference between our language and theirs: we even have a number of sounds in common with the monkeys." He concludes by obliquely summarizing the highlights of Viki's linguistic tutelage: "Unfortunately the young animal died before" her surrogate parents were able to achieve success. The book ends on a hopeful note when the judge, in his genial summing-up, argues: "Mankind resembles a very exclusive club. What we call human is defined by us alone." In other words, it is up to us to admit the tropis to the human community, to share the rights of man. This means searching for a legal basis for agreement to admit new members. But the setting up of such rules and regulations entails a consensus on the definition—or redefinition—of what constitutes language, a task Chomsky has so skillfully and authoritatively undertaken (1980), but which, Sebeok has argued elsewhere (see Appendix II), may be an inexecutable task because of the inherently indeterminate vacuousness of the term.

In a recent publication about "talking dogs" (see chap. 7, this volume), reference is made to Olaf Stapledon's perfervid novel, *Sirius: A Fantasy of Love and Discord* (1944), which deals with the making of a super-sheepdog who develops "true speech," his life and reversion to a feral state, and ultimately his death as an outlaw. What is of interest in this context is that the scientist, Thomas Trelone, who works the remarkable transformation of Sirius, is well acquainted with the Kellogg paradigm (1980), but, "contrary to his original plan," and despite the fact that "apes offered the hope of more spectacular success," opts to use dogs instead. His reasons include that dogs are "capable of much greater freedom of movement in our society" and that he regarded "the dog's temperament on the whole more capable of development to the human level." Thus, à la Gua, the puppy is raised in the familial company of the Trelones' daughter, Plaxy. His dying words were: "Plaxy-Sirius— worth while."

Fanciful fiction featuring apes that learn to attain language capacity reaches its acme in two novels (see Sebeok 1979: chap. 5): Peter Dickinson's detective story, *The Poison Oracle* (1974), the entire plot of which is impelled by this very issue of a chimpanzee's putative propensity; and especially John Goulet's *Oh's Profit* (1975), the protagonist of which is a singularly endowed young signing gorilla whose maleficent antagonists belong to a cabal of transformational linguists, thinly disguised but more or less recognizable, we are told, by the insiders who have read this *roman à clef*.

In diverse imaginative ways, the concerns of this literary genre, from Verne to Goulet, are identical with those some of us prefer to struggle with in the mythic world of scientific objectivity: to draw distinctions between man and beast; to identify the one animal endowed with language, separated from but immersed in a sea of speechless creatures; to delineate the nature of language itself and distill the essence of mankind. As Browning's poem "Bishop Blougram's Apology" professed in an exceptionally nice march of oxymorons:

Our interest's on the dangerous edge of things.
The honest thief, the tender murderer,
The superstitious atheist, demireps
That love and save their souls in new French books—
We watch while these in equilibrium keep
The giddy line midway: one step aside,
They're classed and done with. I, then, keep the line
Before your sagest. . . .—just the men to shrink
From the gross weights, coarse scales, and labels broad
You offer their refinement. Fool or knave?

CONCLUSION

Throughout this discussion, we have skirted the consequential issue so competently examined by a number of authors such as Bronowski and Bellugi, Brown, Chomsky, Lenneberg, Limber, and McNeill in Sebeok and Umiker-Sebeok 1980; by Gipper (1977), in what is the most thoroughgoing as well as satisfying analysis known; and by Chomsky and Premack (1979): namely, is what is being taught the apes really "language"? We have done so for the simple reason that, at present, of the two related questions posed by Chomsky—*What is a human language?* and *What is a language?*—neither the first, which is open to scientific, i.e., biological, explanation, nor the second, which is not, can be finally answered. Although the debate over problems such as these is in itself of appreciable value, there seems to be no point in adding further speculative material to the fires of contention. We concur with the opinion of Ristau and Robbins (1979:268) that, even if the question What is language? were resolvable by scientific method, "just as man's unique and dominant status remained intact when his other 'unique' accomplishments such as tool use and cooperative hunting were observed to occur in other species, so the existence of rudimentary linguistic skills in other species—if demonstrated—will do little to diminish man's radical differences from other species."

In light of the wide attention given this matter in the media and in some popular books, it should be noted that investigators who accuse critics of the ape "language" projects of being biased in favor of a particular and, they claim, outmoded paradigm that defines *language* too narrowly, may themselves be susceptible to what Barber (1976:5-6) calls the Investigator Paradigm Effect, through their own special attachment to certain scientific or popular notions, some of which were discussed above (see also Hediger 1974:40; Sebeok 1979). As one of us has noted elsewhere:

If linguists, such as Chomsky, are to be enjoined from placing what others regard as little more than adroitly presented circus tricks of a handful of captive African apes beyond the pale of language in the technical sense, then, by the same token of a lack of clear definition, the trainers cannot claim a quasi-human language propensity for their charges either. [See Appendix II, this volume.]

Menzel and Johnson (1978:587), reacting to Griffin 1978a, Premack and Woodruff 1978, and Savage-Rumbaugh et al. 1980b, note a final ironic twist to the controversy over anthropomorphism vs. anthropocentrism:

> The study of "animal language," after the fashion of the target articles, may have, if anything, tended to increase rather than decrease expectations of human chauvinism and presumed "biological superiority," especially in the popular press, where it is more often suggested that chimpanzees, gorillas, and perhaps dolphins may deserve special consideration based on the outcome of research projects demonstrating their similarity to humans.

Schubert (1978:597) adds that to "appraise the relative excellence of nonhuman cognitive abilities by measuring the extent to which these conform to those characteristics of our own species" is "a very unbiological approach" (cf. Desmond 1979).

If the debate over the linguistic status of the signs being taught to apes is unlikely to yield significant novel insights into the phylogenesis of language, the new line of investigation alluded to in this chapter—the critical examination of the interactions between humans and between human and ape in such language-training situations—promises a rich harvest of information concerning a variety of subjects, including especially interspecific communication between human and ape. Pfungst (1965) can serve as a guide in this undertaking, for his investigation of Clever Hans is still one of the few successful attempts to discover the actual signs that mediated between the expectations of experimenters and the performances of their animal subjects. He proceeded from indirect evidence—such as his observations that as the distance between Hans and his questioners increased, the animal's accuracy decreased, or that his performance suffered if the questioner did not know the correct answer—to direct evidence, from both observations of performance and laboratory experiments, in which a number of elements of the question-answer procedure were systematically altered (e.g., the visual channel between man and animal was blocked). Through the painstaking application of this methodology, Pfungst was able to uncover several types of visual and auditory cues that Hans's questioners were unwittingly giving. Pfungst's success in this endeavor led Rosenthal to assert (in Pfungst 1965:xxix), "it seems clear that neither the strategy nor the tactics of inquiry employed by Pfungst are in any way outmoded or irrelevant to contemporary psychology."

While the basic methodology of Pfungst may still be followed in contemporary assessments of ape linguistic capacities, today's investigator can take advantage of the vast amount of research on nonverbal communication that has been done in recent years. In moving from indirect evidence of social cuing, some of which has been presented here, to direct evidence, the microanalysis of the intraspecific and interspecific communication among humans and apes must be performed by persons who have some expertise in one or more relevant areas of nonverbal communication, discourse analysis, *dressage,* and the like, with the support of those especially knowledgeable about experimental design, expectancy effects, and other methodological questions. The examination should be applied to all phases of those undertakings designed to teach language-like symbols to apes, including the initial familiarization of the subject(s) with trainers and research facilities, all training and testing procedures, and the informal social interactions among project personnel (and outside observers) and the animals.

This work demands extraordinary caution and attention to possible methodological pitfalls, for, as Arthur G. Miller has perceptively commented, "there is a magical or fantasy-like aspect to the idea that one's expectancies . . . can become true merely by entertaining such anticipations" (1978:401), and, when applied to scientific research, is threatening to those involved.[25] To make up for this, "evidence must be sufficiently powerful to counter, as it were, such *a priori* expectations" on the part of scientific investigators (ibid.). To be fair, the criteria for accepting research designed to provide direct evidence of nonlinguistic explanations for the apes' use of symbols must be at least as stringent as those applied to attempts to prove that the ghost of Clever Hans does *not* live on in the performances of today's experimental apes. In fact, both approaches—the creation of ever more carefully controlled double-blind tests, on the one hand, and the observation and experimental manipulation of a full complement of semiosic behaviors, on the other—must go hand in hand, if, as is to be hoped, an accurate appraisal of ape linguistic capacity is to be finally accomplished.

POSTSCRIPT:
CONFESSIONS, CONVERSIONS, CONCESSIONS, AND CRUSADES

"As early as 1970, I essentially quit concentrating on the attempt to operationally analyze some aspects of human language, develop training procedures for them and instill them in the ape, because it was clear to me that the accomplishments of which the ape was capable with regard to human-type language were very slight. . . . Early demonstrations and misinterpretations, or overinterpretations, of language-like performance in apes led many people to conclude that the differences between ape and man were enormously less than had been contended. However, I never took language-like performances to signal a reduction in the differences between man and other species. I don't believe that the principle of biological continuity implies such a reduction" (Premack in Chomsky and Premack 1979:8).

"When I began my study with a male chimp called Nim Chimpsky, I hoped to demonstrate that apes can, indeed, form sentences. I wanted to . . . show that grammatical rules are needed to describe many of an ape's utterances. . . . I discovered that the sequences of words that looked like sentences were subtle imitations of the teacher's sequences. I could find no evidence confirming an ape's grammatical competence, either in my own data or those of others, that could not be explained by simpler processes. . . . Much as I would have preferred otherwise, a chimpanzee's 'Report to an Academy' remains a work of fiction" (Terrace 1979:65, 76).

"We are far more conservative now than we were seven or eight years ago with respect to what an ape can do. Lana showed some sensitivity to the rules of grammar, but we have no evidence that she productively comprehended syntax and the meaning of words at the same time. . . . her performance was inconsistent. We couldn't call it a reliable behavior" (Rumbaugh in Sobel 1979).

"Frankly, we are not interested in whether or not language is the exclusive domain of man. That question leads all who address it into a quagmire of confusion, despair, and impatience. We want none of that!" (Rumbaugh and Savage-Rumbaugh 1979).

"Koko's data looked like Nim's data before we had consistent, well trained teachers. Now, however, Koko not only has a good grasp of language but she can make puns and rhymes. . . . I agree with Dr. Terrace that no ape's syntax is identical to a human child's. There's a point where the ape falls behind and stays behind. I'm eager to review my own videotapes to see if they show any of the problems Dr. Terrace found. After that, I will try to refute his claim with solid evidence" (Patterson in Sobel 1979).

"Up to this point, the pattern of chimpanzee development has been comparable to the human pattern, but the rate of development has been much slower. Our subjects are still very immature, so that it will be several years before we can make definitive statements about the highest level of achievement, or establish a pattern of failures that could reveal qualitative differences between chimpanzee and human intelligence" (Gardner and Gardner 1980b).

"Let me out" (Washoe in Harvey 1980).

NOTES

1. For numerous examples of earlier criticisms by ape researchers, see Sebeok and Umiker-Sebeok 1980a. For a sampling of recent reports concerning what has come to be called The Great Ape Debate, see, e.g., Benderly 1980; M. Gardner 1980; Greenberg 1980; Marx 1980; Sebeok and Umiker-Sebeok 1979;

Sobel 1979; Wade 1980; *Time,* March 10, 1980, pp.50-57; and *The New Yorker,* May 26, 1980, pp.28-30.

2. Desmond Morris (1979:48-49) relates an amusing anecdote about a tame raven who mistook a highly sensitive portion of the anatomy of the trainer, Konrad Lorenz, for a sample of the strips of meat used in training.

3. The appealing features of infant chimpanzees described by Ann Premack are comparable with the releasers of caretaking responses displayed by human babies. See, e.g., Guthrie 1976 and Desmond Morris 1977. For additional examples of this type of human response to infant apes, see Desmond 1979.

4. Cf. *Haney's Art of Training Animals* (Burroughs, 1869) and William F. Pinchbeck's *The Expositor, Or Many Mysteries Unravelled* (privately published, 1805). Haney's chap. 17 (pp.157-165), dealing with performing monkeys, could be read with profit by every ape trainer. There is also a vast, if more specialized, literature on Japanese performing monkeys (*Macaca fuscata*); see, e.g., Hirose 1980 or the popular Murasaki 1980. The Japanese term referring to monkey training is *gei-do,* from the Chinese *tao;* it is also used in other ritual performances, such as *bushido.* For further details, see Sebeok 1981a.

5. On this point, cf. Ristau and Robbins 1979:291.

6. See Clifford and Bull 1978 for a full review of the many linguistic and cognitive factors that influence the perceptions and memory of eyewitnesses, often leading to inaccurate accounts of events. The material they present fully supports C. S. Peirce's theory of the logical nature of perception and hypothesis (see chap. 2 this volume). In light of the immense amount of evidence brought forward by Clifford and Bull, among others, persons attempting to teach language-like skills to apes would do well to heed the warning, given those involved in juridical proceedings, about the danger of accepting the fictions of the law court—namely, that eyewitnesses see and hear correctly and so testify, and that, if they do not testify with accuracy, cross-examination will straighten them out.

7. This type of situation presents an interesting combination of eristic and heuristic dialogue (Perelman and Olbrechts-Tyteca 1969:39): (1) two of the participants, the trainer and the ape, communicate directly with one another, as specific individuals; (2) two of the participants communicate with the third person, the observer, only indirectly, through one another; and (3) all three actors address a "universal" audience—that is, the reader/viewer of a written or filmed record of their interaction.

8. In a hilarious response to a series of four photographs of Nim, his trainer, and Nim's pet cat in Terrace et al. (1979:892), Musicant et al., with tongue in cheek, reproach Terrace and his colleagues for failing to note "the fluent signing being made by the cat . . . in Kitty Sign Language (KSL)" (1980: 258). As they point out, on close examination of the photographs, the cat appears to be signing, in sequence, "lemme," "outa," "here," followed by "dirty," "well known to fans of Washoe as an all-purpose expletive" (ibid.). "The most significant aspect of the frothing feline's utterances," they continue, "is that she is accomplishing all of this without prompting, unlike Nim" (ibid.).

9. On the Rumbaughs' own use of richly interpreted anecdotes in their work with Lana and other chimpanzees, see Mellgren and Fouts 1978 and Schubert 1978.

10. Cf. Lenneberg (1980a) regarding the difficulty in telling whether Washoe is making metaphors or mistakes.

11. Ristau and Robbins (1979:271-272) discuss another type of Investigator Data Analysis Effect, this one in relation to the Lana project. Lana was obliged to end all her sentences by pushing a "period" key on her computer console. Investigators assumed that if the chimpanzee depressed this key while

a grammatically incorrect sentence was in progress, she meant "erase"; but she might just as well have intended merely to end that sentence, knowing that a reward would be forthcoming only if she did so.

12. For his tabulations of correct and incorrect responses respectively see Timaeus 1974: Tables 52 (p.154) and 53 (p.156).

It might be worth mentioning here that it did not escape Pfungst's attention (1965:88) that the persons involved in cuing Hans had no idea

> that they were giving any such signs. I myself for some time made these involuntary movements quite unwittingly and even after I had discovered the nature of these movements and had thus enabled to call forth at will all the various responses on the part of the horse, I still succeeded in the earlier naive involuntary manner.

The conjurer Ormond McGill refers to this fascinating effect as the "law of reversed effort," which is exploited in many magic performances, spiritualism, and the occult (water-divining, table-tilting, the ouija board, etc.), and also constitutes a hazard in ape "language" researches. McGill explains (*fide* Fisher 1979:92):

> In all such demonstrations utilizing ideomotor response, the amazing part of the experiment is that the actual creators of the motivating force have no idea that they are the cause. In fact, they often strive most sincerely not to make any movement that would assist the effect, but in this the so-called "law of reversed effort" comes into play and the more effort they put forth not to impart movement, the more unconscious movement they actually produce. As long as the assisting spectators conscientiously concentrate upon your directions towards the production of a desired manifestation, the manifestation will occur.

13. On the subject of homology vs. analogy, see also Chomsky 1980; Chomsky and Premack 1979; Hediger 1980; and Lenneberg 1980a, 1980b. For a recent discussion of the linguistically relevant neurophysiological differences between man and ape, see Popper and Eccles 1977:308-309; Desmond 1979. In passing, it might be noted that it is now known "that the sexually dimorphic vocal control pathways of canaries and zebra finches are responsible for song, which in these species is a complex learned motor skill. . . ." See Nottebohm and Arnold (1979:769), who also point out that the behavioral significance of brain sexual dimorphism, particularly in the preoptic area of rats, still awaits investigation. The connectivity of the sexually dimorphic regions in apes remains undescribed.

14. On the problem of misrepresentation through several types of data reduction by the Gardners and Patterson, see Seidenberg and Petitto 1979:183.

15. Note that Timaeus, in his two experiments, was unable to confirm, as Pfungst had alleged, that head nodding was *the* critical cue for Clever Hans. He found, instead, that the most important cues came from the human examiners' eyes (1974:164). Cf. Menzel's report (1975) concerning the importance of eye signals in chimpanzee communication.

16. Thomas Mann's fictional character Felix Krull, preparing himself in boyhood for his adult life as a confidence man, reports his success with training himself to control his pupil reactions (in *Confessions of Felix Krull Confidence Man*):

> I would stand in front of my mirror, concentrating all my powers in a command to my pupils to contract or expand, banishing every other thought from my mind. My persistent efforts . . . were, in fact, crowned with success. At first as I stood bathed in sweat, my colour coming and going, my pupils would flicker erratically; but later I actually succeeded in contracting them to the merest points and then expanding them to great, round, mirror-like pools.

17. As Hill (1980) has noted, even Premack's "highly controlled" studies were "polluted" by vocal English, since his trainers were permitted to say the English translation of a token aloud as they put it on the display board. Verbal accompaniments were also an accepted part of the studies by Fouts, Patterson, and Terrace. Cf. the discussion by Seidenberg and Petitto (1979:178) on the "rich sources of nonlinguistic cuing in Koko's environment."

18. This faith is also demonstrated by persons serving as allegedly "blind" independent observers. For an interesting example of a case where "the judges repeatedly considered themselves 'blind,'" but in effect were guided by presumably unintended verbal and contextual cues, see Marks and Kammann 1978.

19. The double-blind test proposed by Lenneberg (1980a), which calls for four experimenters and which could, in principle, overcome some of the deficiencies noted above, has not, as far as we know, been used.

20. Premack does admit, however, that "Sarah's performance may have relied critically on quite different features of her social relationship with the trainer. He was quick to respond to her summons at the end of every trial, and praise or food was soon to follow" (1978:905).

21. See the discussion by Sebeok (1979: chap. 5) of muscle readers, such as Eugen de Rubini, and their use of such subtle clues as tremors of the floor, faint sounds of feet, movements of arms and clothing, and the like, as cues guiding them to a hidden object.

22. See Sebeok 1979:98 regarding how police officers inadvertently communicate their own expectations concerning the whereabouts of suspected criminals to the bloodhounds being used to track them.

23. See especially Randi's amusing account of Uri Geller's unsuccessful attempts to employ such methods on the "Johnny Carson Show," where special precautions had been taken to prevent cuing by Carson, who used to be a stage magician.

24. See Desmond 1979 for a lengthy discussion of recent reports by Goodall and other field observers of chimpanzee hunting, killing, and even cannibalistic behaviors, the amount of which has long been underestimated.

25. Based on an anecdote by Mottershead (1959)—a notoriously eccentric (past) Director of the Chester Zoo—Leyhausen (1973:377-378), referring to chimpanzees in captivity, says that "contrary to everything anyone thought they knew so far about [their] ability to communicate among themselves, one chimpanzee [was] able to send another to a particular spot without somehow leading it there," and proceeds to interpret the unverified story "that one chimpanzee could send another in a particular direction by means of its eyes." He does not even question the veridicality of the data before attempting an elaborate exegesis, although there is reason to suspect that the "report" may simply have been a case of English drôlerie.

Note added in proof: Since this chapter was sent to press, two books have appeared that are focally pertinent to the matters treated herein.

One is the extremely important volume by Heini Hediger, *Tiere Verstehen* (Munich: Kindler Verlag, 1980), with a comprehensive chapter on the Clever Hans Phenomenon: "Der 'Kluge Hans' kommt wieder" (pp.112-160). The other is Sebeok and Rosenthal (1981), which contains twenty-five contributions dealing with various facets of the Clever Hans Phenomenon in general, and specifically in horses, whales, apes, and people. Most of the authors of these essays are mentioned in this chapter.

Works of fiction, featuring "talking" chimpanzees (Boyle 1980) or gorillas (Crichton 1980), continue to appear and entertain us.

Chapter 9

Prefigurements of Art

In our own day the philosopher neither minimises nor unduly magnifies the mechanical aspect of the Cosmos; nor need the naturalist either exaggerate or belittle the mechanical phenomena which are profoundly associated with Life, and inseparable from our understanding of Growth and Form.
—D'Arcy Thompson 1945:7

To the biologist . . . and to the painter, improvement is a perfectly valid notion, proof against any attacks philosophers may make on it. . . . And the point I want to make is that in the biological process of evolution, chance processes are among the essentials on which improvement depends. They are not the only essential. The other main one is the occurrence of selection; some of the novelties produced by chance are preserved, others are rejected and allowed to disappear. . . . And the practice of modern painters shows that they have accepted chance as a potentially valuable component of the creative process.
—Waddington 1969:107-108

PRELIMINARIES

THAT LANGUAGE is a biotic property specific to man is true—a truism even —in the sense that no other species encountered so far is, in the technical acceptation of this term, language-endowed. Language is a cognitive structure which, like the behavioral extension of any organ of man's body, may be studied along several more or less agreed upon semiosic/ ethological dimensions (Sebeok 1979: chap. 2), including the characters of its initial state (ontogenesis), mature state, and end state (gradual breakdown, partial reconstitution, and eventual termination) (ibid.: chap. 4). With regard to the phylogenesis of language, there has been much random conjecture and some empirical stumbling, but scarcely even translucent enlightenment so far. Verbal sign configurations have been

An unillustrated preprint of this article was circulated in the Toronto Semiotic Circle Monographs series, as Working Paper No. 1 (1978). It has appeared in *Semiotica* 27:3- 73(1979); and a considerably abridged treatment was published in *Animals* 112:4:22- 26, 34-35 (1979). It is my present intention eventually to expand these materials, with many more illustrations, into an independent book.

elaborated throughout history into many complex forms of message-oriented constructs, encompassing both spoken and literary genres, which are best called jointly—as I had suggested nearly a quarter of a century ago (Bascom 1955:246n9; Bauman 1977:4, 49n2)—the "verbal art." Furthermore, language, being "absolutely distinct from any system of communication in other animals" and thus "also the most diagnostic single trait of man" (Simpson 1966:476), has as its corollary, by definition as it were, the tautologic proposition that man has a monopoly on all manifestations of the verbal art. These statements and their implication, while hardly contestable, are surely trivial, because of the equally unchallengeable fact that the communication system of every *other* species stamps it with a unique hallmark, much as language conspicuously segregates out our humanity (see Appendix I this volume). They do, however, suggest one interesting question that I propose to explore, if tentatively, in what follows, namely, whether the optimal design of certain animal communication systems can allow, given certain contextual conditions, for a superimposed aesthetic function. In other words, how reasonable is it to search for prefigurements of aesthetically charged averbal sign configurations in man's animal ancestry? What, for instance, could Julian Huxley have meant when he asserted in passing, during a Darwin Centennial panel discussion, that in the behavior of the Satinbird (*Ptilonorhynchus violaceus*)—a remarkable bowerbird living in the coastal forests of Eastern Australia, and a species certain members of which paint the inside of their bower efficiently, even, to echo Huxley's word, "deliberately"—there is "definitely the beginning of aesthetics" (Tax and Callender 1960:195)? A pioneer ornithologist, Stonor (1940:96-97), had commented on this painting behavior in a similar vein: "Exactly what the motive is behind this painting is obscure; presumably it is an expression of the bird's love of decoration. It has been suggested that it is connected with its liking for dark colours. . . ." This seemingly bizarre habit, Marshall (1954:65) later likewise surmised, "may be an aesthetic extension of a basic drive," namely, the birds' courtship feeding phenomenon—or just the sort of displacement activity of sexual behavior that some Freudians have posited in men. Gannon (1930:39), the discoverer of bower painting in this species, also observed that the male appeared to employ a tool—a wad of bark, like a brush or sponge, held in the tip of the bill—to apply the paint, which is composed of saliva mixed by the bird with charcoal dust, dark berries, or wood pulp. It was subsequently noted that the paint, washed away by the heavy tropical rains, is replaced daily during the height of the sexual season, and fibrous bark, often still saturated with charcoal and saliva, is commonly to be found on the avenue floor between the two painted walls and where fallen leaves are always quickly removed. This bird, when constructing its social signals, exhibits a decided preference for blue, less so for yellowish-green, shunning red altogether, a bias manifested, moreover, in such like-colored ornamental objects as feathers, flowers, leaves, berries, snail shells, cicada integument, and, near human habitations, pieces of blue-colored glass beads, strands of wool, and tinsel (Frisch 1974:238-239). Generalizing about the entire family *Ptilorhynchidae*, of which about nineteen species occur, Dobzhansky (1962:215) remarks that "it is impossible to deny that a well-adorned bower may give the bird a pleasure which can only be called aesthetic." Recall in this context Nicolas Poussin's maxim—a seventeenth-century evocation of the mediaeval doctrine of *delectatio* as a sign—that "la fin de l'art est la délectation," apropos of which Panofsky (1955:10-11) insists that "a work of art always *has* aesthetic significance," regardless of whether it serves some practical —let me qualify: biological—purpose at bottom. We must likewise concede the possibility that "animals perform some of the behavior patterns we observe because they enjoy the resulting experience" (Griffin 1976: 78), regardless of whether such patterns are adaptive, or virtually so, "but result in a pleasantly satisfying feeling" on the animals' part. Whether or not bowers are built, painted, and decorated for the maker's pleasure, the fact remains that the constructions take place, as a rule, during the breeding season and serve as the sites where territorial displays are performed. The key issue, what the differential effect of the bowers may be on the females, remains unresolved, because this has not been systematically tested.[1]

Contrary to Barthes' (1957:222) contention that the semiotician is entitled to treat writing and pictures in the same way because what he retains from them both is "qu'elles sont toutes deux des *signes*," in all living systems that I know of the characteristics of the signs employed are inseparably joined to the kind of information they carry. Similarly, the concept of "secondary modeling system" (Lotman 1967:130-131), which is assuredly among the more salient features of Soviet semiotics, posits a superstructure that persistently confounds two diverse artistic realizations that, I would argue, demand radically different treatment: on the one side, the products of the verbal art and its derivatives, being inescapably built up from signs that are the operands of a natural language, plus certain traditional or newly invented rules for combining them in possible, impossible, contingent, or imperative ways to advance human cognition and communication; and, on the other side, the artistic products of averbal semiotic systems into which verbal signs may, to be sure, encroach in varying degree.

The performances we call the verbal art and those we call the averbal arts generate in the dominant and the minor hemisphere respectively, although the specializations normally have a complementary relationship. As Eccles (Popper and Eccles 1977:351-352) has pointed out, "the minor hemisphere is specialized in relationship to pictures and patterns, and it is musical." This separation of hemispheric functions, by the evidence to date, is genetically coded. The minor hemisphere is best envisaged as "a very superior animal brain" (Sebeok 1977a:1070), a conception that points precisely in the direction in which future researches are most likely to prove fruitful. The two repertoires of signs may, and often doubtless do, "enter into subtle semantic relationships," as Veltruský emphasizes (Matejka and Titunik 1976:254), the resulting meaning being compounded by a process called codified contiguity. This is achieved by the immense and incessant traffic in the corpus callosum linking the two cerebral hemispheres of the intact human brain, for "probably everything that happens in the minor hemisphere leads to a kind of reverberation in the major hemisphere" (Popper, in Popper and Eccles 1977:482). However, I know of no ground that would compel the conclusion that the interpretant of *every* artistic sign must have a verbal component; and should a semiotic system of the second kind be identified in the infrahuman biosphere, it would certainly be altogether delusive to postulate a verbal infrastructure for the sort of hemispheric specialization intimated is, after all, "unique to man" (ibid.: 353).

The authentic singularity of man consists of this, that he alone disposes over a *pair* of communicative codes: "along with our wholly new and wholly distinct system of true language" (Simpson, ibid.), the verbal code, we retain an older system that, for want of a better name (Sebeok, 1976:156-162, 1977a:1063-1067), is frequently, contrastively, and hence negatively designated as a human manifestation of a cross-specific averbal code. The latter comprehends a trio of subcodes recently differentiated into separate categories by Thure von Uexküll (forthcoming): first, endosemiotic averbal sign systems, or the metabolic code (Sebeok 1979: chap. 1), involving humoral and nervous factors that convey information within the bodies of all animals, including man (cf. Autrum 1972); second, somatosemiotic averbal sign systems, which function to compact the unity of every organism (cf. ibid.: Appendix I), a notion kindred to Leibniz's concept of apperception (as expressed in his c.1714 paper, *Principes de la nature et de le grâce, fondés en raison*), which is our conscious reflection of the inner state of the monad; and third, outspreading averbal sign systems, such as are used for communication between organisms and between any organism and its external environment. In man, the output of this entire array of subcodes, but particularly of the third kind, is exquisitely harmonized in performing with his outpouring of verbal messages, although the diverse repertoires each serve separate ends substantially at variance one from the other—a point worth reemphasizing with Bateson (1968:615), who rather clearly saw how wrong it is to assume that in hominid evolution verbal semiosis has, in any sense, replaced "the cruder systems of the other animals" (ibid.:614), that is, averbal semiosis. Had this been the case, our averbal skills and the organs that execute them would inevitably have undergone conspicuous decay. Obviously, they have not; on the contrary, while the verbal art flourished, we have perfected our averbal arts as well— they too "have been elaborated into complex forms of art, music, ballet . . . and the like, and, even in everyday life, the intricacies of human kinesic communication, facial expression and vocal intonation far exceed anything that any other animal is known to produce" (ibid.).

The ideal of semiosic analysis is to combine causal with functional explanation—to show how sign form interrelates dynamically with sign function, both in synchrony and in diachrony. But an evolutionary sequence is hard to come by in an area so complex and multiply amphibological as art. Instances may be temporally ordered but are not necessarily in linked sequence. Guthrie (1976: chap. 9) offers some interesting ideas, in a semiotic frame, "about how some aspects of our aesthetic sense evolved" (ibid.:73), but the part he was concerned with was that which underlies our appreciation of human physical beauty, the valuation of which he traced to two major elements, copulatory lures and status badges. One perhaps insuperable difficulty all investigators have to face is to identify ineffable "signs of artistic enjoyment" in other species (ibid.), all of them being creatures that are speechless.

The only general survey I can find in the entire literature of the life sciences of basic aesthetic principles possibly shared by man with at least the higher animals was drafted in the late 1960s by another ethologist, Rensch, in an essay that was published only much later in the United States (1974) and Great Britain (1976). This authoritative but still, unfortunately, all too inconclusive review, based in large part on the author's well-known experiments aimed to demonstrate the reality of protoaesthetic phenomena, the results of which were found to be in good conformity with those of psychologists (cf. Arnheim 1954) who studied the elements of aesthetic preferences in human subjects, is devoted in the main to scribblings and paintings by monkeys and apes, with but a laconic page (ibid.:345) on "auditive aesthetic sensations." In 1958, Rensch had investigated the efficacy of aesthetic factors in vertebrates, testing preferences for different patterns in a jackdaw, a carrion crow, and six fishes. He showed that while the fishes always preferred irregular patterns, both species of birds preferred the more regular, more symmetrical, and more rhythmical patterns, doing so in statistically significant numbers. In a color choice test, these birds exhibited a preference for gray and black, being the colors of their own plumage. However, "they preferred patterns with two or four different colours to simpler patterns of one colour or two colours respectively" (Rensch 1958:461). A student of his, Tigges (1963), later found that jackdaws preferred pure colors (red, blue, yellow, green) to equally bright mixed ones (orange, brown, violet, lilac).

Although painting experiments were conducted by N. N. Ladygin Kohts with a chimpanzee named Joni, in Moscow, as far back as 1913, and Shepherd (1915) reported that a chimpanzee drew lines with a pencil, and many an anecdotal story found its way into the literature since then, there are only three serious studies of primate aesthetics: the series of papers by Rensch (see especially 1961, on drawings and paintings as perhaps prestages of copying), a posthumous publication by Schiller

(1951), and the engaging book by Morris (1962), especially showing, on the basis of a detailed analysis of one young chimpanzee, Congo, that the splashes of paint or the pencil marks made by apes are not at all random. The immature Congo, given an incomplete pattern, often made marks which tended to complete it. Alpha, the first-born chimpanzee of the Yerkes Colony, if given a piece of paper, with a cross placed on three of the corners, would put a cross in the fourth corner: "she would also in her crude way try to complete designs and pictures which had been given to her deliberately unfinished or unbalanced" (Bourne 1971: 216). One is thus forced to assume the presence, in advance, of a representation in the animal's nervous system that corresponds to the picture displayed.

The most recent survey of ape creativity may be found in the psychologist Andrew Whiten's excellent account (in Brothwell 1976:18-40). Rensch, who had worked with a capuchin monkey and a green monkey as well as chimpanzees, observing their drawing or painting with pencil, colored chalk, or brush, professes to have been astonished "to find also aesthetic factors having a positive effect with apes, monkeys and [even] crows comparable with the effect in man" (1972:90). He believes that our feelings of aesthetic pleasure, as we look at different black and white patterns, are, in the main, attributable to three basic conditions: symmetry, rhythmic repetition of similar component parts, and consistency of curvatures. His results demonstrate that, with these animals, as with man, "the greater facility to apprehend a design, the details of which are rhythmically repeated or otherwise more easily apprehended, the 'complexibility' is connected with positive feelings and arouses aesthetic pleasure" (ibid.:91). Rensch (1976:342) tells of incidents where

> competent art experts, on being shown monkey's paintings without being told who had painted them, sometimes enthusiastically praised the dynamism, rhythm, and sense of balance. In so doing they have not made fools of themselves, but simply confirmed what the experimental biologists had already also established. Of course, when the art historians, museum directors, or architects who had thus been led into pronouncing opinions on such paintings were afterwards told who the "artists" were, they were always rather put out and sometimes even offended at the deception that had been practiced upon them. . . . In view of this it is hardly surprising that in cases where, at modern art exhibitions, a surreptitiously included monkey's painting has received acclaim from the critics, subsequent disclosure of the deception has produced something of a scandal, as has occurred in Sweden, for example.

I intend to return to pongid painting in more detail below.

Rensch further supposes that the tendency of apes, including orangutans, and capuchin monkeys to put scarves, ribbons, chains, and the like, around their neck, and to romp about with them on, is to be interpreted as enjoyment of dressing up; hence, in his view, aesthetic factors would

be involved in this behavior as well. "It is even more likely," he adds
(1972:91), "that birds find aesthetic pleasure in repeating tunes they
hear from other birds or from humans, and in 'composing' new melodies
from phrases either learned or already known."

Following these brief prefatory observations, I would like to re-
examine in some detail the question of the putative aesthetic propensity
of animals, with specific (although uneven) attention to four semiotic
spheres: (1) kinesthetic signs, (2) musical signs, (3) pictorial signs, and
(4) architectural signs. Sketchy as such a review must be, no such comprehensive literature survey has been attempted before, probably for
several reasons. One of these may be due to the fact that cultural
anthropologists who have sought to inquire into the biological roots of
art have typically set out to do so with a preconception common to
many members of the profession. Alland (1977: chap. 2), for one, opens
his chapter on "The Evolution of Art" with this uncompromising sentence: "The creation and appreciation of art in its many forms are
uniquely human activities," adding, a few pages later (ibid.:24): "True
[sic] artistic behavior is seen in no species other than *Homo sapiens.*
Not even a hint of it occurs in the natural behavior of other species." His
brief exploration of its origins, sensitive as it is, suggests that this lies in
play as a biological property, leading him to a debatable definition of
art as "play involving rules" (ibid.:30) (for a semiotic interpretation of
play in vertebrates, cf. Sebeok 1976:139). This same notion was earlier
advanced by Ellen Eisenberg (cf. Pfeiffer 1969:434), subsuming art in a
more inclusive class of behavior patterns, one which includes all forms
of exploration; and, earlier still, by Dobzhansky (1962:217), who felt that
at least some forms of art "are related to play." (The union of the play-
impulse with aesthetic feelings and sentiments, as linked with superfluous
activities and corresponding pleasures, was first propagated by Spencer
[1897:2:627, 647] eighty years ago; he argued that the aesthetic sphere
in general may be expected to occupy an increasing part in human life
because of greater economization of energy resulting from superiority of
organization bringing a growing proportion of the aesthetic activities
and gratifications.) Dobzhansky, however, perceived even in artistic activity an adaptive value, for he saw in it a wellspring of social cohesion,
thus raising once again a utilitarian interpretation of the role of art. This
viewpoint is most fruitfully developed by Jenkins (1958:14 and *passim*),
a thoroughgoing evolutionist, for whom art has its "ultimate source in
the human effort to adapt to the environment," and who insists, more
generally, that any inquiry into the origins of art must move, as he emphatically puts it, *"toward an analysis of the adaptive situation."*
   Klopfer (1970:399), who means by aesthetic preferences simply "a
liking for objects or activities because they produce or induce particular
neural inputs or emotional states, independently of overt reinforcers,"
answers his own question, whether we can attribute aesthetic impulses

Male Satinbird building his bower; and bower of the Orange-crested
gardener. After Frisch 1974:235, 236, Plates 97 and 99.
Based on color photographs and descriptions by Heinz Seilmann
and Max Renner. Reproduced with the permission of
Karl von Frisch. (See p.211.)

Chimpanzee rain dance. Copyright National Geographic Society,
from the Special Publication of *My Friends the Wild
Chimpanzees*. Lawick-Goodall 1967:82-83. (See p.220.)

Finger-paintings by Congo. From Morris 1962, Plates E. and F.
Reproduced by permission of Mrs. D. M. F. Morris.

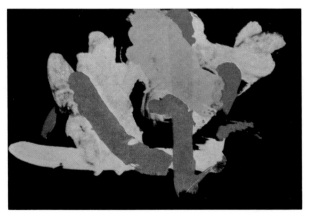

Simple painting by Congo showing the use of vertical, horizontal,
and diagonal lines. From Morris 1962, Plate K. Reproduced
by permission of Mrs. D. M. F. Morris.

Congo painting with bold circular loop. From Morris 1962, Plate L.
Reproduced by permission of Mrs. D. M. F. Morris.

Split fan pattern by Congo with central yellow spot. Collection
Sir Herbert Read. From Morris 1962, Plate H.
Reproduced by permission of Mrs. D. M. F. Morris.

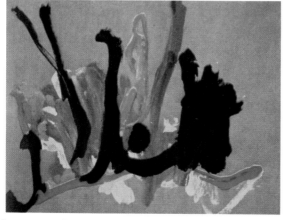

Split fan pattern by Congo with central black spot. From Morris
1962, Plate I. Reproduced by permission of Mrs. D. M. F. Morris.

A male Striated weaverbird. From Hancocks 1973, facing p.48.
(See p.246)

to animals other than man, in the affirmative. The inquiry entails the belief that there must be a biological basis to aesthetics, and thus shifts to a search into the basis thereof: "What are the historical or ultimate reasons for the development of an esthetic sense; by what mechanisms is the development of the species-characteristic preferences assumed?" Klopfer (ibid.:400), too, comes up against the predicament posed by the traditional view that aesthetic preferences are those for which no immediate functional advantage can be perceived; consequently he strikes out in a different direction, seeking for guidance from sensory physiology, while also redefining play as a kind of exploratory activity by which the organism 'tests' different proprioceptive patterns for the goodness of fit.

When ethnologists search for the sources of art, they more often than not mean the verbal art; play thus comes to mean wordplay, which Alland (1977:27), for one, connects with poetry, and which must then be excluded *per definitionem* from the rest of the animal kingdom. Archeologists tend especially to dwell on representative art; as Marshack (1972:275) puts it, "art and symbol are products that visualize and objectify aspects of culture. . . ." Although, on balance, the neuroanatomist Young (1971:519) is undoubtedly right when he says, in the course of his synthesis tracing the sources of human activity from their biochemical basis to the highest levels of consciousness, that "there is no body of facts that yet enables us to understand the origins of aesthetic creation . . . ," the issue remains a tantalizing one, for, as another distinguished biologist put it, "in some situations it becomes really difficult not to impute to animals some sort of aesthetics" (Dobzhansky 1962:215). The dialectic seems to have begun between Darwin, whose theory of sexual selection is based on the assumption that female birds, for example, are able to appreciate the beauty of male plumage (cf. Romanes 1892:380-385), and his contemporary, Wallace, who disputed this view precisely in semiotic terms. Wallace argued that what is involved here is an instinctive interpretation of certain strings of signs emitted by the male. However this may be, it would be unreasonable to expect a perfunctory and iterative scrutiny of the literature of animal behavior to shed much illumination; a deeper search, on the other hand, might at least highlight some fundamental issues—such as the often misunderstood dichotomy of analogy vs. homology, and the even less-understood distinction between phyletic homologies and homologies of tradition.

KINESTHETIC SIGNS

The kinesthetic art—as the multisensory dance when viewed in a semiotic frame is sometimes reductively termed after its most distinctive feature, because in dance (contrasted, particularly, with mime) "movement is often an end in itself" (Royce 1977:197)—is seldom alluded to in the context of animal behavior. Sachs (1937:10) adduced several strik-

ing cases of bird displays he and others in his field, including recently
Royce (ibid.:3-4), explicitly dubbed "dancing." One of his examples is
cited after Maclaren (1926), who witnessed this dance of the stilt birds,
or cranes, in Cape York in Northeastern Australia:

> The birds . . . were long-legged creatures, tall almost as storks, and white
> and gray of feather; and the dance took place in the center of a broad,
> dry swamp. . . . There were some hundreds of them, and their dance was
> in the manner of a quadrille, but in the matter of rhythm and grace excel-
> ling any quadrille that ever was. In groups of a score or more they ad-
> vanced and retreated, lifting high their long legs and standing on their
> toes, now and then bowing gracefully to one another, now and then
> one pair encircling with prancing daintiness a group whose heads moved
> upwards and downwards and sideways in time to the stepping of the pair.
> At times they formed into one great prancing mass, with their long necks
> thrust upward; and the wide swaying of their backs was like unto the
> swaying of the sea. Then, suddenly, as in response to an imperative
> command, they would sway apart, some of them to rise in low, encircling
> flight, and some to stand as in little gossiping groups; and presently they
> would form in pairs or sets of pairs, and the prancing and bowing, and
> advancing and retreating would begin all over again.

His second example, which comes from British Guiana, cited after Appun
(1871:468-469), is, as Royce (1977:4) underlines, "even more interesting
since it describes what is essentially a performer-spectator situation":

> [A] group of some twenty mountain chickens of a brilliant orange-yellow
> color, gathered together in a kind of dance characteristic of these beauti-
> ful birds. In the center one of the cocks executed the dance-like move-
> ments, as he hopped about the open place with wings extended and tail
> outspread. On the branches of the bushes round about, the others sat
> and expressed their admiration of the dancer with the strangest sounds.
> As soon as one cock was exhausted, he joined the spectators, uttering a
> peculiar cry, and another took his place.

These parallels immediately raise several problems, the most obvious
being whether the animal's behavior is "merely" analogous to man's,
whether, that is, shifting to a more familiar parlance, the label "dance"
is "just" a colorful and suggestive metaphor—as it must surely be in
Frisch's designation (1954, 1967) of the kinetic component of the communication system of the honeybee as a "dance"—or whether something
deeper is implied, perhaps indeed a remote phyletic homology.[2] Even if
only an analogy is meant, this is far from valueless, since its study would
throw light on "the laws of function that rule the evolution of a behavior
pattern" (Eibl-Eibesfeldt 1975:233). It is, in fact, highly productive to
compare biological constructs with cultural ones if only to ascertain
whether seemingly similar signifiers trigger comparable interpretants, in
the sense that the wing of an insect (developed from an epidermal fold),
the wing of a bird (developed from a vertebrate extremity), and a wing

of an airplane (manufactured, say, of metal), are all shaped in response to the universal laws of aerodynamics. Armstrong (1963: chap. 15), who devoted an entire chapter to drawing parallels between the dances of birds and men, feels that he is justified in employing the identical label for both sets of motor signs because of

> a natural recognition of the remarkable similarities which actually exist between the dances of birds and men and the identity of the emotional sources from which both take their origin. The resemblances between avian and human dancing are the outcome of emotional drives which underlie the behaviour of all the higher animals; and the natural corollary is that we can use the terpsichorean activities of men to interpret those of birds, and vice versa. Let us not be scared by the bogey of anthropomorphism into the arms of the spectre of Cartesian mechanism. It is not anthropomorphism to believe that man and the higher animals have much in common so far as instinct and emotion are concerned, but an acknowledgment of truth scientifically demonstrated. [Ibid.:195]

Sachs questions, by distinguishing—to recast in modern ethological terminology what he says—phyletic homologies, or those that are transmitted via the genome, from homologies of tradition, that is, those that are passed on via memory, whether animals in fact do dance as man does. The traditional distinction between innate vs. acquired characteristics is not at all as clear-cut as Sachs implies, however, and becomes increasingly inappropriate when one considers the alloprimates. One reason for this is that, for research dealing with homologies, "it is only necessary that information emanating from one common source is passed on. It is not necessary for reproductive relationships to be involved" (Eibl-Eibesfeldt 1975). What we know about dancing in apes is, while doubtless fascinating, unfortunately far from abundant, and even here a further discrimination demands to be promptly introduced, namely, as between studies of animals in captivity, some of which Sachs knew of, and observations of groups in the wild, which are of much more recent vintage. Both sets of data concern chimpanzees—the latter all but exclusively from the popular writings of Lawick-Goodall (for her dramatic descriptions, see, e.g., 1967:75-77, 1971:52-54; Nissen 1932, whose fieldwork was conducted during the dry season, occasionally alludes, nevertheless, to wild chimpanzees performing in parties).

Lawick-Goodall repeatedly refers to a display, which she reports having seen but three times in all her years in the field, as a "rain dance." These group performances, lasting almost half an hour, involved adult males—with females and youngsters in watchful attendance—although often individual males were also observed to "react to the start of heavy rain by performing a rain dance" (1971:54). It is not at all clear from Lawick-Goodall's description of these spectacles what the chimpanzees' behavior pattern could possibly signify. In the human context, what is commonly called a rain dance is performed in many societies as a fertility rite in order to produce rain; it belongs to a class Royce (1977:207) calls metaphorical dances. By contrast, feral chimpanzees, to all appearances, "dislike the rain," reminding the observer of "primitive men . . . defying the elements" (Lawick-Goodall 1967:74, 77). Their carnival display is in reaction to a sudden downpour. What we have here is a striking resemblance in form—sufficiently so, it seems, to account for the labeling— but a dearth of information about referential sign function, and therefore a gnawing question mark about the meaning of the convergence between man and chimpanzee in this arena of expressive movement.

Reports of chimpanzees dancing in the laboratory—including what Sachs (1937:10) claimed to be the "most valuable document"—come from the psychologist Köhler (1922:33-35; cf. 1925:314-315), who was for six years in charge of a research establishment in Tenerife. Köhler frequently observed couples moving in dancelike fashion. He depicted a particular configuration about which he remarked (ibid.:33) that "Die Ähnlichkeit mit einem Tanz war besonders gross," a characterization Sachs wholly concurred with. Nor was this all. Stylized group dances took place, such as the following, which Sachs (1937:10) insisted "was a genuine round dance":

> In mock fighting two of them drag each other about on the ground until they come near a post. Their frolicking and romping quiets down as they begin to circle about, using the post as a pivot. One after another the rest of the animals appear, join the circle, and finally the whole group, one behind another, is marching in orderly fashion around the post. Now their movements change quickly. They are no longer walking but trotting. Stamping with one foot and putting the other down lightly, they beat out what approaches a distinct rhythm, with each of them tending to keep step with the rest. When two posts or boxes stand close to each other, they like to use these as a center, and in this case the ring dance around both takes the form of an ellipse. In these dances the chimpanzee likes to bedeck his body with all sorts of things, especially strings, vines, and rags that dangle and swing in the air as he moves about.

Sachs (ibid.:11) identifies here the prefigurements of a series of basic human dance motifs: "as forms, the circle and ellipse around the post, the forward and backward pace; as movements, hopping, rhythmical stamping, whirling, and even ornamentation for the dance." Köhler (1922:34) further tells us that the sympathetic observer would gladly join in this dance, and that when he initiated the movement around the post "in der besonderen Schrittart, welche für die Tiere dazugehörte," he was immediately followed by a couple of chimpanzees; but when he quit, because of fatigue, his dancing companions would squat and sulk. What Sachs (1937:12) is concerned with here ought to be taken very seriously, but remains as yet unresolved, for, as he summarizes:

> If the dance, inherited from brutish ancestors, lives in all mankind as a necessary motor-rhythmic expression of excess energy and of the joy of

living, then it is only of slight importance for anthropologists and social historians. If it is established, however, that an inherited predisposition develops in many ways in the different groups of man and in its force and direction is related to other phenomena of civilization, the history of the dance will then be of great importance for the study of mankind.

If one defines dance, in the stark fashion of Boas (1955:344), as "the rhythmic movements of any part of the body, swinging of the arms, movement of the trunk or head, or movements of the legs and feet," then clearly the chimpanzees' behavior can legitimately be bracketed with ours. It is plausible, moreover, to regard both underlying structures homologous, implying that they owe their similarity to a common origin, much as laughter and smiling fit into the phyletic scale (cf. Sebeok 1979: chap. 1). The postulation of a homologous relationship does not, however, necessarily imply a distinction between characteristics that are innate vs. those that may be acquired, for homologies may be passed on either via the genome or via memory, that is, by cultural or quasi-cultural mechanisms, in the manner, say, of song traditions in the parasitic weaver finches (*Viduinae*), which were discovered even to transgress species boundaries: these birds learn not only the songs but also the calls of their host species, and close mimicry of the vocalizations of the stepfather results in parallel development that may, in turn, lead to eventual species genesis.

Whether dance behavior is innate or acquired is not known, but it is important to be mindful that information may be communicated to a succeeding generation in several different ways, and therefore, since form depends on the function, convergence can hardly be excluded. In studies of expressive movements, the investigation is particularly complicated by the fact that the specific adaptations are not simply responsive to the environment, but involve subtle selective pressures that cannot yet be formulated in terms of physiological or biochemical correlates—for instance, a concept such as "aesthetic pleasure." Nonetheless, I find myself concurring with Griffin (1976:78), when he exclaims that "this does not seem to [him] to be a sufficient reason for avoiding the concepts themselves, as though they were a dangerous plague." This view accords, I think, with the line taken by such specialists in the dance as Hanna (1977:211), who, while she feels "that the configuration of human behaviour that is called dance is significantly different from the behaviour of other animals, including that which has also been labelled dance," at the same time affirms "that human dance has its roots in phylogenetic and ontogenetic evolution, firstly in predisposing psychobiological processes and secondly in social experience."

MUSICAL SIGNS

"Music," Merriam (1964:27) tells his readers, "is a uniquely human phenomenon . . ."—but his generalization begs the very question that needs exploring. I would therefore prefer to start journeying backward in time from the Janus-like portal that is the sole rational means of access from nature to culture that Lévi-Strauss (1964:24) sagaciously threw open when befittingly noting that

> la musique opère au moyen de deux grilles. L'une est physiologique, donc naturelle; son existence tient au fait que la musique exploite les rythmes organiques, et qu'elle rend ainsi pertinentes des discontinuités qui resteraient autrement à l'état latent, et comme noyées dans la durée. L'autre grille est culturelle; elle consiste dans une échelle de sons musicaux, dont le nombre et les écarts varient selon les cultures.

Boas (1955:340) made two fundamental observations concerning music: first, that the only kind of music that occurs universally is song, "and the source of music must therefore be sought here"; and, second, that two elements, and only two, are common to all song: rhythm and fixed intervals. It is in the class of birds that the rootstock lies to which these remarks must inevitably lead the unprejudiced investigator, fortified by the opinion of so experienced an ornithologist as Thorpe (1974:307), who, in repudiation of a typically naive remark of Suzanne Langer's,[3] proclaims his own stand: "increased familiarity, from long study, certainly for me, increases my conviction that our judgment that bird songs, in some instances and in some degree, represent music is not mistaken."

Within the last two decades several competent and thoughtful studies have appeared appraising a field that in the course of its recent development has even won a name of its own: ornithomusicology (Szoke 1963). One such survey, on the aesthetic content of bird song, was compiled by Hall-Craggs (1969), a British ornithologist. Another, a book-length global reinterpretation of bird song, was undertaken by Hartshorne (1973), a prominent philosopher (perhaps best known to this readership as the senior editor of the Collected Papers of C. S. Peirce). As for the controversial but hardly verifiable central thesis of ornithomusicology—an idea first articulated, I believe, by Montaigne—it is argued that birds evolved elaborate musical utterances long before the appearance of man, who may be supposed to have derived his primitive music under the instigation or, at any rate, influence of their song: men certainly heard it and some may have imitated it. (It should be mentioned here that man often mimics different aspects of animal behavior,[4] and particularly that the imitation of bird dances is quite widespread. One example from Europe is the incorporation of a figure, the Nachsteigen, from the behavior of the mountain cock, into the Bavarian Schuhplatter; see further Armstrong 1965:209ff.) The process of adoption would have been facilitated by the undeniable fact that man and bird share certain requisite physiological foundations: both sense the world most consequentially by optical means, and both address it most saliently by acoustic means.[5] Indeed, in a number of crucial respects, and particularly as to the predisposition of some songbirds, manifesting critical periods in their lives for song learning, to master certain sounds rather than others in a manner reminiscent of the kind of constraints on first language acquisition detectable in human children, and in several other important respects, "these birds are closer to man than any nonhuman primate . . ." (Marler and Gordon 1968:128).[6]

Were the ornithomusicologist's contentions demonstrable, then one could postulate a true homology of tradition, if not a phyletic one: human song would thus be as homologous to bird song as, say, a genetically unrelated second language acquired by a foreign speaker is homologous to the first language learned by a native speaker of that same language. Failing that, we must fall back on the principle of convergent evolution, justified by adequate evidence for formal correspondence. But Szőke's line of argumentation is by no means abrogated or contradicted by the prodigiously erudite Armstrong in his (1963) chapter on "Bird Song as Art and Play." This life-long English student of bird behavior repeatedly remarks that "As evidence increases it becomes more difficult to deny that birds possess some aesthetic sensitivity" (ibid.:267); that "we are justified in postulating the existence of aesthetic appreciation on a lower level among animals" (ibid.:235); and that, "whatever else our aesthetic taste may be, it is an extension and refinement of animal abilities" (ibid.). He quotes an apt observation by Paracelsus, the early sixteenth-century physician and alchemist, who admonished: "Man need not be surprised that animals have animal instincts that are so much like his own. . . . Man may learn from the animals, for they are his parents."[7]

The most elusive problem in demonstrating "that birds have aesthetic taste is the difficulty of proving that any characteristic of bird song is non-utilitarian" (Armstrong ibid.:244). Hartshorne's book (1973, esp. chaps. 2 and 3) is in part addressed to this predicament, which he formulates thus: "To say 'aesthetic' is to say 'not merely or too directly utilitarian.' But we must be careful to balance this consideration against the seemingly contradictory one that unless an aesthetic activity has some connection with utility it will be unlikely to survive evolutionary change" (ibid.:53). Hartshorne speculates that there may be an optimum here between irrelevance to survival needs of the species—notably, as an expression of its territorial requirements (the birds with the "best" songs are usually the ones with the most marked territorial behavior)—and too close or immediate a connection with such needs, as represented by the individual singer in a given context. He postulates "a safety factor," a sort of emergency valve for the outlet of surplus energy, a luxury activity that can always be nullified in exigent circumstances.

Rhythm is the basis of form in bird song, as in all music, much as symmetry is in space or equilibrium in matter. Hall-Craggs (1969:311ff.) discusses its prevalence in some detail, as well as of the transposition of fixed intervals that Boas deemed the second all-important element of music, comparable with melody. Armstrong (1963:244) remarked earlier that "it can hardly be fortuitous that some birds do sing and transpose in accordance with our musical scale." An important series of experiments bearing on this point was carried out by Reinert (1965) with jackdaws (*Corvus monedula*). After being conditioned to distinguish certain rhythmic acoustic signals, the jackdaws were able to identify them even when played by different instruments, that is, with a different timbre, or when the tempo, pitch, or interval was transposed. They could also distinguish between two-four time and three-four time. The birds could perceive acoustical patterns differing in intensity and duration of tone, and recognized a great many variations. In sum, they did not depend on absolute clues only but, as we ourselves do in the perception of phonemes, on relative ones. Ultimately, I suppose, this is a mathematical matter, and eventually Nelson (1973), in fact, undertook a sophisticated quantitative comparative study of this kind, showing similarities of structuring in several taxa, including behavioral organization in bird and man, with respect to acoustic signals.

Many birds, moreover, possess the ability to follow a train of changing pitches, like a scale, and to distinguish it from another train proceeding simultaneously but at a different speed or in a different direction. In other words, these birds appear to have solved what Cherry (1978: 279-282) had designated in man as the "cocktail party problem," the essence of which I take to consist in the capacity to select one particular acoustic string, *viz.*, a tune, from its accompaniment or to distinguish it from another string proceeding at the same time (polyphony). A single individual veery (*Hylocichla fuscescens*) is, for example, able to produce complex polyphonic patternings; nor need there be, in this species, an interval between primary patterns, although it may be present in one voice but not in the other. "At the end of most songs, the two voices come together to cooperate in a characteristic extended trill of *overlapping arpeggios* (song *A*); sometimes this 'cadence' appears to be left to the lower voice alone (song *B*)" (Nelson 1973:288-289). Thorpe, on the basis of his distinguished fieldwork, supplemented by laboratory studies, has clearly confirmed the existence of "something like musical appreciation, albeit on an elementary scale, existing in a good many birds" (1974:205), derived, in part, from discoveries of antiphonal singing, especially in the compulsively duetting African shrike (*Laniarius aethiopicus*) (Thorpe 1972). The notes of the duet constitute polyphonic singing, such that the pitch, timing, and phrasing can, to a large extent, be controlled very exactly, but can also be varied by the singers. Either sex can start and the other finish, either bird can sing the whole pattern alone if the partner is absent, and, when the partner returns, the two birds can either duplicate in perfect time or resume antiphonal singing.

The organized singing patterns of birds have long attracted our attention. In some, the singing is organized to conform with strict sequencing rules; the structure is hierarchical, the levels comparable with

FIG. 9.1. Seven segments showing a characteristic selection of *Laniarius aethiopicus* duet patterns. After Thorpe and North 1965. Reproduced by permission of William H. Thorpe.

FIG. 9.2. Separate figures showing seventeen different duet patterns. After Thorpe and North 1965:221. Reproduced by permission of William H. Thorpe.

the build-up of the human mode of vocal display. Ethologists tend to interpret bird song in terms of the adaptive advantages it confers on the performers and their conspecific audience, while keeping an open mind on the ramifying consequences of the display, which may well surpass a single function and come to encompass the aesthetic dimension. To summarize: "That birds 'sing' is a notion applied popularly to vocal performances that people find aesthetically pleasing, but singing lacks a fully accepted and rigorous descriptive meaning in ethology" (Smith 1977:56).

The ornithomusicological hypothesis becomes muddled when one considers that other animals than birds have variously been alleged to "sing": "Cicadas [i.e., locusts] are noisy, daytime musicians, the male alone singing. The sound is produced by snapping a special structure, the tymbal, with a muscle" (Frings and Frings 1977:79). As with birds, singing is emulative, and this, as Darwin (1901:434) had noted, sometimes gives rise to antiphonic duets or trios. This application of "song" is, however, likely to be metaphorical just as "dance" is in application to the honeybee. Then there is the California singing fish (*Porichthys notatus*), whose song, which varies in tone, pitch, and quality from specimen to specimen, produced under conditions of colonial activity, was carefully described by Charles W. Greene (1924). The striking vocalizations of frogs and toads have also been termed "songs" (Frings and Frings 1977:179), often in reference to the existence of duetting throughout some nineteen genera, or more complex chorusing behavior, the biological function of which has hitherto eluded all investigators. The bellow of the alligator, assumed to convey an assertion of dominance and a challenge to other males within earshot, is likewise often called "song" in the reptile literature. I doubt if phenomena of this sort can be considered as prefigurements in any interesting sense. However, there are at least two groups of mammals in which singing has been reported, and these may be worthier of our regard.

First, there is the case of the humpback whale (*Megaptera novaengliae*), a species whose phonograph recordings have received considerable publicity in the media and on at least American college campuses during the 1970s (George Crumb's exotic composition *Vox Balaenae for Three Masked Players* was directly inspired by the voice of the whale). Mysticete sounds have for some decades been recognized to be varied and complex, but the humpback is the baleen whose rich sonic repertoire has been most thoroughly studied so far (Payne and McVay 1971). The animals certainly "emit a series of surprisingly beautiful sounds" (ibid.:587), including a long train, called a "song," that recurs in cycles lasting up to thirty minutes and perhaps longer. This song is often produced in continuous soliloquy, very loudly, by a single whale for a full eight minutes; there is no evidence of duetting. But its purpose is not really understood; "we can only guess what function this remarkable series of vocalizations serves" (ibid.:597). This being so, no one can yet say whether the performance has, for the whale—in contrast to the human listener—any sort of aesthetic significance, and thus whether the designation "song" is biologically justified.

The climactic question whether songlike behavior has been observed in the order of Primates can be answered affirmatively, but, among the monkeys, it seems, only for some platyrrhine (New World) species, notably, *Callicebus moloch* (titi monkey). In the case of this monkey, Moynihan (1966:119) applies the term song "in a very broad and general sense, to include all series of notes uttered in more or less rapid and regular succession and distinctly set off, by relatively long pauses, from both preceding and succeeding notes." Moynihan characterizes such passages as only moderately rapid throughout all or most of their length, and these he calls "ordinary" songs. He describes four or more other types, and calls these "compound" songs. Among the ordinary songs, he identifies nineteen, but says that this list is certainly not exhaustive. He terms two of the most common compound sequences "full" songs; in these, the normal sequence of pitch changes is from higher to lower, irrespective of the actual notes involved. He explains why they cannot be produced by precisely the same type of motivation—there are qualitative as well as quantitative differences in causation. Full songs of one individual frequently instigate full songs by others. When two or more individuals are within twenty or thirty feet of one another, their songs tend to be very closely synchronized, note by note; synchronization usually breaks down as the distance between individuals increases. This sort of timing probably has one important advantage, to enable singing individuals to judge, with very great precision, their relative positions *vis-à-vis* one another. Like most songbirds, which display an intense dawn chorus, the titi monkey typically vocalizes at daybreak:

> All or almost all the adults . . . begin to sing as soon as it starts to become light, well before sunrise. Their Songs usually are long and full, including (at least) Moans, Resonating Notes and Pumping notes. . . . Dawn Songs probably are seldom or never reactions to external stimuli. . . . They do not appear to have any direct or immediate signal function, insofar as they seldom or never provoke obvious responses from other individuals (except, sometimes, singing in return). [Ibid.:120]

Most of the major components of the *Callicebus* song repertory is assumed by Moynihan to be homologous with that of species in many other genera, occasionally all.

In general, the vocalizations of catarrhine (Old World) monkeys, and especially those of tailless apes, deserve much closer study. Marler and Tenaza (in Sebeok 1977:970) have recently stressed that "a comprehensive acoustical description" of the chimpanzee—which has been studied far more than any other ape—"has yet to be published." With respect to singing behavior, the gibbon may be the most interesting animal of all: as long ago as the 1890s, Blanford (1888-91:97), a well-

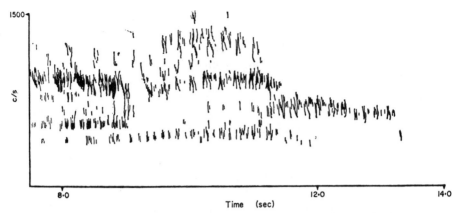

FIG. 9.3. The first part of a full Song phrase by an adult *Callicebus moloch*. After Moynihan 1966:116, Fig. 29. Reproduced by permission of the author and The Zoological Society of London.

known authority on South Asian mammals, wrote about the hoolock (a species of gibbon found in Assam and Upper Burma), that its powerful voice, at a distance,

> much resembles the human voice; [its song] is a peculiar wailing note, audible afar, and . . . one of the most familiar forest sounds. The calls commence at daybreak, . . . several of the flock joining in the cry, like hounds giving tongue. . . . [They] remain silent throughout the middle of the day, but recommence calling towards evening, though to a less extent than in the earlier part of the day.

This is another example of the diurnal rhythm that so frequently characterizes song displays. The same term, "song," is also used for the hoolock and several other varieties of gibbon by Marler and Tenaza (Sebeok 1977a:1001-1009), who distinguish three kinds of choruses based on

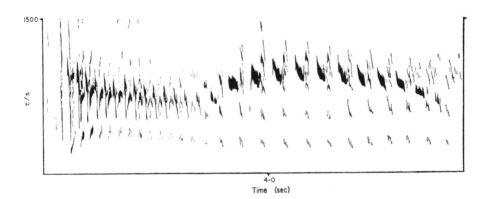

FIG. 9.4. The second and final part of the Song phrase. Reproduced by permission of the author and The Zoological Society of London.

the sex of the singers: those consisting entirely of males singing; those consisting entirely of females singing; and those consisting of duets sung by mated pairs of gibbons. They describe individuals engaged in dyadic countersinging with adjacent neighbors in several species. Predawn chorusing occurs very frequently, with choruses beginning as early as five hours before sunrise. This separates them temporally from dawn bird choruses, and it is assumed that the timing is an evolutionary consequence of interspecific competition for the auditory environment. "Captivity seems to have no effect upon the song structure or the nature of duetting in gibbons," according to these authors (ibid.:1008). In conclusion, Marler and Tenaza supply a long list of unanswered questions about pongid signaling behavior, insisting that, "Above all, new approaches should be sought to characterize the *functions* of different vocalizations, so that more subtle interspecies comparisons of the proportions of a signal repertoire devoted to different kinds of adaptive tasks may be possible" (ibid.:1029). In view of the uncertain state of knowledge about the biological uses of what is nevertheless persistently called "song" in the alloprimates, it seems premature to probe for its aesthetic function, if any.

In concluding this section, and before turning to the representational arts, I should mention that there are birds, among some sixty species of the family *Pipridae*, that *both* sing *and* dance, each species according

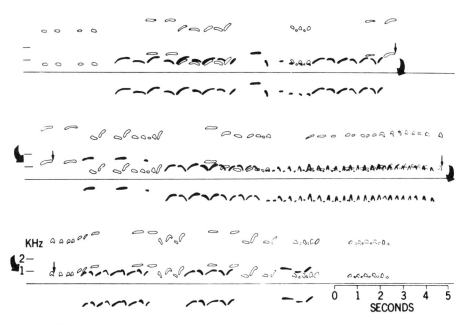

Fig. 9.5. Dueting in gibbons: an example of a male-female duet in the hoolock. From Marler and Tenaza, in Sebeok 1977:1007, Fig. 22. Reproduced by permission of Peter Marler and Indiana University Press.

to its own ritual. Even the earliest explorers of South and Central America noticed them because of their unique dances and the music connected with these dances, as in this entrancing description by Nutting (in 1884; from Slud 1957:333):

> Upon a bare branch which overhung the trail at a distance of about four feet from the ground, two male "Bailadors" were engaged in a "song and dance" act that simply astounded me. The two birds were about a foot and a half apart, and were alternately jumping about two feet into the air and alighting exactly upon the spot whence they jumped. The time was as regular as clock-work, one bird jumping up the instant the other alighted, each bird accompanying himself to the tune of "to-lé-do—to-lé-do—to-lé-do," sounding the syllable "to" as he crouched to spring, "le" while in the air, and "do" as he alighted.

In Costa Rica, where this enchanting bird is known as *el toledo*, people tell the same story in almost exactly the same words while alternately raising each index finger to illustrate the quaintness of the performance. The bird is technically known as *Chiroxiphia linearis* (one of the four so-called Chorus species), or the Long-tailed Manakin, whose antics were recently described, with some variations, anew by Slud (1957). All observers agree that the males do dance and that the *tolédo* call is a constant accompanying feature, although their views differ as to some other details. Slud vividly recounts several distinctive calls associated with the actively dancing males, including the "unmistakable *tolédo*," and characterizes the bird's flight as butterfly-like: "They fly with the weightless bounce of a Morpho," adding: "I am at a loss to explain the mechanics by which the slow beats somehow sustain the retarded flight" (ibid.:336-337). Their airy floating can by no stretch of the imagination be interpreted as a leaping back and forth from branch to branch. Of the dance, he further says:

> Perched crosswise a foot or two apart, both facing in the same direction, the two birds alternately rise straight into the air for a foot or two. Each fluttering rise is preceded by a lowering of the head, and at the top of the rise the bird hangs suspended for an appreciable pause, as though attached to a rubber band. The red crown of the bowed head appears unusually large and bright, the sky-blue back loosely fluffed, the long tail arches and hangs in a graceful curve, and the bright orange legs hang too. A guttural *miaow-raow* punctuates each rise. Gradually the duration of each rise shortens and the rate of successive rise increases. As the tempo mounts, the crest of the risings falls lower and lower and the pitch of the accelerating *miaow-raow's* rises higher and higher until the former degenerate into seemingly uncontrolled flutters and the latter into unintelligible buzzy sounds. Now the birds hardly rise at all and almost bump each other as they flop about like helpless victims of an internal disorder. As though a switch were pulled, the orgiastic frenzy ends suddenly, and the birds cock their heads innocently in calm possession of faculties restored at the instant of reassertion of self-control. [Ibid.:337]

Slud also depicts an alternate dance, which begins after the same pre-liminaries as the preceding one.

> This time, however, the birds stand on the vine or branch lengthwise, both facing in the same direction but with one behind the other, again spaced more than a foot apart. The first bird, uttering his *miaow·raow*, rises straight into the air, where he then hangs momentarily suspended. As he reaches the top of his leap, the rear bird, crouched, his eyes fixed upon the bird in the air, with rapidly flicking wings and arched tail hitches himself forward to the accompaniment of a low ticking, *pk·pk·pk·pk·pk* etc., to a point on the branch directly below the suspended bird and identical to the one from which the first bird rose. The bird in the air now falls diagonally backward to the very spot from which the bird began his ticking, wing-quivering creep. As he alights, the second bird, now in the forward position, rises into the air. At the same instant the first bird, fallen to the rear position, hitches himself forward in his turn. Like balls in a juggling act, the birds replace one another with cyclical regu-larity. The individually uttered *miaow-raow's* accent the recurrent rhythm and the underlying ticking goes on almost without interruption. The tempo may be increased but the performance does not become disor-ganized as in the straight up-and-down dance. . . . The dance ends sud-denly and the birds float "butterfly-like" to the sidelines. [Ibid.:337-338]

PICTORIAL SIGNS

You have already been introduced above to bowerbirds, a group about whose "artistic" productions no less a scientist than Karl von Frisch (1974:244) has said that it has "much similarity with human behavior in comparable situations: those who consider life on earth to be the result of a long evolutionary process will always search for the begin-nings of thought processes and aesthetic feelings in animals, and I believe that significant traces can be found in the bower birds." He (ibid.: 243-244) goes on to quote a wondrous observation by the naturalist Heinz Seilmann about the decorating behavior of a New Guinea species, the Yellow breasted bowerbird (*Chlamydera lauterbachi*):

> Every time the bird returns from one of his collecting forays, he studies the over-all color effect. He seems to wonder how he could improve on it and at once sets out to do so. He picks up a flower in his beak, places it into the mosaic, and retreats to an optimum viewing distance. He be-haves exactly like a painter critically reviewing his own canvas. He paints with flowers; that is the only way I can put it. A yellow orchid does not seem to him to be in the right place. He moves it slightly to the left and puts it between some blue flowers. With his head on one side he then contemplates the general effect once more, and seems satisfied.

Even though Marshall, who, after more than two decades of study, be-came the foremost authority on bowerbirds, had indicated, or tried to, a

utilitarian basis for all such seemingly artistic manifestations, he summed
up his findings thus (1954:185-186):

> I see no reason, provisionally, to deny that bower-birds possess an aesthetic
> sense although, it must be emphasized, we have as yet no concrete proof
> that such is the case. Some bower-birds certainly select for their displays
> objects that are beautiful to *us*. Further, they discard flowers when they
> fade, fruit when it decays, and feathers when they become bedraggled
> and discoloured. . . . The fact that some bower-birds select objects that
> appeal to man's sense of beauty is no proof that such articles have
> a similar effect on the bird. If all bower-birds made collections of bleached
> bones, less would be written of aestheticism. Yet nobody would suggest
> that its pile of dry bones and dead snail-shells is less beautiful to [the
> Great Gray bowerbird] than is the "beautiful" array of blue and red
> berries to [the Yellow-breasted variety]. It would, of course, be unthink-
> able to suggest that bower-birds—or any birds for that matter—do not get
> pleasure from the vocal, architectural, and other activities they perform
> but whether such pleasure has much in common with that of Man, en-
> gaged in comparable pursuits, has yet to be proved.

At any rate, a scientist of the stature of Haldane (1956:II:11) was convinced that "a few animals, such as bower birds, show *sundaradharma*,
behaviour satisfying aesthetic needs. This is most marked in the bower
birds. . . ." Nor does it seem surprising, in the light of conclusions such
as this, that Odoardo Beccari, the first naturalist to discover the display
court of a bowerbird, should have believed that he had stumbled upon
a playhouse built by native children!
    Over and over, we keep encountering the same pivotal aesthetic
paradox: this emerges from a profound confusion about purpose; it drives
us to ferret out compulsively any semblance of utility, usually defined as
adaptive value.[8] We find it difficult to conceive of art as a coherent part
of animal life and can scarcely imagine it as an adornment of the creatures' leisure. All researches in this field are stamped by a tension between
a deeply felt conviction on the part of many distinguished and sensitive
biologists that artistic activity indeed exists in the animal world and the
inability to face its presumed lack of importance, even uselessness. More
generally, Jenkins (1958:130) has argued that the position assigned to
the aesthetic life in Western culture, from Plato onwards, is imbued by
an uneasy fluctuation between these two attitudes, "that art is at once
useless and fraught with significance, purposeless and yet important."
The two poles Jenkins speaks of are perhaps reconciled in a casual comment of Vygotsky's (1971:246): "Apparently the possibility of releasing
into art powerful passions which cannot find expression in normal everyday life is the biological basis of art." Viewed thus, art becomes a kind of
cybernetic device for keeping the organisms' *milieu intérieur*, or, to use
Uexküll's corresponding concept, *Innenwelt* (Sebeok 1978a, chap. 10),
in balance with its surroundings (*milieu extérieur*, or *Umwelt*).

Art, in this homeostatic sense, is surely recognizable in many other biological systems besides that of man. Birds that construct elaborate nests, such as the weavers, build improved nests in their second season, after having practiced during the previous one, now opting for habitations that are "better" in the sense of tidier, neater, more elegant, but not at all demonstrably more useful. One may well ask with the late Waddington (in Brothwell 1976:8), "is it then or is it not an aesthetic 'better'?" Spiders will repair damage made to their webs, but "it is debatable whether this repair is governed solely by utilitarian consideration" (id.). The webs of certain drunken or drugged spiders appear both, one assumes, to them, and certainly to us, very unappealing. And chimpanzees and gorillas, when offered the materials used by human artists, "which are obviously exceedingly unnatural and exotic in relation to a normal primate life, produce paintings and drawings in which some aesthetic qualities may perhaps be discernible" (id.). This is the topic of an overview article by Whiten (in Brothwell 1976, chap. 2), himself a practicing painter. Before, however, turning to ape aesthetics, I should at least mention Dücker's (1963) interesting work on color preferences of forty-two specimens of birds of different families, in eleven species, especially spotted weaver finches. Animals have an innate positive and/or negative feeling-tone for particular colors or patterns; commonly this is related to species-characteristic signs that serve as releasers triggering their responses to each other. The males of many songbird species, Dücker showed, tend to exhibit a preference for the distinctive coloration of their own sex. Rensch (1976:329) found that a green long-tailed monkey (*Cercopithecus aethiops*) favored white, a color that also occurs in the bare skin around the eyes of these monkeys "and is evidently a signal stimulus for the recognition of their own species." Rensch, who had performed several thousand tests with two species of monkey, also reports that, when such innate color triggers are eliminated from the experiments, "higher animals are still found to show some preferences which correspond to the basic aesthetic feelings in man." His monkeys showed a distinct predilection for bright colors over shades of gray, just as human children do. He speculates (ibid.:330) that the probable reason for this is

> that the stimuli which are associated with the sensations of colour and which are generated in the cones of the retina are more powerful than stimuli generated in the rods, which respond only to varying degrees of light and dark, i.e., to different shades of gray. Besides, colours usually stand out more distinctly from their background than grays do and are therefore more easily discernible.[9]

Schiller's study (1951; published posthumously, reported by K. S. Lashley) of more than 200 of Alpha's drawings was a landmark among researches of visual composition in apes. Her drawings, Schiller found, in no case yielded representations. He compared them, in this respect, to scribblings of the human infant from twelve to eighteen months. Nor did he find any evidence of imitative drawing. One feature of interest that emerged was that Alpha's drawings, like those of the Kohts chimpanzee, Joni, underwent a considerable change of style over the six months of nearly daily tests. Twenty months later, however, Alpha returned to her original style. The reason for these fluctuations was not determined. The drawings showed a distinct sense of design and the ability to develop a pattern, including an impressive indication of a tendency for symmetrical arrangement. Schiller felt (1951:109) that this argued "strongly that Alpha has some feeling for a balance of masses on the page." He believed that she was less interested in the effects of her drawings than in the action itself:

> She is not influenced by the color of the figures or background or the visibility of her markings. Pencil lines drawn on or around the figures by the experimenter do not influence the position of her scribblings. She pokes toward the figure with the crayon, exploring its outlines and interior. If she gets an edge loose, she tries to peel the figure off of the sheet. [1951: 110]

Schiller also perceived another factor at work:

> She does not draw with a pointed stick and discards or chews up the crayon when the point breaks and it no longer marks. Given paper and pencil with broken point, she retires to a corner, examines the point, makes a few tentative strokes, then returns to the front of the cage to beg. The fact of marking is thus an essential part of the activity. [Ibid.]

It is, incidentally, worth noting that Alpha was never given any kind of a reward—either food or social—for drawing; Schiller held that she got her reinforcement from the very act of drawing.

Morris (1962) discusses the results obtained with Alpha and compares them with those of his mascot Congo, the second ape artist to be studied in depth. Congo's responses were found to be comparable, when given like tests, with those of Alpha; similar behavior has also been observed in other great apes and in a capuchin monkey who drew lines on the floor of his cage when he was presented with color chalks (Bourne 1971:222; Rensch 1976:339). Several gorillas, from Rotterdam and Basel to Palo Alto, have been known to draw and paint very successfully, as have occasional orangutans. In the mid-1950s, an ape known as Baltimore Betsy became famous from her finger paintings. Her work, and those of two other apes, were shown, without identification, to child psychiatrists.

> One of the psychiatrists interpreted them as coming from an aggressive seven- or eight-year-old boy who had paranoid tendencies. Baltimore Betsy's drawings were said to be from a fiercely belligerent ten-year-old schizoid girl. A second picture by the same animal was also said to be by a ten-year-old girl who was paranoid and showed a strong father identification. [Morris 1962:25; Bourne 1971:224]

FIGS. 9.6 and 9.7. Finger-paintings by chimpanzee Betsy. From Morris 1962, Plates 3 and 4. Reproduced by permission of Mrs. D. M. F. Morris.

Eventually, twelve paintings by Betsy as well as twenty-four Congos were exhibited—and practically all sold—in London. Julian Huxley, who had opened the exhibition, later made the following comments:

> The results show conclusively that chimpanzees do have artistic potentialities which can be brought to light by providing suitable opportunities. One of the great mysteries of human evolution is the sudden outburst of art of a very high quality in the upper Paleolithic period. This becomes more comprehensible if our apelike ancestors had these primitive aesthetic potentialities, to which was later added man's unique capacity for symbol-making. [Morris 1962:27][10]

Morris recapitulates in his justly famous book half a century's picture making with twenty-three chimpanzees, two gorillas, three orangutans, and four capuchin monkeys. Alpha and Congo, who produced some 600 pictures in all, were studied most intensively. The principle that Morris stresses and elaborates (1962:144ff.) is the fact that painting involves actions that are self-rewarding activities, that is, they "are performed for their own sake rather than to attain some basic biological goal. They are 'activities for activities' sake,' so to speak." In human art, this sort of motivation has appeared in many guises. Jenkins's (1958: 126-127) roll call includes such celebrated aesthetic doctrines as

> detachment, catharsis or purgation, isolation, objectification, emotion remembered in tranquility, psychic distance, self-surrender, passivity, pure perception, will-less knowing, reposefulness, equilibrium, synthesis, im-

personalness, contemplativeness, empathy, pleasure objectified, disinterested pleasure, receptivity,

and many others echoing the same meaning. For Morris, the category of self-rewarding activities is essentially biological, of course:

> Most of them are basically physical, meteoric outbursts and are fundamentally similar to human gymnastics and sports, except that they lack any ulterior motives such as the obtaining of health, money, or social standing. They may inadvertently keep the animal mentally and physically healthy and thus indirectly assist in its struggle for survival, but the actual driving force behind these self-rewarding activities appears to be simply the unleashing of surplus nervous energy. [Morris 1962:145]

This immediately suggests a central question: Why, if they have such a strong picture-making potential, have apes neither developed nor utilized it in the wild? This question corresponds closely to a second one, far more widely debated these days: Why, if, as alleged, apes have the cognitive prerequisites for the acquisition of language competency, haven't they elaborated it in nature? No satisfactory answer to the latter question has been put forward thus far; even the rankest activist hasn't proposed that they have done so, outside of science fiction of the likes of Jules Verne and on the planet of the apes. Morris's answer to the former rests on his claim that, as soon as man "had a real language which described objects as well as moods, the gateway was open to the pictorial representation of these objects" (1962:146), or, in other words, that the emergence of this averbal art required the antecedence of verbal signs. This suggestion may appear likely to some, although I personally doubt it and, in any case, it is entirely speculative.[11] More to the point, it sheds no light at all on the previous conundrum. The holistic interpretation of pictures is a function of the right hemisphere, an operation normally exercised in conjunction with the left hemisphere; but the minor hemisphere, which seems specialized for dealing with things all at once, has an extremely limited verbal capacity, even though its performance is said by Eccles (Popper and Eccles 1977:328) to be "superior to that of the brains of the highest anthropoids," while the dominant hemisphere, which tends to deal with things in sequence, is "almost illiterate in respect to pictorial and pattern sense" (ibid.:351).

Morris adduces five further biological principles of picture making beside the basic one, that the accomplishment is in and of itself rewarding. His second principle is that of compositional control, the power of which is illustrated by Alpha's and Congo's adherence to the simple rules of filling a space and keeping within it, balancing, and cadenced repetition. This was previously evidenced from Rensch's investigations with a capuchin and a guenon monkey, and found, as well, in jackdaws and crows. As Morris (1962:161) notes, the vital words here are: "steadiness—symmetry—repetition—rhythm." His third principle, "calligraphic differentiation," is a developmental one, referring to a slow progress of pictorial growth, which, however, is less strikingly exhibited by apes than by children. It is closely related to the fourth principle, thematic variation, or, as we might say in semiotics, the concept of invariance with allowable reformulations.

Whiten rightly regards the last two principles—which the proponent himself had put forward merely as a working hypothesis—of dubious status: "optimum heterogeneity," Morris suggests, governs the composition and point of completion of each picture, meaning by this the stage at which the picture is considered to be finished. Congo, it seems, had a very distinct concept of when a drawing or painting of his came to an end. By contrast, Alpha continued to cover the whole sheet with scribble if the paper was not removed. "Universal imagery" is what gives ape pictures as a whole a recognizable character, Morris finally maintains, but the only image that seems to recur with any regularity (also in capuchin art) is the "fan."

Whiten (Brothwell 1976:32-40) moves beyond the problems of artistic creation that had preoccupied Morris to those of aesthetic appreciation, relying, in the main, on several papers by Humphrey (1971, 1972). Humphrey's initial series of tests was designed to determine if monkeys had favorite colors and preferences for certain brightnesses. The four monkeys tested for color gave the same result: the order of preference in each case was blue, green, yellow, orange, and red. Brightness preference, which was tested by pairing the standard white slide with white slides of differing brightnesses, turned out to be monotonically related to brightness over the range used.

Next, Humphrey tested preferences for pictures, using thirty colored photographs classified as "men" (e.g., a portrait of the keeper), "monkeys" (two infants playing), "other animals" (cow), "foods" (banana), "flower" (daisy), and "abstract painting" (a Mondrian). This order of preference turned out to be: other animals/monkeys/men/flowers/abstract painting/food.

One may well ask, with Whiten (Brothwell 1976:37), "whether such preferences have anything at all to do with aesthetics." Humphrey posits two different patterns that reflect a dichotomy as to the ways both we and monkeys may exploit our senses: we may, he affirms, look at a stimulus "purely for pleasure" or "purely for interest." The pleasure dimension, corresponding to a pure aesthetic, can be either positive or negative but is little affected by novelty, whereas the curiosity dimension is positive and changes only toward indifference as the novelty of the stimulus wanes. In Humphrey's view, the two types of responses operate quite independently, although they often coalesce as to timing, in which case their combined effects will yield a summative expression of preference. Humphrey resumes his findings in five simple principles:

> 1. Two independent kinds of relationship obtain between the monkey and the stimulus, called "interest" and "pleasure/unpleasure."

2. When there is a choice between two stimuli, the monkey ranks them according to their relative interestingness and relative pleasantness.

3. If one stimulus is "appreciably more interesting" than the other, the probability that the monkey will prefer it is 1.

4. If one stimulus is "appreciably more pleasant" than the other, the probability that he will prefer it is 1 unless the other stimulus is appreciably more interesting.

5. If neither stimulus is either appreciably more interesting or pleasant, the probability that he will prefer each is 1/2.

Unfortunately, these principles were derived from monkeys, not apes, but Humphrey was able to predict from his quantitative model with a high degree of accuracy preferences for a stimulus that combined the two distinctive features of interest and pleasure. Visual feedback, we may safely surmise, is an important part of painting for apes, but we can't be sure—and the question still abides why their desire to create visual art remains latent, to surface, if at all, only in captivity, whether spontaneously or under instigation.

Another puzzle which continues to perplex has been well posed by Whiten (ibid.:39), who wonders, "why has nature equipped the chimp and the human with such ability? The interest or curiosity dimension of art can be seen as an offshoot, functionless in terms of survival value. . . . But if a pure aesthetic sense is a functional offshoot of some other functional attribute, what is this?" Humphrey (1973) has wrestled with this difficult question himself, and I find the suggestions of this animal behaviorist particularly intriguing because he believes, as I do, "that a structuralist approach is the key to the science of aesthetics" (ibid.:430), and because he has so fruitfully employed semiotic concepts. Like Lévi-Strauss, whom he cites, his starting point is a conceptualization of an artistic product as a system of signs, but from this obvious notion he goes on to ask how such works acquire their artistic charge. The answer he proposes (ibid.: 432) is that,

> considered as a biological phenomenon, aesthetic preferences stem from a predisposition among animals and men to seek out experiences through which they may *learn to classify* the objects in the world about them. Beautiful "structures" in nature or in art are those which facilitate the task of classification by presenting evidence of the "taxonomic" relations between things in a way which is informative and easy to grasp.

This argument, of course, presupposes that the capacity for effective classification is important for survival, perhaps on a par with eating and sex. If so, techniques of classification were bound to evolve so as to be a source of pleasure to the animal and thus to shape the nonrandom differential reproduction of its genes (natural selection). After all, as Humphrey remarks, both animals and men can be relied on to do best what they most enjoy doing. This point of view, coupled with the idea that no work of art is arbitrary, suggests where an animal's feeling of beauty may come from. In the terminology of René Thom (1975:316), "the work of art acts like the germ of a virtual catastrophe in the mind of the beholder." In other words, although art is always unpredictable, "it appears to us to have been directed by some organizing center of large codimension, far from the normal structures of ordinary thought, but still in resonance with the main emotional or genetic structures underlying our conscious thought."

Humphrey carries his taxonomic metaphor much further, enriching it with the notion of rhyming, or, as I would prefer to denominate the phenomenon more generally, parallelism. He brings experimental evidence to bear from a rich array of studies of exploratory behavior, and from his own investigations of "stimulus novelty" in monkeys. Parallelism involves the psychological notion of "stimulus discrepancy," or what in the early 1950s was called "discrepancy theory," ugly coinages for a fundamental concept with wide applications in the animal world and among human babies.

The propensity to classify seems to have acquired, through evolution, diminishing survival value, but then so did sex: humans can enjoy either, but most *tokens,* though pleasurable *per se,* are not biologically relevant. Only the *type* of activity has a clear-cut biological function.

Finally, let it be noted that Humphrey's pleasure principle seems equivalent to Morris's principle of composition. Pleasure, more likely than curiosity, tends to motivate compositional control, but the reverse holds for calligraphic differentiation and thematic variation. To some extent, all these principles are likely to involve both types of preferences; these components, acting together, may manifest themselves in a principle of optimum heterogeneity. The prefigurements of visual art in our species can thus be understood a little better against its simian backgrounds. This should surprise no one who is even superficially acquainted with the classic book by D'Arcy Thompson, *On Growth and Form* (1945), in which this great zoologist, so far ahead of his time, dealt with the basis for beauty in numberless exquisite structures produced by the plant and animal worlds, and showed that it is possible to construct an abstract, purely geometrical theory of morphogenesis, independent of the substrate of forms and the nature of the forces that create them (Thorpe 1974:302; Thom 1975:8).

ARCHITECTURAL SIGNS

"A building is not only an object but also a sign," Bogatyrev (in Matejka and Titunik 1976:18) noted in 1936, and Jakobson later elaborated on this dictum by stressing that "[a]ny edifice is simultaneously some sort of refuge and a certain kind of message" (1971:703). The utility—i.e., technological interest—of different architectural configurations is thus generally taken for granted. What remains in question is their correlation with the corresponding universe of signifieds, in particular as regards its aesthetic dimension, and the direction of the artistic movement: is it from external form, considered as a signifier, toward internal organization, which becomes the signified, or is it the converse? The architectural work of art, everyone seems to agree, is devoted to the realization of several ends. It stands at the confluence of multiple interests. Its character is syncretic *par excellence.*

In looking at the endlessly manifold abodes constructed by animals—which serve perhaps to trap prey, to protect or comfort the architect or its kind, especially the young, or to attract the attention of a potential mate—we must look for the artistic value that may be involved, although subordinated to the principal interest of the "survival machine," as Dawkins (1978:21, 25) calls the temporary receptacles housing the colony of genes inhabiting every plant and animal. If there is such a subsidiary purpose, falling passively under the sway of "mere" biological advantage, or supplementing it, an effort must be made to ferret out this aesthetic component. Such a quest is far from trivial, for, in the end, it is tantamount to asking: What is art?

The sources for the materials utilized by animals to erect their dwellings are twofold: either the substances are produced from within their own bodies, or they are assembled from the environment surrounding them. In the latter case, members of some species may exhibit subtle preferences, which may justly be termed aesthetic, in their very selection of particular habitats. Indeed, Klopfer (1970:400) even supposes that "the most convincing evidence for the existence of esthetic preferences come from the literature on habitat selection. . . ." This discerning ethologist (1969:57-58) has consistently allowed for constraints due to psychological factors, the most intriguing cases of which are posed by those situations in which the preferences cannot be related to physical abilities, "as when a particular color of flower or shape of leaf or complex of factors is preferred to any other"—as in Ripley's narrative (see chap. 9n1). It is difficult enough to isolate the relevant feature of a complex *Gestalt;* to provide an explanation for the underlying sensory or neural basis for preferences that are termed aesthetic remains generally a difficult research problem for the future.

In the process of building, animals employ essentially the same techniques that we do: digging, masonry, plaiting, weaving, and so on. For Vitruvius—the failed Augustinian architect and engineer later turned influential writer—the universal *homo faber* was the architect, to whom the Romans assigned the art of building as well as the craft of fabricating machinery (i.e., secondary tools; see Sebeok 1972:85). Vitruvius (1826: 3), in spelling out what architecture is, maintained that "two considerations must be constantly kept in view" in the execution of his art and craft, "namely, the intention, and the matter used to express that intention. . . ." Whatever one's opinion may be about the intrusion of intention, volitional control, or, more broadly, of teleological considerations, into the domain of semiotics,[12] there can scarcely be any doubt that man fully shares the second attribute mentioned by Vitruvius with the speechless creatures.

In respect to the concept of *animal laborans*, the animal "which labors and 'mixes with,' " or "which with its body . . . nourishes life," but which "still remains the servant of nature and the earth" (Arendt 1958:136, 139), it is, in truth, hard to perceive essential differences among the species. Such discriminations as may exist must be sought in Arendt's redefined and refined view of the classic *homo faber*, an anthropocentrically utilitarian figure she nonetheless so insistently, although eloquently, opposed to *animal laborans—homo faber*, "who makes and literally 'works upon,' " whose production is tantamount to what she calls reification, the creation, that is, of a uniquely human world in the face of nature. Only *homo faber*, she claims, "conducts himself as lord and master of the whole earth" (ibid.:139). For her (ibid.:173), *homo faber*, "in his highest capacity," assumes, of course, the functions "of the artist, of poets and historiographers, of monument-builders or writers, because without them the only product of their activity, the story they enact and tell, would not survive at all." This bleak and in the end still narrowly parochial view implies that none of the works of nature, which manifestly come into being without man's intervention, let alone his midwifery, can have aesthetic or even economic value. As Karl Marx has put the same idea in *Das Kapital* (1933:3:698): "Der Wasserfall, wie die Erde überhaupt, wie alle Naturkraft hat keinen Wert, weil er keine in ihm vergegenständlichte Arbeit darstellt." This attitude to nature and to natural productions degrades objects into means, where animals are always presumed to be building something not for its own sake but for the sake of instrumentality, or expediency toward the realization of some putative biological end. The absurdity of this Sophistic devaluation of nature was despised by many Greeks, as Arendt (1958:157) noted, and its inherent authropocentrism perhaps most persuasively resolved in Plato's celebrated argument against Protagoras, whose subjective idealism fails to accord—as I have tried to show elsewhere (Sebeok 1978a)—with the most elementary lessons of the modern life science.

The field of "natural architecture" is exceptionally fortunate in that there exists a splendid book devoted to that subject in its entirety ranging from the invertebrates, particularly the arthropods, to the birds and on to the highest mammals, inclusive of apes. This compendium, which requires no specialized knowledge for its enjoyment, was written by Karl von Frisch (1974) in collaboration with his son, Otto. It bore the original title, *Tiere als Baumeister*—which translates into "Animals as Master Builders"—both more powerful and more suggestive, as well as less overburdened or presumptuous, than the English rendering on the title page.[13]

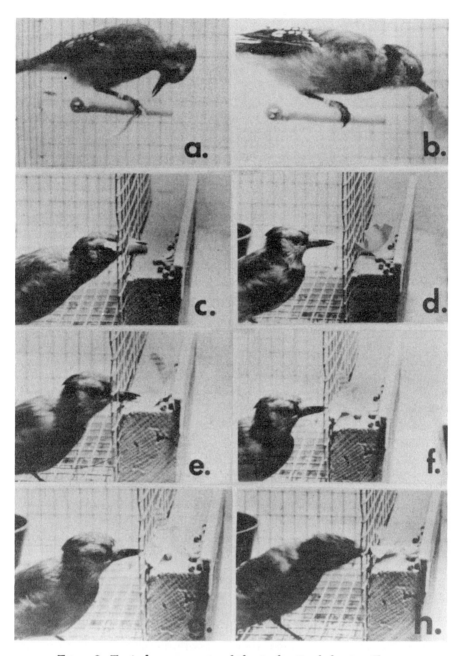

FIG. 9.8. Typical components of the tool-using behavior. From Thony B. Jones and Alan C. Kamil, "Tool-Making and Tool-Using in the Northern Blue Jays," *Science* 180 (June 8, 1973):1076-78. Copyright 1973 by the American Association for the Advancement of Science, and reproduced with their permission.

The architectural activity of animals is best regarded as a manifestation of tool-using behavior—a sophisticated way of manipulating objects and exploring their uses to adaptive advantage. According to Frisch (1974:22), the use of tools that are not parts of their bodies is rare among animals: "They mostly use the organs of their bodies, chiefly their mouth parts and their legs."[14] Rare though the use of extrinsic artifacts may be over-all, statistically speaking, newly discovered instances continue to be published. A case in point is a learned behavioral sequence recently detected in Northern blue jays (*Cyanocitta cristata*), which involves tool making, to wit, by the tearing and alteration of pages from a newspaper, and employing these as tools to rake in food pellets that otherwise lay out of reach (Jones and Kamil 1973).

Even the larva of the green lacewing (*Chrysopa slossonae*) uses a tool in the climax of a complicated sequence that has been inelegantly dubbed "trash-carrying behavior" (Eisner et al. 1978). This insect form

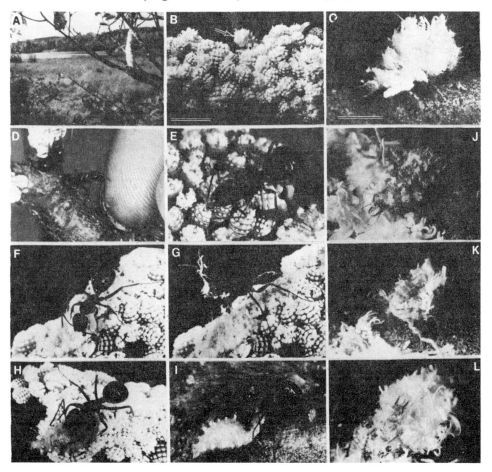

FIG. 9.9. Wooly alder aphid. From Eisner et al. 1978:791, Fig. 1.
By permission of Thomas Eisner, Cornell University.

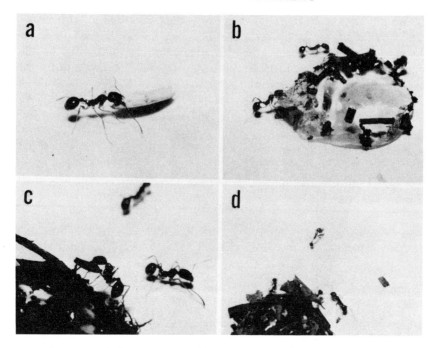

FIG. 9.10. *Aphaenogaster rudis* carrying a tool. From Fellers and Fellers 1976, Fig. 1. By permission of Joan H. Fellers.

FIG. 9.11. *Aphaenogaster treatae* placing tools (pieces of plant material) on honey. By permission of Joan H. Fellers.

disguises itself as, i.e., mimics, its own prey by plucking some of the waxy "wool" from the bodies of the alder aphids amidst colonies of which it lives and feeds, and then applies this material to its own back. The exogenous shield thus constructed protects the larva from assault by the ants that ordinarily "shepherd" the aphids.

Some social insects, notably, several species of *Aphaenogaster—* none of which are mentioned by Frisch, despite the relatively large amount of space (1974:72-150) he otherwise devotes to the constructions of eusocial insects—use pieces of leaf, mud, and sand grains as tools for carrying soft foods from distant sources to the colony, a maximally efficient way of exploiting available resources (Fellers and Fellers 1976).

I recite these random examples of recently uncovered cases of tool-using activity to adumbrate my hunch that such forms of behavior anticipate the more advanced forms of animals' building activities. In ethological jargon, the question becomes: how does tool-using behavior become ritualized (Sebeok 1979: chap. 2)? Or, in semiotic parlance: how does a tool, with a primary amplifying function, acquire a superim-

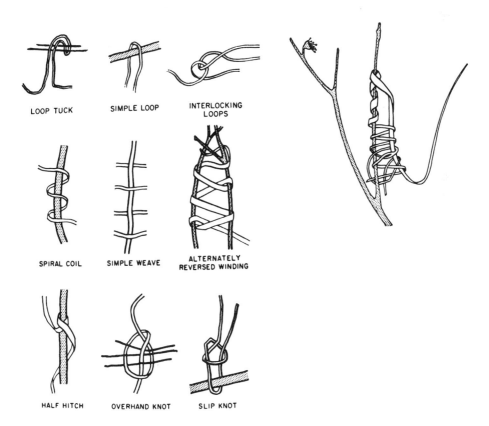

LOOP TUCK   SIMPLE LOOP   INTERLOCKING LOOPS

SPIRAL COIL   SIMPLE WEAVE   ALTERNATELY REVERSED WINDING

HALF HITCH   OVERHAND KNOT   SLIP KNOT

FIG. 9.12. Diagrams illustrating some of the elaborate weaving. From Hancocks 1973:52-53.

posed sign-function (Sebeok 1976:30)? The answer to this question, at this stage in the development of both ethology and diachronic semiotics, is precisely the same as to the deceptively innocent one, "What passes in the mind of a bowerbird when he builds and decorates his bower?" Frisch replies (1974:244-245), "Naturally, I cannot answer [my own] question. No one can." His denial notwithstanding, Frisch proceeds to declare his conviction that in these birds, no less than in chimpanzees, "not only insight into the consequences of their actions but also evidence of aesthetic feelings can be found."

No purpose would be served by rehearsing here even a sampling from among the host of striking examples of exterior and interior designs masterfully adduced by Frisch. The multitalented bowerbirds figure prominently, as do a large variety of other kinds of birds, including those consummate nest builders, the weavers, and especially *Malimbus cassini,* noted for the care and precision of the working male, reminiscent in his technique of a human basket weaver or one with a loom. Among the many mammals whose imposing labors are illustrated, the impressively productive accomplishments of the beaver (*Castor fiber,* or the American kind, *C. canadensis*), however, do deserve to be singled out. The fantastic edifices of this "architectural mute"—the evocative epithet was coined, in 1868, by Lewis H. Morgan (1970:101)—are exemplified by the construction of dams, lodges, burrows, and canals. The opinion that "there is no other animal that can by its labor transform the landscape in the same way as can the beaver and man" (Wilsson 1969:1) is shared by all informed observers. This preeminent master builder, particularly busy in the mountains, checks turbulent brooks and, with its dams, protects the fields and pastures below from becoming silted up with sand and gravel. The artificial reservoirs thus created are soon stocked with trout and other fishes and turned into a refuge for water birds. The very magnitude of some beaver projects is stupefying—the largest dam is that on the Jefferson River, near Three Forks, Montana: one can follow it for some 2,300 feet. Although the beavers' basic engineering skills are innate—"the principles of their art are theirs by inheritance" (Frisch 1974:278)—their brains are exceptionally well developed in comparison with those of other rodents, and their correspondingly superior adaptability to changing ecological situations is emphasized by knowledgeable ethologists. Morgan (1970:99) even felt "at liberty to infer an intention on the part of the beaver," and others believe that beavers profit from example or experience.

By contrast, there is nothing remarkable about the building activities of the Great Apes. Adult chimpanzees, in some regions, are known to fashion fresh nests up in the trees nightly, as do orangutans and gorillas, although heavy males among the latter tend to sleep on the ground. Köhler's (1925: esp. chap. V, on "Building") experiments with chimpanzees that solve the problem of getting fruit situated beyond the reach of their arms by manufacturing a suitable tool for bridging the distance

FIG. 9.13. Beaver dam, solid bank. From Morgan 1868, Plate IX.

from themselves to the food—by fitting two bamboo rods together, for instance, or by erecting a tower from packing cases—are widely known, although his interpretation is still debated. While the actions of Köhler's chimpanzees were portrayed as conveying an impression of deliberation and purpose, the animals seemed to have but a very modest sense of

FIG. 9.14. Beaver dam, solid bank. From Morgan 1868, Plate X.

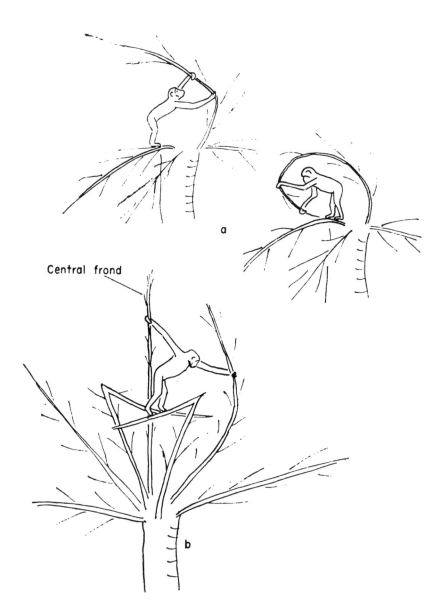

Central frond

FIG. 9.15. Adolescent female attempting to make a nest in a palm tree. From Lawick-Goodall 1968:198, Fig. 13. By permission of the publishers.

FIG. 9.16. Chimpanzee making double-stick. From Köhler 1925, Plate III. By permission of Routledge & Kegan Paul Ltd.

either statics (ibid.:161, 163-164) or balance. Some never managed to solve the problem at all.

The penumbra of an absorbing lifelong research commitment is delineated in two arresting sentences at the end of Frisch's study (1970: 286): "The evolutionary roots of human behavior reach far back into the behavior patterns of animals. Those who are fascinated by these connections need only fasten on one such puzzle, the architecture of animals perhaps. . . ." The prefigurements of architecture, however, are but one detail in the mosaic of the much vaster, much deeper, mystery of the precultural emergence of the averbal arts.

CONCLUDING REMARKS

At the outset of this essay, I drew a sharp distinction between the verbal art and the averbal arts, proclaiming my conviction that, while it seems unavailing to search for the prefigurements of language-based sign systems, a scrutiny of the roots of the four other semiotic spheres discussed might prove illuminating. Differences in the neurological processing of verbal vs. averbal patterns of input and output are solidly and rationally grounded in separate dominions of the human brain. The evolutionary antecedents are also assuming shape, although they remain blurred at the edges.

The late Bronowski (1977:112; cf. Sebeok 1976:119) wondered whether "any animal language [has] figures of speech," by which he appeared to question whether an animal ever uses the same sign-vehicle corresponding to two or more different significates. The answer to the latter must unequivocally be in the affirmative, since the context in which any gesture is delivered decisively shapes its "correct" interpretation. But Bronowski's "figures of speech," as he used the expression in his exploratory article on "Human and Animal Language," is itself merely a figure of speech—a rhetorical device of his own. It has little to do with verbal art.

FIGS. 9.17 and 9.18. Chimpanzee on insecure construction, and having achieved a four-story structure. From Köhler 1925, Plates IV and V. By permission of Routledge & Kegan Paul Ltd.

To be sure, it has been widely reported that the creation of signed metaphors as well as metonyms was recorded in different home-raised chimpanzees. In 1976 (Sebeok 1979: chap. 6), I recounted that both sorts of tropes were alleged to have occurred: "whereas Washoe created 'waterbird' for duck, a metonymic or indexical expression, being a sign in real reaction with the object noted . . . , Lucy generated 'candy fruit' for watermelon, a metaphoric or iconic term, possessing the qualities signified. . . ." Lately, however, I—and others (e.g., Martin Gardner, personal communication)—have come to feel that such interpretations must be reviewed if not with suspicion at least with caution. Both chimpanzees were getting a steady stream of unconscious feedback from their trainers. Thus only her handler was present in the canoe when Washoe glimpsed her first duck and made a sign for "water" followed by a sign for "bird." There was no awareness of the possibility that Washoe, dragging her hand in the water, didn't sign "water," next noticed the bird, and only then signed "bird." The behavior of the trainer, who (for all we know) repeated the two signs, could easily have taught Washoe a new sign, namely, the "water-bird" sign, which she would associate from then on with ducks. The circumstances were, *mutatis mutandis,* similarly indeterminate for Lucy's "candy fruit," "cry fruit" (for onion), and for every other such case that I am aware of. All of these are subject to other, less portentous, construals, the simplest among which is the pervasive emission of subthreshold involuntary cuing of the destination by the source, or the "Clever Hans" experience (Sebeok 1979: chaps. 4 and 5). In sum, there is no hard evidence whatsoever for the existence of figures of speech, in the literal sense, among the speechless creatures—a prototypal *contradictio in adiectivo . . .* !

A second leitmotif of my article skirted the profound problem of aesthetic significance—particularly in opposition to our juxtaposition with utility—viz., purposiveness or directedness, tantamount, in some contexts, to the Aristotelian art of *chrēmatisttikē,* or the amassment of wealth with no limit in respect of its end, but in this context simply to the preservation and improvement of the gene pool, or the longterm environment of the gene. The question whether animals are endowed with "consciousness" has remained wide open (Griffin 1976), being no doubt poorly posed, but many distinguished life scientists concur that some animals on some occasions behave toward some objects *as if* the organisms were motivated by a recognizably aesthetic incentive. This much is clarion clear, for instance, as regards the bowerbirds.

The essence of the aesthetic impulse surely lies in the structures organisms extract and reconstruct from among salient features of their environment. Albrecht Dürer (Conway 1889:182), among a host of commentators, believed this to be so; according to him, "Denn wahrhaftig steckt die Kunst in der Natur, wer sie heraus kann reissen, der hat sie." Others make a separation between natural or organic beauty, and artificial or aesthetic beauty, contrasting the realm of living things with that of "living" forms. But the two are obviously bonded, since all the percipients themselves are a part of nature. The spectacles through which we see the world are partly an apparatus for bringing into focus certain aspects of our existence (*Umwelt*), but they are, at the same time, a means for relating harmoniously varied facets of the universe to each other. To paraphrase a saying of Henri Poincaré, aesthetic sensibility plays the part of a delicate sieve. The challenge, of course, is to define explicitly what those relations—of balance and order that delight—are in the characteristic idiom of each art, as well as in the all-embracing architectonics of the living megacosm. The concept of delight thus undergoes a radical transmutation: it is elevated into a function that biologists can recognize, objectify, cope with in familiar terms. The "artistic animal" is not defined by a heightened sensitivity to movement, sound, color, shape, but by its innate and/or learned capacity to elicit a stable dynamic structure from the fluid environment, whether inorganic,

organic, or a subtle blend of both. The sign systems thus created, which serve an underlying semantic function, take in time an aesthetic turn. How this happens is magesterially brought out in an 1865 Platonic dialogue on the origin of beauty that Gerard Manley Hopkins had composed for his tutor at Oxford (House and Storey 1959:86-114).

The dialogue between the Professor of the newly founded chair of Aesthetics (no doubt Walter Pater) and a student takes place in the tranquil setting of a college garden, and the dialectic "battledore" quickly comes to concentrate on "one of the most finely foliaged of trees," the chestnut. The Professor points to the leaves of the tree to illustrate the principle of symmetry or, more generally, of the structural relations inherent in nature. The Professor asks:

> ". . . now what is symmetry? Is it not regularity?"
> "I should say, the greatest regularity. . . ."
> "So it is. But is it not that sort of regularity which is measured by length and breadth and thickness? Music for instance might be regular, but not symmetrical ever; is it not so?"
> "Quite so. . . ."
> "Let us say regularity then."
> The Professor next draws attention to the oak, "an unsymmetrical tree."
> "Then beauty, you would say perhaps, is a mixture of regularity and irregularity."
> "Complex beauty, yes. But let us inquire a little further. What is regularity? Is it not obedience to law? And what is law? Does it not mean that several things, or all the parts of one thing, are like each other?"
> [The Professor continues:]
> ". . . regularity is likeness or agreement or consistency, and irregularity is the opposite, that is difference or disagreement or change or variety."

But do these distinctions apply to all things? Beauty is certainly a relation, but *what* is this relation? The sense of beauty in fact is a comparison. The conversation now moves on to the subject of poetry: rhythm, meter, and rhyme.

> "Now you remember I wished beauty to be considered as a regularity or likeness tempered by irregularity or difference: the chestnut-fan was one of my instances. In rhythm we have got the regularity, the likeness; so my aim is, as rhythm is agreed to be beautiful, to find the disagreement, the difference, in it. . . . Rhythm therefore is likeness tempered with difference. . . ."
> "What is rhyme? . . . Is it not an agreement of sound—?"
> "With a slight disagreement, yes. . . . In fact it seems to me rhyme is the epitome of [our] principle. All beauty may by a metaphor be called rhyme. . . ."

If rhyme is taken as the poetic paradigm for beauty, consisting of comparison for likeness' sake (metaphor, simile) as well as for unlikeness' sake (antithesis, contrast), what is the convenient word that gives us the common principle for all such kinds of equations? Hopkins proffers *parallelism,* and moves on to analyze parallelism "both structural and unstructural," parallelism of expression and parallelism of sense, and suspense and countervailing tension, of the arousal of expectation and its denial, in short, of parallelism, is also the pervasive pivotal device finally to illustrate his dictum that "The structure of poetry is that of continuous parallelism" (ibid.:84).[15]

Now it is evident—to recapitulate briefly—that the conspicuous use of reiteration, of a statement of a theme with variations, of the creation of common to all manifestations of the art of animals discussed in this essay: what is criterial of their kinesthetic art is rhythmic somatic motion; at the heart of their music are "les rythmes organiques" and the transposition of fixed intervals; the cardinal substantives that characterize their picture making are "steadiness—symmetry—repetition—rhythm"; and the mark of their virtuoso architecture is surely geometrical symmetry—broken in multiform ways—which transmutes the ulterior modularity of physical reality into macroscopic projects of utility as well as beauty.

Hopkins's insight about the source of beauty was amplified by Humphrey a little over a century later (1973:432). He asked: "What is the biological advantage of seeking out rhyming elements in the environment?" The answer he proposed was this:

> Considered as a biological phenomenon, aesthetic preferences stem from a predisposition among animals and men to seek out experiences through which they may *learn to classify* the objects in the world about them. Beautiful "structures" in nature or in art are those which facilitate the task of classification by presenting evidence of the "taxonomic" relations between things in a way which is informative and easy to grasp.

This proposition demands a tripartite justification.

One must explain, to begin with, why the knack for classification should be important for biological survival. If the function of categorization is to sort out sensory experience—to identify, with essential economy, good, bad, and indifferent forms, or, in semiotic phrasing, to sift out the presence of such forms "endowed with signification" that trigger appropriate longterm releasers—then the evolution of efficient classificatory techniques is bound to be of survival value. Humphrey (ibid.:433) argues that "just as with eating or with sex, an activity as vital as classification was bound to evolve to be a *source of pleasure* to the animal. Both animals and men can, after all, be relied on to do best what they enjoy doing."[16]

Second, it is necessary to show why a maneuver such as Hopkins called parallelism should be optimally advantageous to the classificatory animal. It seems clear that the fundamental role of the central nervous system is precisely to provide the creature with a local map simulating its position in the environment, to enable it to sort out, among other vital intelligence, the images of biologically and/or socially important organisms, viz., to distinguish prey from predator. This is surely best accomplished by an arrangement of such images into a distinctive feature matrix, or in terms of "likeness tempered with difference." Parallelism is the organizing principle employed in many of the most successful taxonomical procedures, including the Linnaean (more generally, it imbues set theory).

> If it is helpful for the taxonomist to look for "rhymes" in his materials, so it is helpful for the animal to do so. It is for this reason that we have evolved to respond to the relation of beauty which rhyme epitomises. At one level we take pleasure in the abstract structure of rhyme as a model of well-presented evidence, and at another we delight in particular examples of rhyme as sources of new insight into how things are related and divided. [Humphrey 1973]

The third step is to seek evidence, beyond the prevailing propensity of man and animals to classify their surroundings, for the surmise that animals also are attracted in particular to parallelism. To amass a modicum of such testimony was, in fact, the main objective of this study: to adduce instances of parallelism in the animal world that have no demonstrable natural value but that nevertheless give people as well as the animals involved something akin to aesthetic pleasure, even when the process or the product is disunited from its proper biological context.

The universal propensity to classify dictates that animals generate units of signification, or significata, by stipulating redundancies. Several arrangements are possible, such as nondimensional (taxonomic) classification or dimensional (paradigmatic) classification, in both of which classes are formed by means of intersection (Dunnell 1971:44-45). When classes and sub-classes are created, they may be defined by features that are either inherent in nature as the sole feasible solution or, as in man and his tamed creatures, arrays that are arbitrary to a degree (cultural categories, individual idiosyncrasies). Yet even certain human populations may be "forced to meet nature on its own terms and to categorize those aspects of the natural environment which are relevant to it in a biologically realistic way" (Bulmer 1970:1082). The conception of class, whether based on naturally imposed or arbitrarily chosen qualities, sometimes acquires a certain elegance and power elevating it beyond a mere organizational tool, and we can then say that the production carries an aesthetic charge.

Lévi-Strauss and Piaget have both been concerned with primordial questions of human classification. The inquiry of Lévi-Strauss, instigated by a linguistic model, postulates a proclivity in all of us to think in opposites and contrasts, to pry perceptual information from the environment constrained by certain predetermined structures, and to consolidate and combine these percepts in classifying, naming, and mythic systems. Through a series of ordered transformations, these systems relate themes and variations on them that are effable, for instance, in artistic products that themselves are embodiments of mind.

Animals create a taxonomy appropriate to their species and ecological niche. Thus predators, for instance, distinguish different categories of prey—by size, appearance, odor, and other signifiers—thus forestalling wastefully indiscriminate attacks. *Vice versa,* many potential prey distinguish among different kinds of predators, as we observe from their use of sundry warning signs, variations in their flight distances and flight reactions, e.g., depending on whether the enemy is up in the air or down on the ground. It is less well known, however, that animals give each other and carry proper names (Sebeok 1976:138-140; 1981) that individuate each from every other. As Hediger (1976:1357), who devoted a perceptive and semiotically sensitive study to the use of proper names in the animal kingdom, pointed out: "Its proper name is part of its [the animal's] personality. Therefore it distinguishes between its own self and the non-self."[17] Hediger also pleads for research on the appearance of proper names in evolution, for this may "open a new door to the delicate problem of self-consciousness in animals." Concern with naming, moreover, focuses attention on parallelism as a special case. Parallelism of this kind evokes a sort of pleasure familiar to all observers of children's behavior. Humphrey (1973:435-436) comments on this pronounced tendency in children, which is promoted, among other devices, through picture books designed especially for them. The passion for collecting, he feels, is yet another manifestation of the pleasure both mature children and men take in classification. Among the animals, it is not an accident that bowerbirds are among the most sedulous of collectors, each species according to its predilection. Thus the display ground of the Great Gray "may contain an almost inconceivable accumulation of pale or reflective rubbish"—but sometimes also bright specimens of gold or pieces of precious opal—yet every bit of their harvest of treasure "is chosen with great discrimination" (Marshall 1954:92).

Piaget has demonstrated that young children are limited in performing internally consistent classificatory tasks. Shown an aggregate of diverse objects and asked to place together those that go together, the child will come up with a range of volatile groupings of phenomena that are not yoked by a simultaneous awareness of a whole and its parts, either physically or conceptually. A sense of hierarchy comes later, at a mature stage of operational intelligence; accordingly, sophisticated art usually emerges in human ontogeny as an accessory only to adult cognitive capacity. Comparisons of animal artistic productions with those by children were made as early as 1935, when Nadie Kohts juxtaposed drawings by her chimpanzee, Joni, with those by her son, Roody. She showed that early scribbles by Joni and early scribbles by Roody resembled each other greatly. However, while later drawings by Joni evidenced greater complexity but no imagery, those by Roody exhibited, in addition, mimetic qualities, to wit, the recognizable icon of a face (cf. Fig. 3 in Brothwell 1976:21).

When Mukařovský delivered his seminal 1934 lecture, on "L'art comme fait sémiologique," he meant his study to underline and exemplify certain aspects of the dichotomy—which he never questioned—between the natural sciences and the humanities, as well as to bring out the importance of semiotic considerations for aesthetics and for the history of art (Matejka and Titunik 1976:8). Referring, in conclusion, to this programmatic paper, I should like to note the paradoxical aspect of the proposed enterprise: a consistently carried out characterization of every work of art as an autonomous sign composed of an artifact (the signifier), an aesthetic object (its signification), and an abstract, context-oriented relationship to the thing signified, tends precisely to obliterate the factitious schism it is supposed to uphold.[18]

NOTES

1. Even these remarks may need to be modified in the light of such casual but expert observations as Ripley's (in Eisenberg and Dillon 1971:8-9), concerning a species of gardener bowerbird (*Amblyornis*) in New Guinea. Ripley reports how he pondered in awe the proportionately huge, six-foot, tepee-like structure made by one of these birds; he describes how he would be drawn back, day after day, to one or another of the bowers near his camp, to watch the placing of particular fruits, berries, or flowers in neat, foot-square beds. He then continues:

> I found that these bowers are virtually a year-round preoccupation with the male birds rather than an extra-long seasonal one, and that the female may come and visit the bower during the nonbreeding season as well. Furthermore, the young males watch the adult birds and so, during the several years of their maturation period, may have a chance to profit by the example of their elders. By this process of transfer of training as well as an enhancement of innate instincts is taking place. I say this because I was able to observe critical selections for color and tone of objects. In one case a flower that I had picked, which was not being used to make up one of the flower beds, was rejected out of hand by the male bird presumably for reasons of color. In another case a flower, not otherwise picked by a male bird, was accepted and, after being slightly rearranged, was included in the bed, even though the flower was of a different species. The color, a pinkish red of this orchid, matched very well the pinkish red of the bed flowers from a vine.

Ripley then goes on to narrate how he was able to create a new vogue among two of the bowerbirds. These observations, as raw data, are highly suggestive and of heuristic value, if not, of course, conclusive.

2. I am not, of course, concerned here with spectacles, like circus acts,

where animals have purportedly been trained by dint of a trans-species operation to "dance" in exhibitions. Hanna (1977:212) observes:

> It is true that a human can dance mechanically or perform a dance pattern con-
> ceptualized and created by someone else, in the same way that a nonhuman
> can be trained to perform a dance by a human. We have all seen "dancing"
> chimpanzees, horses, dogs, bears, parrots, or elephants.

The latter, however, are only skillfully induced semiotic illusions. The animals'
biologically appropriate movements are accompanied by the contrived music,
not the other way about:

> Une bonne musique est surtout importante dans le travail régulier et tout à
> fait indispensable dans les airs de danse. En dehors des figures régulieres, il
> importe seulement qu'elle soit précipitée ou lente suivant la vivacité ou la
> lenteur des mouvements. Les ours, les chevaux, les éléphants, les chiens danseurs
> par exemple, nécessitent une musique particulièrement bien adaptée, tandis que
> les singes, les perroquets, etc., etc., ne réclament que des flonflons à peu près
> quelconques. [Hachet-Souplet 1897:32-33]

The principles of animal humanization in the circus are explained by Bouissac
(1976:116ff.), such as, for instance, causing them to "dance" in pairs (waltz)
or alone (ballet): "The most efficient training in this vein evokes a behavior
from the animal that, within the constructed situation, subtly creates the impression that the animal has humanlike motivations, emotions, and reasoning."
Iconicization of movements is attained through musical accompaniment, by "re-
ducing them to a rhythm, either to achieve complete harmony, as in the case
of liberty horse acts, or to achieve individual regularity, as in 'haute école' acts
(dancing horses)" (ibid.:131). The same was true, *a fortiori*, of flea circuses
(Andrews 1977:100-106), common in my childhood, and a few of which still
operate abroad (the famous American one, at Huber's Museum, in New York's
Times Square area, closed a generation ago). A program note preserved in the
British Museum's Mansell Collection of an exhibition held, in the 1830s, at
Regent Street, in London, speaks of "Two Fleas dressed as Ladies, and Two as
Gentlemen dancing as Waltzers, Twelve Fleas in the Orchestra playing on
different Instruments of proportionable size. . . ." The occasion was, by all
appearances, a lavish affair, "A ball with frock-coated gentlemen partnering
silk-clad ladies, whilst a twelve-piece orchestra played audible flea-music; the
Great Flea Mogul complete with harem, and a 120-gun ship of the line drawn
by a single flea" (ibid.:103f.). On the bizarre case of the carterpillar (*Cerura
borealis*) that dances to musical notes between 300 and 360 hertz (roughly
from E to F-sharp above middle C), see Maugh (1980).

    3. Thorpe dismisses Langer's absurd view that the singing of birds, being
"unconscious," is not art. For a critical consideration of her writings on music,
see further Henle (1958:202-220).

    4. Linguists will recognize this observation as a generalization of the so-
called bow-wow theory of the origin of speech, supposed to have arisen as a
consequence of onomatopoeia.

    5. This notwithstanding, there are also profound differences, since song-
birds possess twin sound-producing organs—one in each bronchus—whereas in
man, as indeed in all mammals, there is but a single vocal source. Our understanding of the acoustical and physiological processes involved in the singing
of birds is still very far from satisfactory. For details, see the excellent but
neglected work of Greenewalt (1968).

    6. Cf. Nottebohm's remark (1972:133) that "The gap separating human

vocal exploits from those of other primates is enormous." The same investigator is principally responsible for the dramatic discovery of lateralization of vocal control in several songbirds, notably the canary, in the brain of which localization of vocal control was found with an overlying left hemispheric dominance (Nottebohm, Stokes, and Leonard 1976). Vocal learning is thus a trait shared by bird and man, with, perhaps, a very few other species. See, however, Falk 1980:76n1.

7. Cf. also the comment of two anthropologists, cited in Wescott (1974: 288), "emphasizing bird-song both as an analog to and a model for human song. . . ."

8. So already in Romanes (1892:410): "All cases where beauty can be pointed to in organic nature are seemingly due . . . to utility."

9. See Davis (1974:216-219) on the complexities of the neurophysiological mechanisms of encoding color and form in monkeys.

10. The animal paintings at Lascaux, Altamira, and other famous decorated caves of the Upper Paleolithic (c. 35,000 to 10,000 B.C.) do not seem to me directly related to the issues discussed here. The prehistoric art forms of the last Ice Age—which, it is now known, include remarkably lifelike engraved "portraits" of men and women, as well as elaborate musical instruments such as a percussion orchestra of six pieces and the six-stop flutes excavated one at a Ukrainian site and another, dating from the same period, in France—are far too sophisticated to be productively compared with ape art.

11. Ferguson (1977:835) has recently documented convincingly that much of the creative thought of the designers of our technology is nonverbal, nor is it easily reducible to words. The importance of his article lies in the fact that the origins of this component of technology lie not in science but in art. McNeill (1973:91) has cogently remarked that even if free-ranging chimpanzees had indeed evolved a capacity for language-like communication, "we should not expect it to resemble human language. . . ." This view accords with the opinion of Washburn (1978:410) about apes in general, that "the structure of their natural communications will be like that of monkeys."

12. I have previously alluded to these issues and some of their implications (Sebeok 1976:35n65, and 127), discriminating sharply between subjective and objective varieties of teleology. I was therefore surprised that several reviewers of my book, notably Martynov (1978:178), took exception to my strictures, introducing, in the process, several levels of confusion into the argument. Martynov also regrets that I failed to cite the well-known book by Ackoff and Emery (1972), who devote their chaps. 10 and 11 to semiotics, but they simply rehearse notions already dealt with much better in various writings of Charles Morris. Matters of artistic intent are obviously pertinent to the subjects dealt with here, but space precludes the possibility of their detailed consideration. Concisely put, in my view, intention had best be regarded as a convention, and the intent of any sign simply its use.

13. Perhaps this obvious translation was avoided because it would have echoed the title of another book, *Master Builders of the Animal World*, published at about the same time (Hancocks 1973). The author of this book is an architect.

14. For the first approach to a semiotic typology of organismal vs. artifactual human and animal sign systems, see Sebeok 1976:30-32. For further references to the use of tools by birds, see Jones and Kamil 1973:1078n2. Guilmet (1977) is concerned with reconstructing the behavioral context which coevolved with tool using and tool making in the hominid lineage. He argues that the method of socialization practiced by a tool-making group would affect the degree of formal standardization presented by the tools themselves.

15. For an elaboration and application of Hopkins's path-breaking studies to grammatical parallelism by a modern master, see Jakobson (1966).

16. Humphrey (1979:47) argues that when exploratory behavior becomes an all-encompassing passion, it has exceeded its evolutionary function and turns into a perversion of sorts.

17. On the notion of the "Semiotic Self," see Sebeok 1979: Appendix I.

18. Regrettably, Hediger's 1979 study on creativity in animals reached me only after my own essay had already been typeset.

Chapter 10

The Ultimate Enigma of "Clever Hans":
The Union of Nature and Culture

Tell me, where is fancy bred,
or in the heart or in the head?
How begot, how nourished?
Reply, reply.
—*The Merchant of Venice*

THE SCOPE of application of the epithet "Clever Hans" turned out to be very elastic indeed. Almost from the birth of the appellation, especially after it was reinforced by the initial appearance of Pfungst's 1907 study, in German, unregenerate skeptics simply refused to accept the findings of Stumpf's commission of inquiry, which was charged with the examination of Mr. von Osten's eponymous horse. Among them were the obsessive jeweler, Krall (1912), and a 1911 Belgian Nobel Prize winner, the symbolist playwright, Maeterlinck (1914).[1] Nearly two decades later, the late Joseph Banks Rhine, a self-styled psychic adventurer, instead of employing Ockham's razor to shave away pseudo-explanatory entities, dubbed the mare Lady Wonder "the greatest thing since radio," ascribing the filly's alleged powers to telepathy (Rhine and Rhine 1928-29, and 1929-30) (later, this act was proved to be an instance of a well-known mentalist trick, called in the business "pencil reading" [Gardner 1957]). In the late 1970s one was still distressed to read assertions, by a self-proclaimed "centaur," that horses communicate by means "more subtle than man himself: extra-sensory perception and telepathy" (Blake 1977:26).

In contemporary psychology and some adjacent disciplines, the narrow, literal, and simplistic view of the Clever Hans episode prevails, to wit, that what was involved in that uproar constituted a perhaps amusing aberration in the history of science, featuring a canny stallion that operant-conditioned the learned world of Berlin and beyond, and, as countless other smart horses before and since, as well as pigs, dogs, a goat or two, and many geese and other birds have, succeeded in duping

This paper was delivered at the Conference on the Clever Hans Phenomenon: Communication with Horses, Whales, Apes, and People, held under the auspices of the New York Academy of Sciences, May 6-7, 1980. A version has appeared in Sebeok and Rosenthal (1981:199-205).

the gullible public at large. Those who cling to this ingenuous definition of the happening are unable to grasp the cross-specific, indeed, universal pervasiveness of the effect. The general implications of it were, however, perfectly understood by the reviewer of the first American edition of the classic account, when he remarked that "Mr. Pfungst has made a lasting contribution to both human and animal psychology, which cannot be passed over lightly by any serious student in either field" (Johnson 1911: 666).

According to a particularly disturbing interpretation, exemplified recently by several leading workers (Savage-Rumbaugh et al. 1980a:54) with the allegedly language-like behaviors of chimpanzees, the Clever Hans Effect *may* apply to horses, but "oversimplifies" the problem, for "[t]he chimpanzee behaviors . . . even if they are meaningless . . . are far too complex to be controlled by a simple 'go' or 'no go' cue." Although it has been shown, in painstaking detail (see chap. 8 this volume), that many experimental results in this field achieved so far can be more parsimoniously explained in terms of the Clever Hans Effect than otherwise, there seems to remain a lingering doubt about the pertinence of the effect to primates, including particularly humans. Polanyi (1958: 169-170) has correctly argued that even philosophers are susceptible to influence by the Clever Hans Effect, specifying that "this is exactly how [they] make their descriptions of science, or their formalized procedures of scientific inference, come out right." I would like to augment Polanyi's observation—and for this assertion I adduced evidence elsewhere (Sebeok 1979: chap. 5)—that the principle is a naturally connate part of every verbal and nonverbal interaction of all human dyads, as well as an ineradicable component of each and every instance of man-animal communicative interchanges, specifically scientific experiments. As Hediger has so perceptively noted:

> Every experimental method is necessarily a human method and must *per se* constitute a human influence on the animal. . . . The concept of an experiment with animals—be it psychological, physiological or pharmacological—without some direct or indirect contact between human beings and animals is basically untenable. [1974:29]

The fundamental reason for the ubiquity of the Clever Hans Phenomenon in the realm of biology is best understood when it is viewed as a special case of the physical law imposing the ultimate limitation on the knowability of the "real" state of affairs: the quantum of action couples the observer (subject) with the system observed (object), such that, as in wave mechanics, an observation necessarily changes the observed system (Davies 1979:156-158). (In the human/animal context, a further perturbation may frequently be caused by the intrusion of the Pathetic Fallacy [Sebeok 1972, chap. 2].)

The omnipresence of the Clever Hans Phenomenon in all dyads—whether only one partner is human or both are—seems to me no longer at issue, although its paradigmatic operation in the ontogenesis of infant behavior remains to be shown in full detail in its differential role across cultures.

In this chapter, I wish to reopen an ancient and perhaps perennial problem area by redrawing it in the context of the Clever Hans Phenomenon. This indeed constitutes a profound enigma, which can be stated in several isomorphic ways, depending on one's philosophical preconceptions and terminological preferences. As Jakob von Uexküll (1980) might have phrased it: How are semiotic strings—verbal or nonverbal—emanating from the organism's *Umwelt* transmuted into beneficial or harmful effects in the body's *Innenwelt?* Or, to adapt Lévi-Strauss's opposition: How are subjective states—let us call them "Culture"—transformed into objective states, that is, "Nature"? The model presupposed here is a dualist-interactionist mock-up (sometimes known as "the correlation hypothesis"), involving the flow of information across the interface between the brain and the conscious self, in the tradition of Sherrington's philosophical position, as clarified to an extent by Popper and Eccles in their famous discussions of World 1 and World 2 (see, for example, Eccles 1979). My personal image of the brain is that of a physical network, or structure, of neurons. I define "mind" as a system of signs, or representations, of what is commonly called "the world," or, more exactly, the "*Umwelt*" (von Uexküll) or "ground" (Peirce 1935-1966:1.292). This model implies confidence that there exist one-one relationship patterns between the physical fabric of the brain onto which are coded the signs of the mind. Since we are ignorant of the linking principles, the enigma is, of course, how this coding is accomplished. Or just how do signs represent?

Cannon's classic paper (1942) reports many instances of mysterious, sudden, and apparently psychogenic, death, from all parts of the globe, traceable to Voodoo: The victim is cursed by a witch doctor, or perhaps because of the violation of a powerful taboo. However, if the warlock removes the spell, recovery is immediate. Faith, obviously, is a pivotal factor, just as it is in the workings of the placebo effect (although suggestibility cannot be clearly separated from spontaneous change, as Lasagna has recently underlined [1980]), as well as in Christian Science, the central tenet of which was pronounced by Mary Baker Eddy as: "Mortal belief is all that enables a drug to cure material ailments [since] the so-called laws of health are simply laws of mortal belief" (1934:174). The same may be true of hypnosis, which, Sacerdote tells us, "may be in many ways the most powerful of placebos" (Holden 1977:808). The sudden death syndrome has been described not only in man, but also in rats (Richter 1957) and many other animals, and has been variously ascribed to shock or to hopelessness. At any rate, what seems to be involved is overactivity primarily of the parasympathetic system. In an interesting book, *Scared to Death*, Barker (1968) has shown that if terrified animals are first given chlorpromazine before being severely constrained, the proportion of dying is much reduced; this is likewise the case when they are administered atropine, which neutralizes parasympathetic effects. However, if given mecholyl, or similar parasympathetic stimulants, the "Voodoo" effect is intensified.

Although Cannon's ideas are fascinating, have generated nearly forty years of controversy, and disclosed a shadowy outline of a novel area of exciting research possibilities, the fundamental conundrum remains in sharp contradiction to the adage, "Sticks and stones will hurt my bones, but words can never harm me." We know that indeed they can, as they can cause—at least since 1224—spontaneous stigmatization. There are now about fifty more or less reasonably reliable cases in the literature, beginning with that of St. Francis of Assisi, for which no satisfactory medical explanation has been offered (Thurston 1952).

What is missing, in all such cases, is the mind-to-body conversion mechanism, although it seems increasingly likely that the psychogenic activation of the secretion of certain brain chemicals may be implicated; for example: pain-diminishing endorphins (which are endogenous opiate-like substances, such as dynorphin), interferon (which counters viral infections), and steroids (which reduce inflammations). It is speculated that these or similar mechanisms may be operative in the whole range of so-called miracle cures as well as their opposites. Thus, the cues, both verbal and nonverbal, we may further postulate, are transformed by the appropriate receptor into signals from nerve cell to nerve cell, releasing specific chemicals that affect the brain by coupling with action sites on yet other classes of nerve cells. These chemicals cohere with their receptors like keys in their unique locks, and, by so fitting, switch off activities in the cell. Sometimes, in the manner of hormones, their influence may spread much more widely. The effects of peptides in the nervous system represent a chemical semiotic system that the brain uses to communicate with itself. Herbert Benson's current investigation of the survival patterns of Tibetan lamas under winter conditions at altitudes of 14,000 feet, allegedly by the practice of Tumo yoga, supplemented by the use of herbal remedies, may throw considerable light on systems such as these, especially considering the Tibetan world view, which emphasizes three components as essential in dyadic interactions: the patient's faith, the healer's belief, and, interestingly, the *karma* (literally, "deed" or "action," that binds men to the world) linking the two (Sobel 1980).

In passing, I should also like to mention the serendipitous discovery by Robert Nerem that laboratory animals given special attention—greeting and cuddling several times daily—significantly reduced fatty deposits (i.e., cholesterol) in contrast to the control group (Anonymous 1980). Since the Clever Hans Effect, as I said at the outset, is narrowly, but nonetheless commonly, confined by psychologists to animals, it may be worth reminding ourselves of the fact that psychosomatic practice is a recognized component of veterinary medicine. Brouwers, a well-known Belgian veterinarian, claims that "Mental factors . . . play their part in veterinary medicine just as in human medicine" and supports this statement by many apt examples from many species (1956). Chertok and Fontaine, in a fascinating paper (1963), collected numerous further instances of psychosomatic disturbances, ranging from eczemas in dogs to pseudopregnancy in cats, mares, and heifers, as well as in bitches. A whole series of organic and functional disturbances occur in captive animals as a result of situational stress arising from alterations in interindividual relationships, embodied in both verbal and nonverbal projections from man to animal. As in the human context, these authors tell us that while a good deal is known about such relationships on the psychological level (transference), next to nothing is known about the somatic basis of these relationships. Kalogerakis (1963) has shown that smell is certainly one of the surface mediators, but it would be valuable to know why some animals react to cues by behavioral change, others by somatic or functional upsets.

Permit me to conclude with one more example, recently and rightly marveled at by Lewis Thomas (1979: chap. 13), namely, the homely wart. Its removal "by rubbing . . . with somewhat that afterwards is put to waste and consume" aroused the curiosity of Francis Bacon; "I do apprehend the rather, because of mine own experience," he tells us (1900:V:160). Thomas meditates over an experiment by Surman et al. (1973), who designed a test for the hypothesis that warts are treatable by hypnotherapy. Their tentative findings supported their hypothesis and suggest that hypnosis has a general effect on host response to the causative virus. An earlier experiment by Sinclair-Gieben and Chalmers (1959) went much further. It demonstrated that hypnosis can influence lesions selectively: that is, it was suggested to the patient that the warts on one side of the body (the more affected) would disappear (the other side serving as a perfectly matched control). In nine of the ten patients, the warts on the "treated" side disappeared, while those on the control side remained unchanged. The heart of the mystery lies less in how the power of cuing resulted in the power of curing than in how the immunological system of the human body—which we assume is both deaf and blind—can be induced to perform its healing function by deploying its lymphocytes upon command, by turning off bilateral arterioles in a hierarchical manner, confined, that is, to but one side of the body. If a selected work is done by a chemical mediator, it would be nice to know how and which, and in response to what.

Thus the omnipresence of the Clever Hans Phenomenon in human everyday life, including human/animal contact situations in a rich variety, affords an appropriate occasion to deliberate upon what Freud so picturesquely dubbed "the mysterious leap" (cf. Deutsch 1959) from the mind (psychology) to the body (neurophysiology). It may also constitute a convenient investigative tool with the aid of which the Cartesian gap can, to a degree, be further narrowed. For a final resolution to the correlation version of the identity hypothesis, and the attendant coding problems, we must look to further assiduous researches in the field of brain electrochemistry, for, plainly, the Clever Hans Effect is too important to be left to psychologists.

NOTE

1. For details see T. A. Sebeok, "Dialogue about Signs with a Nobel Laureate," *American Journal of Semiotics* 1 (1982).

Appendixes

I. The Eye Is Quicker than the Hand

DESMOND MORRIS
Manwatching: A Field Guide to Human Behavior

George Gaylord Simpson, writing in 1966 about the biological nature of man, claimed that language is our "most diagnostic single trait." This characterization is true, in the sense that no other species encountered so far is (in the technical sense) language-endowed, while, at the same time, the pretension is trivial, in the sense that the communication system of every other species stamps it with a unique hallmark, much as language conspicuously segregates out our humanity. Bee, blenny, beaver, bear, or baboon, each group communicates by way of its very own code, one that is critically distinct from all other codes identified in the organic world, although it is a common occurrence in nature that two or more species may develop ties—mechanisms for code-switching—that enable them to communicate across taxonomic boundaries, to the extent required for the welfare of all concerned.

The true singularity of man consists of this, that he alone has a *pair* of codes at his disposal: a verbal code, and what, for want of a better name, is frequently, contrastively, and hence negatively designated as his nonverbal code. These twin devices are exquisitely orchestrated in performance, yet serve separate ends substantially at variance one from the other; indeed, man's repertoire of nonverbal signs functions in ways that lexical and grammatical strings are unsuited to, and vice versa. The two components of this bifold structure have fundamentally diverse phylogenetic roots, and respond to disparate cultural constraints. Moreover, as Gregory Bateson (1968) has cogently argued, it is totally wrong to assume that, in hominid evolution, language has in any manner replaced the "cruder systems of the other animals." On the contrary, the two have blossomed side by side, and both processes "have been elaborated into complex forms of art, music, ballet, poetry, and the like, and even in everyday life the intricacies of human [nonverbal communication] far exceed anything that any other animal is known to produce."

The distinction between the two complementary types of human semiosis did not escape the genius of C. S. Peirce when he developed, at the threshold of this century, his detailed classification of the sciences. He spoke of "the vast and splendidly developed science of linguistics" as

This review originally appeared under the title "Talking with the Body," in the *Times Literary Supplement* No.3957, p.84 (January 27, 1978).

belonging to a domain "embracing studies of mental performances and products." Then he noted the kindred domain "of incarnations, or ensoulments of mind," referring to this latter category "all studies of the minds of insects and . . . of octopuses, of sexual characteristics, of the seven ages of human life, of professional and racial types, of temperaments and characters." Broadly speaking, it is this second order of phenomena, focused exclusively upon man, especially of the Western Hemisphere, that constitutes the subject-matter of Desmond Morris's handsome book, itself a splendidly adroit blend of verbal and nonverbal signs.

Morris wisely stays clear of the terminological entanglements that have bedevilled nonverbal communication studies since Kleinpaul, in 1888, circumscribed his field of inquiry, in an oxymoron, as *Sprache ohne Worte*. The scope of this department of knowledge has fluctuated widely, and continues to do so. At one extreme—implied, for instance, in Malinowski's extended essay of 1935 on the language of magic and gardening in the Trobriand Islands—the area staked out is hardly distinguishable from the study of the entirety of culture. At the other extreme application may be confined to movements, or lack of them, of parts of the human face and limbs, in some versions supplemented by information about the digitally unarticulated stirrings of the vocal apparatus. The approach of Morris, who, happily, innovatively, and most appropriately, puts himself in the position of a naturalist observer of the behavior of people or "man-watcher," is eclectic, but he understandably tends to stress those aspects which best lend themselves to visual display. Indeed, much of the burden of this book is carried by the high number of pictures, in black and white and in color. These are so intimately and elegantly mixed in with the text that Marshall McLuhan, for once, stands vindicated: Morris's medium really does become his message.

The reader, that is, the viewer, is drawn into the contents of this book from the first glimpse of the jacket. Surprisingly enough, this is not quite the same in the United States as in Great Britain. In the U.S. we are presented with a close-up shot of a hugely dilated left pupil, presumably female (*bella donna*?), either conveying uncontrollable sexual arousal, or, having been administered atropine, waiting to be fitted with eyeglasses. The British version displays an enormous, surrealistically dilated right pupil, presumably male, ogling a naked youth who may well be in the status of pupillarity. Morris's hypothetical comments about the underlying implications of this dramatic variation in packaging could in itself make a fascinating contribution to comparative ethology.

The text consists of more than seventy bite-size morsels, crisp segments that cover just such topics as Peirce had succinctly enumerated. For instance, what Peirce meant by "sexual characteristics" is what Morris handles, in part, under the heading of Gender Signals, or cues that express and emphasize masculinity or femininity of individuals. What Peirce poetically rendered as "the seven ages of human life," Morris discusses, in part, under the heading of Infantile Signals, but he might well have balanced this chapter, on early childhood, with a corresponding one on second childhood: the signs of old age constitute a subject, bordering on social gerontology, that is bound to take on central importance for an ever increasing portion of the world's population in the years ahead. Another surprising omission is an at least cursory presentation of the signs of ill health, in brief, of medical symptomatology. John Hughlings Jackson propagated the term *asemasia* (introduced, in 1878, by the American physician Hamilton) for the condition when our nonverbal signing capacity undergoes dissolution, and it would have been highly instructive to have an illustrated exposition of this tragic but common affliction.

What, we may reasonably ask, is the purpose of bird-watching, the presumed analogue of "manwatching"? Either it is a harmless and conceivably even edifying hobby, or it is an indispensable technique of field ornithology for the construction of a bird's ethogram, defined as a precise inventory of any animal's totality of action systems (as Jennings designated, as far back as 1906, what we are now accustomed to calling behavior patterns), the verified representation of which is the sine qua non of scientific research in this area.

What Morris gives us in *Manwatching* is a great deal more than a collage of intuitive, episodic vignettes. Yet it falls far short of a complete, coherent ethogram of our species. What he does provide is a mosaic of glimpses, fragments which may, some day, help in the construction of a new science of human ethology; in the meantime, many of these bits and pieces will entertain a growing international public whose appetite has been whetted, over the past two decades, to receive just this kind of easily digestible intelligence about features of its own semiotic self. Morris writes in his usual jargon-free style, the simple transparency of which goes superbly with the rich, well-selected, and aptly captioned iconography. This is in itself no mean accomplishment in the hag-ridden domain of nonverbal communication studies, where a feeble grasp of thin subject matter is often disguised by a scarcely penetrable patter. His generally acute perceptions give off an air of easy assurance. His handling of the literature is comprehensive, thorough, and up to date, although the documentation cited, disappointingly, includes only two items in languages other than English. (The pertinent portion of one of them, as Morris is aware, is available in English as well, and the other, De Jorio's [1832] classic study of gesture in ancient art and literature compared with the gestures in common use in the Naples of the day, has already been translated from the Italian and should shortly appear in English.)

Since the eye is the pivotal sense that has guided the make-up of this book, and as it may well be considered emblematic of the entire enterprise, an imperative reference, which Morris should by all means have singled out for at least passing mention, is the book, published in 1975, by his fellow-ethologist Otto Koenig: *Urmotiv Auge*, significantly subtitled

"Neuentdeckte Grundzüge menschlichen Verhaltens," a bulky tome containing 766 pictures, some in color, and 162 drawings. Had a timely English version been made available, this book and its presentation would have given Morris's own production fair competition. As it is, *Manwatching* will saturate the market and maintain its well-deserved primacy.

II. BUT WHO'S LISTENING?

EMILY HAHN

Look Who's Talking!

Glendower's boastful claim, "I can call spirits from the vasty deep," coupled with Hotspur's sardonic retort, "Why, so can I, or so can any man; But will they come when you do call for them?" is prototypical of exchanges played out over and over again in two contemporary arenas of scientific endeavor—one extraterrestrial, the other pastoral—seemingly remote from each other yet astonishingly agnate as regards their psychological source, aim, and, to a fair extent, techniques for realizing contact. It is surely no coincidence that these paired provinces of knowledge, liberally laced with lore, severally resonating to Harlow Shapley's cardinal question: "In this universe of stars, space, and time, *are we alone?*" evoke returns that were long anticipated in man's myths. They came to be canalized, with increasing sophistication, in diverse works of science fiction—nicely exemplified, on the one hand, by the Martian and Venusian romances of Edgar Rice Burroughs, on the other, by the same fertile author's 23 Tarzan adventure novels—and began to take their present philosophical as well as vulgar shapes in the early 1960s. (For the record, Shapley's categorical decision was that *"we are not alone"* in this universe, but, so far, the most profitable service of his slogan has been its anticlimactic exploitation as promotional copy by Columbia Pictures for *Close Encounters!*)

One of the two domains (known, since 1971, by the acronym CETI) features terrestrial portals extended out toward "vasty deep" space. These gates are kept ajar—at considerable expense to the polity—in the faith either that messages generated "here" will travel through them to perceivers thought to be lurking among advanced extraterrestrial civilizations, or, having been targeted *vice versa*, may reach properly programmed telluric interpreters at any moment now. Thus, in thickening traffic, messages are dispatched by mankind to communicate with putative receivers "out there," as via the carefully designed and coded sign complex

---

This review originally appeared in a somewhat shortened form in the *Times Literary Supplement* No.1041 (September 22, 1978), under the title "Clever Hans & Co."

engraved on a gold-plated plaque characterized by a relatively sophisticated set of syntactic and semantic markers, carried aboard Pioneer 10, launched one morning in March 1972. A decade or so before
that, Project Ozma was mounted—vainly, as it turned out—to scan Tau
Ceti passively for semiosic activity in the constellation of Cetus, the
whale.

Beneath the flood tide of attack on the problem of two-way interstellar
communication—an international cooperative search being conducted
by a host of radio astronomers, biochemists and exobiologists, mathe-
maticians, and other enthusiasts who have produced an impressive and
flourishing body of scientific literature, although without, alas, as yet a
shred of known subject matter—there surges a powerful undercurrent of
irrationalism and pseudoscience. This embarrassment might well be called
mass UFOria. The ins and outs of this hysterical debate about alien
forces in our midst cannot be pursued here, but the mutual charges
of "emotional bias" are worth pointing out, since they immediately bring
to mind parallel accusations agitating the other field dedicated to dispel-
ling modern man's anomie epitomized by his communicative isolation.
This inquiry, to probe the multitude of speechless creatures with whom
we share the earth, constitutes the main theme of Emily Hahn's informed
account, wherein she deplores the fact that there are still stubborn hold-
outs (she points her finger at Noam Chomsky in particular) "who refuse
to take seriously the work being done with" animals—exemplified here
by the chimpanzee Washoe—in order "to determine their capacity to
communicate in human fashion" (p.137).

Of Hahn's credentials there can be no doubt. Among her 47 previous
books, *Animal Gardens* (1967) and *On the Side of Apes* (1971)
abundantly testify to her profound empathy for all manner of animate
beings. Her readiness to journey to far ends of the globe and into
remote byways of scholarship in pursuit of even fugitive clues that might
attest to the ability of animals to think and reason vouches for the
immediacy and freshness of her information. Her reportorial quest for the
rational animal is in good conformity with one of the two principal
traditions leavening both sides of this arduous quest in the history of
ideas as the dialectic launched in the seventeenth century continues to
unfold. This is the stance foreshadowed in a prophetic book by the
French physician Julien Offray de la Mettrie, his 1747 *L'Homme machine*,
a work that persistently argues for the assimilation of human to animal
nature, in its firm repudiation of Cartesian dualism and on the basis
of data drawn from comparative anatomy and experimental psychology.
His lively exposition of a consistent materialism offered an heuristic hypothesis for the study of behavior and thus became a major forerunner
of a host of twentieth-century treatises, partly speculative, partly empirical. The most recent contribution in this vein is Donald R. Griffin's
extraordinary essay *The Question of Animal Awareness: Evolutionary*

Continuity and Mental Experience (1976), which Hahn of course cites with warm approval (pp.134-136).

The wellsprings of Hahn's predilections are quite clear, but the opposing view is hardly represented at all. Two examples of this kind of distortion must suffice. Hahn alludes to a jeweler named Karl Krall and his "collection of wonderful horses at Elberfeld" (p.23) and by subtle implication casts serious doubt for the untutored reader on the indubitably established principle of the Clever Hans Fallacy—the eponymous semiotic phenomenon whereby the destination of a message decisively but unwittingly influences the behavior of the source, as, for instance, by minuscule muscle tremors or changes in pupil diameter—and its corollaries that, she rightly surmises, "would put an end to . . . hopes of communication between our world and that of the nonhuman animals" (p.16). (Elizabeth Mann Borgese, in her alluringly naive 1968 book, *The Language Barrier: Beasts and Men,* used Krall's with the same indulgence.) The jejune procedures and conclusions of the amateurish Krall, who published a voluminous account of his "experiments" in *Denkende Tiere* (1912), were fully disposed of in an altogether masterful analysis by his contemporary Stefan von Máday in a point-for-point rebuttal, *Gibt es denkende Tiere?* (1914). Yet this meticulous, conclusive study is completely ignored by Hahn (as by the gushing Borgese before her).

Or take a second equine example: Hahn recites the self-styled exploits of a trainer named Henry N. Blake, who believes, or claims he does, that horses can communicate among each other and with humans by ESP or, as he writes in his latest (1977) book, that they "can and do have the ability to communicate by telepathy." Now it is perfectly clear from both of his books that Blake is a victim of the Clever Hans Fallacy—in fact, I have seldom come across a more transparent case of unconscious sensory cuing. It is irresponsible to insinuate otherwise, even if not explicitly endorsing crude folk beliefs about the psychic powers of animals. Hahn is certainly not naive, and it is hard to understand why she quotes Blake yet fails to mention any of the several illuminatingly realistic handbooks dealing with the training of horses to perform in circuses—especially the authoritative manuals by Pierre Hachet-Souplet (1897, *et seq.*)—or, specifically to the issue, the aforementioned Máday's very close to definitive study, *Psychologie des Pferdes und der Dressur* (1912).

Although she is aware of it, Hahn greatly underestimates the pernicious inevitability of the Clever Hans Fallacy. This pervasive source of error patently infects not only every contact between men and animals—notably so in situations of *apprentissage* and *dressage*—but all dyadic couplings between men, women, and infants and can even, as Joseph Weizenbaum has shown of late, significantly intrude into and distort our (as well as, *a fortiori,* the supposedly mechanically controlled chimpanzee Lana's) relationships with computers. When the Clever Hans Fallacy, or Pygmalion effect, further adulterated by the Pathetic Fallacy—the attribution of human affection to natural objects, including other animals and plants—strikes such installations where especially humanoid marine mammals or pongids are catechized intensively to ascertain their postulated propensity for language, it is hardly surprising that the prophecies are self-fulfilled in consequence of the complicated, evanescent, mostly automatic and out-of-awareness verbal and averbal maneuverings that take place.

On this point, it is essential not to be misunderstood: no one who knows elementary biology can doubt that all animals are able to communicate in their fashion with their conspecifics, as well as with members of such other species as share their ecosystem. The intraspecific communicative code of each animal species is singular, although a proclivity for code switching may also, to the extent necessary for survival, be wired in or partially acquired through experience. In circumstances where the animal's ecosystem embraces humans a severe perturbation usually arises, particularly so when one is injected artificially into an otherwise natural setting. Hahn, paraphrasing Lana's head operator, the psychologist Duane M. Rumbaugh, thinks it safe to conclude "that language as a form of communication is not totally unique from animal communication" (p.147). Well, the truth of this pretension—which I take to be pivotal to and the ultimate *raison d'être* for her book—hinges on what is meant by "language," and what the redundant expression "totally unique" is intended to imply. For perfectly valid reasons of logic, the term "language" is indeed vague, just as other verbal signs, such as "dawn" or "dusk," are inherently indeterminate and indefinite. As Charles S. Peirce used to teach, if a term is sufficiently specific, it raises no relevant questions; but the more precise we become, he tirelessly repeated, the more we are likely to err. Hahn chooses to stress this inherent vacuousness when she says that "without a generally accepted definition of language the question cannot be answered definitively"; yet she does conclude, such indeterminacy notwithstanding, that "many people are satisfied that the apes' productions are certainly relative to the language behavior of man" (pp.146-147). But what kind of people has she in mind? The gulls of yesteryear, who believed that a *deus* would emerge *ex machina* from the mind of one of Lilly's dolphins? Or scientists of the stature of John C. Eccles—surely with no linguistic axe to grind—who forcefully expressed his doubt that "these clever learned responses [of signing apes] can be regarded as a language even remotely resembling human language"?

If linguists, such as Chomsky, are to be enjoined from placing what others regard as little more than adroitly presented circus tricks of a handful of captive African apes beyond the pale of language in the technical sense, then, by the same token of a lack of clear definition, the trainers cannot claim a quasi-human language propensity for their charges either. Not surprisingly, by the way, the psychologists who have postulated and claimed cognitive capacities of this sort for "their" chimpanzees—ranging from subjects living in simulated naturalistic conditions to caged brutes subjected to forced-choice tests—have developed bitter rivalries. Mutual imputations of misinterpretation and worse—finagling—are rampant, so that the impression of idyllic concord conveyed by Hahn is quite misleading.

Linguists these days tend to agree that there is only one universal semiotic system or, to use S. K. Shaumyan's terminology, a single genotype language that models semantic processes realized by phenotype grammars, i.e., natural languages, providing correspondence rules connecting this genotype language with the thousands of extant phenotypes, each of which is unique. Similarly, the communication system of every other kind of animal is unique—species-specific, as biologists like to put it; in fact, this very uniqueness is criterial of specific taxonomic ranking, as, for example, in separating four kinds of very similar arctic gulls by just one small but absolutely crucial recognition index, signified solely by eye-ring coloration. At the same time, all communication systems share by definition a number of features the existence of which, among other things, enables ethologists to institute studies of ritualization, i.e., explorations in the evolution of the sign function. Taxonomic proximity between two species does not, however, imply near-identity of their respective systems of communication. Even though the average human polypeptide is more than 99 percent identical with its counterpart in the chimpanzee, there are obviously marked differences in our form and behavior, including especially semiosic comportment, probably because of differences in our array of regulatory genes. Language very likely emerged as a consequence of retarded human development, giving rise to our major adaptive distinction from the alloprimates. The differential character of our regulatory systems needs much more investigation, but there seems little doubt as to its importance in evolutionary change. A recognition that the underlying (genetic) continuity of process itself contains the seeds for surface saltation, amounts to, as Stephen Jay Gould brilliantly argues, a "reconciliation of our gradualistic bias with the appearance of discontinuity," or, to put it in another way, of evolution with revolution. The semiotic systems of the Great Apes evolved quantitatively into man's averbal communicatory systems, but his language and the type of intellectual organization of which it is a palpable manifestation are qualitative innovations, which, nonetheless, can be explained quite well in standard biological ways.

Whether scanning the skies for fabulously garrulous companions or looking around in our own backyard for ingenuously articulate (if certainly speechless) partners to alleviate our cosmic loneliness, Hotspur's interrogative can at present only be rejoined in the negative. No spirits have materialized so far from either above or below.

III. THE DOMAIN OF THE SACRED

JOHN BLACKING
The Anthropology of the Body

> If any thing is sacred the human
> body is sacred.
> —Walt Whitman,
> *I Sing the Body Electric* (1855)

This superior collection—bringing together most of the papers presented at a conference sponsored by the Association of Social Anthropologists, on the Anthropology of the Body, and reported to have been "intended to focus on the human body as the link between the nature and the culture present in all human activities"—fleshes out, as it were, an observation of Taine's, as reported by the eminent historian H. A. L. Fisher, in an article he published in 1941, "Paris at High Noon." Taine, according to Fisher, "pointed out that history was made by men, that men had bodies, that bodies were now healthy, now disordered, and that the state of the body inevitably affected the action of the mind. The study of the human body was part of the historian's duty" (1941:418b). It is evidently part of the anthropologist's professional commitment as well, but its scrutiny of the body has traditionally been relegated to that segment of the field which is severally qualified—at least in the United States—as physical anthropology, bioanthropology, and the like. In Blacking's view, the divorcement of physical and cultural/social anthropology is no longer useful, this because of the reciprocal reasons that the human body is shaped, or at least influenced, by culture, while certain apparently cultural phenomena—his prime example is language—are biologically based.

Almost all of the nineteen papers assembled here—including Blacking's fascinating exploratory introduction, leading the reader "Towards an Anthropology of the Body"—take it for granted that there exists a tacit consensus about the boundaries circumscribing the body, although Francis Huxley, in "The Body and the Play Within the Play," adverts to the problematic character of the commonly postulated relationship between self and nature, such that the embodiment of the "self" synecdochically "stands for" nature (inclusive, of course, of culture and society). However, this still leaves open the definition of the "self," continuously debated from Plato's dramatistic (i.e., dialectic) exposition in the *Timaeus,* to Lévi-Strauss's structuralist conversion of the Platonic model in his also synecdochically Totemic Operator—admittedly just a program, one that remains "reserved for the ethnology of a future century. . . " (1962:200).

This review originally appeared in the *Journal of Social & Biological Structures* 3(1980):227-229.

Provisionally, we can postulate that every enculturated human being possesses a pair of "bodies," or selves, one embedded inside the other. The contained infrastructure can best be apprehended in immunological, viz., biochemical terms: invasion of this physical body is initially signified by the immune response—that is, a specific reaction by the individual animal aimed at neutralizing or obliterating foreign bodies, or antigens, such as a population of bacteria. The response of the system also features adaptivity, i.e., the upgrowth of a memory, and a crucial characteristic that enables it to react to *unexpected* stimuli, or, in other words, to manifest amplifying semiotic overtones. The enveloping superstructure, or the semiotic self as such, is necessarily anchored both biologically and socially; invasion of this outer bubble, or social membrane of irregular and elastic size and shape, triggers what Freud designated "signal-anxiety"—it serves as an early warning system for the former. The arena for the immune reaction is circumscribed by the body's largest organ, the skin, which filters matter-energy flows. The semiotic self is normally contained between the skin and an outer perimeter, or information-filtering threshold, discovered by Heini Hediger in 1935. Hediger distinguished between two extreme ways of vertebrate behavior: contact types and distance types. Man clearly represents the second sort of species, being surrounded by a well-defined individual distance and intolerant of physical propinquity (save in special circumstances, such as when engaged in reproductive activities). The cross-cultural implications of Hediger's model were later explored, in preliminary forays, by Edward T. Hall (1959, 1966), under the rubric of "proxemics," while the psychological ones were probed by Robert Sommer, in his deplorably neglected book, *Personal Space* (1969). Blacking assigns proxemics to the microscopic aspects of human movement and holds that an anthropology of the body constitutes a crossroads where "the micro and macro" meet. Another author, J. B. Loudon, returns to this point in the context of his consideration of the biological basis of social relationships through the medium of "body products," a phrase that he limits (too restrictively, I think) to excretion.

A pivotal notion, scarcely touched on in this book, was articulated and beautifully illustrated by Jonathan Miller in *The Body in Question* (1978: chap. 7): that the possession of a body "may be the necessary condition of being a person but it is not a sufficient one." Each neonate must learn to personate, to distinguish, that is, between *ego* and *alter*. Here, again, a double agent is at work: the body comes to be perceived as one object in a world abounding with other objects; but the body is also felt as a medium of experience and the arena of action. It is this second conformation that enables us to demarcate our perception of the "outside" world from the universe of embodied sensations. The implications of this dual configuration were brilliantly blocked out by Jakob von Uexküll, beginning in the first decade of this century, in his delineation of the *Funktionskreis* concept, which connotes a vast program of as yet hardly begun research, based on a cybernetic cycle between what he called the *Innenwelt* (or the organism's inwardly staged model of the world) and its *Umwelt* (or, roughly, the organism's cognitive map). Before the advent of modern, i.e., post-Peircean, semiotics, and especially its contemporary formalization by René Thom, von Uexküll's theoretical contributions were not only, so to speak, floating in limbo, but were largely misunderstood and disparaged by ethologists, especially Konrad Lorenz (cf. Sebeok 1979: chap. 10; see now, further, Uexküll 1980).

The limitations of space will not permit me to comment on the many other superb articles in this book, but I cannot, in conclusion, refrain from singling out Gilbert Lewis's "Fear of Sorcery and the Problem of Death by Suggestion," because this essay comes face-to-face with the ultimate enigma Marcel Mauss (1926:311-330) marked as cases "où la nature sociale rejoint très directement la nature biologique de l'homme" (ibid.:329). The problem can be restated thus: how does the body transmute (verbal and nonverbal) semiotic strings into physiological action as wonderful as getting rid of warts (Thomas 1979: chap. 13), or inducing both subjective improvement and objective changes in angina pectoris (Benson and McCallie 1979), or causing sudden death in animals and man in all parts of the globe (Cannon 1942, and his many followers, especially Richter 1957)? At present, we can only surmise that such strings may activate, given the right conditions, the secretion of powerful substances such as endorphins, dynorphins, interferons, or steroids, by coupling with action-sites, or receptors, or nerve cells in the manner of a lock-and-key arrangement and also perhaps spreading their influence throughout the body as hormones. It is worth recollecting in this connection Darwin's antithetical proposition (1872: chap. 3) that the transmission of messages by vocal means may well be rooted in the agony of pain.

References

Ackoff, Russell L., and Fred E. Emery
1972 *On Purposeful Systems*. Chicago: Aldine-Atherton.

Alland, Alexander, Jr.
1977 *The Artistic Animal: An Inquiry into the Biological Roots of Art*. Garden City: Anchor Press/Doubleday.

Andrews, Michael
1976 *The Life that Lives on Man*. New York: Taplinger.

Anonymous
1891 "Wild Animal Training." *The Strand Magazine* 2:291-301.
1979 "Story about Chimp Stirs Furor at OU." *The Tulsa Tribune*, November 29.
1980 "Try a Little TLC." *Science 80* 1(2):15.

Apel, Karl-Otto
1973 "Charles W. Morris und das Programm einer pragmatisch integrierten Semiotik." In *Zeichen, Sprache und Verhalten*, ed. by Charles William Morris, 9-66. Düsseldorf: Schwann.

Appun, Karl
1871 *Unter den Tropen*. Jena: H. Costenoble.

Arendt, Hannah
1958 *The Human Condition*. Chicago: University of Chicago Press.

Armstrong, Edward A.
1963 *A Study of Bird Song*. London: Oxford University Press.
1965 *Bird Display and Behavior: An Introduction to the Study of Bird Psychology*. New York: Dover.

Arnheim, Rudolf
1954 *Art and Visual Experience*. Berkeley: University of California Press.

Aschoff, Lee
1980 "'Talkative' Turtle Is Missing." *Milwaukee Sentinel*, June 2.

Autrum, Hansjochem
1972 "The Communications Network of the Human Body." In *Man and Animal: Studies in Behaviour*, ed. by Heinz Friedrich, 77-81. London: MacGibbon & Kee.

Ayim, Maryann
1974 "Retroduction: The Rational Instinct." *Transactions of the Charles S. Peirce Society* 10:34-43.

Bacon, Francis
1900 *The Works of Francis Bacon*, ed. by James Spedding, Robert Leslie Ellis, and Douglas Denon Heath. Boston: Houghton, Mifflin and Company.

Baer, Eugen
1979 "Tom Sebeok's Thomism." *Semiotica* 28:349-370.

Barber, Theodore X.
1976 *Pitfalls in Human Research: Ten Pivotal Points*. New York: Pergamon.

Baring-Gould, William S.
1967 (ed.) *The Annotated Sherlock Holmes*. 2 vols. New York: Clarkson N. Potter.

Barker, John Charles
1968 *Scared to Death*. London: F. Muller.

Barthes, Roland

1957 *Mythologies*. Paris: Seuil.

1975 *Roland Barthes*. Paris: Seuil.

Bartley, William Warren III

1973 *Wittgenstein*. Philadelphia: J. B. Lippincott.

Bascom, William R.

1955 "Verbal Art." *Journal of American Folklore* 68:245-252.

Bateson, Gregory

1968 "Redundancy and Coding." In *Animal Communication: Techniques of Study and Results of Research*, ed. by Thomas A. Sebeok, 614-626. Bloomington: Indiana University Press.

Bauman, Richard

1977 *Verbal Art as Performance*. Rowley: Newbury House.

Bell, Joseph

1893 "Mr. Sherlock Holmes," Introduction to the Fourth Edition of *A Study in Scarlet*. London: Ward, Lock. [Previously published in the *Bookman* (London).]

Benderly, Beryl Lieff

1980 "The Great Ape Debate: Can Gorillas and Chimps Use Language or Not?" *Science 80* 1(5):60-65, 95.

Benson, Herbert and David P. McCallie, Jr.

1979 "Angina Pectoris and the Placebo Effect." *New England Journal of Medicine* 300:1424-1429.

Bernstein, Basil B.

1974 "Social Class, Language and Socialisation." In *Current Trends in Linguistics. Linguistics and Adjacent Arts and Sciences*, ed. by Thomas A. Sebeok, 12:1545-1562. The Hague: Mouton.

Bernstein, Richard J.

1965 (ed.) *Perspectives on Peirce*. New Haven: Yale University Press.

Blacking, John

1977 *The Anthropology of the Body*. London: Academic Press.

Blake, Henry N.

1975 *Talking with Horses: A Study of Communication between Man and Horse*. London: Souvenir Press.

1977 *Thinking with Horses*. London: Souvenir Press.

Blanford, William T.

1889-91 *The Fauna of British India: Mammalia*. London: Taylor and Francis.

Blumenthal, Arthur L.

1974 "An Historical View of Psycholinguistics," in *Current Trends in Linguistics. Linguistics and Adjacent Arts and Sciences*, ed. by Thomas A. Sebeok, 12:1105-1134. The Hague: Mouton.

Boas, Franz

1955 [1927] *Primitive Art*. New York: Dover.

Bogatyrev, Petr

1971 *The Functions of Folk Costume in Moravian Slovakia*. The Hague: Mouton.

Borgese, Elizabeth Mann

1968 *The Language Barrier: Beasts and Men*. New York: Holt, Rinehart and Winston.

Bottéro, Jean

1974 "Symptômes, signes, écritures." In *Divination et Rationalité*, ed. by Jean-Pierre Vernant et al., 70-197. Paris: Seuil.

Bouissac, Paul

1976 *Circus and Culture: A Semiotic Approach*. Bloomington: Indiana University Press.

1979 "A Compass for Semiotics." *Ars Semeiotica* 2:205-221.
Boulding, Kenneth E.
1961 [1956] *The Image.* Ann Arbor: University of Michigan Press.
Bourne, Geoffrey H.
1971 *The Ape People.* New York: G. P. Putnam's Sons.
Boyle, T. Coraghessan
1980 "Descent of Man." In *Descent of Man and Other Stories,* 3-16. New York: McGraw-Hill.
Braun, John
1978 "Martin Gardner." *The Linking Ring* 58/4:47-48.
Breland, Keller and Marian Breland
1966 *Animal Behavior.* New York: Macmillan.
Bronowski, Jacob
1967 "The Reach of Imagination." *Proceedings of the American Academy of Arts and Letters and National Institute of Arts and Letters,* Second Series, No. 17:31-42 (the Blashfield Address).
1974 "Language in a Biological Frame." In *Current Trends in Linguistics, Linguistics and Adjacent Arts and Sciences,* ed. by Thomas A. Sebeok, 12: 2539-2559. The Hague: Mouton.
1977 *A Sense of the Future: Essays in Natural Philosophy.* Cambridge: MIT Press.
Bronowski, Jacob and Ursula Bellugi
1980 "Language, Name and Concept." In *Speaking of Apes: A Critical Anthology of Two-Way Communication with Man,* ed. by Thomas A. Sebeok and Jean Umiker-Sebeok, 103-113. New York: Plenum. (First published 1970.)
Brothwell, Don R.
1976 (ed.) *Beyond Aesthetics: Investigations into the Nature of Visual Art.* London: Thames and Hudson.
Brouwers, J.
1956 "Le rôle du système nerveux en pathologie générale." *Annales de Médicine vétérinaire* 44:245-270.
Brown, Roger
1968 "The Development of Wh Questions in Child Speech." *Journal of Verbal Learning and Verbal Behavior* 7:277-290.
1980 "The First Sentences of Child and Chimpanzee." In *Speaking of Apes: A Critical Anthology of Two-Way Communication with Man,* ed. by Thomas A. Sebeok and Jean Umiker-Sebeok, 85-101. New York: Plenum. (First published 1970.)
Brunswik, Egon
1929 "Prinzipienfragen der Gestalttheorie." In *Beiträge zur Problemgeschichte der Psychologie: Festschrift zu Karl Bühler's 50. Geburtstag,* ed. by Egon Brunswik et al., 78-149. Jena: Gustav Fischer.
1955 [1952] "The Conceptual Framework of Psychology." In *International Encyclopedia of Unified Science,* ed. by Otto Neurath, Rudolf Carnap, and Charles Morris, 1:10:655-760.
Brunswik, Egon et al.
1929 (eds.) *Beiträge zur Problemgeschichte der Psychologie: Festschrift zu Karl Bühler's 50. Geburtstag.* Jena: Gustav Fischer.
Bühler, Charlotte
1965 "Die Wiener Psychologische Schule in der Emigration." *Psychologische Rundschau* 16:187-196.
Bühler, Charlotte and Hildegard Hetzer
1929 "Zur Geschichte der Kinderpsychologie." In *Beiträge zur Problemge-*

schichte der Psychologie: Festschrift zu Karl Bühler's 50. Geburtstag, ed. by Egon Brunswik et al., 204-224. Jena: Gustav Fischer.

Bühler, Karl
1905-08 "Tatsachen und Probleme zu einer Psychologie der Denkvorgänge." *Archiv für die gesamte Psychologie* 9:297-365 (1907), 12:1-23 (1908), 24-92 (1908).
1918 *Die geistige Entwicklung des Kindes.* Jena: Gustav Fischer.
1927 *Die Krise der Psychologie.* Jena: Gustav Fischer.
1933 "Die Axiomatik der Sprachwissenschaften." *Kanstudien* 38:19-90.
1965² [1934] *Sprachtheorie: Die Darstellungsfunktion der Sprache.* Stuttgart: Gustav Fischer.
1968² [1934] *Ausdrucktheorie: Das System an der Geschichte aufgezeigt.* Stuttgart: Gustav Fischer.
1969 *Die Uhren der Lebewesen: Studien zur Theorie der Raumzeitlichen Orientierung.* In *Österreichische Akademie der Wissenschaften. Philosophisch-Historische Klasse,* Sitzungsberichte 265:3:10:73-160. Vienna: Hermann Böhlaus Nachf.

Bulmer, Ralph
1970 "Which Came First, the Chicken or the Egg-Head?" In *Échanges et Communications,* ed. by Jean Pouillon and Pierre Maranda, 2:1069-1091. The Hague: Mouton.

Burroughs, W. H.
1869 *Haney's Art of Training Animals. A Practical Guide to Amateur or Professional Trainers. Giving Full Instructions for Breaking, Taming, and Teaching All Kinds of Animals . . . .* New York: Jesse Haney & Co.

Campbell, Maurice
1935 *Sherlock Holmes and Dr. Watson: A Medical Digression.* London: Ash.

Cannon, Walter B.
1942 " 'Voodoo' Death." *American Anthropologist* 44:169-181.

Carlsmith, J. Merrill, Phoebe C. Ellsworth, and Elliott Aronson
1976 *Methods of Research in Social Psychology.* Reading, Mass.: Addison Wesley.

Castañeda, Hector-Neri
1978 "Philosophical Method and the Theory of Predication and Identity." *Noûs* 12:189-210.

Cawelti, John G.
1976 *Adventure, Mystery, and Romance: Formula Stories as Art and Popular Culture.* Chicago: University of Chicago Press.

Chauvin-Muckensturm, Bernadette
1974 "Y a-t-il utilisation de signaux appris comme moyen de communication chez le pic epeiche?" *Revue du Comportement Animal* 9:185-207.

Cherry, Colin
1978³ *On Human Communication: A Review, a Survey, and a Criticism.* Cambridge: MIT Press.

Chertok, L. and M. Fontaine
1963 "Psychosomatics in Veterinary Medicine." *Journal of Psychosomatic Research* 7:229-235.

Chevalier-Skolnikoff, Suzanne
1976 "The Ontogeny of Primate Intelligence and Its Implications for Communicative Potential: A Preliminary Report." In *Origins and Evolution of Language and Speech,* ed. by Steven R. Harnad, Horst D. Steklis, and Jane Lancaster. Annals of the New York Academy of Sciences 280. New York: New York Academy of Sciences.

Chomsky, Noam
1979 *Language and Responsibility.* New York: Pantheon Books.

1980 "Human Language and Other Semiotic Systems." In *Speaking of Apes: A Critical Anthology of Two-Way Communication with Man*, ed. by Thomas A. Sebeok and Jean Umiker-Sebeok, 429-440. New York: Plenum. (First published 1979.)

Chomsky, Noam and David Premack
1979 "Species of Intelligence." *The Sciences* 19 (9):6-11,23.

Christopher, Milbourne
1970 *ESP, Seers & Psychics*. New York: Thomas Y. Crowell.
1973 *The Illustrated History of Magic*. New York: Thomas Y. Crowell.

Claus, Peter J.
1976 "A Structuralist Appreciation of 'Star Trek.'" In *The American Dimension: Cultural Myths and Social Realities*, ed. by W. Arens and Susan P. Montague, 15-32. Port Washington, N.Y.: Alfred Publishing Co.

Clifford, Brian R. and Ray Bull
1978 *The Psychology of Person Identification*. London: Routledge & Kegan Paul.

Cohn, Robert Greer
1977 "Mallarmé's Windows." *Yale French Studies* 54:23-31.

Collier, John
1969 [1931] *His Monkey Wife: or Married to a Chimp*. London: Chatto & Windus.

Constant, J. and J. Dubois
1975 "Discours sur la méthode double aveugle." *Revue de Neuropsychiatrie infantile* 23:329-343.

Conway, William M.
1889 *Literary Remains of Albrecht Dürer*. New York: Cambridge University Press.

Cooper, Peter
1976 "Holmesian Chemistry." In *Beyond Baker Street: A Sherlockian Anthology*, ed. by Michael Harrison, 67-73. Indianapolis: Bobbs-Merrill.

Crichton, Michael
1980 *Congo*. New York: Alfred A. Knopf.

Dale-Green, Patricia
1966 *Dog*. London: Rupert Hart-Davis.

Darwin, Charles
1872 *The Expression of the Emotions in Man and Animal*. London: John Murray.
1901 [1874] *The Descent of Man*. London: John Murray.

Davies, P. C. W.
1979 "Reality Exists Outside Us?" In *Lying Truths: A Critical Scrutiny of Current Beliefs and Conventions*, ed. by Ronald Duncan and Miranda Weston-Smith, 144-158. Oxford: Pergamon.

Davis, Roger T.
1974 *Monkeys as Perceivers*. New York: Academic Press.

Dawkins, Richard
1978 *The Selfish Gene*. New York: Oxford University Press.

De Jorio, Andrea
1832 *La Mimica degle Antichi Investigata del Gestire Napoletano*. Naples: Del Fibrano.

Desmond, Adrian J.
1979 *The Ape's Reflexion*. New York: The Dial Press.

Deutsch, Felix
1959 (ed.) *On the Mysterious Leap from the Mind to the Body: A Workshop Study on the Theory of Conversion*. New York: International Universities Press.

De Waal, Ronald Burt
1974 *The World Bibliography of Sherlock Holmes and Dr. Watson: A Classified and Annotated List of Materials Relating to Their Lives and Adventures.* New York: Bramhall House.
Diaconis, Persi
1978 "Statistical Problems in ESP Research." *Science* 201:131-136.
Diels, Hermann
1901 *Herakleitos von Ephesos.* Berlin: Weidmansche Buchhandlung.
Dobzhansky, Theodosius
1962 *Mankind Evolving: The Evolution of the Human Species.* New Haven: Yale University Press.
Doyle, Arthur Conan
1923 *Through the Magic Door.* Garden City: Doubleday, Page.
1924 *Memories and Adventures.* Boston: Little, Brown.
n.d. *The Complete Sherlock Holmes.* Garden City: Doubleday.
Dücker, Gerti
1963 "Spontane Bevorzügung arteigener Farben bei Vögeln." *Zeitschrift für Tierpsychologie* 20:43-65.
Dunnell, Robert C.
1971 *Systematics in Prehistory.* New York: The Free Press.
Eccles, John C.
1979 *The Human Mystery. Lecture 10. The mind-brain problem: Experimental Evidence and Hypothesis.* Heidelberg: Springer International; New York: Springer-Verlag.
Eco, Umberto
1979 *The Role of the Reader: Explorations in the Semiotics of Texts.* Bloomington: Indiana University Press.
Eddy, Mary Baker
1934 [1875] *Science and Health with a Key to the Scriptures.* Boston: Trustees under the will of Mary Baker G. Eddy.
Efron, David
1972 [1941] *Gesture, Race and Culture.* The Hague: Mouton.
Ehrenfeld, David W.
1972 *Conserving Life on Earth.* New York: Oxford University Press.
Eibl-Eibesfeldt, Irenäus
1975² *Ethology: The Biology of Behavior.* New York: Holt, Rinehart and Winston.
Eisele, Carolyn
1976 (ed.) *The New Elements of Mathematics by Charles S. Peirce.* 4 vols. The Hague: Mouton.
Eisenberg, John F. and Wilton S. Dillon
1971 *Man and Beast: Comparative Social Behavior.* Washington: Smithsonian Institution Press.
Eisner, Thomas, Karen Hicks, Maria Eisner, and Douglas S. Robson
1978 " 'Wolf-in-Sheep's-Clothing' Strategy of a Predatious Insect Larva." *Science* 199:790-794.
Eitner, Lorenz
1955 "The Open Window and the Storm-Tossed Boat, an Essay in the Iconography of Romanticism." *Art Bulletin* 37:281-290.
Ekman, Paul and Wallace V. Friesen
1969 "The Repertoire of Nonverbal Behavior: Categories, Origins, Usage, and Coding." *Semiotica* 1:49-98.
Ellsworth, Phoebe C.
1978 "When Does an Experimenter Bias?" *The Behavioral and Brain Sciences* 1 (3):329,393.

Epstein, Robert, Robert P. Lanza, and B. F. Skinner
1980 "Symbolic Communication between Two Pigeons (*Columba livia domestica*)," *Science* 207:543-545.

Erwin, Joseph, Terry L. Maple, and G. Mitchell
1979 (eds). *Captivity and Behavior. Primates in Breeding Colonies, Laboratories, and Zoos.* New York: Van Nostrand.

Evans, William E. and Jarvis Bastian
1969 "Marine Mammal Communication: Social and Ecological Factors." In *The Biology of Marine Mammals,* ed. by Harald T. Andersen. New York: Academic Press.

Exline, Ralph V. and Absalom M. Yellin
1971 *Eye Contact as a Sign between Man and Monkey.* Proceedings of the XIX International Congress of Psychology. London: International Congress of Psychology.

Falk, Dean
1980 "Language, Handedness and Primate Brains: Did the Australopithecines Sign?" *American Anthropologist* 82:72-78.

Feinberg, Gerald and Robert Shapiro
1980 *Life Beyond Earth.* New York: William Morrow and Co.

Fellers, Joan H. and Gary M. Fellers
1976 "Tool Use in a Social Insect and Its Implications for Competitive Interactions." *Science* 192:70-72.

Ferguson, Charles A.
1971 *Language Structure and Language Use.* Stanford: Stanford University Press.

Ferguson, Eugene S.
1977 "The Mind's Eye: Nonverbal Thought in Technology." *Science* 197:827-836.

Field, George Wallis
1970 *Hermann Hesse.* New York: Twayne Publishers.

Fisch, Max H.
1964 "Was There a Metaphysical Club in Cambridge?" In *Studies in the Philosophy of Charles Sanders Peirce,* 2d series, ed. by Edward C. Moore and Richard S. Robin, 3-32. Amherst: University of Massachusetts Press.
1977 "Peirce's Place in American Thought." *Ars Semeiotica* 1:21-37.
1979 "Charles Morris (1901-1979)." *Semiotic Scene* 3:159-160.

Fisher, Herbert A. L.
1941 "Paris at High Noon: Portrait of a Student." *The Atlantic Monthly* 167:416-423.

Fisher, John
1979 *Body Magic.* New York: Stein and Day.

Fouts, Roger S.
1973 "Acquisition and Testing of Gestural Signs in Four Young Chimpanzees." *Science* 180:978-980.

Fouts, Roger S. and Joseph B. Couch
1976 "Cultural Evolution of Learned Language in Chimpanzees." In *Communication Behavior and Evolution,* ed. by Martin E. Hahn and Edward C. Simmel, 141-161. New York: Academic Press.

Fouts, Roger S., Joseph B. Couch, and Charity R. O'Neil
1979 "Strategies for Primate Language Training." In *Language Intervention from Ape to Child,* ed. by Richard L. Schiefelbusch and John H. Hollis, 295-323. Baltimore: University Park.

Fouts, Roger S., Roger L. Mellgren, and William Lemmon
1973 "American Sign Language in the Chimpanzee: Chimpanzee-to-Chim-

panzee Communication." Paper presented at the Midwestern Psychological Association Meeting, Chicago.

Fouts, Roger S. and Randall L. Rigby
1980 "Man-Chimpanzee Communication." In *Speaking of Apes: A Critical Anthology of Two-Way Communication with Man,* ed. by Thomas A. Sebeok and Jean Umiker-Sebeok, 261-285. New York: Plenum. First published 1977.

Fouts, Roger S., Gary Shapiro, and Charity O'Neil
1978 "Studies of Linguistic Behavior in Apes and Children." In *Understanding Language through Sign Language Research,* ed. by Patricia Siple, 163-185. New York: Academic Press.

Fox, Michael W.
1971 *Behavior of Wolves, Dogs and Related Canids.* New York: Harper & Row.
1978 *The Dog: Its Domestication and Behavior.* New York: Garland STPM Press.

Fox, Michael W. and James A. Cohen
1977 "Canid Communication." In *How Animals Communicate,* ed. by Thomas A. Sebeok, 728-748. Bloomington: Indiana University Press.

Friedman, Neil
1967 *The Social Nature of Psychological Research.* New York: Basic Books.

Frings, Hubert and Mabel Frings
1977² *Animal Communication.* Norman: University of Oklahoma Press.

Frisch, Karl von
1954 *The Dancing Bees.* London: Methuen.
1967 *The Dance Language and Orientation of Bees.* Cambridge: Harvard University Press.
1974 *Animal Architecture.* New York: Harcourt Brace Jovanovich.

Furness, William H.
1916 "Observations on the Mentality of Chimpanzees and Orangutans." *Proceedings* of the American Philosophical Society 55:281-290.

Galdikas, Biruté M. F.
1978 "Orangutans and Hominid Evolution." In *Spectrum: Essays Presented to Sutan Takdir Alisjahbana on His 70th Birthday,* ed. by S. Udin. Jakarta: Dian Rakyat.

Gannon, Gilbert R.
1930 "Observations on the Satin Bower Bird with Regard to the Material Used by It in Painting Its Bower." *Emu* 30:39-41.

Gardner, Beatrice T. and R. Allen Gardner
1975 "Evidence for Sentence Constituents in the Early Utterances of Child and Chimpanzee." *Journal of Experimental Psychology* 104 (3):244-267.
1980a "Comparative Psychology and Language Acquisition." In *Speaking of Apes: A Critical Anthology of Two-Way Communication with Man,* ed. by Thomas A. Sebeok and Jean Umiker-Sebeok, 287-330. New York: Plenum. First published 1978.
1980b "Two Comparative Psychologists Look at Language Acquisition." In *Children's Language,* vol. 2, ed. by Keith E. Nelson. New York: Halsted, forthcoming.

Gardner, Martin
1957 *Fads and Fallacies in the Name of Science.* New York: Dover.
1966 "Dermo-optical Perception: A Peek Down the Nose." *Science* 151: 654-657.
1976 "The Irrelevance of Conan Doyle." In *Beyond Baker Street: A Sherlockian Anthology,* ed. by Michael Harrison, 123-135. Indianapolis: Bobbs-Merrill.

1979 "How to be a Psychic, Even If You Are a Horse or Some Other Animal." *Scientific American* 240 (5):18.

1980 "Monkey Business." *The New York Review of Books* 27 (4):3-6.

Garvin, Paul L.

1964 "Note." *Language* 40:633-635.

1966 "Karl Bühler's Contribution to the Theory of Linguistics." *Journal of General Psychology* 75:212-215.

Gillett, John D.

1973 "The Mosquito: Still Man's Worst Enemy." *American Scientist* 61: 430-436.

Ginzburg, Carlo

1980 "Morelli, Freud and Sherlock Holmes: Clues and Scientific Method." *History Workshop* 9:7-36.

Gipper, Helmut

1977 "Die Sonderstellung der menschlichen Sprache gegenüber der Verständigungsmitteln der Tiere." *Mitteilungen der Berliner Gesellschaft für Anthropologie, Ethnologie, und Urgeschichte* 5 (1):26-67.

Gogol, Nikolai

1960 *The Diary of a Madman and Other Stories,* trans. by Andrew R. MacAndrew. New York: The New American Library.

Goldenson, Robert M.

1973 *Mysteries of the Mind: The Drama of Human Behavior.* New York: Doubleday.

Gomperz, Heinrich

1908 *Weltanschauungslehre* 2/1: *Einleitung und Semasiologie.* Jena: E. Diederichs.

Gould, Stephen Jay

1978 "Morton's Ranking of Races by Cranial Capacity." *Science,* 200:503-509.

Greenberg, Joel

1980 "Ape Talk: More than 'Pigeon' English?" *Science News* 117:298-300.

Greene, Charles W.

1924 "Physiological Reactions and Structure of the Vocal Apparatus of the California Singing Fish." *American Journal of Physiology* 70:496-499.

Greene, Graham

1969 [1940] *Collected Essays.* Harmondsworth: Penguin.

Greenewalt, Crawford H.

1968 *Bird Song: Acoustics and Physiology.* Washington: Smithsonian Institution Press.

Greimas, Julien Algirdas

1970 *Du sens: Essais sémiotiques.* Paris: Seuil.

Griffin, Donald R.

1976 *The Question of Animal Awareness: Evolutionary Continuity of Mental Experience.* New York: Rockefeller University Press.

1978a "Prospects for a Cognitive Ethology." *The Behavioral and Brain Sciences* 1 (4):527-538.

1978b "Experimental Cognitive Ethology." *The Behavioral and Brain Sciences* 1 (4):555.

Grzimek, Bernhard

1975 (ed.) *Grzimek's Animal Life Encyclopedia.* New York: Van Nostrand Reinhold.

Guilmet, George M.

1977 "The Evolution of Tool-Using and Tool-Making Behaviour." *Man* 12:33-47.

Günther, Arnold Fritz
  1968 "Der Zeichenbegriff bei K. Bühler und G. H. Mead," in *Forschungs-bericht* 68-2/4, Institut für Phonetik und Kommunikationsforschung der Universität Bonn. Hamburg: Helmut Buske.
Guthrie, Edwin Ray and George Plant Horton
  1946 *Cats in a Puzzle Box.* New York: Rinehart.
Guthrie, R. Dale
  1976 *Body Hot Spots: The Anatomy of Human Social Organs and Behavior.* New York: Van Nostrand Reinhold.
Hachet-Souplet, Pierre
  1897 *Le dressage des animaux et les combats de bêtes, révélation des procédés employés par les professionels pour dresser le chien, le singe, le cheval, l'éléphant. les bêtes féroces, etc.* Paris: Firmin Didot.
Hahn, Emily
  1978 *Look Who's Talking!* New York: Thomas Y. Crowell.
Haining, Peter
  1978 *The Jules Verne Companion.* London: Souvenir Press.
Haldane, John Burdon Sanderson
  1956 "The Argument from Animals to Men: An Examination of Its Validity for Anthropology." *The Journal of the Royal Anthropological Institute of Great Britain and Ireland* 86(II):1-14.
Hall, Edward T.
  1959 *The Silent Language.* Garden City: Doubleday.
  1966 *The Hidden Dimension.* Garden City: Doubleday.
Hall, Trevor H.
  1978 *Sherlock Holmes and His Creator.* London: Duckworth.
Hall-Craggs, Joan
  1969 "The Aesthetic Content of Bird Song." In *Bird Vocalizations: Their Relations to Current Problems in Biology and Psychology,* ed. by Robert A. Hinde, 367-381. Cambridge: Cambridge University Press.
Haller, Rudolf
  1959 "Das 'Zeichen' und die 'Zeichenlehre' in der Philosophie der Neuzeit." *Archiv für Begriffsgeschichte* 4:113-157.
Hamon, Philippe
  1968 "Zola romancier de la transparence." *Europe* (May):385-391.
Hancocks, David M.
  1973 *Master Builders of the Animal World.* New York: Harper & Row.
Hanna, Judith L.
  1977 "To Dance Is Human: Some Psychological Bases of an Expressive Form." In *The Anthropology of the Body,* ed. by John Blacking, 211-232. London: Academic Press.
Hansell, C. E. M.
  1980 *ESP and Parapsychology: A Critical Reevaluation.* Buffalo: Prometheus Books.
Hardwick, Charles S.
  1977 (ed.) *Semiotic and Significs: The Correspondence between Charles S. Peirce and Victoria Lady Welby.* Bloomington: Indiana University Press.
Hartshorne, Charles
  1973 *Born to Sing: An Interpretation and World Survey of Bird Song.* Bloomington: Indiana University Press.
  1979 "Charles Morris." *Semiotica* 28:193-194.
Harvey, Paul
  1980 "Animals Can Talk." *Bloomington* [Indiana] *Herald-Telephone,* January 7.

Haycraft, Howard
1941 *Murder for Pleasure: The Life and Times of the Detective Story.* New York: D. Appleton-Century.
Hayes, Cathy
1951 *The Ape in Our House.* New York: Harper.
Healy, Alice F.
1980 "Can Chimpanzees Learn a Phonemic Language?" In *Speaking of Apes: A Critical Anthology of Two-Way Communication with Man,* ed. by Thomas A. Sebeok and Jean Umiker-Sebeok, 141-143. New York: Plenum. (First published 1973.)
Hediger, Heini
1938 "Ergebnisse tierpsychologischer Forschung im Zirkus." *Die Naturwissenschaften* 26 (16):242-252.
1968 *The Psychology and Behavior of Animals in Zoos and Circuses.* New York: Dover.
1969 *Man and Animal in the Zoo: Zoo Biology.* New York: Delacorte.
1974 "Communication between Man and Animal." *Image Roche* 62:27-40.
1976 "Proper Names in the Animal Kingdom." *Experientia* 32:1357-1364.
1979 "Kreativität beim Tier." In *Seele und Leib—Geist und Materie,* ed. by Maja Svilar, 193-216. Bern: Peter Lang.
1980 "Do You Speak Yerkish? The Newest Colloquial Language with Chimpanzees." In *Speaking of Apes: A Critical Anthology of Two-Way Communication with Man,* ed. by Thomas A. Sebeok and Jean Umiker-Sebeok, 441-447. New York: Plenum. (First published 1979.)
Heinroth, Oskar
1910 "Beiträge zur Biologie, namentlich Ethologie und Psychologie der Anatiden." *Verhandlungen des V. Internationalen Ornithologen-Kongresses* 5:589-702.
Henle, Paul
1958 (ed.) *Language, Thought, & Culture.* Ann Arbor: University of Michigan Press.
Herrnstein, R. J., Donald H. Loveland, and Cynthia Cable
1977 "Natural Concepts in Pigeons." *Journal of Experimental Psychology: Animal Learning and Memory* 2:285-302.
Hess, Eckhard H.
1975 *The Tell-Tale Eye: How Your Eyes Reveal Hidden Thoughts and Emotions.* New York: Van Nostrand Reinhold.
Hesse, Hermann
1949 *Magister Ludi.* New York: Frederick Ungar. [Trans. from *Das Glasperlenspiel* (1943), by Mervyn Savill.]
Hewes, Gordon W.
1973 "Primate Communication and the Gestural Origin of Language." *Current Anthropology* 14:5-24.
Higham, Charles
1978 *The Adventures of Conan Doyle.* New York: Pocket Books.
Hill, Jane H.
1980 "Apes and Language." In *Speaking of Apes: A Critical Anthology of Two-Way Communication with Man,* ed. by Thomas A. Sebeok and Jean Umiker-Sebeok, 331-351. New York: Plenum. (First published 1978.)
Hiller, Barbara F.
1980 "Conversations with Koko." *Gorilla* 3 (1):3.
Hilton, George W.
1968 *The Night Boat.* Berkeley: Howell-North Books.
Hirose, Shizumu
1980 *Saru.* Tokyo: Hosei University Press. [In Japanese.]

Hitchings, J. L.
1946 "Sherlock Holmes the Logician," *The Baker Street Journal* 1 (2) (old series):113-117.
Holden, Constance
1977 "Pain Control and Hypnosis," *Science* 198:808.
Horálek, Karel
1948 "La fonction de la 'structure des fonctions' de la langue." *Recueil Linguistique de Bratislava* 1:39-43.
Horan, James D.
1967 *The Pinkertons: The Detective Dynasty that Made History*. New York: Crown Publishers.
House, Humphrey and Graham Storey
1959 *The Journals and Papers of Gerard Manley Hopkins*. London: Oxford University Press.
How, Harry
1892 "A Day with Dr. Conan Doyle." *The Strand Magazine* 4 (2):182-188.
Hrushovski, Benjamin
1960 "On Free Rhythms in Modern Poetry: Preliminary Remarks Toward a Critical Theory of Their Structures and Functions." In *Style in Language*, ed. by Thomas A. Sebeok, 173-192. New York: John Wiley & Sons.
Huizinga, Johan
1949 [1938] *Homo Ludens: A Study of the Play Element in Culture*, trans. by R. F. C. Hull. London: Routledge & Kegan Paul.
Humphrey, Nicholas K.
1971 "Colour and Brightness Preferences in Monkeys." *Nature* 229:615-617.
1972 "Interest and Pleasure: Two Determinants of a Monkey's Visual Preference." *Perception* 1:395-416.
1973 "The Illusion of Beauty." *Perception* 2:429-439.
1979 "The Biological Basis of Collecting." *Human Nature* 2:44-47.
Jakobson, Roman
1963 "Parts and Wholes in Language." In *Parts and Wholes*, ed. by Daniel Lerner, 157-162. New York: The Free Press of Glencoe.
1966 "Grammatical Parallelism and Its Russian Facet." *Language* 42:399-429.
1971a *Selected Writings I: Phonological Studies*. The Hague: Mouton.
1971b *Selected Writings II: Word and Language*. The Hague: Mouton.
Janik, Allan and Stephen Toulmin
1973 *Wittgenstein's Vienna*. London: Weidenfeld and Nicolson.
Jastrow, Joseph
1935 *Wish and Wisdom: Episodes in the Vagaries of Belief*. New York: D. Appleton-Century.
Jenkins, Iredell
1958 *Art and the Human Enterprise*. Cambridge: Harvard University Press.
Johnson, Harry Miles
1911 "Review of Oskar Pfungst, Clever Hans (the Horse of Mr. von Osten): A Contribution to Experimental, Animal, and Human Psychology." *Journal of Philosophy* 8:663-666.
1912 "The Talking Dog." *Science* 35:749-751.
1913 "Audition and Habit Formation in the Dog." *Behavior Monographs* 2 (8):1-78.
Jolly, Alison
1978 "The Chimpanzees' Tea-party." *The Behavioral and Brain Sciences* 1 (4):579-580.
Jones, Louis Clark
1950 "Revenant." In *Standard Dictionary of Folklore and Legend* 2:933-934. New York: Funk & Wagnalls.

Jones, Thony B. and Alan C. Kamil
  1973 "Tool-Making and Tool-Using in the Northern Blue Jay." *Science* 180: 1076-1078.
Jutzler-Kindermann, Henny
  1954 *Können Tiere Denken? Ja.* Schopfheim: Henny Jutzler-Kindermann.
Kafka, Franz
  1917 "Ein Bericht für eine Akademie." *Der Jude* 2 (November): 559-565.
  1936 [1924] *The Great Wall of China: Stories and Reflections,* trans. by Willa and Edwin Muir. New York: Schocken Books.
Kahn, Charles H.
  1979 *The Art and Thought of Heraclitus.* Cambridge: Cambridge University Press.
Kalogerakis, Michael G.
  1963 "The Role of Olfaction in Sexual Development." *Psychosomatic Medicine* 25 (5):420-432.
Kamp, Rudolf
  1977 *Axiomatische Sprachtheorie: Wissenschaftstheoretische Untersuchungen zum Konstitutionsproblem der Einzelwissenschaften am Beispiel der Sprachwissenschafttheorie Karl Bühlers.* Berlin: Duncker & Humblot.
Kartunnen, Lauri
  1973 "Presuppositions of Compound Sentences." *Linguistic Inquiry* 4:169-193.
Katz, David
  1937 *Animals and Men: Studies in Comparative Psychology.* London: Longmans, Green.
Kellogg, Winthrop N.
  1980 "Communication and Language in the Home-Raised Chimpanzee." In *Speaking of Apes: A Critical Anthology of Two-Way Communication with Man,* ed. by Thomas A. Sebeok and Jean Umiker-Sebeok, 61-70. New York: Plenum. (First published 1968.)
Kellogg, Winthrop N. and Louise A. Kellogg
  1933 *The Ape and the Child: A Study of Environmental Influence on Early Behavior.* New York: Hafner.
Ketner, Kenneth Laine and James Edward Cook
  1975 (eds.) *Charles Sanders Peirce: Contributions to* The Nation. *Part One: 1869-1893* (Graduate Studies, Texas Tech University, No. 10). Lubbock: Texas Tech Press.
King, Mary-Claire and A. C. Wilson
  1975 "Evolution at Two Levels in Humans and Chimpanzees." *Science* 188:107-116.
Kloesel, Christian J. W.
  1979 "Charles Peirce and the Secret of the Harvard O. K.." *The New England Quarterly* 52 (1):55-67.
Klopfer, Peter H.
  1969 *Habitats and Territories: A Study of the Use of Space by Animals.* New York: Basic Books.
  1970 "Sensory Physiology and Esthetics." *American Scientist* 58:399-403.
Koestler, Arthur
  1973 *The Case of the Midwife Toad.* New York: Vintage Books.
Köhler, Wolfgang
  1922 "Zur Psychologie des Schimpansen." *Psychologische Forschung* 1:2-46.
  1925 *The Mentality of Apes.* London: Routledge & Kegan Paul.
Kotarbinski, Tadeusz
  1966 *Gnosiology: The Scientific Approach to the Theory of Knowledge,* trans. by Olgierd Wojtasiewicz. Oxford: Pergamon Press.

Krall, Karl
1912² *Denkende Tiere: Beiträge zur Tierseelenkunde auf Grund eigener Versuche.* Leipzig: Friedrich Engelmann.
Kreskin (George Kresge)
1973 *The Amazing World of Kreskin.* New York: Random House.
Krug, Josef
1929 "Zur Sprachtheorie." In *Beiträge zur Problemgeschichte der Psychologie: Festschrift zu Karl Bühler's 50. Geburtstag,* ed. by Egon Brunswik et al., 225-258. Jena: Gustav Fischer.
Lapp, John C.
1975 "The Jealous Window-Watcher in Zola and Proust." *French Studies* 29 (2):166-176.
1976 "Proust's Windows to Reality." *Romantic Review* 67 (1):38-49.
Larguier des Bancels, Jean and Eduard Claparède
1913 À propos du chien de Mannheim." *Archives de Psychologie* 13:377-379.
Lasagna, Louis
1980 "The Powerful Cipher." *The Sciences* 20:31-32.
Lawick-Goodall, Jane van
1967 *My Friends the Wild Chimpanzees.* Washington: National Geographic Society.
1968 *The Behavior of Free-Living Chimpanzees in the Gombe Stream Reserve.* Animal Behaviour Monographs 1 (3):161-311.
1971 *In the Shadow of Man.* Boston: Houghton Mifflin.
Laziczius, Julius von
1939 "Das sog. dritte Axiom der Sprachwissenschaft." *Acta Linguistica* 1:162-167. Reprinted in *Selected Writings of Gyula Laziczius,* ed. by Thomas A. Sebeok, 64-70. The Hague: Mouton.
1942 *Ältalános nyelvészet: alapelvek és módszertani kérdések.* Budapest: Magyar Tudományos Akadémia.
Leach, Maria
1961 *God Had a Dog: Folklore of the Dog.* New Brunswick: Rutgers University Press.
Lebzeltern, Gustav
1969 "Karl Bühler—Leben und Werk." In *Österreichische Akademie der Wissenschaften. Philosophisch-Historische Klasse,* Sitzungsberichte 265:3: 10:7-70. Vienna: Hermann Böhlaus Nachf.
Leech, Al
1948 *Don't Look Now.* Chicago: Magic, Inc.
Leibniz, Gottfried Wilhelm
1962 *Mathematische Schriften,* ed. by Karl I. Gerhard. Hildesheim: Georg Olms.
Lenneberg, Eric H.
1975 "A Neuropsychological Comparison between Man, Chimpanzee and Monkey." *Neuropsychologica* 13:125.
1980a "A Word between Us." In *Speaking of Apes: A Critical Anthology of Two-Way Communication with Man,* ed. by Thomas A. Sebeok and Jean Umiker-Sebeok, 71-83. New York: Plenum. (First published 1969.)
1980b "Of Language Knowledge, Apes, and Brains." In *Speaking of Apes: A Critical Anthology of Two-Way Communication with Man,* ed. by Thomas A. Sebeok and Jean Umiker-Sebeok, 115-140. New York: Plenum. (First published 1971.)
Lévi-Strauss, Claude
1958 *Anthropologie Structurale.* Paris: Plon.
1962 *La pensée sauvage.* Paris: Plon.
1964 *Le cru et le cuit.* Paris: Plon.

Leyhausen, Paul
1973 "The Biology of Expressions and Impressions." In *Motivation of Human and Animal Behavior: An Ethological View,* ed. by Konrad Lorenz and Paul Leyhausen. New York: Van Nostrand Reinhold. (First published 1967.)
Lieberman, David A.
1979 "Behaviorism and the Mind: A (Limited) Call for a Return to Introspection." *American Psychologist* 34:319-333.
Lilly, John Cunningham
1967 *The Mind of the Dolphin: A Nonhuman Intelligence.* Garden City: Doubleday.
1978 *Communication between Man and Dolphin: The Possibilities of Talking with Other Species.* New York: Crown.
Limber, John
1980 "Language in Child and Chimp?" In *Speaking of Apes: A Critical Anthology of Two-Way Communication with Man,* ed. by Thomas A. Sebeok and Jean Umiker-Sebeok, 197-220. New York: Plenum. (First published 1977.)
Linden, Eugene
1980 "Talk to the Animals." *Omni* (January):88-90, 107-109.
Linehan, Edward J.
1979 "The Trouble With Dolphins." *National Geographic* 155 (4):506-540.
Lockard, Joan S.
1978 "Speculations on the Adaptive Significance of Cognition and Consciousness in Nonhuman Species." *The Behavioral and Brain Sciences* 1 (4):583-584.
Locke, John
1975 *An Essay Concerning Human Understanding,* ed. by Peter H. Nidditch. Oxford: Clarendon Press.
Lorenz, Konrad
1954 *Man Meets Dog.* London: Methuen.
1971 *Studies in Animal and Human Behavior 2.* Cambridge: Harvard University Press.
Lotman, Jury M.
1967 "Tezisy k probleme 'Iskusstvo v rjadu modelirujuščix sistem.' " *Trudy po znakovym sistemam* 3:130-145.
Lubbock, Sir John
1886 "Note on the Intelligence of the Dog." *Fifty-fifth Meeting of the British Association for the Advancement of Science,* 1089-1091. London: John Murray.
Lykken, David T.
1974 "Psychology and the Lie Detector Industry." *American Psychologist* 29:725-739.
MacKenzie, William
1913 "Le problème du chien pensant de Mannheim." *Archives de Psychologie* 13:312-376.
Maclaren, Jack
1926 *My Crowded Solitude.* New York: R. M. McBride & Co.
McLuhan, Marshall
1965 *Understanding Media: The Extensions of Man.* New York: McGraw-Hill.
McNeill, David
1980 "Sentence Structure in Chimpanzee Communication." In *Speaking of Apes: A Critical Anthology of Two-Way Communication with Man,* ed. by Thomas A. Sebeok and Jean Umiker-Sebeok, 145-160. New York: Plenum. (First published 1973.)

Máday, Stefan von
1914 *Gibt es denkende Tiere? Eine Entgegnung auf Krall's "Denkende Tiere."* Leipzig: Wilhelm Engelmann.
Maeterlinck, Maurice
1914 *The Unknown Guest*, trans. by Alexander Teixeira de Mattos. New York: Dodd, Mead and Company.
Malmi, William A.
1980 "Chimpanzees and Language Evolution." In *Speaking of Apes: A Critical Anthology of Two-Way Communication with Man*, ed. by Thomas A. Sebeok and Jean Umiker-Sebeok, 191-196. New York: Plenum. (First published 1976.)
Marks, David and Richard Kammann
1978 "Information Transmission in Remote Viewing Experiments." *Nature* 274 (5672):680-681.
1980 *The Psychology of the Psychic*. Buffalo: Prometheus Books.
Marler, Peter
1980 "Primate Vocalization: Affective or Symbolic? In *Speaking of Apes: A Critical Anthology of Two-Way Communication with Man*, ed. by Thomas A. Sebeok and Jean Umiker-Sebeok, 221-229. New York: Plenum. (First published 1977.)
Marler, Peter and Andrew Gordon
1968 "The Social Environment of Infant Macaques." In *Biology and Behavior: Environmental Influences*, ed. by David C. Glass, 113-129. New York: Rockefeller University Press.
Marshack, Alexander
1972 *The Roots of Civilization: The Cognitive Beginnings of Man's First Art, Symbol and Notation*. New York: McGraw-Hill.
Marshall, Alexander J.
1954 *Bower-Birds: Their Displays and Breeding Cycles*. Oxford: Clarendon Press.
Martinak, Eduard
1901 *Psychologische Untersuchungen zur Bedeutungslehre*. Leipzig: Johann Amrosius Barth.
Martynov, V. V.
1978 "Review of Sebeok 1976." *Literatury i jazyka* 37 (2):178-179.
Marx, Jean L.
1980 "Ape-Language Controversy Flares Up." *Science* 207:1130-1133.
Marx, Karl
1933 *Das Kapital. Marx-Engels Gesamtausgabe*, Part II. Zürich: Ring-Verlag.
Matejka, Ladislav and Irwin R. Titunik
1976 (eds.) *Semiotics of Art: Prague School Contributions*. Cambridge: MIT Press.
Maugh, Thomas H.
1980 "Saturday Night Weaver." *Science 80* 1(5):85.
Maurer, David W.
1974 *The American Confidence Man*. Springfield, Ill.: Charles C. Thomas.
Mauss, Marcel
1968 "Effet physique chez l'individu de l'idée de mort suggérée par la collectivité." In *Sociologie et Anthropologie*, 311-330. Paris: Presses Universitaires de France.
Meinong, Alexius
1977 *Über Annahmen*, ed. by Rudolf Haller. Graz: Akademische Druck- und Verlagsanstalt.
Mellgren, Roger L. and Roger S. Fouts

1978 "Mentalism and Methodology." *The Behavioral and Brain Sciences*
1 (4):585-586.
Menzel, Emil W., Jr.
1975 "Natural Language of Young Chimpanzees." *New Scientist* 65:130.
Menzel, Emil W., Jr., and Marcia K. Johnson
1978 "Should Mentalistic Concepts Be Defended or Assumed?" *The Behavioral and Brain Sciences* 1 (4):586-587.
Menzel, Rudolfine and Rudolf Menzel
1948 "Sprechende Hunde?" *Österreichischer Boxerhund*, Mitteilungsblatt 10 (February).
Merriam, Alan P.
1964 *The Anthropology of Music*. Evanston: Northwestern University Press.
Merton, Robert K.
1957 "Priorities in Scientific Discovery: A Chapter in the Sociology of Science." *American Sociological Review* 22: 635-659.
Messac, Régis
1929 *Le "Détective Novel" et l'influence de la pensée scientifique*. Paris: Librairie Ancienne Honoré Champion.
Miles, Helen Lyn White
1979 "Conversations with Apes: The Use of Sign Language by Two Chimpanzees." Dissertation, University of Connecticut.
Millar, Ronald
1972 *The Piltdown Men*. London: Victor Gollancz.
Miller, Arthur G.
1978 "And in This Corner, from Cambridge, Massachusetts . . . ." *The Behavioral and Brain Sciences* 1 (3):401-402.
Miller, Eugene F.
1979 "Hume's Reduction of Cause to Sign." *The New Scholasticism* 53: 42-75.
Miller, Jonathan
1979 *The Body in Question*. New York: Random House.
Moore, Bruce R. and Susan Stuttard
1979 "Dr. Guthrie and *Felis domesticus* or: Tripping over the Cat." *Science* 205:1031-1033.
Morgan, Lewis H.
1970 [1868] *The American Beaver and His Works*. New York: Burt Franklin.
Morris, Charles
1948 *The Open Self*. New York: Prentice-Hall.
1956 [1942] *Paths of Life: Preface to a World Religion*. New York: George Braziller.
1966 *Festival*. New York: George Braziller.
1970 *The Pragmatic Movement in American Philosophy*. New York: George Braziller.
1971 *Writings on the General Theory of Signs*. The Hague: Mouton.
1976 *Image*. New York: Vantage Press.
Morris, Desmond
1962 *The Biology of Art: A Study of the Picture-Making Behavior of the Great Apes and Its Relationship to Human Art*. New York: Alfred A. Knopf.
1977 *Manwatching: A Field Guide to Human Behavior*. New York: Harry N. Abrams.
1979 *Animal Days*. London: Jonathan Cape.
Morris, Desmond, Peter Collett, Peter Marsh, and Marie O'Shaughnessy
1979 *Gestures: Their Origins and Distribution*. New York: Stein and Day.
Morris, Ramona and Desmond Morris

1966a *Men and Pandas.* New York: New American Library.
1966b *Men and Apes.* New York: McGraw-Hill.
Mottershead, G. S.
1959 "Experiments with a Chimpanzee Colony at Chester Zoo." *International Zoo Yearbook* 1:18-20.
Mounin, Georges
1980 "Language, Communication, Chimpanzees." In *Speaking of Apes: A Critical Anthology of Two-Way Communication with Man,* ed. by Thomas A. Sebeok and Jean Umiker-Sebeok, 161-177. New York: Plenum. (First published 1976.)
Moynihan, Martin
1966 "Communication in the Titi Monkey, Callicebus." *Journal of Zoology* 150:77-127.
Mukařovský, Jan
1976 [1936] "Art as Semiotic Fact." In *Semiotics of Art: Prague School Contributions,* ed. by Ladislav Matejka and Irwin R. Titunik, 3-9. Cambridge: MIT Press.
Murasaki, Yoshimasa
1980 *The Revival of Monkey Training: The Art and Method in Monkey Training.* Kyoto: Buraku mondai kenkyu-jo. [In Japanese.]
Murphy, Gardner and Robert O. Ballou
1960 (eds.) *William James on Psychical Research.* New York: The Viking Press.
Musicant, Robert A., William R. Lovallo, Sherrilyn Gillespie, and William Leber
1980 "Cat Signing?" *Science* 207:258.
Nelson, Keith
1973 "Does the Holistic Study of Behavior Have a Future?" In *Perspectives in Ethology,* ed. by Paul P. G. Bateson and Peter H. Klopfer. New York: Plenum.
Nissen, Henry W.
1932 "A Field Study of the Chimpanzee: Observations of Chimpanzee Behavior and Environment in Western French Guinea." *Comparative Psychology Monographs* 8 (36):1-222.
Nolen, William A.
1974 *Healing: A Doctor in Search of a Miracle.* Greenwich, Conn.: Fawcett.
Nordon, Pierre
1966 *Conan Doyle.* London: John Murray.
Nottebohm, Fernando
1972 "The Origins of Vocal Learning." *The American Naturalist* 106:116-140.
Nottebohm, Fernando and Arthur P. Arnold
1979 "Songbirds' Brains: Sexual Dimorphism." *Science* 206:769.
Nottebohm, Fernando, Tegner M. Stokes, and Christina M. Leonard
1976 "Central Control of Song in the Canary, *Serinus canarius,*" *Journal of Comparative Neurology* 165:457-486.
Observations de physique générale I
1718 In *Histoire de l'Académie Royale des sciences. Avec les Memoires de mathématique et de physique.* Année 1715, Histoire. Paris.
Panofsky, Erwin
1955 *Meaning in the Visual Arts: Papers in and on Art History.* Garden City: Doubleday.
Parfit, Michael
1980 "Are Dolphins Trying to Say Something, Or Is It All Much Ado about Nothing?" *Smithsonian Magazine* 11(7):72-81.

Patterson, Francine G.
  1978a "Conversations with a Gorilla." *National Geographic* 154 (4):438-465.
  1978b "The Gestures of a Gorilla: Sign Language Acquisition in Another Pongid Species." *Brain and Language* 5:72-97.
  1979a "Linguistic Capabilities of a Lowland Gorilla." In *Language Intervention from Ape to Child,* ed. by Richard L. Schiefelbusch and John H. Hollis, 325-356. Baltimore: University Park Press.
  1979b "Linguistic Capabilities of a Lowland Gorilla." Dissertation, Stanford University.
  1980 "Gorilla Talk." *The New York Review of Books* 27(15):45-46.
  1981 "Ape Language." *Science* 211:86-87.

Payne, Roger S. and Scott McVay
  1971 "Songs of the Humpback Whales." *Science* 173:587-597.

Pazuchin, Roscislaw V.
  1963 "Učenie K. Bjulera o funkcijach jazyka kak popytka psiochologičeskogo resenija lingvističeskich problem." *Voprosy Jazykoznanija* 5:94-103.

Peirce, Charles Sanders
  1929 "Guessing." *The Hound and Horn* 2:267-282.
  1935-66 *Collected Papers of Charles Sanders Peirce,* ed. by Charles Hartshorne, Paul Weiss, and Arthur W. Burks. Cambridge: Harvard University Press. [References are either to volumes and paragraphs (not pages) or to unpublished manuscripts from the Peirce Edition Project located at Indiana University—Purdue University at Indianapolis.]

Pelc, Jerzy
  1977 "On the Prospects of Research in the History of Semiotics." *Semiotic Scene* 1 (3):1-12.

Perelman, Chaïm and Lucie Olbrechts-Tyteca
  1969 *The New Rhetoric: A Treatise on Argument.* Notre Dame: University of Notre Dame Press.

Petitto, Laura A. and Mark S. Seidenberg
  1979 "On the Evidence for Linguistic Abilities in Signing Apes." *Brain and Language* 8:162-183.

Pfeiffer, John E.
  1969 *The Emergence of Man.* New York: Harper & Row.

Pfungst, Oskar
  1965 *Clever Hans (The Horse of Mr. von Osten),* ed. by Robert Rosenthal. New York: Holt, Rinehart & Winston.

Phillips, David P.
  1978 "Airplane Accident Fatalities Increase Just after Newspaper Stories about Murder and Suicide." *Science* 201:748-749.

Pilisuk, Marc, Barbara Brandes, and Didier van der Hove
  1976 "Deceptive Sounds: Illicit Communication in the Laboratory." *Behavioral Science* 21:515-523.

Plischke, Hans
  1914 *Die Sage vom Wilden Heere im deutschen Volke.* Eilenburg: C. W. Offenhauer.

Plomin, Robert and A. R. Kuse
  1979 "Genetic Differences between Humans and Chimps and among Humans." *American Psychologist* 34:188-190.

Ploog, Detlev and Theodore Melnechuk
  1971 "Are Apes Capable of Language?" *Neurosciences Research Program Bulletin* 9:600-700.

Polanyi, Michael

1958 *Personal Knowledge: Towards a Post-Critical Philosophy.* Chicago: University of Chicago Press.
Popper, Karl R. and John C. Eccles
1977 *The Self and Its Brain: An Argument for Interactionism.* New York: Springer International.
Posner, Roland
1979 "Charles Morris und die verhaltenstheoretische Grundlegung der Semiotik." *Zeitschrift für Semiotik* 1:49-79.
Pratt, J. Gaither
1977 *Parapsychology: An Insider's View of ESP.* Metuchen: The Scarecrow Press.
Premack, Ann J.
1976 *Why Chimps Can Read.* New York: Harper & Row.
Premack, David
1971 "Language in Chimpanzee?" *Science* 172:808-822.
1972 "Teaching Language to an Ape." *Scientific American* 227:92-99.
1976 *Intelligence in Ape and Man.* Hillsdale, N. J.: Lawrence Erlbaum Associates.
Premack, David and Guy Woodruff
1978 "Does the Chimpanzee Have a Theory of Mind?" *The Behavioral and Brain Sciences* 1 (4):515-526.
Premack, David, Guy Woodruff, and Keith Kennel
1978 "Paper-marking Test for Chimpanzee: Simple Control for Social Cues." *Science* 202:903-905.
Randi, James
1975 *The Magic of Uri Geller.* New York: Ballantine Books.
1978a "New Evidence in the Uri Geller Matter." *The Skeptical Inquirer* 2:25-30.
1978b "Tests and Investigations of Three 'Psychics.' " *The Skeptical Inquirer* 2 (2):25-39.
Ransdell, Joseph
1977 "Some Leading Ideas of Peirce's Semiotic." *Semiotica* 19:157-178.
Rapaport, David
1951 (ed.) *Organization and Pathology of Thought: Selected Sources.* New York: Columbia University Press.
Reinert, Jürgen
1965 "Takt- und Rhythmusunterscheidung bei Dohlen." *Zeitschrift für Tierpsychologie* 22:223-271.
Rensberger, Boyce
1977 *The Cult of the Wild.* Garden City: Anchor Press/Doubleday.
Rensch, Bernhard
1958 "Die Wirksamkeit ästhetischer Faktoren bei Wirbeltieren." *Zeitschrift für Tierpsychologie* 15:447-461.
1961 "Malversuche mit Affen." *Zeitschrift für Tierpsychologie* 18:347-364.
1972 *Homo Sapiens from Man to Demigod.* New York: Columbia University Press.
1976 "Basic Aesthetic Principles in Man and Animals." In *The Nature of Human Behaviour,* ed. by Gunter Altner, 322-345, 445-447. London: Allen & Unwin.
Revzin, Isaac I.
1964 "K semiotičiskomu analizu detektivov (na primere romanov Agaty Kristi)." *Programma i tezisy dokladov v letnej škole po vtoričnym modelirujuščim sistemam,* 16-26 avg., 38-40. Tartu.
1978 [1964] "Notes on the Semiotic Analysis of Detective Novels: With Examples from the Novels of Agatha Christie." *New Literary History* 9:385-388.

Rhine, Joseph Banks and Louisa E. Rhine
   1928-29 "An Investigation of a 'Mind-Reading' Horse." *Journal of Abnormal and Social Psychology* 23:449-466.
   1929-30 "Second Report on Lady, the 'Mind-Reading' Horse." *Journal of Abnormal and Social Psychology* 24:287-292.
Richter, Curt P.
   1957 "On the Phenomenon of Sudden Death in Animals and Man." *Psychosomatic Medicine* 19:191-198.
Ristau, Carolyn A. and Donald Robbins
   1979 "Book Review: A Threat to Man's Uniqueness? Language and Communication in the Chimpanzee?" *Journal of Psycholinguistic Research* 8 (3): 267-300.
Ritter, Paul
   1911 "Ein berühmter Vorgänger des sprechenden Hundes." *Friedrichshafener General-Anzeiger* 6 (January):19.
Robin, Richard S.
   1967 *Annotated Catalogue of the Papers of Charles S. Peirce*. Amherst: University of Massachusetts Press.
Romanes, George John
   1892 *Darwin, and After Darwin: An Exposition of the Darwinian Theory and a Discussion of Post-Darwinian Questions*. Chicago: Open Court.
Rosebury, Theodor
   1969 *Life on Man*. New York: The Viking Press.
Rosenthal, Robert
   1976 *Experimenter Effects in Behavioral Research*. New York: Irvington Publishers.
   1978 "How Often Are Our Numbers Wrong?" *American Psychologist* 33: 1005-1008.
Rosenthal, Robert and Donald B. Rubin
   1978 "Interpersonal Expectancy Effects: The First 345 Studies." *The Behavioral and Brain Sciences* 3:377-415.
Rossi-Landi, Ferruccio
   1975 "Signs about a Master of Signs." *Semiotica* 13:155-197.
Rowdon, Maurice
   1978 *Elke & Belam*. New York: G. P. Putnam's Sons.
Royce, Anya Peterson
   1977 *The Anthropology of Dance*. Bloomington: Indiana University Press.
Rumbaugh, Duane M.
   1977 (ed.) *Language Learning by a Chimpanzee: The Lana Project*. New York: Academic Press.
   1980 "Language Behavior of Apes." In *Speaking of Apes: A Critical Anthology of Two-Way Communication with Man*, ed. by Thomas A. Sebeok and Jean Umiker-Sebeok, 231-259. New York: Plenum. (First published 1977.)
Rumbaugh, Duane M., Timothy V. Gill, Ernst von Glaserfeld, Harald Warner, and Pier Pisani
   1975 "Conversations with a Chimpanzee in a Computer-Controlled Environment." *Biological Psychiatry* 10:627-641.
Rumbaugh, Duane M. and E. Sue Savage-Rumbaugh
   1979 "A Response to Herbert Terrace's Paper, 'Linguistic Apes.' " Manuscript.
Sachs, Curt
   1937 *World History of the Dance*. New York: Norton.
Sanders, Richard J. and Herbert S. Terrace
   1979 "Conversations with a Chimpanzee: Language-like Performance with-

out Competence." Paper presented at the annual meeting of the American Psychological Association.

Saul, M.
  1843 "The Architecture of Birds." *The Builder* 16 (May 27):190.

Savage-Rumbaugh, E. Sue
  1980 "Straight from the Horse's Mouth." Paper read at the New York Academy of Sciences Conference on The Clever Hans Phenomenon: Communication with Horses, Whales, Apes, and People, May 6.

Savage-Rumbaugh, E. Sue and Duane M. Rumbaugh
  1979 "Initial Acquisition of Symbolic Skills via the Yerkes Computerized Language Analog System." In *Language Intervention from Ape to Child,* ed. by Richard L. Schiefelbusch and John H. Hollis, 277-294. Baltimore: University Park Press.

Savage-Rumbaugh, E. Sue, Duane M. Rumbaugh, and Sally Boysen
  1978 "Symbolic Communication between Two Chimpanzees (*Pan troglodytes*)." *Science* 201:641-644.
  1980a "Do Apes Use Language?" *American Scientist* 68:49-61.
  1980b "Linguistically-Mediated Tool Use and Exchange by Chimpanzees (*Pan troglodytes*)." In *Speaking of Apes: A Critical Anthology of Two-Way Communication with Man,* ed. by Thomas A. Sebeok and Jean Umiker-Sebeok, 353-383. New York: Plenum. (First published 1978.)

Savage-Rumbaugh, E. Sue, Duane M. Rumbaugh, S. T. Smith, and J. Lawson
  1980 "Reference: The Linguistic Essential." *Science* 210:922-925.

Scheglov, Yuri K.
  1975 [1968] "Toward a Description of Detective Story Structure." *Russian Poetics in Translation* 1:51-77.

Scheglov, Yuri K. and A. K. Zholkovskii
  1975 [1971] "Towards a 'Theme—(Expression Devices)—Text' Model of Literary Structure." *Russian Poetics in Translation* 1:3-50.

Scheibe, Karl E.
  1978 "The Psychologist's Advantage and Its Nullification: Limits of Human Predictability." *American Psychologist* 33:869-881.

Schiefelbusch, Richard L. and John H. Hollis
  1979 (eds.) *Language Intervention from Ape to Child.* Baltimore: University Park Press.

Schiller, Friedrich
  1967 *On the Aesthetic Education of Man in a Series of Letters,* ed. and trans., with an Introduction, Commentary, and Glossary of Terms, by Elizabeth M. Wilkinson and L. A. Willoughby. Oxford: Clarendon Press.

Schiller, Paul
  1951 "Figural Preferences in the Drawings of a Chimpanzee." *Journal of Comparative Physiological Psychology* 44:101-111.

Schmid, Bastian
  1938 *Begegnung mit Tieren.* Munich: Knorr & Hirt.

Schor, Naomi
  1969 "Zola: From Window to Window." *Yale French Studies* 42:38-51.

Schubert, Glendon
  1978 "Cooperation, Cognition and Communication." *The Behavioral and Brain Sciences* 1 (4):597-600.

Scott, John Paul and John L. Fuller
  1965 *Genetics and the Social Behavior of the Dog.* Chicago: University of Chicago Press.

Sebeok, Thomas A.
  1960 (ed.) *Style in Language.* Cambridge: The Technology Press of the Massachusetts Institute of Technology.

1972 *Perspectives in Zoosemiotics.* The Hague: Mouton.
1976 *Contributions to the Doctrine of Signs.* Lisse: Peter de Ridder Press.
1977a (ed.) *How Animals Communicate.* Bloomington: Indiana University Press.
1977b "Zoosemiotic Components of Human Communication." In *How Animals Communicate,* ed. by Thomas A. Sebeok, 1055-1077. Bloomington: Indiana University Press.
1977c (ed.) *A Perfusion of Signs.* Bloomington: Indiana University Press.
1978a *Considerazioni sulla semiosi.* Urbino: Centre Internazionale di Semiotica e di Linguistica 77/A.
1978b "Note Concerning Martin Gardner's Caricature of Charles Morris." *Semiotica* 23:3-4.
1979 *The Sign & Its Masters.* Austin: University of Texas Press.
1981 "Naming and Playing in Animals, with Reference to Playing: A Hypothesis." *Recherches sémiotiques/Semiotic Inquiry,* in press. [Paper delivered at a Colloquium on Playing and Performing: The Semiotics of Entertainment, June 6, 1980, Victoria University, Toronto.]
1981a "Japanese Monkey Performances: An Ancient Art Revived." *Explorers Journal* 59 (1):34-37.
Forthcoming. *Clever Hans.* Bloomington: Indiana University Press.
Sebeok, Thomas A. and Robert Rosenthal
1981 (eds.) *The Clever Hans Phenomenon: Communication with Horses, Whales, Apes, and People.* Annals of the New York Academy of Sciences 364.
Sebeok, Thomas A. and Jean Umiker-Sebeok
1979 "Performing Animals: Secrets of the Trade." *Psychology Today* 13 (6): 78-91.
1980 (eds.) *Speaking of Apes: A Critical Anthology of Two-Way Communcation with Man.* New York: Plenum.
Segre, Cesare
1979 *Structures and Time: Narration, Poetry, Models.* Chicago: University of Chicago Press.
Seidenberg, Mark S. and Laura A. Petitto
1979 "Signing Behavior of Apes: A Critical Review." *Cognition* 7:177-215.
Shapiro, Gary
1975 "Teaching Language to a Juvenile Orangutan" [abstract only]. *American Journal of Physical Anthropology* 42:329.
Shepard, Paul
1978 *Thinking Animals: Animals and the Development of Human Intelligence.* New York: Viking Press.
Shepherd, William T.
1915 "Some Observations on the Intelligence of the Chimpanzee." *Journal of Animal Behavior* 5:391-396.
Silverman, Paul
1978 *Animal Behavior in the Laboratory.* New York: Pica Press.
Simpson, George Gaylord
1966 "The Biological Nature of Man." *Science* 152:472-478.
Sinclair-Gieben, A. H. C. and Derek Chalmers
1959 "The Evaluation of Treatment of Warts by Hypnosis." *Lancet* 2:480-482.
Slud, Paul
1957 "The Song and Dance of the Long-Tailed Manakin, *Chiroxiphia Linearis.*" *The Auk: A Quarterly Journal of Ornithology* 74:333-339.
Smart, Benjamin H.
1831 *Outline of Sematology.* London: John Richardson.

Smith, Edgar W.
1952 *The Later Adventures of Sherlock Holmes,* vol. III. New York: Heritage Press.

Smith, W. John
1977 *The Behavior of Communicating: An Ethological Approach.* Cambridge: Harvard University Press.

Sobel, Dava
1979 "Researchers Challenge Conclusion That Apes Can Learn Language." *New York Times,* October 21.
1980 "Placebo Studies Are Not Just 'All in Your Mind.'" *New York Times,* January 6.

Sollas, William J.
1915[2] *Ancient Hunters.* New York: Macmillan.

Sommer, Robert
1969 *Personal Space: The Behavioral Basis of Design.* Englewood Cliffs: Prentice-Hall.

Spencer, Herbert
1897 *The Principles of Psychology.* New York: D. Appleton.

Spitzer, Leo
1945 "La enumeración caótica en la poesía moderna." In *Collección de estudios estilisticos* 1. Buenos Aires: Instituto de Filologia.

Stapledon, Olaf
1944 *Sirius: A Fantasy of Love and Discord.* London: Secker & Warburg.

Starrett, Vincent
1971 [1934] *The Private Life of Sherlock Holmes.* New York: Haskell House Publishers.

Steiner, George
1979 "Wien, Wien, nur du allein." *The New Yorker,* June 25, 101-105.

Steiner, Wendy
1978 "Modern American Semiotics (1930-1978)." In *The Sign: Semiotics around the World,* ed. by Richard W. Bailey, Ladislav Matejka, and Peter Steiner, 99-118. Ann Arbor: Michigan Slavic Publications.

Stonor, Charles R.
1940 *Courtship and Display among Birds.* London: Country Life.

Stratton, George M.
1921 "The Control of Another Person by Obscure Signs." *Psychological Review,* 28:301-314.

Straub, R. O., Mark S. Seidenberg, Thomas G. Bever, and Herbert S. Terrace
1980 "Serial Learning in the Pigeon." *Journal of Experimental Analysis of Behavior,* in press.

Studdert-Kennedy, Michael
1979 "The Beginnings of Speech." *Status Report on Speech Research,* April-June:35-64. New Haven: Haskins Laboratories.

Sullivan, Walter
1980 "Scientists Move toward Dialogue with Dolphin." *New York Times,* April 7, C1-2.

Surman, Owen S., Sheldon K. Gottlieb, Thomas P. Hackett, and Elizabeth L. Silverberg
1973 "Hypnosis in the Treatment of Warts." *Archives of General Psychology* 28:439-441.

Szőke, Peter
1963 "Ornitomuzikológia." *Magyar Tudomány* 9:592-607.

Tax, Sol and Charles Callender
1960 (eds.) *Issues in Evolution.* Chicago: University of Chicago Press.

Temerlin, Maurice K.

    1975 *Lucy: Growing Up Human: A Chimpanzee Daughter in a Psychotherapist's Family.* Palo Alto: Science and Behavior Books.

Terrace, Herbert S.

    1979 "How Nim Chimpsky Changed My Mind." *Psychology Today* 13 (6): 65-76.

    1980a *Nim: A Chimpanzee Who Learned Sign Language.* New York: Knopf.

    1980b "Is Problem-Solving Language?" In *Speaking of Apes: A Critical Anthology of Two-Way Communication with Man,* ed. by Thomas A. Sebeok and Jean Umiker-Sebeok, 385-405. New York: Plenum. (First published 1979.)

    1980c "More on Monkey Talk." *The New York Review of Books* 27 (19):59.

    1981 "A Report to the Academy, 1980." *Annals of the New York Academy of Sciences* 364:94-114.

Terrace, Herbert S. and Thomas G. Bever

    1980 "What Might Be Learned from Studying Language in the Chimpanzee?" In *Speaking of Apes: A Critical Anthology of Two-Way Communication with Man,* ed. by Thomas A. Sebeok and Jean Umiker-Sebeok, 179-189. New York: Plenum. (First published 1976.)

Terrace, Herbert S., Laura A. Petitto, Richard J. Sanders, and Thomas G. Bever

    n.d. "Can an Ape Create a Sentence?" Manuscript. Columbia University.

    1979 "Can an Ape Create a Sentence?" *Science* 206:891-902.

    1980 "On the Grammatical Capacities of Apes." In *Children's Language,* vol. 2, ed. by Keith E. Nelson. New York: Gardner Press.

    1981 "Ape Language." *Science* 211:87-88.

Thom, René

    1975 *Structural Stability and Morphogenesis: An Outline of a General Theory of Models.* Reading: W. A. Benjamin.

Thomas, Lewis

    1979 *The Medusa and the Snail: More Notes of a Biology Watcher.* New York: Viking Press.

Thompson, Claudia R. and Russell M. Church

    1980 "An Explanation of the Language of a Chimpanzee." *Science* 208:313-314.

Thompson, D'Arcy Wentworth

    1945 *On Growth and Form.* Cambridge: Cambridge University Press.

Thompson, Stith

    1955-58 *Motif-Index of Folk-Literature.* Bloomington: Indiana University Press.

Thorpe, William H.

    1972 *Duetting and Antiphonal Song in Birds: Its Extent and Significance* (*Behaviour,* Monograph Supplement 18). Leiden: Brill.

    1974 *Animal Nature and Human Nature.* Garden City: Anchor Press/ Doubleday.

Thorpe, William H. and M. E. W. North

    1965 "Origin and Significance of the Power of Vocal Imitation: With a Special Reference to the Antiphonal Singing of Birds." *Nature* 208:219-222.

Thurston, Herbert

    1952 *The Physical Phenomena of Mysticism.* London: Burns Oates.

Tigges, Margarete

    1963 "Muster- und Farbbevorzügung bei Fischen und Vögeln." *Zeitschrift für Tierpsychologie* 20:129-142.

Timaeus, Ernst

    1974 *Experiment und Psychologie: Zur Sozialpsychologie psychologischen Experimentierens.* Göttingen: C. J. Hogrefe.

Tracy, Jack
1977 (ed.) *The Encyclopedia Sherlockiana or, A Universal Dictionary of the State of Knowledge of Sherlock Holmes and His Biographer John H. Watson, M. D.* Garden City: Doubleday.
Trubetzkoy, Nikolaj Sergeevič
1939 *Grundzüge der Phonologie. Travaux du Cercle Linguistique de Prague* 7. Prague.
Truzzi, Marcello
1973 "Sherlock Holmes: Applied Social Psychologist." In *The Humanities as Sociology,* ed. by Marcello Truzzi, 93-126. Columbus, Ohio: Charles E. Merrill.
1980 "Book Note [of Sebeok and Umiker-Sebeok 1980]." *Zetetic Scholar* 6:180.
Tuteur, Werner
1957-58 "The 'Double-Blind' Method: Its Pitfalls and Fallacies." *American Journal of Psychiatry* 114:921-922.
Uexküll, Jakob von
1980 *Kompositionslehre der Natur: Biologie als undogmatische Naturwissenschaft,* ed. by Thure von Uexküll, III (4):291-388. Frankfurt am Main: Ullstein.
Uexküll, Thure von
Forthcoming Positionspapier über das Thema "Semiotik der Angst."
Umiker-Sebeok, Jean
1976 "Comments on 'Language, Communication, Chimpanzees,' by G. Mounin." *Current Anthropology* 17 (1):17-18.
Umiker-Sebeok, Jean and Thomas A. Sebeok
1980a "Introduction: Questioning Apes." In *Speaking of Apes: A Critical Anthology of Two-Way Communication with Man,* ed. by Thomas A. Sebeok and Jean Umiker-Sebeok, 1-59. New York: Plenum.
1980b "More on Monkey Talk." *The New York Review of Books* 27(19): 59-60.
Ungeheuer, Gerold
1967 "Die kybernetische Grundlage der Sprachtheorie von Karl Bühler." In *To Honor Roman Jakobson: Essays on the Occasion of His 70th Birthday* 3:2067-2086.
Verne, Jules
1870 *Vingt mille lieues sous les mers.* Paris: J. Hetzel.
1976 *Twenty-Thousand Leagues under the Sea,* ed. by Walter James Miller. New York: Thomas Y. Crowell.
Vitruvius Pollio, Marcus
1826 *The Architecture of Marcus Vitruvius Pollio, in Ten Books,* trans. by Joseph Gwilt. London: Priestly and Weale.
Vygotsky, Lev Semenovich
1971 *The Psychology of Art.* Cambridge: MIT Press.
Waddington, Conrad H.
1969 *Behind Appearance: A Study of the Relations between Painting and the Natural Sciences in This Century.* Edinburgh: Edinburgh University Press.
Wade, Nicholas
1980 "Does Man Alone Have Language? Apes Reply in Riddles, and a Horse Says Neigh." *Science* 208:1349-1351.
Walker, Philip
1969 "The Mirror, the Window, and the Eye in Zola's Fiction." *Yale French Studies* 42:52-67.
Warden, Carl John and Lucian Hynes Warner

1928 "The Sensory Capacities and Intelligence of Dogs, with a Report on the Ability of the Noted Dog 'Fellow' to Respond to Verbal Stimuli." *The Quarterly Review of Biology* 3:2-28.

Washburn, Sherwood L.
1978 "Human Behavior and the Behavior of Other Animals." *American Psychologist* 33:405-418.

Wellek, Albert
1959 "Ein Dritteljahrhundert nach 'Krise der Psychologie.'" *Zeitschrift für Experimentelle und Angewandte Psychologie* 6/1:109-117.
1968 "Karl Bühler." *International Encyclopedia of the Social Sciences* 2: 199-202.

Wescott, Roger W.
1974 (ed.) *Language Origins*. Silver Spring: Linstok.

White, Lynn, Jr.
1979 "The Ecology of Our Science." *Science 80* 1(1):72-76.

Wilson, Edward O.
1975 *Sociobiology: The New Synthesis*. Cambridge: Harvard University Press.

Wilsson, Lars
1969 *My Beaver Colony*. London: Souvenir.

Witmer, Lightner
1909 "A Monkey with a Mind." *The Psychological Clinic* 3:179.

Wolfe, John B.
1936 "Effectiveness of Token-Rewards for Chimpanzees." *Comparative Psychology Monograph* (12) 5.

Wood, Forrest G.
1973 *Marine Mammals and Man: The Navy's Porpoises and Sea Lions.* Washington: Robert B. Luce.
1979 "*Delphinus Loquens?*" *American Scientist* 67:652.

Wood, George H. and Remi J. Cadoret
1958 "Tests of Clairvoyance in a Man-Dog Relationship." *Journal of Parapsychology* 22:29-39.

Woolf, Virginia
1933 *Flush: A Biography*. New York: Harcourt, Brace.

Young, John Z.
1971 *An Introduction to the Study of Man*. Oxford: Clarendon.
1977 *What Squids and Octopuses Tell Us about Brains and Memories.* Forty-Sixth James Arthur Lecture on Evolution of the Human Brain. New York: American Museum of Natural History.
1979 "Memory and Its Models." In *Scientific Models & Man*, ed. by Henry Harris, 44-55. Oxford: Clarendon Press.

Yunis, Jorge J., Jeffrey R. Sawyer, and Kelly Dunham
1980 "The Striking Resemblance of High-Resolution G-Banded Chromosomes of Man and Chimpanzee." *Science* 208:1145-1148.

Zeman, J. Jay
1980 "Charles W. Morris (1901-1979)." *Transactions of the Charles S. Peirce Society* 16, in press.

Zeuner, Frederick E.
1963 *A History of Domesticated Animals*. New York: Harper & Row.

Ziman, John
1978 *Reliable Knowledge: An Exploration of the Grounds for Belief in Science*. Cambridge: Cambridge University Press.

Ziolkowski, Theodore
1977 "Talking Dogs—From Kafka to Snoopy." *TV Guide*, June 25:22-23.

Index of Names

Ach, Narziss 94
Ackoff, Russell L. 258
Adler, Alfred 98
Alland, Alexander, Jr. 216, 217
Allen, Woody 7
Ally (chimpanzee) 157, 158, 160, 188, 189, 199
Alpha (chimpanzee) 215, 233, 234, 235, 236, 237
Ames, Edward Scribner 76, 88
Andrews, Michael 257
Aristotle 104
Arli (dog) 128
Armstrong, Edward A. 219, 222, 223
Arnheim, Rudolf 214
Arnold, Arthur P. 208
Aronnax, Pierre (fictional character) 69, 70, 73
Aschoff, Lee 171
Auersperg, Prince 107
Austin (chimpanzee) 135, 156, 159, 160, 189, 192, 195, 196, 197
Autrum, Hansjochem 213
Avebury, Lord. *See* Lubbock, Sir John
Ayim, Maryann 24, 51

Babcock, Michael J. 171
Babcock, Rosemary A. 171
Bacon, Francis 96, 264
Baer, Eugen vi, 4
Bangs, George H. 22
Barber, Theodore X. 142, 144, 162, 164, 165, 166, 179, 203
Baring-Gould, William S. 40
Barker, John Charles 262
Barrymore (fictional character) 66
Barthes, Roland 6, 7, 11, 55, 56, 212
Bartley, William Warren III 91, 97, 104
Bascom, William R. 211
Bastian, Jarvis 170
Bates, John (fictional character) 14
Bateson, Gregory 213, 267
Beccari, Odoardo 232
Beecher, Henry Ward 33, 43
Belam (dog) 129
Bell, Dr. Joseph 38, 39, 40, 41, 42, 46, 48
Bell, Mrs. Joseph 40
Bellugi, Ursula 203
Benderly, Beryl Lieff 207
Bennett, Leon 71
Benson, Herbert 263, 277
Berganza (fictional dog) 119
Berkeley, George 25
Bernard, Claude 42, 103
Bernatzik, Hugo 107
Bernstein, Basil B. 8
Bernstein, Richard J. 25
Betsy (chimpanzee) 234, 235
Bever, Thomas G. 145, 158, 159, 194
Blacking, John 275, 276

Blake, Henry N. 127, 171, 260, 272
Blanford, William T. 227
Bläumker, Clemens 93
Blumenthal, Arthur L. 94
Boas, Franz 221, 222, 223
Bogatyrev, Petr N. 100, 239
Bohr, Niels 162
Booee (chimpanzee) 199, 200
Boot, W. H. J. 72
Borgese, Elizabeth Mann 126, 128, 129, 272
Bottéro, Jean 12
Bouissac, Paul vi, 4, 123, 127, 130, 139, 173, 257
Boulding, Kenneth E. 83
Boulle, Pierre 201
Bourne, Geoffrey H. 215, 234
Boye (dog) 118
Boyle, T. Coraghessan 209
Boysen, Sally 144
Braun, John 90
Breland, Keller 139, 171
Breland, Marian 139, 171
Brentano, Bernard von 94, 103
Brock, H. M. 67
Brogyanyi, Bela 117
Bronowski, Jacob 3, 12, 124, 203, 249, 250
Brothwell, Don R. 215, 233, 237, 256,
Brouwers, J. 263
Brown, Roger 146, 157, 160, 172, 187, 203
Browning, Robert 202
Bruller, Jean 201
Brunswik, Egon 94, 105
Buck (fictional dog) 119
Buddha 88
Bühler, Berta 93, 106
Bühler, Charlotte 93, 95, 96, 97, 98
Bühler, Inge 97
Bühler, Karl 12, 13, 91, 92, 93, 94, 95, 96, 97, 98, 99, 100, 101, 102, 103, 104, 105, 106, 107, 108
Bühler, Ludwig 93, 106
Bull, Ray 146, 207
Bulmer, Ralph 254
Burks, Arthur W. 18
Burns, Susan 109
Burroughs, Edgar Rice 270
Burroughs, W. H. 175, 207

Cable, Cynthia 156
Callendar, Charles 211
Calrissian, Lando (fictional character) 8
Camhy, Daniela G. 107
Campbell, Maurice 38
Cannon, Walter 103, 262, 263
Carlsmith, J. Merrill 166
Carnap, Rudolf 79, 89
Caro (fox) 132
Carson, Johnny 209
Cassirer, Ernst 104